Purnell's Encyclopedia of
SPORT

Contributors

Norman Barrett
Howard Bass
Bob Fisher
Richard Garrett
John Goodbody
Colin Graham
C. M. Jones
Tony Morris
Gilbert Odd
Geoffrey Page
Charlie Rous
Sidney Saltmarsh
Alan Smith
Martin Tyler
Andy Wilson
Graeme Wright

Norman Barrett Editor
Karen Spink Design

This book was planned
and edited for Purnell
by Publicare

ISBN 361 02812 1
Printed in Tenerife
by Litografía A. Romero, S. A.
(Spain). D. L. 927 - 74

Purnell's Encyclopedia of SPORT

Norman Barrett

Purnell Books, Maidenhead

Contents

Foreword

by **Dr Roger Bannister**
Chairman of the Sports Council

It takes courage for a publisher to launch an encyclopedia of sport. However good the contributors may be and however reliable the information they furnish, he must still be uneasily aware that, even as his book is going to press, those taking part in something like 100 sports are creating history.

Nevertheless, such an offering will be gratefully received. This book is a giant dam against the raging tide of time passing. Sportsmen and sports lovers everywhere can pause to consider the size, quality, and diversity of what has been achieved up to now, the better to judge what is possible in the future. And of course any well-edited encyclopedia is of inestimable value to historians and researchers.

As chairman of the Sports Council, established as an executive body under Royal Charter, I am acutely conscious of the fluctuations in, and the complex problems of, sport.

At our headquarters and in our nine regions we are in constant touch with the governing bodies of sport, local authorities, local sports councils and voluntary organizations, and are ready to give advice on the improvement of a sport, whether in its coaching schemes, preparation training, and international competition, or in its administration or its facilities.

As for the money side of it, the Government grant to the Sports Council has risen from £3.5 million in our first year to £6.5 million in the current financial year, but, set against inflation, this still is insufficient for us to meet the known demand for sports facilities throughout the country. More than three times as much is needed.

Last year, close on £1 million went to the governing bodies of sport for their administration, coaching, preparation training, development, and international events, as against just over £500,000 in the previous year; and, over two years, 97 major schemes for sports and leisure centres, swimming pools, golf courses, athletics and cycle tracks, sailing facilities, etc, in every part of England have been aided to the extent of some £2.5 million. But again, there is so much more to be done.

In return, each sport has co-operated wholeheartedly with us and with local authorities to make our Sport for All campaign a real force in the land. And they are equally as keen on the enlargement of the campaign, to provide for whole families to take sporting weeks or weekends at multi-sports centres and holiday camps.

All told, there is a tremendous upsurge of interest in leisure activities, and it is most timely that Purnell should bring out this *Encyclopedia of Sport* with its global treatment of each sport and its wealth of records and 'memorable moments'.

Roger Bannister
July, 1974

Acknowledgements

The Editor gratefully acknowledges the assistance of the following in authenticating material for this encyclopedia: Harold Abrahams, All-England Netball Association, All-England Women's Hockey Association, Amateur Basket Ball Association, Amateur Gymnastics Association, Angling News Services, Badminton Association of England, John Blake, British Olympic Association, English Lacrosse Union, Grand National Archery Society, Hockey Association, International Squash Rackets Federation, Major-General E. H. G. Lonsdale, National Small Bore Rifle Association, Jack Rollin, Irving Rosenwater, Squash Rackets Association, Oscar State.

The artwork in this book was done by William Walton Associates (colour) and Paul Buckle. Photographs were supplied by the following: Harold Abrahams, Angling News Services, Associated Press, Australian Information Service, John Blake, British Olympic Association, Camera Press, Information Canada Photograph Library, Central Press, Colorsport, Mike Cornwell, Patrick Eagar, Fox Photos, Ray Green, Japan Information Centre, Noeline Kelly, Keystone Press, George Kirkley, E. D. Lacey, London Express News and Feature Services, The Mansell Collection, New Zealand High Commission, Novosti, Gilbert Odd, Pictorial Press, Press Association, Radio Times Hulton Picture Library, South African Embassy, Sport and General, Syndication International, Topix, United Press International.

Aerosport

Above: *A Zlin Trener, one of the most popular aircraft used for competition aerobatics. The sport has had world championships since 1960, and competitors loop, roll, turn, and spin in a series of sequences marked by a panel of judges.* Far left: *In precision parachuting, the contestant opens the 'chute almost immediately and steers it towards the target by means of open panels in the canopy. There are also events for style, in which the contestant performs a series of free-fall manoeuvres against the clock. The sport is also called skydiving.* Left above: *Gliding as a sport has flourished since World War II, with world championships instituted in 1948. Contests include free distance, speed over a triangular course, and out-and-home events. Speeds of 145 mph have been attained, and average speeds of nearly 100 mph have been recorded over 100 km triangular courses.* Left below: *In Formula One racing, 17-ft span monoplanes powered by 100 hp engines reach speeds of 200 mph round a 3-mile circuit.*

Angling

Fishing began in the mists of time when men needed to catch fish to live. No one knows exactly how long ago it all started, but bone hooks have been found that date back 50,000 years. Paintings from ancient Egypt show men fishing with rod and line. From the need to catch fish to live grew the urge to fish for pleasure . . . and so developed angling.

Today, angling is a world-wide sport. In many countries, it is the biggest participant sport of all. In Britain, for example, a survey carried out by the National Anglers' Council found that nearly three million people are anglers.

Angling is split into three types: sea fishing, game fishing (that is, fishing for salmon and trout), and coarse fishing (coarse fish such as roach and bream caught in rivers, canals, and lakes).

For many, angling means simply a pleasurable day by the waterside. For some, it is a determined hunt for a fish of record proportions. For others, in sea and freshwater, it is a competition in a match setting to see who can catch the most.

The only authoritative world body in record terms is the International Game Fish Association, who, from their headquarters in Florida, keep a world-wide watch on record fish taken from the sea. No official world records exist for freshwater fish. In this field, anglers seem to have been careless, which could explain why so many of them have been presumed liars by the lay public! Britain is one of the few European countries with a record fish committee, and it is only since the 1950s that they have had one. In world terms, a freshwater fish list is published as authentic by the American magazine *Field and Stream*, but its comprehensiveness must be open to doubt, because so many of the fish listed are solely from the American continent.

The only governing body in angling with claims to world status is the Confédération Internationale de la Pêche Sportive, with headquarters in Italy. It is this body that runs the world freshwater angling championships, inaugurated in 1957.

Coarse fishing is popular in Europe, particularly in Britain, France, Belgium, and Italy. But in Scandinavia, the Americas, and most of the rest of the world, it is little practised. The British coarse fisherman is considered one of

Above: *Hydrogen balloons – the classic form of ballooning – are more complex and expensive than hot air balloons, but generally have a better performance. International balloon races are held regularly, the most famous being the one across the Alps. Records may be set in various categories for distance, duration, and altitude.* Right: *One form of sport parachuting is relative work, in which teams form a particular pattern or go through a sequence of free-fall patterns against the clock.* Below right: *Line-up for the start of the 1924 King's Cup Air Race, an event designed to further the progress of civil aviation in Britain. First held in 1922, it reached its height of popularity in the 1930s.* Below: *Record-breaking lone flier Sheila Scott with her Piper Comanche in 1969.*

AEROSPORT 'MOSTS'

World championship titles

Aerobatics – men	2	USSR
Sport parachuting – men	5	USSR
– women	5	USSR
Gliding – individual	2	H. Huth (W. Ger)

Ballooning records

Distance	255 miles	M. Wiedertehr (US)
Altitude	35,971 ft	J. R. P. Not (GB)

Gliding records

Distance	907.7 mi	H.-W. Grosse (W. Ger)
Altitude	46,266 ft	P. F. Bikle Jr (US)

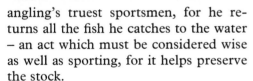

Angling is a sport with many facets: Above left: *Salmon fishing on the tranquil waters of Loch Tay, in Scotland.* Above: *Striking into a big marlin in turbulent ocean waters.* Far left: *Hooking a rainbow trout in a quiet New Zealand stream.* Left: *Coarse fishing in the flooded meadows of the Avon, Hampshire.*

angling's truest sportsmen, for he returns all the fish he catches to the water – an act which must be considered wise as well as sporting, for it helps preserve the stock.

Coarse fishermen use rods and lines with a variety of baits, of which maggot, 'caster' (the chrysalis of the maggot), bread, and worms are the most often used. The roach is the most popular fish with English coarse fishermen. Others are bream, chub, barbel, tench, carp, perch, and pike.

There are three types of coarse fisherman: the man who just likes a quiet day's fishing; the specimen hunter, a dedicated man, usually a member of a group, who concentrates on catching big fish with selective baits; and the match fisherman, who fishes against others in competitions.

Contestants in match fishing occupy stakes about 15 yards apart, and the winner is the man who catches the biggest weight. The world's record match catch of 168 lb 11 oz was taken in the River Ansager in Denmark by an English angler, Robert Atkinson of Canterbury, in September 1973.

Believed to have originated in Britain, *game fishing* is now universally pursued all over the world. The main species sought are trout (brown and rainbow), sea trout (a species of trout that migrates to the sea), and salmon.

The true game angler insists that the only sporting way to catch a fish is with an artificial fly. This consists of various materials tied on the shank of a hook in an attempt to imitate the colour and shape of a natural fly. There are many hundreds of accepted patterns of fly. These break down into two types: the dry fly (fished on the surface with the aid of a floating line) and the wet fly (fished under the surface).

Worldwide, *sea fishing* is the biggest single branch of angling, not just because it provides fish for the pan but also because access to it costs nothing unless a boat is employed. The biggest monsters caught on rod and line come from the warmest waters, as the IGFA list demonstrates. The Caribbean and the sea south of Australia are classic big game fish grounds.

A famous French father and son team at the 1969 world championships at Bad Oldesloe, in West Germany. Robert Tesse, three times individual winner, watches his son Jacques fishing.

9

Unlike the coarse and game fishermen, sea anglers have no close season. No branch of fishing is progressing faster in terms of growing numbers and improvements in technique, especially in the field of boat fishing. It has been found that sunken wrecks are the home of real monsters. With the use of modern depth-sounding equipment, more and more of these wrecks are being located.

Beach and pier anglers do not catch nearly as many fish as boatmen, nor are their fish as big. But they, too, have produced technical innovations, especially in the field of long casting. For bait, sea anglers have traditionally used things like lugworm and ragworm (dug from beaches), mussel, crab, and slices of fish such as mackerel. Latterly, they have gone in for artificial spinning baits.

Casting is a sport in itself. The International Casting Federation stages annual championships, with 10 events, for accuracy and distance.

WORLD RECORD SEA FISH

	(lb–oz)				line/(lb)
Albacore	70–0	South Africa	8.2.72	B. Cohen	130
Amberjack	149–0	Bermuda	21.6.64	P. Simons	30
Barracuda	83–0	Nigeria	13.1.52	K. J. W. Hackett	50
Bass, Calif. Black Sea	563–8	California	20.8.68	J. D. McAdam Jr	80
Bass, Calif. White Sea	83–12	Mexico	31.3.53	L. C. Baumgardner	30
Bass, Channel	83–0	Virginia	5.8.49	Z. Waters Jr	50
Bass, Giant Sea	680–0	Florida	20.5.61	Lynn Joyner	80
Bass, Sea	8–0	Massachusetts	13.5.51	H. R. Rider	50
Bass, Striped	72–0	Massachusetts	10.10.69	E. J. Kirker	50
Blackfish or Tautog	21–6	New Jersey	12.6.54	R. N. Sheafer	30
Bluefish	31–12	N. Carolina	30.1.72	J. M. Hussey	50
Bonefish	19–0	Zululand (SA)	26.5.62	B. W. Batchelor	30
Bonito, Oceanic	39–15	Bahamas	21.1.52	F. Drowley	50
	40–0	Mauritius	19.4.71	J. R. P. Cabache Jr	50
Cobia	110–5	Kenya	8.9.64	E. Tinworth	50
Cod	98–12	Massachusetts	8.6.69	A. J. Bielevich	20
Dolphin	85–0	Bahamas	29.5.68	R. Seymour	50
Drum, Black	109–0	Virginia	5.2.72	S. Dennis	50
Flounder	30–12	Chile	11.1.71	A. N. Moreno	20
Kingfish	78–12	Dominican Rep.	26.11.71	F. Viyella	50
Marlin, Black	1560–0	Peru	4.8.53	A. C. Glassell Jr	130
Marlin, Atlantic Blue	845–0	Virgin Is.	4.7.68	E. J. Fishman	80
Marlin, Pacific Blue	1153–0	Guam	21.8.69	G. D. Perez	180
Marlin, Striped	415–0	New Zealand	31.3.64	B. C. Bain	80
Marlin, White	159–8	Florida	25.4.53	W. E. Johnson	50
Permit	50–8	Florida	15.3.71	M. E. Earnest	20
Pollack	43–0	New Jersey	21.10.64	P. Barlow	50
Runner, Rainbow	30–15	Hawaii	27.4.63	H. Goodale	130
Roosterfish	114–0	Mexico	1.6.60	A. Sackhelm	30
Sailfish, Atlantic	141–1	Ivory Coast	26.1.61	T. Burnand	130
Sailfish, Pacific	221–0	Galapagos Is.	12.2.47	C. W. Stewart	130
Shark, Blue	410–0	Massachusetts	1.9.60	R. C. Webster	80
	410–0	Massachusetts	17.8.67	Martha Webster	80
Shark, Mako	1061–0	New Zealand	17.2.70	J. B. Penwarden	130
Shark, Man-eater or White	2664–0	S. Australia	21.4.59	A. Dean	130
Shark, Porbeagle	430–0	Channel Is.	29.6.69	D. Bougourd	80
Shark, Thresher	729–0	New Zealand	3.6.59	Mrs V. Brown	130
Shark, Tiger	1780–0	S. Carolina	14.6.64	W. Maxwell	130
Snook or Robalo	52–6	Mexico	9.1.63	Jane Haywood	30
Swordfish	1182–0	Chile	7.5.53	L. Marron	130
Tanguigue	81–0	Pakistan	27.8.60	G. E. Rusinak	80
Tarpon	283–0	Venezuela	19.3.56	M. Salazar	30
Tuna, Allison or Yellowfin	296–0	Mexico	7.3.71	E. C. Malnar	80
Tuna, Atlantic Big-eyed	321–12	New York	9.9.72	Vito Lo Caputo	50
Tuna, Pacific Big-eyed	435–0	Peru	17.4.57	R. V. A. Lee	130
Tuna, Blackfin	38–0	Bermuda	26.6.70	A. L. Dickens	30
Tuna, Bluefin	1065–0	Nova Scotia	19.11.70	R. G. Gibson	130
Wahoo	149–0	Bahamas	15.6.62	J. Pirovano	130
Weakfish	19–8	Trinidad	13.4.62	D. B. Hall	80
Weakfish, Spotted	15–3	Florida	13.1.49	C. W. Hubbard	50
	15–6	Florida	4.5.69	M. J. Foremny	30
Yellowtail	111–0	New Zealand	11.1.61	A. F. Plim	50

The biggest catch on record, Alf Dean's 2,664-lb man-eating shark. Dean hooked this monster, nearly 17 feet long, at Denial Bay, near Ceduna, in South Australia. Larger sharks have been caught by harpoon.

ANGLING WORLD CHAMPIONSHIPS (3-hour matches)

Most successful angler	Robert Tesse (Fr)	1st 3, 2nd 1, 3rd 2
Most successful team	France	1st 6, 2nd 5, 3rd 4
Record team weight	57 lb 13 oz 4 dr	Italy, 1957
Record individual weight	20 lb 5½ oz	H. Levels (Neth) 1972
Record no. fish caught	652	J. Isenbaert (Bel) 1967

Archery

One of the fastest growing individual sports, archery received the recognition its growth warranted with the return of target archery to the Olympic arena at Munich in 1972. Its participants number hundreds of thousands in more than 50 member nations of the Fédération Internationale de Tir à l'Arc (FITA).

Royalty, in the form of Henry VIII and George IV, played its part in the development of the sport. And George IV, while Prince of Wales, started the Toxophilite Society which, with a Royal prefix is now one of some 750 archery societies in Britain affiliated to the Grand National Archery Society (GNAS), which itself was founded in 1861.

FITA was founded in 1931, the year that saw the first target world championships. With the exception of the World War II years, these championships were held annually until 1950. Now they are held every two years, with European target and field championships held in the alternate years. The field world championships, also biennial, were first contested in 1970.

The technological advances since World War II have brought a new era to archery with the development of new designs, materials, and aids for bows and arrows. Scores today often double those of the yew longbow and wooden arrow era. World records in the sport are established at world championships and at designated tournaments held by member countries of FITA.

Target archery, the most popular form of the sport, permits the use of any form of bow. At club level, shoots are held over varying distances with a maximum range of 100 yards for men; 80 yards for women and juniors. The target at this distance is 4 feet in diameter with a centre (the *gold*; 9 points) just over 9 inches across. Working outwards, there are red, blue, black, and white rings worth 7, 5, 3, and 1 points respectively. Archers shoot in groups of two to six at a target, each archer shooting two sets of three arrows in rotation before scores are taken and arrows collected. This done, shooting recommences. A round can comprise 6 to 12 dozen arrows shot over different distances.

Under FITA rules, two sizes of target face are used, with each colour divided into an inner and outer scoring zone. Points range from 10 for an inner gold to 1 for an outer white. Men shoot three

Equipment has changed as much as dress over the years, from the basic bows and cumbersome costume of 1908 (left) to the sophisticated weapons and functional uniform of today (above).

dozen arrows at each of the following distances: 90, 70, 50, and 30 metres. Women and juniors shoot the same number from 70, 60, 50, and 30 metres. At the two shorter distances, a target face 80 cm across is used, and the arrows are scored and collected after every three shots. The maximum score for a FITA round is 1,440.

Field archery has two main styles, with separate competition classes in each – freestyle and instinctive (or barebow), though Britain also has the 'traditional'. The instinctive class excludes mechanical aids to aim or indication of draw length. The black and white targets vary in size according to the range.

There are many other forms of archery, including the use of animal-shaped targets and shooting for distance.

In field archery, the distance to the target is not always known and in the instinctive class mechanical aids to aim and draw are not allowed. The outer, black ring of the small target counts 3 points, the inner, white ring with the black centre spot counts 5.

ARCHERY ACHIEVEMENTS

World record FITA Single Round		
—men	1,268 pts	John Williams (US)
—women	1,236 pts	Emma Kakhovka (USSR)
World record FITA Double Round		
—men	2,528 pts	John Williams (US)
—women	2,426 pts	Anna Keunova (USSR)
Most world titles		
—men	4	H. Deutgen (Sweden)
—women	7	Janina Kurkowska (Pol.)

Association football

Banks, Gordon (England), rightly won acclaim as the world's premier goalkeeper following the 1966 World Cup, and consolidated his position in the 1970 tournament. Strongly built and particularly courageous, he inspired confidence in team-mates and demoralized opponents with his brilliance. Banks began with Chesterfield in 1958–59, but the next season saw him at Leicester, and in 1963 he won his first cap against Brazil at Wembley. He went to Stoke for £52,500 in 1967. Elected Footballer of the Year in 1972, he later sustained a serious eye injury in a car crash, and this led to his retirement in 1973.

Beckenbauer, Franz (W. Germany), Bayern Munich's poised and elegant half-back, put the Germans on the road to victory against England in the 1970 World Cup quarter-finals. His fine run and accurate shot well illustrated his attacking capabilities, which his country's policy had squandered in the 1966 final by using him to police Bobby Charlton. He won a Cup-Winners Cup medal in 1967 and in 1972 was voted European Footballer of the Year after Germany's European Championship win.

Best, George (N. Ireland), brought to British football a magical quality that made him the idol of thousands. But the

pressures of fame are demanding and led to frequent 'retirements'. At his peak he can be unplayable, his balance and ball control taking him swerving through packed defences. His courage and coolness in front of goal have resulted in numerous goals, some quite exceptional. He was Europe's and England's Footballer of the Year in 1968, when he played a vital part in Manchester United's European Cup success.

Of all the football codes, association football, or soccer, is the one that has retained the 'foot' part of the game in its purest form. Whereas in other codes handling is just as much a part of the game as kicking – more in some sports, such as rugby and American football – in soccer only the goalkeeper may handle the ball. As a result, much finer skills than just kicking the ball have been developed with the feet and other parts of the body – head, thighs, chest, etc. Soccer is, in fact, the only sport in which players *literally* use their heads. As a result, at its best, soccer has developed into an infinitely variable spectacle of dazzling ball control, mazy dribbling, harmonious passing and positioning, explosive shooting, and courageous defence. At its worst, however, soccer can be a spoiling, ultra-defensive game, in which bad sportsmanship, cheating, foul

The incomparable Pelé, flanked by his jubilant team-mates, Tostão and Jairzinho, in a moment of triumph in the 1970 World Cup, brilliantly won by Brazil.

play, and poor control are more prominent than the finer points, and work-rate and physical endeavour are more prized than flair and skill.

Most of the ancient civilizations played games in which a ball or similar object was kicked. But it was not until the 19th century in England that association football as we know it today grew out of the violent mob football that had been played in the streets and fields of England, on and off, for centuries. The first set of rules was drawn up at Cambridge University in 1846. In 1862, Mr J. C. Thring, one of those responsible for the Cambridge rules, drew up his 'Ten Rules' for 'The Simplest Game'.

At this time, there were a number of

clubs springing up, especially in London, and there was an even greater need for one definitive set of rules. With this object in mind, the representatives of the clubs met in October 1863 to form the Football Association. Eleven clubs were enrolled as the original members, but they soon fell out when it came to drawing up the rules. It was now that the supporters of the dribbling and the carrying games went their separate ways and football became two separate games: soccer and rugby. But the dispute was not over handling the ball. It was over

Blanchflower, Danny
(N. Ireland) captained Spurs to the 'double' in 1961, the FA Cup in 1962, and the Cup-Winners Cup in 1963. An intelligent and skilful right-half, he was the ideal general of a fluent talented side, his long, accurate passes setting his forwards into action time and again. He moved to Barnsley from Glentoran in 1948–49 and was at Aston Villa from 1951 to 1954, when he went to Tottenham. England's Footballer of the Year in 1958 and again in 1961, he won a record 56 Northern Ireland caps.

Danny Blanchflower with the FA Cup.

Memorable moments in sport

The magic Magyars

Dateline: Wembley, 25 November 1953. The scoreline, when it came up in large headlines in every footballing country in the world, could scarcely be believed – England 3 Hungary 6. England's first home defeat by foreign opposition – apart from little Eire's largely forgotten 2-0 win at Everton four years earlier – was achieved by perhaps the finest team the world has yet seen. The speedy, fluent, confident Hungarians gave a display that would have shattered any side. England, ill-prepared, possibly over-confident after so many invincible years, were not in the same class. Not that England played badly. Their first two goals were brilliantly taken, but the Hungarians were so good that their margin must have been greater had they not slackened off in the last half-hour.

'No European nation has beaten us here, and none ever will.' That was the average insular Englishman's feeling before the match. The Hungarians were unknown in England (the equally insular press had largely ignored their remarkable record of success over the preceding few years), and England were thought to be heading for yet another victory ... simply because they were England. But from the first minute, when Nandor Hidegkuti slashed a 20-yard rising shot beyond Merrick, the Hungarians delivered a lesson: a lesson in ball control, in accuracy, in moving into position, in finishing.

The use of a deep centre-forward (Hidegkuti), with the inside men (Sandor Kocsis and Ferenc Puskas) acting as spearheads, confused the English defence. Likewise they had no answer to the sudden onslaughts by Bozsik, nominally right-half, whose thunderbolts from outside the penalty area produced two goals, one a deflection by Puskas from a free-kick.

The England defence – Alf Ramsey, Billy Wright and all – were left gasping as Hidegkuti completed a hat-trick and the brilliant Puskas, turning on the proverbial sixpence, sent Wright chasing shadows while he rifled in the best goal of the lot with his inimitable left foot.

Postscript: The 'Magic Magyars' went on to demonstrate their brand of scintillating football to the world for another $2\frac{1}{2}$ years until they disbanded at the time of the Hungarian Uprising. From June 1950 to November 1955, they lost only one match – the World Cup final to Germany, when Puskas was not fully fit. A measure of their greatness is their goal record during this 51-match run – 220–58 ... and they scored in every match!

Ferenc Puskas (far right) leaves the England defence spellbound and the Wembley crowd speechless with his first and Hungary's third goal. England's captain, Billy Wright, Johnston (5), 'keeper Merrick, and Alf Ramsey (2) seem to be looking in different directions as the ball nestles in the corner of the net.

Bremner, Billy (Scotland), put his volatile temperament behind him to put Leeds United among the greats. With the dynamic little redhead organizing the defence, firing the attacks, Leeds consistently dominated the late 1960s and early 1970s – though often missing the prizes. An outside-right who eventually became a right-half, he formed a midfield pairing with Johnny Giles that was the envy of most clubs. First capped by Scotland in 1965, he was later given the captaincy. England's Footballer

of the Year in 1970, he has won League, FA Cup, League Cup, and Fairs Cup medals.

Busby, Sir Matt (Scotland), won a permanent place in soccer history for his rebuilding of Manchester United after World War II, when they did not even have a home ground, and again after the famous 'Busby Babes' had perished at Munich. As a player, he was a skilful half-back with Manchester City and Liverpool, and captained Scotland during the war. As a manager, he believed in letting players make full use of their natural talents, and his formidable scouting system ensured he found the best. The climax of his career was United's European Cup victory in 1968.

Chapman, Herbert, soccer's first major innovator, was the guiding force behind the great Huddersfield side of the 1920s and the Arsenal of the 1930s. At Huddersfield he turned an ordinary side into League Champions, and at Highbury he created a side rich in talent. With Charlie Buchan he devised the 'third-back' game, and he converted Alex James into the player to make his W-formation tick. If somewhat negative, his thinking was also highly functional – as his teams proved.

The 'mob football' played in the streets of London in the early 1300s. The game was banned for the first time in 1314, during the reign of King Edward II.

hacking – the unpleasant practice of kicking an opponent's shins. The supporters of the handling game wanted hacking to remain part of the game, and when they were defeated at a meeting on December 1 they withdrew from the Football Association.

The Football Association grew slowly at first, but it also grew strongly. In 1871, it introduced the FA Cup as a competition for the clubs affiliated to it, and a year later it organized the first official international, between England and Scotland. As a result, the Scottish Football Association was founded in 1873. The Scots had a profound influence on soccer in two respects. They initiated the passing game, and they gave football its first professionals. Professionalism was illegal, but in the early 1880s, especially in Lancashire, it was not uncommon for clubs to entice Scottish players south and to reward them for their skills. The effect of this was to take the stronghold away from the truly amateur clubs in the South to the Northern clubs, such as Blackburn and Preston.

The Football Association were unable to ignore the rise of professionalism, and in 1885 they wisely decided to legalize it. Three years later the Football League was founded, and the modern game was well on its way. European countries soon followed Britain's lead in establishing national associations and league and cup competitions. Internationals were

played, and in 1904 the Fédération Internationale de Football Association (FIFA) was born. Founded by seven countries – Belgium, Denmark, France, the Netherlands, Spain, Sweden, and Switzerland – FIFA now has more than 140 national associations affiliated to it.

Soccer was first included in the Olympics in 1908. Great Britain won the first two titles, but since the 1950s communist-bloc countries have prevailed, with their 'state-paid amateurs'. The first World Cup was staged in Uruguay in 1930, and major European club competition took hold in the 1950s.

The Laws of soccer, still administered by the International Football Association Board set up in 1882, have not kept pace with the development of the game. In 1891 referees and linesmen replaced umpires and the penalty kick was introduced, and in 1912 the use of hands by the goalkeeper was restricted to the penalty area. A major change to the offside law, requiring two instead of three defenders between attacker and goal, came in 1925, and the Laws were rewritten in 1938. Vague, inadequate, and capable of a wide range of interpretation, they badly need rewriting again – not to change the game radically, but to allow it to catch up with the times. For in the

1970s, with players changing clubs for hundreds of thousands of pounds (Barcelona paid Ajax £922,300 for Johan Cruyff in 1973) and TV audiences measured in hundreds of millions for World Cup and other big games, soccer has come a long way since the days of the 'gentleman amateur'.

The World Cup

The idea of a world soccer championship is as old as FIFA itself, but it was not until 1929 that FIFA gave Uruguay the go-ahead to stage the first World Cup tournament in 1930. Now it rivals the Olympic Games as the world's most important sporting occasion. Its prize was, up to 1970, the Jules Rimet Trophy, named after the Frenchman who was president of FIFA from 1920 to 1954. In 1970, Brazil won it for the third time to keep the cup permanently. A new prize, called the FIFA World Cup, was presented by FIFA.

The British countries, in dispute with FIFA, did not take part in any of the pre-war tournaments. And the choice of Uruguay to host the first meant that the

England's Geoff Hurst becomes the first man to score 3 in a World Cup final with this spectacular goal against Germany in 1966.

strongest European countries did not make the trip. The 13 entries were seeded into four groups, with Uruguay and Argentina, as expected, coming through to the final, beating Yugoslavia and the United States (with six former British professionals) by the same score, 6-1, in the semi-finals. Uruguay, despite going in at the interval 2-1 down, won a fast and furious match 4-2 in front of a 100,000 crowd.

Uruguay did not defend their trophy, and Italy won the next two World Cups – both contested on a knock-out basis – the first at home, the second in France. In 1934, the 16 qualifiers out of 32 entries contested the finals. Austria, with their 'Wunderteam', including the great Sindelar and Smistik, were the disappointment of the tournament, going down 1-0 in the semi-finals to Italy, who went on to beat Czechoslovakia 2-1 in the final, Schiavio scoring their extra-time winner.

Italy's only two survivors in 1938 were inside-forwards Meazza and Ferrari. Between them was the prolific Piola, whose five goals in four matches helped Italy retain the trophy. Hungary were their 4-2 victims in the final.

It was another 12 years before the next World Cup competition, and this time it

Charles, John (Wales), physically strong, skilful and dominant in the air, was a world-class player at both centre-half and centre-forward. In 1950, and just 18, he became the youngest Welsh international, and in 1958 he helped Wales reach the World Cup quarter-finals. Leeds converted Charles into a centre-forward, and 42 League goals in 1953–54 and 38 in 1956–57 proved his ability. But later in 1957 he went to Juventus for an unprecedented £65,000 fee. He won 3 league and 2 cup medals in Italy before returning to Leeds in 1962. But several months later he was back in Italy, with Roma. Sadly, his greatness had passed and the next three seasons saw him in Wales, with Cardiff, before going into non-League football.

Bobby Charlton in action against Romania in the 1970 World Cup, near the end of his illustrious international career.

Charlton, Bobby (England), survived the Munich disaster to become the most-capped and most-loved footballer in English soccer. Few honours eluded him. He was European and English Footballer of the Year in 1966 and won World Cup, European Cup, Football League, and FA Cup medals. His 106 caps and 49 goals were both England records.

Manchester United took him as a youngster, and even then the powerful left-foot shot, the defence-splitting passes, the astute little flicks, and the ability to beat his man were apparent. United employed him as an inside-forward, but Alf Ramsey saw him as England's deep-lying centre-forward for the 1966 World Cup. His 106th cap came against West Germany in the 1970 World Cup. He retired in 1973 to manage Preston.

Cruyff, Johan (Netherlands), European Footballer of the Year in 1971 and 1973, possesses all the qualities essential for a striker in an era of massed defences. But Cruyff is more than a mere striker: in the manner of Di Stefano, he is an orchestrator, setting up attacks and finishing them with deadly accuracy. He helped Ajax Amsterdam win the European Cup in 1971, scored both goals when they retained it in 1972, and captained them to their third triumph in 1973. He then went to Barcelona for a world record £922,300 and straightaway inspired them to their first championship success for 14 years.

Dean, Dixie (England), put himself in the record books, perhaps for all time, when he scored 60 goals for Everton when they won the 1927–28 1st Division Championship. His tally for all matches that season was an astonishing 82.

Bill Dean, as he preferred to be known, was powerfully built and his heading was superb. He specialized in coming in to meet crosses from the wing. But he was by no means just a goal-scoring centre-forward, and he made many openings for team-mates with his precise deflections. With Dean leading their attack, Everton won the League Championship twice and the FA Cup once. He scored a record 379 goals in the Football League in a career that began with Tranmere Rovers in 1923–24 and ended with Notts County in 1938–39. Capped 16 times, he scored 18 goals for England.

returned to South America, to Brazil. England took part for the first time, and, as in 1930, the group system was used. And for the only time a final pool, rather than semi-finals and a final, determined the winner.

It was expected that Brazil and England would be contenders for the trophy, but this was not to be. England were beaten by the United States in one of football's greatest upsets, and then lost to Spain. Sweden provided another surprise by leading their group ahead of Italy.

The final pool was made up of Brazil, Spain, Sweden, and Uruguay. Brazil started in magnificent style, beating Sweden 7-1 and Spain 6-1. All they had to do was draw with Uruguay, who had drawn with Spain, to win the cup. In the event, an iron Uruguayan defence held out until just after half-time, when Brazil scored. But then the Brazilian pressure eased, and the Uruguayans scored twice to rob Brazil of their prize – in front of nearly 200,000 spectators.

Brazil's defeat was unexpected, but Hungary's defeat in Switzerland in 1954 was a greater shock. This was the Hungary of Grosics, Bozsik, Czibor, Hidegkuti, Kocsis, and, above all, Puskas. Just three weeks before the World Cup they had defeated England 7-1. What happened was that the Hungarians were out-thought by the West German manager, Sepp Herberger. Both teams were in the same group, but, as two teams from each group qualified for the quarter-finals in

this World Cup, the Germans could afford to lose to Hungary. Herberger played six reserves against a full-strength Hungary. The Hungarians won 8-3, but they did not know the full strength of the Germans. In addition, and perhaps more significant, Puskas was injured and did not play again until the final. There, Hungary and West Germany met again, but this time the Germans were at full strength. At first it was all Hungary, as Puskas and Czibor scored. But that was all, and the Germans netted three times to defeat a side thought unbeatable.

The 1958 and 1962 World Cups belong to Brazil. In 1958, for the first time, Wales, England, Scotland, and Northern Ireland all qualified. Wales and Northern Ireland outdid their fellow-British by making the quarter-finals. The Irish were outplayed by France 4-0, but it took a goal by Pelé to put Brazil through against Wales. Meanwhile, West Ger-

The goal that denied Hungary the World Cup in 1954. Gyula Grosics just fails to hold Helmut Rahn's shot, and Germany win 3-2, Hungary's first defeat for four years.

many and Sweden also entered the semi-finals. Pelé got a hat-trick against France, and he then picked up two more in the final as the Brazilians unleashed all their brilliance on Sweden, to win 5-2. France's Fontaine scored a record 13 goals in the tournament.

Nine of the Brazilian side travelled to Chile in 1962 for what is considered the most disappointing of World Cup tournaments. The football was, on the whole, defensive, and the vicious play was seen at its worst in the Group 2 match between Chile and Italy. Players kicked and punched their opponents, and the police had to enforce a sending-off. Brazil, with Pelé injured in the first match, found an able deputy in Amarildo, and beat Czechoslovakia 3-1 in the final.

The great surprise of the 1966 tournament in England was the appearance in the quarter-finals of the little North Koreans, who drew with Chile and then beat Italy in their group. More sensational was their 3-0 lead over Portugal after only 24 minutes of their quarter-final.

But then Eusebio scored four times and the Portuguese eventually won 5-3. England, playing Alf Ramsey's methodical but sometimes dull football until they beat Portugal 2-1 in a splendid semi-final with two Bobby Charlton goals, faced West Germany in the final. It was a match of changing fortunes. First West Germany led through Haller, only for Hurst to equalize minutes later. In the 78th minute Peters scored, and the trophy seemed England's, but Weber equalized in injury time. What happened in extra time is history. Geoff Hurst's two goals, one still disputed, gave him the first hat-

Memorable moments in sport

Pelé's dummy

Dateline: Guadalajara, Mexico, 17 June 1970. The incomparable Brazilian star Pelé enriched soccer with countless memorable moments. Lightning speed of thought as well as of movement helped him amass more than a thousand goals, and his almost telepathic ability to find team-mates with perfect passes made many more. Yet the moment that is perhaps treasured above all by his innumerable admirers was not a goal but a 'near miss', not a shot or a pass but a 'dummy'.

The climax of Pelé's career was the 1970 World Cup, in Mexico, where he was the star of stars. Brilliant combinations with Jairzinho, Tostão, Rivelino, and Gerson, spectacular goals against Czechoslovakia and Romania, and a looping shot from behind the half-way line that caught the Czech 'keeper out of goal and only just scraped past the post – all these focused the spotlight on the 'Black Diamond', and few could have thought that he had any fresh footballing tricks to display. But he still had one or

Pelé does a 'U-turn' round the stranded 'keeper.

two up his sleeve, as he showed against Uruguay in the semi-finals.

A long, low diagonal pass from the left split the Uruguayan defence wide open, with Pelé haring in from the right unchallenged. But 'keeper Mazurkiewicz was advancing rapidly to block his path to goal. He checked, to see which way Pelé would take the ball, and found himself rooted to the ground in confusion as Pelé continued running full pelt to his right, ignoring the ball, which shot past him to his left. Pelé then 'changed gear', swerved behind the 'keeper, caught up with the ball and screwed it just wide as other defenders were coming back to cover.

Geoffrey Green of *The Times* once wrote that back in the thirties he had watched the Arsenal 'magician' Alex James split a defence by 'waving a foot' over the ball, and this had revealed to him a whole new vision of the game. Pelé's dummy in Mexico must have had a similar inspiring effect on millions of fans watching it on TV who had perhaps felt that soccer had nothing new to offer.

Di Stefano, Alfredo (Argentina and Spain), European Footballer of the Year in 1957 and again in 1959, is regarded by many as the most complete footballer of all time. Tall and well built, he possessed excellent control and acceleration, passed astutely – often seemingly intuitively – was a fine header, and finished with power and accuracy. To these qualities he added exceptional stamina that allowed him to dictate play from any point of the field when well into his 30s.

He first played for River Plate in 1944, and won 7 caps for his native Argentina before joining the rebel Colombian League. In 1953 he went to Spain, for whom he played 31 times. But it was for Real Madrid he performed his magic, scoring more than 500 goals for them, a record 49 in his 58 European Cup matches.

Leaving Real in 1964 he played for Espanol, before turning to management – with almost immediate success. He was Argentina's Manager of the Year in 1970 for his feats with Boca Juniors, and the following season he took Valencia to the Spanish League Championship.

Doherty, Peter (N. Ireland), a tall, gifted ball player with an

elusive swerve and a powerful left-foot shot, is universally recognized as Northern Ireland's finest inside-forward. He won wide acclaim also as the manager who took the national side to the quarter-finals of the 1958 World Cup. A player in the Di Stefano mould, he had a great influence on all his teams, although his playing career was somewhat tempestuous and chequered. His clubs numbered Glentoran, Blackpool, Manchester City, where he won a Championship medal in 1937, Derby County, for whom he scored in the 1946 FA Cup triumph, Huddersfield, and finally Doncaster Rovers.

Edwards, Duncan (England), made his league debut for Manchester United at 16 in April 1953, and two years later, at 18 years 183 days, became the youngest player capped for England. His talent was enormous. Physically powerful, a superb shot with either foot, he may well

have emerged as the finest wing-half ever to play for England. Sadly fate intervened. On 21 February 1958, aged 21 and winner of 18 caps and two League Championship medals, Duncan Edwards died, a victim of the Munich air disaster.

Eusebio (Portugal), European Footballer of the Year in 1965, came to prominence with Benfica in the early 1960s. Mozambique born and nicknamed the 'Black Panther', he is a natural footballer, easy moving and graceful. He scored two goals in Benfica's 5-3 defeat of Real Madrid in the 1962 European Cup final and his explosive right-foot shooting helped them to the 1963, 1965, and 1968 finals. Portugal first capped him at 19, and it was virtually his performance that took them through their quarter-final against North Korea in the 1966 World Cup. He scored 4 goals in that match, and his 9 in the tournament made him top scorer.

trick in a World Cup final, and they gave England a 4-2 victory.

The 1970 World Cup is remembered mainly for Brazil's scintillating football, which won them the Jules Rimet Trophy outright. But there were other memories – England's fine defensive performance against Brazil in their group match, with Bobby Moore and Gordon Banks outstanding; Germany's comeback from two down in their quarter-final against England and their remarkable fight before losing to Italy 4-3 in the semi-finals; golden goals from Czechoslovakia's Petras, Peru's Cubillas, Russia's Byshovets, and nine from Germany's Müller. Brazil beat Italy 4-1 in the final. And Pelé, Tostão, Jairzinho (who scored in all Brazil's matches), Rivelino, Gerson, and company demonstrated to the world 'what football is all about'.

International club competition

The idea of a European competition for clubs had been tossed around since the 1920s, and in 1927 the Mitropa Cup was started, catering for mid-European countries. It was the French newspaper *L'Equippe* that initiated the first European Champion Clubs Cup (known universally as the European Cup), and 16 clubs entered the first competition, in 1955–56. (Chelsea, England's entry, withdrew on the advice of the Football League.) Not all the entrants were league champions, but from 1956–57 onwards only league winners and the holders were eligible. The rounds are on a home-and-away basis, with the final being held on a predetermined ground.

The first five years of the competition

Eusebio (left) scores the first of his four goals against North Korea in the 1966 World Cup quarter-final at Goodison Park.

Real masters

Dateline: Hampden Park, 18 May 1960. At the end of the 1960 European Cup final at Hampden Park, the immense Scottish crowd of more than 127,000 remained to give Real Madrid a deafening ovation. It showed to what extent one of the most critical and chauvinistic audiences in the world had been impressed by the brilliance of the Spanish team, which calmly rode the shock of an early goal to destroy a far from inept Eintracht Frankfurt side.

As it transpired, this match, the fifth of Real's European Cup triumphs, was almost their swan-song. At the same time, it was surely the zenith of the marvellous partnership between Alfredo

Di Stefano, arms in the air, scores Real Madrid's second goal to put them ahead.

Di Stefano, the balding Argentinian centre-forward of all work, and Ferenc Puskas, the tubby Hungarian with the killing left foot.

Eintracht, who had hit six goals in each semi-final leg against Rangers, had a remarkable pair of veterans in the 33-year-old scheming inside-forward Pfaff and the 35-year-old right-winger Kress. It was Kress who put Eintracht ahead after 18 minutes from a pass by Stein, the big, strong centre-forward. That lead lasted just eight minutes. Canario, the Brazilian right-winger, crossed and Di Stefano lashed the ball home. Three minutes later an error by Loy allowed Di Stefano to score another, and later Puskas left-footed a third from the narrowest of angles – eight yards from the near post and a yard from the goal-line. When, just after half-time, the Hungarian scored from a rather harsh penalty, that seemed to be that. It was not.

Real's combination, the variety of their moves, were superb. Often they played possession football with a web of short, neat passes before suddenly accelerating for goal. Puskas scored twice more, Stein made it 2-6, Di Stefano raced through alone for his hat-trick, and finally Stein got a consolatory third. There remained no more but the epithets . . . and memories for those who had seen what many still regard as the finest game ever.

Finney, Tom (England), is often compared with Stanley Matthews, yet he was the more complete player. He was brilliant on either wing, an incisive inside-forward if necessary, or a creative deep-lying centre-forward. England capped him 76 times in four different positions, and he scored a then record 30 goals in those matches. He remained faithful to Preston, collecting a Cup runners-up medal in 1954. That year, and in 1957, he was voted Footballer of the Year. Like Matthews he could twist and turn to the byline and cross pin-point centres, but he could also cut in and shoot powerfully with either foot.

Gallacher, Hughie (Scotland), one of the 'Wembley Wizards', was the complete centre-forward. Quick-witted and superbly balanced, he had near perfect ball control, speed, and a baffling swerve. He was remarkable in the air, despite being only 5 ft 6 in tall. He netted 22 goals in 19 internationals. In a tempestuous career north and south of the border, he played for 8 clubs, scoring 387 League goals, most of them for Airdrie, Newcastle, and Chelsea.

Gento, Francisco (Spain), nicknamed 'Paco', appeared in all Real Madrid's European finals from 1956 to 1971, captaining them to a 6th European Cup victory in 1966. A small, compact left-winger, with a fine turn of speed and instant acceleration, he had the most remarkable ball control. He combined almost intuitively with Di Stefano. As well as setting up numerous goals, he scored some vital ones, especially his extra-time winner in the 1958 European Cup final.

Greaves, Jimmy (England), played his first League game in 1957 and retired in 1971 having scored 491 goals. Of these, 357 were in League matches for Chelsea, Spurs, and West Ham, and 44 came in 57 England appearances. Nine others were for AC Milan, during a brief, unhappy spell there in 1961, when Chelsea sold him for £80,000. Spurs brought him back to England for £99,999, and in 1970 they traded him to West Ham as part of a record deal for Martin Peters.

A marksman with a powerful left-foot shot and wonderful reflexes, he led the First Division goalscorers 5 times and he boasted the remarkable record of scoring in his first match for all his teams. With his premature retirement at 31, football lost a true artist.

Association football

Haynes, Johnny (England), the first England £100-a-week footballer, could have found greater fortune with numerous clubs, yet he remained faithful to Fulham, even when it meant seasons of 2nd Division football. Not that this affected England selection: the last 22 of his 56 internationals, which included the 1962 World Cup, were as captain. An inside-forward of masterly technique, he will always be remembered for his superb passing to the wings or through the centre.

Jairzinho (Brazil) became, in 1970, the first player to score in every match of a World Cup tournament when he scrambled in Pelé's header to put Brazil 3-1 up on Italy in the final. As Garrincha's successor on the right wing, he showed with his deceptive ball control and immaculately placed crosses that a class winger could still open defences, no matter how packed or brutal.

James, Alex (Scotland), a popular figure immediately recognizable in his baggy pants, was the linkman between defence and attack during Arsenal's great days of the 1930s, an inside-left of genius. Arsenal bought him in 1929 from Preston, where he had

were dominated by one club – Real Madrid. And the excitement this club generated by its fluent, attacking style of play ensured the European Cup of immediate success. There was no emphasis, as there was later, on defensive tactics in away matches. Real knew only one game: the attacking game. With such players as Di Stefano, Rial, Gento, Kopa, and later Puskas up front and Santamaria, Muñoz, and Zarraga behind them, they played it brilliantly.

Real won their sixth trophy in 1966, and although other fine sides won the trophy more than once – Benfica of Portugal and AC Milan and Internazionale of Italy each won it twice – it was not until Dutch champions Ajax completed a hat-trick in 1973 that a comparable side held sway. Ironically, their star Johan Cruyff was promptly whisked away to a Spanish club, and Ajax's run came to an end. The first British side to win the European Cup was Celtic in

1967; the first English side, Manchester United, in 1968, when George Best and Bobby Charlton outgunned Benfica and Eusebio at Wembley.

But British sides have made their presence felt in the two other major European competitions, the Cup-Winners Cup and the UEFA Cup (formerly Inter-Cities Fairs Cup). The former was first held in 1960–61. For national cup-winners (or runners-up if the winner qualifies as holder or is in the European Cup), it is run on similar lines to the European Cup. No club had won it more than once by the early 1970s, but British clubs had won 5 of the 14 competitions contested to 1974, and reached 4 of the other finals.

The Fairs Cup began in 1955 with a long-drawn-out affair between cities – represented by composite sides or single clubs – that did not finish until 1958, when Barcelona beat London in a two-legged final. The final has remained a

a reputation as a goalscorer, but Herbert Chapman turned him into a goal-maker, whose long, raking passes to raiding wingers were perhaps the main reasons for Arsenal's 4 Championships and 3 Cup finals in 7 seasons. It was a minor mystery, however, that he won no more than 8 caps

Two European Cup finals at Wembley, and two of the game's stars exhibit similar ball skills: George Best (above right), for Manchester United against Benfica in 1968, and Johan Cruyff (right), for Ajax against Panathinaikos in 1971.

Leeds captain Billy Bremner heads the only goal of the 1970–71 Fairs Cup semi-final tie against Liverpool at Anfield. Leeds went on to win the trophy for the second time.

two-legged affair, but more usually over two weeks than the two months of the first. Dominated at first by Spanish clubs – Barcelona, Valencia, Real Zaragoza – it was 'taken over' by English clubs when Leeds beat Ferencvaros in the 1968 final, having lost to Dynamo Zagreb of Yugoslavia the previous year. The roll of English clubs after Leeds runs: Newcastle, Arsenal, Leeds again, Tottenham (the first of the UEFA Cups), Liverpool.

UEFA Cup entry is open to a certain number of clubs from each member country, depending on its club strength. England's allocation, for example, is four. The holders gain automatic entry.

A facet of European club competition has been the means of deciding a draw over two legs. Originally, deciders were played on a neutral ground, but gradually all three competitions introduced the away-goals rule, under which away goals count double in the event of a tie. Games still tied were decided by a toss, but now penalties are taken – five each side alternately, and then in ones until a winner emerges.

The success of the Champion Clubs Cup in Europe inspired a counterpart in the New World – the South American Cup, or Copa Libertadores de America. First staged in 1960, it is run in groups which produce more groups for a semi-final round, which in turn produces two teams for a two-legged final. The previous year's winners are exempt until the semi-final round. The champions and the runners-up of the countries entering have been eligible since 1965.

Independiente of Argentina won the trophy for a record fourth time in 1973, Peñarol of Uruguay and Estudiantes de La Plata of Argentina both having won it three times. The only other country to provide a winner has been Brazil, with Santos in 1962 and 1963, although Chile's Colo-Colo took Independiente to a third match in 1973. The competition has a history of disputes and incidents – all 22 players in one match in 1971 were jailed for fighting – and the final has often been a war of attrition instead of a soccer showpiece.

With club champions being produced in Europe and South America, the two dominant soccer-playing continents, it was only natural that they should meet in a World Club Championship. But the competition, which did not receive FIFA's official approval until the late 1960s, has been littered with all that's

Kocsis, Sandor (Hungary), though not tall, was renowned for his remarkable heading ability. Inside-right of the 'Magic Magyars', he led the 1954 World Cup goalscorers with 11, and scored 75 in his 68 internationals. He did not return with Honved after the 1956 Hungarian Uprising, and eventually went to Spain, where he won further honours with Barcelona.

The airborne Kocsis in action against England in 1953.

Law, Denis (Scotland), with his lightning reflexes, superb heading, and ability to convert the half-chance into a goal, was one of Europe's most exciting footballers of the 1960s. Manchester City paid Huddersfield a record £55,000 for him in 1960 and sold him to Torino in 1961 for £100,000. A year later Manchester United brought him back to England for £115,000 to add flair and brilliance to their attack. In 1964 he was European Footballer of the Year. He scored a record 30 goals for Scotland, and after going to Manchester City in 1973 on a free transfer, made a surprising international comeback at the age of 33.

Lawton, Tommy (England), rivals Dixie Dean as Britain's best ever centre-forward. He had the same menace in the air and was formidable on the ground, strong on the ball, with a fierce shot. Everton paid Burnley £6,500 in 1936 when he was only 17, and in 1938–39 he scored 34 goals when they won the Championship. That season he won the first of 23 caps. In 1945 he went to Chelsea, and then in 1947 came his amazing move to Third Division Notts County for the first £20,000 fee. After helping them to promotion he went to Brentford and Arsenal, but later returned to Notts as manager.

Real Madrid's international forward line that ruled Europe in the late 1950s, from the left: Raymond Kopa (France), Hector Rial (Argentina), Alfredo Di Stefano (Argentina), Ferenc Puskas (Hungary), 'Paco' Gento (Spain).

McGrory, Jimmy (Scotland), Celtic's prolific goalscoring centre-forward between the wars, put away 550 goals in his first-class career. In British league football, he is the only leading scorer to have averaged more than a goal a match. In 1928 he scored 8 against Dunfermline, and in 1936 notched 4 against Motherwell in 5 minutes. He was manager of Kilmarnock, and then, from 1945 to 1965, of Celtic.

Mackay, Dave (Scotland), became a legend in his own time, the man who kept coming back. As an all-purpose left-half with Hearts and then Spurs, he won almost every honour going. He was a dynamic, driving member of the Spurs 'double' side of 1960–61 and an astute captain to Wembley in 1967, having twice come back after breaking a leg. In 1968 he embarked on a new career as a stopper at Derby County, immediately captaining them back to Division I. He was

joint Footballer of the Year in 1969. In 1971 he went to Swindon as player-manager. He became Nottingham Forest's manager in 1972, and Derby's in 1973.

Matthews, Sir Stanley (England), was the first footballer to be knighted, an honour received a month before his 50th birthday. That day he played in his star-studded testimonial, climaxing a career that began with Stoke in 1932 at 17 and encompassed some 700 League games and 54 full internationals. He had been a schoolboy international centre-half, but it was on the right-wing that he won world renown for his skills
(continued on opposite page)

No wonder the Scottish left-back's hair is standing on end – he's about to be made a fool of in a wartime international at Wembley by England's right-winger, the great Stanley Matthews, 'wizard of dribble'.

worst in sport – ill-feeling, bad sportsmanship, and violence.

The first world champions were Real Madrid, and in the next six years Peñarol, Santos, and Internazionale (Milan) each won it twice. For some years after this, with Argentinian clubs representing South America, the competition degenerated into a vicious farce, the Racing Club v Celtic (1967) and Estudiantes v Manchester United (1968), AC Milan (1969), and Feyenoord (1970) encounters being particularly disgraceful. Ajax pulled out of the competition in 1971 and 1973, allowing the European runners-up to enter, although they took their chance in 1972 and beat Independiente.

Soccer round the world

The continental confederations look after football in their own areas: in Europe the body is the Union of European Football Associations (UEFA); in South America, Confederación Sudamericana de Fútbol (CONMEBOL); in Africa, the African Football Confederation; in North and Central America and the Caribbean, Confederación Norte-Centroamericana y del Caribe de Fútbol (CONCACAF); in Asia, the Asian Football Confederation; and in Oceania (Australasia, etc), the Oceania Football Confederation (OFC).

Most of these bodies run competitions for national teams. The European Football Championship (formerly the Nations Cup) was first held in 1958. Although it has not captured the public imagination as the World Cup has, or attracted the partisan following of the international club cups, it provides keen competition. It is played with eight groups of four (each playing each, home and away), to produce eight teams for the quarter-finals, played on a two-legged home-and-

Celtic's little Jimmy Johnstone takes on two Racing Club defenders in the abortive 1967 World Club Championship.

away basis. Semi-finals, final, and third-place match are played in the same country.

Russia won the first championship (1958–60) and lost to Spain in the final of the second (1962–64), both of these being played on a knock-out basis. Italy hosted the third competition (1966–68) and won it – just. They played a goalless draw in the semi-final with Russia and went through on the toss of a coin. In the final they pulled back Yugoslavia's 1-0 lead in the last few minutes and won a replay two days later 2-0 against very tired opponents. Germany's team that won the fourth championship (1970–72) played some fine football, and beat Russia 3-0 in the Brussels final.

A number of other international competitions are held in Europe, between groups of countries or their clubs. The most long-lasting, indeed the oldest international competition in the world, is the British International Championship. An annual competition between England, Northern Ireland, Scotland,

Memorable moments in sport

Monty's magic save

Dateline: Wembley, 5 May 1973. No Second Division side had won the FA Cup for 42 years, and Sunderland were thrown in at Wembley against cup-holders Leeds United, one of the strongest club sides in the world. But the under-dogs, inspired by hordes of Wear-side followers who had lifted them in previous rounds, were not overawed. They matched Leeds for skill, for endeavour, and for spirit. And they took the lead with a Porterfield goal after 31 minutes.

The incident upon which the match turned, however, came midway through the second half. Leeds were throwing everything at them. Right-back Reaney sent a high ball to the far post. Left-back Cherry, who had earlier popped up in dangerous positions, again burst through on the blind side of the Sunderland defence, alone and unchallenged. He met Reaney's cross perfectly, heading it down towards the far corner. Goalkeeper Montgomery, who had moved across to meet the danger, flung himself to his left and just managed to get his hands to the ball. But he could only parry it – onto the right foot of the oncoming

Lorimer . . . *Peter Lorimer's right foot*!

Lorimer made contact six yards from an empty net. But Montgomery, momentarily flat out on the ground, somehow lifted himself and dived towards the probable trajectory of the ball, flinging up an arm in a moment of sheer instinctive genius and deflecting it onto the crossbar and to eventual safety.

The TV camera captured another sporting cameo at the end of the match as Sunderland manager Bob Stokoe – in trilby and raincoat, yet elegant as a gazelle – sprinted onto the pitch. There were 11 heroes in his Sunderland team, yet he ran straight into the arms of . . . Jim Montgomery.

Below left: Cherry homes in on Reaney's cross and Clarke (right) prepares to acclaim a goal. But Montgomery, below right, flings himself back across his goal to parry the point-blank header. The ball falls to Lorimer (7), who lashes it towards the net with his mighty right foot from no more than six yards. But again Montgomery blocks the ball, bottom left, knocking it onto the cross-bar, eventually to be cleared by a team-mate. Bottom right: The game is over, Sunderland have won, and their ecstatic manager Bob Stokoe runs straight over to his goalkeeper for a congratulatory embrace.

and his longevity. His tantalizing body swerve, devastating acceleration, superb ball control, and pin-point passing made him the nightmare of opposing backs.

Stoke sold him to Blackpool in 1947 for a mere £11,500, and he played in three Cup finals, collecting his winners medal in the drama-packed 'Matthews final' of 1953. In 1962 he returned to Stoke for £2,500, and his presence alone doubled the gates. It also helped Stoke back to Division I in 1963, when was Footballer of the Year. He had previously won the award in 1948 and had been European Footballer of the Year in 1956.

Mazzola, Sandrino (Italy), having led Inter-Milan's attack when they won the European Cup and World Club Championship in successive

years, emerged in the 1968 European Championship as a constructive inside-forward, and it was in this midfield role that he guided Italy to the final of the 1970 World Cup. His father was the Torino star Valentino Mazzola.

Mercer, Joe (England), ranks among the foremost British footballing personalities. As an attacking wing-half with Everton, he won Championship honours in 1939; in a more defensive role he captained Arsenal to the Championship in 1948 and 1953 and to Wembley in 1950 and 1952. In 1950 he was Footballer of the Year. Management at Sheffield United and Aston Villa ended in a breakdown, but Manchester City coaxed him back, and with Malcolm Allison's help he took them back to Division I in 1966. Then, from 1968 to 1970 he saw them win the Championship, the Cup, the League Cup, and the Cup-Winners Cup. In 1972, he became manager of Coventry, and in 1974 was made caretaker manager of England when Sir Alf Ramsey was sacked.

Meredith, Billy (Wales), linked with Stanley Matthews as the greatest outside-right of all time, was a winger of the classic mould, dribbling the ball to the corner flag before crossing immaculately. But he was not averse to popping up in goalscoring situations, as in the 1904 Cup final for Manchester City. He had joined City in 1894, but in 1906 went to Manchester United, winning League and Cup honours before returning to City in 1921.

and Wales, it was first held in 1884. Each country plays each other once. England and Scotland have dominated the Championship, and the match between these two sides has always been keenly contested.

South America had an international championship long before Europe. First held in 1917, the South American Championship was staged at irregular intervals, until in 1967 it faded away, overshadowed by the South American Cup, for clubs. Of the 29 tournaments that took place, Argentina won 12, Uruguay 11, and Brazil only 3. Peru, Paraguay, and Bolivia also managed to get their names on the trophy.

The African Football Confederation (founded 1956) and the Asian Football Confederation (1954) both have competitions for nations and for champion clubs. CONCACAF also holds an international championship.

World football has for long been dominated by Europe and South America, but there have been signs of rapid growth in other continents. North Korea popped up in the 1966 World Cup and shamed Italy 1-0 to reach the quarter-finals, where they shocked Portugal, leading 3-0 before Eusebio took charge and led Portugal to a 5-3 victory. But perhaps the greatest sensation in international soccer was England's defeat at the hands of the United States in the 1950 World Cup in Brazil. The 1-0 scoreline at Belo Horizonte still sends shivers down the spines of English fans. But few people remember that the United States reached the semi-finals of the first World Cup in 1930 – they lost 6-1 to Argentina. With soccer spreading in American schools, how long can it be before the United States are a real force in world football? And another country gave notice in 1973 of their progress by

Memorable moments
in sport

The Wembley Wizards

Scotland's centre-forward Hughie Gallacher (left) watches the ball whistle past the post, a welcome escape for the bemused and overworked England defence.

Dateline: Wembley, 31 March 1928. Scotland's most famous victory was achieved by the team known as 'The Wembley Wizards' – the team who humbled England to such an extent that Alex James, the most magical wizard of them all, proclaimed 'We could have had ten'.

The tiny Scottish attack, with Alec Jackson easily the tallest at 5 ft 7 in, swept England aside by playing the pure style of Scottish football: ground passes alternating with individual dribbles. It was a day on which all the front five – Jackson, Dunn, Gallacher, James, and Morton –

hit peak form together, the sort of day that comes once in a lifetime, if at all.

Doyen critic Ivan Sharpe summed it up like this: 'England were not merely beaten. They were bewildered – run to a standstill, made to appear utterly inferior by a team whose play was as cultured and beautiful as I ever expect to see.' And 30 years later Sharpe was still insisting that he had not seen a display to match it.

Scotland were lucky on two counts. First, heavy rain made the Wembley turf, unused for almost a year, markedly different from the mud of the normal March pitch. It was ideal for their style of play. Second, England winger Smith hit a post in the second minute. A dry day, or an early goal against them, could have resulted in an entirely different match.

But football is full of such theories, whereas the record books are concerned only with the facts. The facts of this celebrated match are that Scotland streaked to a sensational 5-1 success, with Jackson scoring three times (four Huddersfield team-mates were in the England side) and James (then a goalscorer with Preston before he became a goalmaker with Arsenal) hitting two beauties past the overworked Hufton. Kelly scored England's goal direct from a free-kick – one of only six shots his team managed throughout the game.

Football club colours

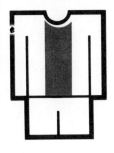

Ajax
(Netherlands)

Arsenal
(England)

Barcelona
(Spain)

Bayern Munich
(West Germany)

Benfica
(Portugal)

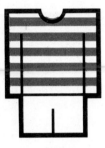

Celtic
(Scotland)

Chelsea
(England)

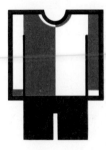

Ferencvaros
(Hungary)

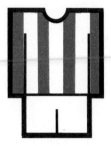

Feyenoord
(Netherlands)

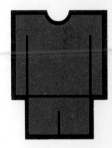

Independiente
(Argentina)

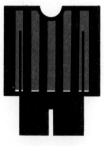

Inter-Milan
(Italy)

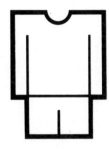

Leeds United
(England)

Liverpool
(England)

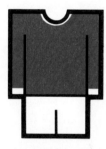

Manchester City
(England)

Manchester United
(England)

AC Milan
(Italy)

Nacional
(Uruguay)

Newcastle United
(England)

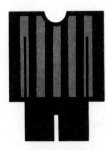

Peñarol
(Uruguay)

Racing Club
(Argentina)

Rangers
(Scotland)

Real Madrid
(Spain)

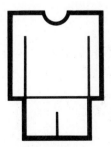

Santos
(Brazil)

Tottenham Hotspur
(England)

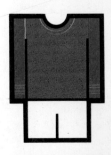

West Ham United
(England)

VIỆT NAM DÂN CHỦ CÔNG HÒA

BƯU CHÍNH

30

OLYMPIA ROMA MCMLX

XVII

40 f

MAGYAR POSTA

962. AUTÓ MOTORSPORT

MAGYAR POSTA

10

40 GR

3P

County Cricket 1873-1973

7½P

County Cricket 1873-1973

9P

County Cricket 1873-1973

MAGYAR POSTA 20 f

XIX olimpijada

Mexico · 1968

010

JUGOSLAVIJA

CUBA   CORREOS
1970   1

XI JUEGOS CENTROAMERICANOS Y DEL CARIBE

ČESKOSLOVENSKO

TOKIÓ
1964

30 f

MAGYAR
POSTA

LONDON-WEMBLEY

1953. XI. 25.

1953
EPSTADION

6:3

MAGYAR POSTA

2 Ft

WORLD CUP CHAMPIONS

Italy 2nd.

2   YEMEN

MEXICO 70

WORLD CUP CHAMPIONS
Brazil 1st.

4   THE MUTAWAKELITE KINGDOM
OF YEMEN

WORLD CUP CHAMPIONS

W. Germany 3rd.

6   YEMEN

160 LEI   POSTA

R.P. ROMINA

20 c

Republique RWANDAISE

HRY XIX· OLYMPIÁDY 1968 MEXIKO

30 h

ČESKOSLOVENSKO

HRY XIX· OLYMPIÁDY 1968 MEXIKO

60 h

ČESKOSLOVENSKO

REPUBLICA   17 c

CORREO
AÉREO   DOMINICANA

БЪЛГАРИЯ

GUYANA 5c SOUTH AMERICA · GUYANA 6c SOUTH AMERICA · GUYANA 25c SOUTH AMERICA

XVIII IGRZYSKA OLIMPIJSKIE TOKIO 1964 · POLSKA 40 GR

MISTRZOSTWA ŚWIATA W KLASIE FINN 1965 · POLSKA 30 GR

POLSKA 20 gr

REPUBLICA DOMINICANA 3c CORREOS

REPUBLICA DOMINICANA 5c CORREOS

MANX GRAND PRIX GOLDEN JUBILEE 1923 1973 · ISLE OF MAN 3P

II. EUROPÄISCHE JUNIORENSPIELE LEICHTATHLETIK LEIPZIG 1968 · 20 DDR

REPUBLICA DOMINICANA 11c CORREO AEREO

REPUBLICA DOMINICANA 10c CORREO AEREO

MANX GRAND PRIX GOLDEN JUBILEE 1923 1973 · ISLE OF MAN 3½P

X TÉLI OLIMPIA · MAGYAR POSTA 30 F · GRENOBLE

W KOSZYKÓWCE MĘŻCZYZN · XIII MISTRZOSTWA EUROPY · POLSKA 90 GR

20 c · REPUBLIQUE RWANDAISE

FUJEIRA · WINTER OLYMPICS GRENOBLE 1968 · POSTAGE 2 RIYALS

IX Zimowe Igrzyska Olimpijskie · Innsbruck 1964 · Polska 20 GR · F. WINIARSKI

IX Zimowe Igrzyska Olimpijskie · Innsbruck 1964 · Polska 30 GR · F. WINIARSKI

MEXICO 68 · 20 b · POSTA ROMANA

IX Zimowe Igrzyska Olimpijskie · Innsbruck 1964 · Polska 40 GR · F. WINIARSKI · PWPW

FUJEIRA · WINTER OLYMPICS GRENOBLE 1968 · POSTAGE 3 RIYALS

Racing colours of leading owners

Her Majesty
The Queen

Queen Elizabeth
The Queen Mother

Mr John J. Astor

Lady Beaverbrook

Mr T. F. Blackwell

M. M. Boussac

Lord Derby

Mrs J. L. Hislop

Mr L. Brook Holliday

Lord Howard
de Walden

Mr F. R. Hue-Williams

Mr H. J. Joel

Mr Stanhope Joel

Mr K. N. Maharaj

Mr P. Mellon

Duke of Norfolk

Mr G. A. Oldham

Mr G. J. Van der Ploeg

Mr David Robinson

Mr C. A. B. St
George

Sir Michael Sobell

Mrs P. Tweedy

Lady Zia Wernher

Anne Duchess of
Westminster

M D. Wildenstein

Joe Jordan of Leeds powers in a header for Scotland against Czechoslovakia at Hampden Park in September 1973, watched by captain Billy Bremner (far left) and the evergreen Denis Law (far right). This goal gave Scotland a 2–1 victory and ensured their qualification for the 1974 World Cup finals.

qualifying for the World Cup for the first time – Australia. Severe competition from three other football codes has held soccer back in Australia, but the spotlight of the World Cup can only encourage the game there.

The lifeblood of soccer round the world is found in the national leagues and cups, in which fiercely partisan supporters follow the fortunes of their chosen teams week in and week out. Some countries, such as Spain and Hungary, run their leagues on a 'pyramid' system in which there is a top division with promotion from and relegation to two or more second divisions and then perhaps nine third divisions and more regional leagues. In England and Scotland the leagues are based on a much simpler structure. Scotland has just two divisions (with another scheduled for 1975–76), England four. In England, the Football League has been in existence since 1888–89, the oldest in the world. It is also regarded as perhaps the toughest, with a First Division of 22 teams. And by the early 1970s, 22 different teams had won the Championship, with Arsenal and Liverpool the most successful, recording eight wins each. The Scottish League, on the other hand,

has been dominated largely by two clubs, Rangers and Celtic. First held in 1890–91, it had by the early 1970s been won by only 8 other clubs—14½ times.

The Scottish Cup is similarly dominated by the same two Glasgow clubs, whereas the FA Cup has nearly 40 winners. Inaugurated in 1872, two years earlier than its Scottish counterpart, the FA Cup provides traditionally exciting soccer, with a showpiece final at Wembley. By the early 1970s, no team had managed to equal Aston Villa's record of seven wins, six of which were made before Wembley's first final in 1923.

Many other countries have league competitions going back a long way. Knock-out cup competitions, however, were not so popular until the advent of the European Cup-Winners Cup in 1960. But although European club tournaments have revitalized many national competitions, they have also meant an increase in the number of games played. The extra pressure on players – taking part in some sixty or seventy highly competitive matches a season – with the consequent lowering of standards and the win-at-all-costs attitude – has been one of the problems of soccer in the seventies ... along with television, violence on and off the field, antediluvian administration, poorly defined laws, down to lack of wingers – all of which continue to make soccer a major talking point for millions even when it is not so entertaining as in days of yore.

Moore, Bobby (England), received the World Cup in 1966, climaxing a hat-trick of winning Wembley finals. He captained West Ham when they won the FA Cup in 1964 and the Cup-Winners Cup in 1965. In 1964 he was Footballer of the Year, and he was the 1966 World Cup Player of the Tournament. A tall, cultured defender, he played in the 1962 World Cup and was England's captain again in 1970. Happiest as a second stopper in a No. 6 shirt, he stamps his authority on play immediately, tackling, covering, and distributing faultlessly, and stifling attacks by intelligent anticipation. He won a record 108 caps before going to Fulham in 1974.

Müller, Gerd (W. Germany), European Footballer of the Year in 1970, led the 1970 World Cup goalscorers with 10, 6 from hat-tricks against Bulgaria and Peru. A strong shot with either foot, a

powerful header of the ball, he converts the slightest chance, often the seemingly impossible ones. With Müller as their marksman, Bayern Munich enjoyed League, Cup, and Cup-Winners Cup success after 1966.

Pelé (Brazil) is the best known of all footballers, and probably the finest. His talents are legendary: the intuitive ability to produce the unexpected, the selfless touches that set up goals for team-mates, the ball control that allows him to outwit the closest marking, and the soaring header and shooting power that have brought more than 1,000 goals. He was a world star at 17 when Brazil first won the World Cup. In 1970, when his presence dominated that World Cup, he was indisputably the king, heading the first goal of the final and making two others.

Born into an impoverished, coloured family, he has become one of the world's richest sportsmen. Santos, who made him their first-choice inside-left when he was 16, have benefited greatly from their star, triumphing in competitions from the Sao Paulo League to the World Club Championship.

Association football

Puskas, Ferenc (Hungary and Spain), the 'Galloping Major' of the magnificent Hungarians of the 1950s, possessed one of the fiercest left-foot shots in football history. England felt its power when they fell 6-3 at Wembley in 1953; Eintracht Frankfurt were 4 times on the receiving end in the 1960 European Cup final; and Benfica had to allow a hat-trick before beating Real Madrid 5-3 in the 1962 final.

Though captain of Hungary for many of his 84 internationals — in which he scored 83 goals — Puskas preferred exile to returning to Hungary in 1956 with the touring Honved, and two years later Real Madrid signed him. Europe was again to be awed by the brilliant ball control and fulminating shot of the stocky inside-left. He played 4 times for Spain in 1961–62. In 1971 he made his fourth European Cup final as manager of Greek club Panathinaikos.

Ramsey, Sir Alf (England), enigmatic manager of England when they won the World Cup in 1966 and lost it in 1970, made his name in the managerial field with Ipswich, guiding them from Division III to the League Championship in 5 seasons. In doing so, he emulated his performance as a Spurs player of winning the 2nd and 1st Division titles in successive seasons. Spurs bought him from Southampton in 1949, and he won the nickname 'The General' for his steady, constructive play at right-back for club and country. The resolute qualities displayed in the player were later evident in the manager, with his preference for players with a high work-rate rather than the spectacular individualist.

Sir Alf Ramsey with the Jules Rimet Trophy his England side won in 1966.

Laws of soccer

The Laws of football may be altered only at the annual meeting of the International Football Association Board. This body meets every June, and is made up of representatives of the four British Football Associations and of FIFA. The British associations each have one vote and FIFA has four, and alteration of the Laws requires a three-quarters majority.

The field of play is marked out as in the diagram. For international matches the range of dimensions is 110–120 yards by 70–80 yards. The ball, made of leather or any other material approved by the International Board, has a circumference of 27 to 28 inches and must weigh 14 to 16 ounces at the beginning of the game.

Soccer is played between two teams of 11 players. The maximum number of substitutes allowed in any competition is two, selected from five nominated players. In most British competitions only one is permitted, and he must be nominated before the match. The 11 players on a team consist of 10 outfield players and a goalkeeper, who is the only one allowed to handle the ball (but only within his own penalty area).

The game is controlled by a referee, whose decisions are final. He uses a whistle to start and stop the game, and is assisted by two linesmen, who signal by means of a flag. They patrol the touch-lines, outside the field.

The duration of the game is 90 min, divided into two periods of 45 min with a half-time interval of up to 5 min. The referee should make allowance at the end of each period for time lost through stoppages.

Before the start of play, opposing captains toss a coin, the winner choosing either to kick off or which end to start from. The teams change ends at half-

Some offences are more deliberate than others. The Laws, however, give the referee little scope to deal justly with 'professional' fouls.

time. At the start of the game, the ball is placed on the centre-spot and all the players must be in their own half of the field. No players from the side not kicking-off may be nearer than 10 yards from the ball. The ball must travel at least its own circumference into the opposing half of the field and the kicker may not play the ball again until it has been touched by another player. The game is restarted in the same way after a goal has been scored (by the team conceding the goal) and after the half-time interval (by the team who did not kick off).

The game is restarted after any other temporary suspension (not covered by the various kicks or the throw-in) by means of a *dropped ball*. The referee drops the ball at the place where it was when play was suspended, and no player is allowed to play the ball until it has touched the ground.

For a goal to be scored, the ball must pass wholly over the goal-line, between the posts and under the cross-bar, provided it does so in accordance with the Laws. The team scoring the greater number of goals is the winner; if an equal number of goals are scored, the game is a 'draw'. In certain circumstances, such as cup replays, 'extra time' (usually 15 minutes each way) is added in an attempt to get a result.

There are nine offences punishable by the award of a *direct free-kick*: kicking or attempting to kick an opponent; tripping; jumping at an opponent; violently charging an opponent (a fair charge is made shoulder to shoulder); charging from behind (unless being obstructed);

This probably indicates that the teams should change ends before the kick-off, but referees are often to be found pointing in two directions at once. Lack of an adequate signalling system in soccer makes communication difficult.

holding; pushing; striking or attempting to strike an opponent; or handling the ball. If any of these fouls is committed in the penalty area, a *penalty-kick* is awarded, whether or not the ball was in the area at the time of the offence.

An *indirect free-kick* is awarded for such offences as dangerous play and intentional obstruction (running or standing between an opponent and the ball without attempting to play the ball) and for certain technical offences such as *offside*. A player is offside if he is nearer his opponents' goal-line than the ball *at the moment the ball is played*, unless there are two of his opponents nearer to their own goal-line than he is or the ball last touched an opponent. A player cannot be offside in his own half or direct from a goal-kick, corner-kick, throw-in, or dropped ball. A player does not have to touch the ball to be offside, and a referee need not penalize a player in an offside position if in his opinion the player is not interfering with play or seeking to gain advantage.

A player may be *cautioned* for persistent infringement of the Laws, for dissent, and for ungentlemanly conduct. A player may be *sent off* for serious offences or for persistent misconduct after receiving a caution.

When a free-kick is being taken, opposing players must stand at least 10 yards from the ball. A goal can be scored from a direct free-kick. But another player (of either side) must touch the ball before a goal can be scored after an indirect free-kick. For a penalty-kick, all players except the taker and the opposing goalkeeper must be outside the penalty area (but within the field of play) and at least 10 yards from the ball. The kick is taken from the penalty-spot.

If the ball passes over a touch-line, a *throw-in* is awarded at the place it went out to the side opposing the player who

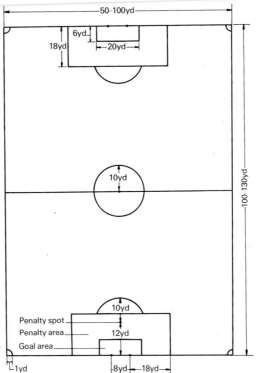

Dimensions of an association football pitch.

last touched the ball. The thrower must use both hands to deliver the ball from behind and over his head. If the ball passes over the goal-line (except when a goal is scored), a *goal-kick* is awarded to the defending team if the ball was last played by a member of the opposing side, or a *corner-kick* is awarded to the attacking team if the ball was last played by a defender. The kicks are taken from the side the ball went out. A goal-kick is taken from within the goal-area, and all opposing players must be outside the penalty area. For a corner-kick, the ball must be placed wholly within the quarter-circle at the corner-flag. Opposing players must be at least 10 yards from the ball. A goal can be scored direct from a corner-kick.

Revie, Don (England), the man who made the great Leeds side of the 1960s and 1970s, came to the fore as a scheming inside-forward with Leicester and then,

after a short stay at Hull, became the deep-lying centre-forward of Manchester City's 'Revie plan'. In 1955, when Manchester City lost at Wembley, he was Footballer of the Year, and the next season he collected his Cup winners medal. Transfers followed to Sunderland and Leeds, and it was at Leeds that, as manager, he was able to give full expression to his ideas, building them from a mediocre 2nd Division side into one of Europe's top teams. In 1974 he became England team manager.

Seeler, Uwe (W. Germany), winner of a record 72 caps, scored in 4 World Cups, captaining the Germans to the final and semi-finals respectively in 1966 and 1970. By 1970 he

had reverted to midfield, but with his acrobatic headers and deadly finishing he was not far removed from the striker who had led the West German League scorers on 5 occasions.

Shankly, Bill (Scotland), having enjoyed a distinguished career that saw him as Preston's right-half in the 1937 and 1938 Cup finals, managed Carlisle, Grimsby, Workington, and Huddersfield before going to Liverpool in 1959. Since then he has become a legend — shrewd, gruff but kind, witty, often quoted — and he developed the formidable and successful Liverpool sides of the 1960s and 1970s.

Bobby Moore won a record 108 caps for England in an international career that lasted from 1962 to 1973 and included the 1966 World Cup in which he captained England to victory.

SOCCER 'MOSTS'

World Cup

Wins	3	Brazil (1958–62–70)
Appearances	10	Brazil (1930–1974)
Individual	5	Antonio Carbajal (Mexico) 1950–54–58–62–66
Goals	14	Gerd Müller (West Germany) 1970–74
	13	Just Fontaine (France) 1958
in final	3	Geoff Hurst (England) 1966
Highest score	9	Hungary (v S. Korea, group match) 1954
	9	Yugoslavia (v Zaïre, group match) 1974
in final	5	Brazil (v Sweden) 1958
Aggregate	12	Austria 7 Switzerland 5 (quarter-final) 1954

Internationals

Appearances	110*	Pelé (Brazil)
	108	Bobby Moore (England)
	106	Bobby Charlton (England)
consecutive	70	Billy Wright (England)
Goals	90*	Pelé (Brazil)
	83	Ferenc Puskas (Hungary, Spain)
	75	Sandor Kocsis (Hungary)

Career Goals

	1,329†	Artur Friedenreich (Brazil)
	1,195	Pelé (Brazil; to end of 1973) 1,209 games
	1,006	Franz 'Bimbo' Binder (Austria & Germany) 1930–50, 756 games

Olympic Games

Wins	3	Hungary (1952–64–68)
Highest score	17	Denmark (17-1 v France 'A', 1908)

International club competition

European Cup

Wins	6	Real Madrid (Spain) 1956–57–58–59–60–66
Individual	6	Paco Gento (Real Madrid)
Finals	8	Paco Gento (Real Madrid)
Goals	49	Alfredo di Stefano (Real Madrid)
Highest score	12	Feyenoord, Netherlands (v KR Reykjavik, 1st rnd) 1969–70
in final	7	Real Madrid (7-3 v Eintracht Frankfurt) 1959–60
Aggregate (2 legs)	18	Benfica, Portugal (8, 10 v Stade Dudelange, prel rnd) 1965–66

South American Cup

Wins	4	Independiente (Argentina) 1964–65–72–73
Highest score	11	Peñarol, Uruguay (11-2 v Valencia, Venezuela) 1970

National League Championships

Argentina	11	River Plate		Irish Republic	10	Shamrock Rovers
Austria	25	Rapid Vienna		Italy	15	Juventus
Belgium	16	Anderlecht		Netherlands	16	Ajax
Brazil – Rio de Janeiro	20	Fluminense		Poland	10	Gornik Zabrze; Ruch Chorzow
São Paulo	16	Palmeiras				
Czechoslovakia	13	Sparta Prague		Portugal	20	Benfica
England	8	Arsenal; Liverpool		Scotland	34	Rangers
France	7	St-Etienne		Spain	15	Real Madrid
Germany, East	6	Vorwaerts		Uruguay	32	Peñarol
Germany, West	9	Nuremberg		USSR	10	Dynamo Moscow
Hungary	22	Ferencvaros		Yugoslavia	11	Red Star Belgrade
Ireland, Northern	29	Linfield				

Attendance Records

World Cup	199,850	Brazil v Uruguay, Maracana Stadium (Brazil) 16.7.50
European Cup	135,826	Celtic v Leeds (semi-final), Hampden Park (Scotland) 15.4.70
final	127,621	Real Madrid v Eintracht Frankfurt, Hampden Park, 18.5.60
British	149,547	Scotland v England, Hampden Park, 17.4.37
Scottish Cup	146,433	Celtic v Aberdeen, Hampden Park, 24.4.37
FA Cup	126,047	Bolton v West Ham, Wembley, 28.4.23
Scottish League	118,567	Rangers v Celtic, Ibrox, 2.1.39
Football League	83,260	Manchester United v Arsenal, Maine Road, 17.1.48

Transfers

	£922,300	Johan Cruyff (Ajax Amsterdam to Barcelona) 1973
British	£350,000‡	Bob Latchford (Birmingham to Everton) 1974

* Recognized by FIFA, but includes matches not universally regarded as full internationals, such as games against regions or clubs; more widely accepted are 92 games/76 goals.

† Undocumented, but recognized by FIFA.

‡ Valuation in a 'player-exchange plus cash' deal.

Johan Cruyff cost Barcelona a record £922,300 when they lured him away from Ajax in 1973. It was money well spent, though, for he inspired the Spanish club to their first league title for 14 years and he brought the crowds swarming back.

British Records

Teams

Highest score	Arbroath 36 Bon Accord 0 (Scot. Cup, 1st rnd) 5.9.1885	
International	England 13 Ireland 0, 18.8.1882	
FA Cup	Preston 26 Hyde 0 (1st round) 15.10.1887	
final	Bury 6 Derby 0, 1903	
Scottish final	Renton 6 Cambuslang 0, 1888	
League Div. I	West Bromwich Albion 12 Darwen 0, 4.3.1892	
	Nottingham Forest 12 Leicester Fosse 0, 21.4.1909	
away	Newcastle United 1 Sunderland 9, 5.12.1908	
	Cardiff 1 Wolverhampton Wanderers 9, 3.9.55	
Scottish Div. I	Celtic 11 Dundee 0, 26.10.1895	
away	Airdrieonians 1 Hibernian 11, 24.10.59	

Goals/season

League Div. I	128 Aston Villa (42 games) 1930–31	
Scottish Div. I	132 Heart of Midlothian (34 games) 1957–58	

Points/season

League Div. I	67 Leeds United (42 games) 1968–69	
Scottish Div. I	76 Rangers (42 games) 1920–21	

Players

International appearances — England		108	Bobby Moore
	N. Ireland	59	Terry Neill
	Scotland	55	Denis Law
	Wales	68	Ivor Allchurch
Football League appearances		764	Jimmy Dickinson (Portsmouth)
Scottish League appearances		626	Bob Ferrier (Motherwell)
International goals — England		49	Bobby Charlton (106 games)
	N. Ireland	13	Billy Gillespie (25 games)
	Scotland	30	Denis Law (55 games)
	Wales	23	Trevor Ford (38 games)
Single match		6	Joe Bambrick, Ireland (v Wales) 1.2.30

League goals

Football League —	Season	60	Dixie Dean (Everton, 39/42 games) 1927–28
	Match	7	James Ross (Preston v Stoke) 6.10.1888
		7	Ted Drake (Arsenal away to Aston Villa) 14.12.35
	Any division	10	Joe Payne (Luton v Bristol R., Div III S) 13.4.36
	Cup tie	9	Ted MacDougall (Bournemouth v Margate, 1st rnd) 20.11.71
	Career	434	Arthur Rowley 1946–65
	Div. I	357	Jimmy Greaves 1957–71
	one club	349	Dixie Dean (Everton) 1925–38
Scottish League —	Season	52	William McFadyen (Motherwell, 34/38 games) 1931–32
	Match	8	Jimmy McGrory (Celtic v Dunfermline) 14.1.28
	Cup tie	13	John Petrie (Arbroath v Bon Accord) 5.9.1885
	Career	410	Jimmy McGrory 1922–38
	Div. I	397	Jimmy McGrory 1922–38
	one club	397	Jimmy McGrory (Celtic) 1922–38

Above: *Ted Drake of Arsenal, who equalled the First Division goalscoring record with 7 goals against Aston Villa in 1935.*

Jimmy McGrory, Celtic's prolific centre-forward, set numerous Scottish goal-scoring records between the wars.

Far left: *Bill 'Dixie' Dean, whose record 60 First Division goals for Everton in the 1927–28 season has never remotely looked like being beaten since.*
Left: *Jimmy Greaves, who scored a record 357 goals in England's First Division, for Chelsea, Spurs, and West Ham.*

Stein, Jock, went to Celtic in 1951 from the obscurity of non-League football in Wales. Three years later the sturdy centre-half was captaining Celtic to a Scottish League and Cup double. That in itself was a Cinderella story, but Stein was to reach greater heights as a manager. In 1960 he saved Dunfermline from relegation, and led them to a Scottish Cup triumph the next year. A short spell with Hibs in 1964, and then he was back at Celtic. With his arrival came an era of glory, with a perpetual list of League, Cup, and League Cup honours climaxed by the European Cup victory of 1967.

Wright, Billy (England), when he led England against Scotland in April 1959, became the first footballer to win 100 caps. When he retired in August that year he had 105. He had captained England since 1948. Originally an inside-forward, he soon staked his claim to the right-half berth, but in the 1954 World Cup he moved to centre-half, where his courage, determination, and remarkable leap were ideally suited.

Wright played more than 500 games for Wolves, captaining them to victory in the Cup in 1949 and in the Championship in 1954, 1958, and 1959. He was Footballer of the Year in 1952. Yet when he had joined Wolves, Frank Buckley almost sent him home because he was too small. In 1962 he became manager of Arsenal, but though doing much that was good, he did not produce immediate results and was replaced in 1966.

Yachin, Lev (USSR), well over 6 ft tall and given to courageous and spectacular saves, ranks high on any list of all-time great goalkeepers. Winner of a record 74 Russian caps, he starred in the 1958 World Cup (the first of three), and in the 1960 and 1964 Nations Cups, in which Russia were winners and runners-up respectively. All his domestic football was played for Moscow Dynamo, but one of his most brilliant performances was for the Rest of the World against England in 1963.

Young, George (Scotland), his country's most capped player when he retired in 1957, dominated the defence in one of Rangers' great periods. Tall and strongly built, yet surprisingly mobile, he was equally commanding at centre-half or right-back. He captained his country in 50 of his 75 representative appearances (53 peace-time internationals) and won 6 League and 4 Cup winners medals.

In the 1800s, before catenaccio, *centre-backs, or even crosses, football was chiefly a dribbling game. It was the Scots who introduced passing to the game, in the 1870s.*

Soccer terms

Blind side The side of one or more players away from the ball or the play.

Catenaccio A tactical system, basically defensive, with a *sweeper* operating behind four backs, three midfield players, and two strikers.

Centre A pass from near the touchline into the goalmouth.

Centre-back(s) The player(s) positioned between the left and right full-backs.

Cross Same as *centre.*

Dribbling The art of running with the ball at the feet, particularly as a means of beating opponents.

Linkman Same as *midfield player.*

Marking Covering a player so that his team-mates cannot pass to him effectively. There are two main methods of marking: *man-to-man*, in which a defender concentrates on a particular opponent, and *zonal*, in which a defender covers the player or players in a certain section of the field.

Midfield player A player who links the defence with the attack. Basically he operates in the centre of the field, but should move up or back as play dictates.

Over the top/ball A term used when a player, going in to make a tackle, kicks over the top of the ball and fouls an opponent. Regarded as one of the worst crimes in the game, but sometimes difficult to detect without the aid of a slow-motion replay.

Overlapping When a player goes up outside the ball-carrier, often the winger, to receive the ball, or when he takes over the role of the winger.

Running off the ball Players not in possession moving into a good position to receive the ball, or to divert the attentions of defenders from other players.

Screening Keeping the ball away from an opponent by shielding it with the body or legs while playing it.

Set-piece Any dead-ball situation at which practised moves can be attempted.

Shoulder-charge A lawful charge, shoulder to shoulder, on an opponent. The ball must be within playing distance.

Sliding tackle When the tackler slides in to rob his opponent of the ball.

Square ball/pass A cross-field pass.

Stopper Originally the centre-half in the third-back game. Now more usually one of two centre-backs.

Striker A player who operates mostly upfield to score goals.

Sweeper The player behind the defensive four in a *catenaccio* line-up.

Tackle from behind Misapplied term for the foul committed by a player going for the ball via the back of an opponent's legs.

Tactical foul Euphemism for a foul committed so that the opposing side loses its advantage. Handling a through ball and tripping are common examples. Soccer is one of the few sports that does not equip its referees to deal satisfactorily with such tactics.

Target man Usually a striker who collects the clearances from defence and holds the ball until support arrives.

Third-back game The tactical system in which the centre-half moved back from midfield to play as a centre-back. Resulted from the change in the offside law in 1925.

Through ball A pass through or over a defence for a team-mate to run on to.

Trapping The art of controlling the ball with foot, chest, stomach, thigh, or sometimes head before making use of it.

W formation The formation of the forwards in the third-back game. The inside-forwards moved back to fill the area left vacant by the centre-half, leaving the wingers and centre-forward ahead of them, and so forming a W.

Wall The line-up of defending players between the ball and the goal at a free-kick to prevent a direct shot at goal.

Wall pass A pass immediately deflected on by the receiver for the original passer to run on to. Sometimes referred to as a 'quick one-two'.

Athletics

The first sport in the Olympic Games, athletics is a conglomerate of activities in which any fit person, male or female, can participate. A multiplicity of running and obstacle (hurdle) races, four types of throwing (three for women), and all-round competitions make up what Americans call 'track and field': add to these cross-country, long-distance road running, and walking and you have 'athletics'.

Nobody knows for sure when athletics in a form remotely resembling what it is today came into existence. The ancient Greeks set great store by their sports, and special occasions such as funerals were often celebrated with special Games, as well as such regular festivals as the Olympic, Nemean, and Pythian Games. In the Celtic countries of northern Europe, feats and trials of strength were all part of the heroic heritage of life. One thing, however, is certain; that amateur athletics originated in England in the 19th century, specifically in the public schools and the universities of Oxford and Cambridge. The most important date in this period is 1864, when the teams of Oxford and Cambridge first met in a competition. The sport grew, with national and international events being promoted, until, in 1896, we come to the first modern Olympic Games, held in Athens.

The Olympic Games have been of paramount importance in the history of athletics, for the ideals laid down by Baron Pierre de Coubertin were fundamentally amateur, and from that date (1896) onwards only amateur athletics has been of any importance. The International Amateur Athletic Federation

Akii-Bua, John (Uganda), produced one of athletics' most scintillating performances when he won the 1972 Olympic 400 m hurdles in a world record 47.8 sec by some 7 yards. One of 43 sons and daughters of a father

and 8 wives, Akii-Bua was the first 'technical' event athlete to break into world class from Uganda.

Avilov, Nikolai (USSR), won the Olympic decathlon title at Munich in 1972. Fourth in 1968 in only his fourth decathlon, he produced 6 personal bests at Munich for a world record 8,454 points.

Balas, Iolanda (Romania) completely dominated women's high jumping from 1957 to 1966, winning two Olympic titles (1960, 1964), two European championships (1958, 1962), and setting 14 world records. She exceeded 6 ft in 50 competitions, using the outmoded scissors style and her height (6 ft 0¾ in) to their best advantage. When she retired in 1967 her world record stood at 6 ft 3¼ in, set in 1961.

Bannister, Roger (GB), ensured a permanent place for himself in sporting history as the first man to run a mile in less than 4 minutes, at Oxford on 6 May 1954. Later that year he won the Empire Games mile (in 3 min 58.8 sec) and the European 1,500 m title. He then retired from athletics, but sport reclaimed him in 1971 when he was appointed chairman of Britain's new Sports Council.

A dramatic photo-finish picture of the 1952 Olympic 100 metres final. The winner was Lindy Remigino (US), third from top, followed by Jamaica's McKenley, second from top, McDonald Bailey (GB), second from bottom, and F. D. Smith (USA), third from bottom – all in the same time.

31

The phenomenal Filbert Bayi (613) breaks the world record in winning the 1974 Commonwealth Games 1,500 metres, with two gallant New Zealanders, John Walker (483) and Rod Dixon (453), second and fourth. Kenya's Ben Jipcho, who came third, is eclipsed in more ways than one.

Bayi, Filbert (Tanzania), a sergeant in Tanzania's People's Defence Force, won the 1974 Commonwealth Games 1,500 m with a typical example of the sensational front-running that had electrified the athletics world in 1973. He gave notice of his potential in January 1973 when, at 19, he beat Kenya's Kip Keino by 20 yd in the All-African Games 1,500 m to become his country's first ever winner. He went on to delight Europe with a 6-week summer tour in which he won 7 of 9 races. His victims included Dave Wottle (US), Emiel Puttemans (Belgium), and Ben Jipcho (Kenya). Jipcho was the man who twice beat him — with a second-fastest ever 3 min 52 sec mile (Bayi ran 3:52.6). At Christchurch, however, Bayi turned the tables on Jipcho, winning in a world-record 3 min 32.2 sec, 0.9 sec faster than Jim Ryun's 6½-yr-old mark.

Beamon, Bob (USA), will always be remembered for his mind-bending long jump of 29 ft 2½ in (8.90 m) at the Mexico City Olympics in 1968. It added 1 ft 9¾ in to the world record and seemed destined to remain unbeaten for decades. Enormous natural talent, utilized to its full in ideal conditions, gave the 6 ft 2¾ in Beamon his fame, but he found it difficult to live with, and never again approached his best.

Bikila, Abebe (Ethiopia), was the first marathon runner to win two Olympic titles (1960, 1964). As an 'unknown' in 1960, he ran barefoot to win in 2 hr 15 min 16.2 sec, a world best time. He had his appendix removed only six weeks before the 1964 race, but still won in 2 hr 12 min 11.2 sec, another world best, finishing fresh and a record 4 min 8 sec in front of the next man. Sadly, a leg injury hampered him in the 1968 race, from which he retired. In 1969 severe spinal injuries received in a car crash ended his athletics career, and he died four years later.

Modern athletics grew out of the clubs that sprang up in England in the early 1800s. The first cross-country club, the Thames Hare and Hounds (right), was founded in the 1860s.

(IAAF), founded in 1913, perpetuates the amateur law, and only sporadic and — so far — abortive attempts to popularize professional athletics have been made.

Athletics is basically a young person's sport, and with the amateur concept operative this means that the best performers are likely to be those with time to train. University men have traditionally excelled in athletics, and in Eastern Europe the armed forces have had their share of top performers. The leading national teams come from the USSR, East Germany, and the United States, while striving to rival them are the nations of Western Europe, notably West Germany, Finland, Britain, and France, and the up-and-coming developing countries of which Kenya and Ethiopia are outstanding examples.

Track events

The *sprints* are the shortest events on the track, and are measures of the runner's speed — of foot and reaction. The Olympic events classified as sprints are the 100, 200, and 400 metres, and their English equivalents are 100, 220, and 440 yards. These events are all run

in lanes so that there is no jostling for position and no collisions between runners travelling at top speed. Whereas the 100 dashes are run on a straight course (as is the 200 in some cases, especially in America), the 200 and 400 are normally run on a curved track, a 400-metre lap being standard on running tracks. These curved runs necessitate a staggered start, with the men on the outside running a good deal of the race 'blind'. While this is a disadvantage in itself, the less tight bend is a compensating advantage.

The start is a crucial factor in the sprints, and the crouch start is normal. Starting blocks are used in the sprints (and in the 800 metres), but they were sanctioned by the IAAF only in 1938. Previously, sprinters had dug small holes in the cinder tracks to give them a firm start.

Sprinting has always been an American preserve, and among their top names have been such Olympic champions as Eddie Tolan (1932), Jesse Owens (1936), Bobby Morrow (1956), and Tommie Smith (1968). Europeans have struggled to get on terms, but only one European, Valeriy Borzov (1972), has completed the Olympic 100–200 double.

Women's sprinting is more European-oriented, with Renate Stecher (East Germany) leading the way with world 100 and 200 metres records in the early 1970s. Australians Marjorie Jackson and Betty Cuthbert were prominent in the 1950s, and perhaps the world's greatest sprinter in grace, speed, and success was Wilma Rudolph, who won both Olympic titles in 1960, reflecting America's great wealth of Negro talent.

The 400 metres is often an event for specialists, and the epitome of the one-lap runner was Lee Evans, a black American who won the 1968 Olympic title in 43.8 sec. The equivalent on the women's side must be Monika Zehrt, the East German winner of the 1972 Olympic title.

Middle-distance running is the basis of an athletics meeting. These longer events give spectators a chance to get involved, and the distances range from 800 to 10,000 metres. The Olympic events and their English 'equivalents' are 800 metres/880 yards, 1,500 metres/ 1 mile, 5,000 metres/3 miles, 10,000 metres/6 miles, although only the mile seems to have a chance of surviving

Memorable moments in sport

The Tan Streak from Ohio State

Dateline: Ann Arbor, Michigan, 25 May 1935. Imagine the buzz of the crowd leaving the Ferry Field in Ann Arbor on the last Saturday of May 1935, the day of the annual 'Big Ten' inter-university meet. There could have been only one name on the lips of any impartial spectator, that of Jesse Owens, the 'Tan Streak from Ohio State'.

Owens, it had been rumoured, had recently exceeded 26 feet in the long jump, and had also been peaking towards this day with a series of very fast sprint times. So the stage was set, despite the fact that Owens was suffering with a slightly strained back.

But the soreness disappeared with the starter's shot in the 100 yards. Away he sped to record 9.4 sec and equal the world record. Then, to the long jump pit, with the announcer focusing the crowd's attention on him. By now psychologically geared up, Owens unleashed his smooth power to cut the sand no less than 26 ft 8¼ in from the take-off board. This single jump sufficed, of course, to win the immediate competition, but it added no less than 6 inches to the existing world record, and

The 220 yd (below) and the long jump (right).

in its metric form – 8.13 metres – was the first 8-metre jump. It was to be 25 years before it was beaten.

Then, before the adrenalin had time to drain away, Owens was back in action, running the straight 220 yards in 20.3 sec, a world record for that distance and for the slightly shorter 200 metres that remained unequalled and unbeaten for 14 years. And to round off this afternoon of miracles, Owens won the straight 220 yards low hurdles by 5 yards in 22.6 sec – a world record that was also a record for 200 metres. Barely 45 minutes had elapsed since the start of the 100 yards.

Blankers-Koen, Francina (Netherlands), won 4 gold medals at the 1948 Olympics, more than any other woman athlete at one Games. Sixth in the high jump at the 1936 Games, she competed during the war in German-occupied Holland. She arrived at the London Games with two gold medals from the European championships (hurdles and relay) and as holder of seven world records – 100 yd (1944), 100 m (1948), 80 m hurdles (1948), high jump (1943), long jump (1943), 4 × 110 yd relay (1948), and 4 × 200 m relay (1944). In London she won the 100 and 200 m and 80 m hurdles, and anchored the Dutch team to relay victory – her 11th race of the Games, and her 11th win. She later picked up two more world records, 220 yd (1950) and pentathlon (1951), and in 1950 won three more European gold medals, for the sprints and the hurdles.

Borzov, Valeriy (USSR), picked out early as having the ideal characteristics for a sprinter, justified the theory with a series of victories in major competitions. European 100 m champion in 1969, he added the 200 m to his repertoire to complete a sprint double in the 1971 championships. At the Munich Olympics the following year the Ukrainian, who disliked running the bend in the 200 m, pulled off the first 100–200 m double by a European in an Olympic Games and helped the USSR to silver in the relay.

Boston, Ralph (USA), was the most consistent long-jumper in the world from 1960 to 1968. Rarely beaten, he was Olympic champion in 1960, 2nd in 1964, and 3rd in 1968. In 1960, with a jump of 26 ft 11¼ in, he beat Jesse Owens's 25-year-old world mark, becoming only the 9th holder of this record. In 1961 he became the first 27-ft jumper, and the first man to beat the long-jump record twice. His 6th and final world mark was 27 ft 5 in, in 1965.

Brumel, Valeriy (USSR), had his high-jumping career cut short by a road accident in 1965 when he was 23 and already something of a legend. Olympic silver medallist at 18 in 1960, he assumed the world leadership in 1961 and was paramount until his accident, winning the 1962 European championship and 1964 Olympic title. Six world records – the last 7 ft 5¾ in – were also part of the Brumel legend.

Burghley, Lord David (GB), president of the AAA since 1936 and the IAAF since 1946, won the Olympic 400 m hurdles in 1928. In the 1930 Empire Games he won both hurdles and a third gold in the 4 × 440 yd.

Clarke, Ron (Australia), was the king without a crown: he set 17 world records in middle and long distances but never won a major international title. His first world records came in 1963 (6 miles and 10,000 m), though in 1956 he had held the world junior mile record – and carried the Olympic torch on its final lap in Melbourne. Beaten in the 1964 Olympics (3rd in 10,000 m, 9th in 5,000 and marathon), Clarke set out on an orgy of record breaking which made him the world's fastest man at distances from 3 miles to 1 hour (he later added the 2 miles). But his competitive weaknesses were cruelly exposed in the 1966 Commonwealth Games (2nd in 3 and 6 miles), the 1968 Olympics (unplaced), and the 1970 Commonwealth Games (2nd in 10,000 m).

Cuthbert, Betty (Australia), was the shy heroine of the 1956 Olympics, in which she completed the sprinter's treble of 100, 200, and 4 × 100 m titles.

Subsequent lack-lustre performances in major competition caused her to drop out of athletics in 1961, but she came back to such good effect that she broke her 11th individual world record in 1963 and surprised a lot of people by winning the 1964 Olympic 400 m.

Memorable moments in sport

Bannister breaks the 4-minute bogey

Dateline: Iffley Road, Oxford, 6 May 1954. In 1945, Gunder Haegg set a world mile record in neutral Sweden of 4 min 1.3 sec, after he and fellow-Swede Arne Andersson had reduced Sydney Wooderson's pre-war record of 4 min 6.4 sec in a series of steps. The world mark in this Blue Riband of the track had been reduced only four times in the 1930s, and only once in the 1920s. And Haegg's 1945 time had stood for so long that it, and the 4-minute barrier, began to assume almost divine dimensions.

Then, in 1954, three athletes – from diverse parts of the world – began to approach Haegg's mark. The magic 4 minutes was a possibility again, and the race was on – not on one track, but on several, thousands of miles apart.

When Roger Gilbert Bannister and his training companions Chris Brasher and Chris Chataway plotted their tactics for a mile race in Oxford for the Amateur Athletic Association against the University, they knew that this might be Bannister's last chance. Bannister, fourth

in the 1952 Olympic 1,500 metres, had a time of 4 min 2.0 sec. But Australia's John Landy had half a dozen similar times to his credit, and the young American Wes Santee had clocked 4 min 2.4 sec.

The afternoon of that Thursday was wet and blustery. But, providentially, soon after 6 p.m., as the runners went to their marks, the wind dropped. Brasher led for the first lap, with Bannister trailing him in 57.7 sec. Brasher kept going for $2\frac{1}{2}$ laps, and Bannister passed the half-mile in 1 min 58.3 sec. When Brasher flagged, Chataway – a formidable 5,000 metres competitor – took over, dragging Bannister through the $\frac{3}{4}$ mile in 3 min 0.7 sec. Now was the chance for the fast-finishing Bannister – but did he have enough in reserve? With 250 yards to go he summoned himself for his supreme effort, and sped past Chataway. Surging round the last bend and up the final straight with his ground-eating stride, he was stretched to the limit. As he broke the tape, he collapsed with exhaustion. It was close, and there was no doubt it was a world record. But what about the magic 4 minutes? Whispers from the centre of the track filtered up to the stands 'He's done it!' But still the 1,200 spectators who had just been shouting their lungs out were hushed, waiting. Then came the announcement, which seemed to take almost as long as the race, as Norris McWhirter tantalizingly recited Bannister's credentials and the list of records he had just smashed, from meeting to world record, until he came to '. . . the time is THREE . . .' The rest of the announcement was lost as the crowd went wild.

Epilogue: Just 46 days later, Landy – also paced by Chataway – clocked 3 min 57.9 sec in Finland, lopping 1.5 sec off Bannister's time. The two met in Vancouver in August, in the Commonwealth Games, and Bannister beat Landy in a classic final in 3 min 58.8 sec. Thereafter, the 4-minute mile became commonplace. But Bannister's achievement was a 'first' that would never be forgotten – a truly memorable moment in the history of sport.

spreading metrication, with the United States the last bastion of the other English equivalents.

Such events have always exercised a strong fascination for the European countries, who have dominated them as the Americans have the sprints. And despite seven decades of continual improvements in training techniques, the Europeans are still just leading the next strongest forces in the world at these events, the Kenyans. As a measure of the improvements in men's times, take the 10,000 metres record: the first recognized mark was Jean Bouin's 30 min 58.8 sec in 1911, and in 1973 this was reduced by Britain's Dave Bedford to 27 min 30.8 sec. Even in the shortest distance, the improvements are marked: in 1973 the 800 metres record was 1 min 43.7 sec, some 8 seconds faster than the 1912 record. The greatest mathematical improvements, however, must be still to come in women's events, for until the 1970s women had not been encouraged to run more than 800 metres.

But middle-distance running is not about times – it is about racing. There are basically two kinds of runners in these events – those who run in front and try to draw the finishing sting from their rivals (Ron Clarke, Dave Bedford) and those who run behind, waiting to slip past the leaders and win on the line (Dave Wottle, Chris Chataway). The best runners are those who can run either way, and of these the classic example is Paavo Nurmi, who could run and win using either tactic. Nurmi was one of a group of runners in the 1920s and 1930s who were nicknamed the 'Flying Finns', so apparent was their dominance of world middle-distance running. It is worth recalling a few more: Hannes Kolehmainen, Ville Ritola, Lauri Lehtinen, Gunnar Höckert, Taisto Maki, Ilmari Salminen, Viljo Heino. And Finland's remarkable comeback in the

Davis, Glenn (USA), only man to win the Olympic 400 m hurdles twice (1956–60), set world records for 200 m, 400 m, and 440 yd hurdles, and 440 yd flat. He also ran a 45.3 sec third leg in the relay in Rome to help the American team to a world record and himself to a third Olympic gold.

De la Hunty, Shirley (Australia), a durable female sprinter-cum-hurdler, competed in three Olympics, winning a silver and two bronze medals in 1948 (as Shirley Strickland), a gold (80 m hurdles) and a bronze in 1952, and – after giving birth to a son – in 1956 retained her hurdles title and won a third gold in the relay. In the 1950 British Empire Games she won three gold and two silver medals.

Didrikson, Babe (USA), possessed an amazing sporting talent. In track and field she excelled in so many events that in 1932 she won the American women's team championship alone! At the Olympics in 1932 she won the hurdles and javelin and was placed second in the high jump (with a world record height the same as the winner's). Mildred Didrikson was also outstanding in basketball and baseball, and after her track days were over she became, as Mrs Zaharias, one of the world's most successful golfers. She won tournament after tournament in the 1940s and early 1950s, before dying of cancer in 1956.

Competing in the American women's championships for her club, the Employers Casualty Company, the 18-year-old Babe Didrikson won five of the eight events she contested, all in about $2\frac{1}{2}$ hours, and amassed enough points to win the team title single-handed.

Dillard, Harrison (USA), world-record holder in the high hurdles, failed to qualify for the US Olympic team in his event in 1948, entered the 100 m trial, qualified in 3rd place, and then went so far as to win that event in the Olympics and take a second gold in the relay. In 1952, he did qualify for the hurdles, won, and was again a relay gold medallist.

Elliott, Herb (Australia), can claim to be the complete miler, for although he retired from sport in 1961 when still only 22, he had achieved everything a runner could desire. Coached by the extraordinary Percy Cerutty, he was Olympic 1,500 m champion with a world record 3 min 35.6 sec in 1960; Commonwealth Games ½ and 1 mile champion in 1958; three times Australian champion; unbeaten in 1,500 m and 1 mile races; and between January 1958 and September 1960 beat 4 minutes for the mile on no fewer than 17 occasions, including a world-record 3 min 54.5 sec in 1958 in Dublin. Where other milers would begin their surge for the finish at the bell, Elliott, with relentless power, would begin his with nearly two laps to go. He probably never reached his full potential.

George, Walter (GB), the first 'king of distance', set world bests for 1 mile to 1 hour in the 1880s. He won British championships from 880 yd upwards, before turning pro in 1884. Decades ahead of his time in training methods, he set amateur marks that were unequalled for years, and his mile in 4 min 12¾ sec as a professional in 1886 was unbeaten for 29 years and remains a classic mark in athletics history.

Haegg, Gunder (Sweden), flourished as a middle-distance runner during World War II while Sweden were neutral. Training in forests using the new *fartlek* (speed play) method helped him set 15 world records at 7 distances, including a mile in 4 min 1.3 sec in 1945, after an epic series of duels with his rival and compatriot Arne Andersson. Their activities stopped abruptly, however, when they were declared professional in that year. All of Haegg's world marks stood for at least 6 years, the 3 mile and 5,000 m records for nearly 12.

The explosive start of a 100 metres – where quick reactions can gain half a yard or more.

Top: *Chris Chataway beats Vladimir Kuts in a world record 5,000 metres at the White City in a 1954 London–Moscow match.* Above: *Ann Packer (GB) wins the 1964 Olympic 800 metres final.* Right: *A study in concentration and effort as Russia's Valeriy Borzov prepares to receive the baton from Yuri Silov in the 1972 Olympic 4 × 100 m relay.*

1970s was led by Juha Vaatainen, Lasse Viren, and Pekka Vasala.

The *hurdles* are the obstacle races of the track. Men compete at 110 metres and 400 metres, the hurdles themselves numbering 10 and being 3 ft 6 in high for the shorter distance and 3 ft for the longer. The main women's event is the 100 metres hurdles – 10 hurdles 2 ft 9 in high, though a 400 metres event has been tried.

The first great hurdler was Alvin Kraenzlein of the United States, and it was he who developed the 'leading leg' style of clearance. His winning time in the 1900 Olympic 110 metres event was 15.4 sec; the 1972 winner was Rod Milburn (USA), in 13.24 sec. In the 400 metres, a name that stands out is Britain's David Hemery, winner of the 1968 title. But his title and even his

outstanding world record were taken in 1972 by a Ugandan, John Akii-Bua, whose time of 47.82 sec is good going on the flat, let alone over 10 hurdles.

The middle-distance obstacle race is the *steeplechase*, which is often said to be the toughest race in the track repertoire. Run over 3,000 metres, it includes 28 solid hurdles 3 ft high and 7 water jumps. A development of cross-country running but transferred to the track, this race was largely the preserve of Europeans until the emergence of the Kenyans in the late 1960s. Historically, the greatest steeplechaser was Volmari Iso-Hollo, a Flying Finn who was Olympic champion in 1932 and 1936. But even his achievements paled beside that of the Kenyan Ben Jipcho, who ran the race in a staggering 8 min 14.0 sec in 1973.

Going over the water jump, Kenya seem to dominate the Commonwealth Games steepleshase at Christchurch in 1974, and indeed, Ben Jipcho (404), the world record holder, duly won it.

Field events

There are two groups of field events – the jumps and the throws. The jumps comprise the high jump, pole vault, long jump, and triple jump. The throws are the shot, discus, hammer, and javelin. Women compete in only the high and long jumps, and the shot, discus and javelin.

The *high jump* favours those with a powerful spring in their legs, which is more important than height. The jumper also needs a gymnast's control of his or her body in the air. There are two main techniques in current use, but in both of them the jumper tries to keep his body low over the bar. In the straddle style, the jumper actually seems to roll around the bar, straddling it with his legs. The second main technique in use today is the 'Fosbury Flop', named after its first exponent, Dick Fosbury, Olympic champion in 1968. In this jump, the bar is cleared by the jumper on his back, and though it is mechanically less efficient than the straddle it enables the jumper to make more use of his speed and spring.

Two outstanding names in modern high jumping are those of Valeriy Brumel (USSR) and Iolanda Balas (Romania), who both held the world record and Olympic title simultaneously and pushed the world record into hitherto unknown areas.

The *pole vault* is an acrobatic and athletics event combined, and demands

Harbig, Rudolf (Germany), won a relay bronze medal in 1936, in the Nazi Olympics, but Hitler's war-mongering prevented him from achieving Olympic fame. His remarkable run of 55 successive victories from August 1938 to September 1940 including an outstanding 800 m in 1 min 46.6 sec in 1939, which lopped 1.8 sec off the previous record and lasted for 16 years, and a new 400 m world mark of 46.0 sec. He died at the Eastern Front in 1944.

Hemery, David (GB), achieved an outstanding world-record win in the 1968 Olympics 400 m hurdles (48.1 sec) and was 3rd in this event in

1972. And he completed a 'set' of Olympic medals with a 4 × 400 m silver in 1972. He was also an accomplished high hurdler, winning the short event in the 1966 and 1970 Commonwealth Games, and being runner-up in the 1969 and 1971 European championships.

Jackson, Marjorie (Australia), the 'Blue Streak', had an outstanding record of success as a sprinter, winning both titles in the 1952 Olympics and at the 1950 and 1954 Commonwealth Games, as well as winning three Commonwealth relay golds. Her 10.4 sec 100 yd at Sydney in 1952 knocked a phenomenal three-tenths of a second off her own world mark. In all she set 10 world records (5 original, 5 equalled) at individual sprint distances before retiring from athletics at the age of 22.

Dick Fosbury introduced a new dimension to high jumping with his famous 'flop' in the 1970s.

The first 18-foot pole vaulter, Chris Papanicolaou of Greece, shows how it's done in an event that was revolutionized in the early 1960s with the advent of the fibreglass pole.

Järvinen, Matti (Finland), one of a great family of track and field stars, improved the javelin world record 10 times in the 1930s, from 234 ft 9 in (1930) to 253 ft 4 in (1936). He won the 1932 Olympic title, but a back injury relegated him to 5th in 1936. He was twice European champion. His father, Werner, won the 1906 (Interim) Olympic discus, and the most successful of his three brothers was Akilles, who won two decathlon silver medals, and set a world record in 1930.

Jipcho, Ben (Kenya), set a most amazing world record of 8 min 14.0 sec for the 3,000 m steeplechase in 1973 as well as running a mile in 3 min 52.0 sec, performances that ranked him among the world's best middle-distance runners. Never afraid to run two races in an afternoon, Jipcho was runner-up to Keino in the 1972 Olympic steeplechase, and won the 1974 Commonwealth steeplechase and 5,000 m before turning professional at the age of 30.

Keino, Kipchoge (Kenya), an exuberant and spectacular runner, ubiquitously featured in all sorts of middle-distance events in the 1960s and early 1970s. Though he seldom set records — only two world marks in his career — he was a superb racer. He romped home first in the 1966 Commonwealth Games 1 and 3 miles; high altitude living gave him an advantage in the 1968 Olympics in which he won the 1,500 m and was 2nd in the 5,000; and at the 1970 Commonwealth Games he won the 1,500 m and came third in the 5,000. His most flamboyant gesture (of many) was to enter — and win — the 1972 Olympic steeplechase (as the programme prevented his running the 5,000 m) as well as coming 2nd in the 1,500 m. After Munich, Keino turned professional.

great strength as well as skill. Modern poles, made of fibre-glass, have tremendous flexibility and spring, and the top vaulters utilize this spring to clear more than 18 feet. The vaulter runs towards the bar, plants the pole in a specially constructed 'box' which holds the end of the pole while he is lifted into the air, and catapults himself over the bar. The type of pole used has changed over the years, from ash to hickory, bamboo, metal, and fibre-glass. But vaulters still concede the title of 'greatest' to Cornelius Warmerdam, an American who simply put all the components of vaulting together so well that he set a world record of 15 ft 7¾ in in 1942 with a bamboo pole; it was not until 1957 that Bob Gutowski beat it with a metal pole.

Technological advances gave athletics the first 16 ft vault in 1962, 17 ft in 1963, and 18 ft in 1970. In the Olympics, the United States won every gold medal until 1972, when Wolfgang Nordwig of East Germany snatched the title.

The *long jump* is the simplest field event, and for years to come, if not for ever, the event will be associated with the name of Bob Beamon, who cleared 29 ft 2½ in to win the 1968 Olympic title. His record — 1 ft 9½ in farther than anyone else's best — seems destined to last for decades. This event relies almost entirely upon natural talent — speed and spring — which can be harnessed to provide distance, and Beamon combined these two qualities and used them to their best effect in the Olympic arena. Another man who did the same was Jesse Owens, whose leap of 26 ft 8¼ in in 1935 lasted 25 years as a world record. British long-jumping tradition is thin, but a year of glory came in 1964, when Mary Rand and Lynn Davies both won Olympic gold medals in Tokyo.

The *triple jump* places exceptional demands on the athlete. In essence, it is

Two great American throwing men: Randy Matson (left), the first 70-foot shot putter, and Al Oerter, four-time Olympic discus champion.

Above: *Nigeria's Modupe Oshikoya won the 1974 Commonwealth long jump, was 2nd in the pentathlon, and 3rd in the hurdles.* Below: *Klaus Wolfermann, 1972 Olympic javelin champion.*

Kolehmainen, Hannes (Finland), was the original 'Flying Finn'. At the 1912 Olympics he won three titles – the 5,000 and 10,000 m and the 8,000 m cross-country, and after World War I, at the 1920 Games, he won the marathon. Known as 'Hannes the Mighty', Kolehmainen set world records from 3,000 to 30,000 m. And although he never set a world 10,000 m mark, he won that title in the 1912 Games by no less than $\frac{3}{4}$ of a minute.

Kuts, Vladimir (USSR), had a short but distinguished middle-distance career in which he won the 1956 Olympic 5,000 and 10,000 m and the 1954 European 5,000 m. In the European race he completely surprised the great Zatopek by maintaining a fast pace, and he was never caught, beating Zatopek's world record into the bargain. A true 'iron-man' of athletics, he ran his races from the front, with frequent punishing bursts of speed to kill his opponents off. In all, he set 8 world records (over 5,000 m, 10,000 m, and 3 miles). Three times he lost his 5,000 m record, but three times he won it back, reducing it to 13 min 35.0 in 1957, before recurrent stomach ailments led to his retirement.

Landy, John (Australia), a remarkably consistent athlete, was the world's leading miler in the mid-1950s. A front runner, he set a world mile record of 3 min 58.0 sec in 1954 (which included the 1,500 m record), but just missed the big

prizes – he was beaten by Roger Bannister to the first 4-minute mile and in the 1954 Empire Games mile, and he came 3rd in the 1956 Olympic 1,500 m. Renowned for his sportsmanship, Landy on one occasion actually stopped in a race to pick up a fallen rival, but he still won!

a trial for distance made up of a hop, a step, and a final jump, and the world's best cover distances in excess of 55 ft. Of modern champions, three – all of whom were also world record holders – stand out: Adhemar Ferreira da Silva (Brazil), Olympic champion in 1952 and 1956; Jozef Schmidt (Poland), champion in 1960 and 1964; and Viktor Saneyev (USSR), champion in 1968 and 1972.

In the throwing events there is a built-in advantage for athletes who are both strong and big. This emphasis on strength and size is nowhere more apparent than in the *shot*, in which a 16-lb ball (8 lb 13 oz for women) is projected from a 7-ft circle by a punching movement from under the chin. Because bulk is an important factor in this – and in other throwing events – drugs called anabolic steroids have been used to promote rapid growth. The prolific improvement in throwing records has been widely attributed to these 'bulk bombs', which are of course banned, and remained almost undetectable until a medical break-

Lusis, Janis (USSR), was the only athlete to win 4 European titles (1962–66–69–71) in one event, the javelin. He also won a 'complete set' of Olympic

medals – bronze (1964), gold (1968), and silver (1972).

Mathias, Bob (USA), was the youngest Olympic athletics champion (17 years 9 months) when he won the 1948 decathlon, and the first man to retain this title – and with a world record total – four years later. Mathias, 6 ft 3 in tall and 15½ stone, was unbeaten in decathlons in his amateur career, which ended soon after his 1952 success when he was only 22 – an age when most decathletes have not yet elected to go for this punishing event. Mathias later became a US Congressman.

Morrow, Bobby (USA), won three sprint gold medals – 100, 200, and 4 × 100 m – in the 1956 Olympics. A Texan, Morrow elicited favourable comparisons with the great Jesse Owens, the only other man to accomplish this feat, and equalled world records on a number of occasions. He continued to reign supreme in the USA in 1957 and 1958.

Myers, Lon (USA), almost legendary 19th-century athlete, won 8 national titles in one week in 1880 – the American and the Canadian 100, 220, 440, and 880 yd championships. Small and light, but with long legs, he won the US 440 yd title from 1879 to 1884 before turning pro.

Only 21, England's Ian Chipchase won the 1974 Commonwealth hammer, the 'old man's' event.

through in 1973. In the women's events, some throwers have been alleged to be as much man as woman, precipitating the introduction of sex tests.

The second throw is the *discus*, which is basically a plate weighing 2 kg (1 kg for women). It is thrown with a round-arm action from a circle of 8 ft 2½ in diameter, and has to land within a 45° arc. The most successful discus thrower – and the most durable Olympic athlete ever – was Al Oerter, champion four times, from 1956 to 1968. The discus has also proved an event for those who persevere: Ludvik Danek (Czechoslovakia), who was Olympic champion in 1972, and Lia Manoliu (Romania), women's champion in 1968, both reached the top after many years of trying.

The *javelin* – a spear weighing 800 gm (600 gm for women) – is one of the ancient Greek throwing implements (the other being the discus), and its origins are obviously martial. The manner of throwing is to run up to a line and project the javelin forward without fouling the line. In this way, the world's best men are just exceeding 300 ft, women 200 ft.

The *hammer* – an iron ball attached to a wire, and the whole weighing 16 lb – is the only throw not indulged in by women. It is thrown in a rotating style similar to the discus. This throw is one of the most complicated, and possibly for this reason hammer throwers tend to be older men. Anatoliy Bondarchuk, Olympic winner in 1972, took up the event when he was 27 years old.

All-round events

Two athletics events exist to find the most proficient all-rounder – for men the 10-event decathlon, and for women the 5-event pentathlon.

The *decathlon* is athletics' most gruelling event, and lasts two days. On the first come the 100 metres, long jump, shot, high jump, and 400 metres; on the second, the 110 metres hurdles, discus, pole vault, javelin, and 1,500 metres. The whole event is organized on a points basis. The points awarded for each event are computed from existing standards – world records, average times for the world's top ten, and so on – so that performances in the different events in

Jim Thorpe, perhaps the greatest all-rounder ever, competing in the 1912 Olympics.

Nurmi, Paavo (Finland), was one of the first great stars of the track. He carried on the Finnish tradition of distance running begun by Hannes Kolehmainen, and in three Olympics won a record 9 gold medals and a record 12 medals altogether. And his total of 22 world records has never been surpassed. Crowds all over Europe and America flocked to see the 'Phantom Finn', who ran with a stopwatch in his hand and was able miraculously to maintain his form even when required to run seven races in six days — something he did in the 1924 Olympics, winning them all, including the 1,500 and 5,000 m in the same afternoon. Having won the 10,000 m and cross-country in the 1920 Olympics, he then went four years without

defeat, breaking record after record, culminating in his five gold medals at the Paris Olympics. He continued to break his records, running dozens of races a year and rarely meeting defeat. In the 1928 Olympics he won the 10,000 m, and was aiming for the marathon in 1932 when he was banned by the IAAF for infringing the amateur code.

The career of Northern Ireland's great pentathlete Mary Peters is encapsulated in the five events, above. Top left: the hurdles, with Mary winning the 1974 Commonwealth title. Top right: The shot, and the 1973 AAA title. Centre: The high jump, her best event in her 1972 Olympic triumph. Above: The long jump, and the 1970 Commonwealth title. Above right: The 200 metres in 1972.

the decathlon can be compared. For instance, the tables drawn up in 1962 made 10.2 sec for 100 metres and 7 ft 1½ in for the high jump each worth 1,000 points, with more or fewer points awarded according to whether a performance is above or below the standard.

The way in which standards have altered is typified by the 1,500 metres: 1,000 points for 3 min 54.0 sec in 1934 and 3 min 40.2 sec in 1962.

The Olympic champion decathlete can claim to be the world's greatest athlete, and among this select company are the Americans Glenn Morris (1936, and later a celluloid Tarzan) and Bob Mathias (1948 and 1952, the only man to win twice), and Russia's Nikolai Avilov, the 1972 champion and world record holder.

The women's *pentathlon* is not such a grinding task, but it is spread over two

O'Brien, Parry (USA), dominated shot-putting in the 1950s with 10 world records and 2 Olympic titles. He introduced a new style, in which he began by facing the 'wrong' way. Ridiculed at first, the 'O'Brien style' brought him his first world mark (59 ft 0¾ in) in 1953 and took him unbeaten through 116 successive competitions. Eight times US champion (plus one discus title), he set his last world record (63 ft 4 in) in 1959, and came 2nd and 4th in the next two Olympics.

Oerter, Al (USA), in four Olympics won four discus gold medals – a record unique in Olympic history. A supreme competitor when the chips were down, he won his first title in 1956 as a 20-year-old. At Rome he won with his penultimate throw, and in 1962 he became history's first 200-ft thrower. A slipped disc and damaged ribs did not prevent his competing at the Tokyo Olympics: of course, he won, again with his last-but-one throw. In 1968, for the third time he produced a personal best (212 ft 6 in) in the Olympic final. Oerter, who four times broke the world record himself, had the current world-record holder behind him in each of his Olympic victories.

Owens, Jesse (USA), has no peer in the sphere of sprinting and long jumping. In record-breaking his feats of 25 May 1935 stand unparalleled anywhere for one afternoon's work. And his only Olympic appearance, in 1936, was unprecedented and subsequently unrivalled. He won individual gold medals in the 100 and 200 m and the long jump, and a fourth in the 4 × 100 relay. Such a talent in the son of a poor farmer was a natural prey to professional promoters, and soon Owens was racing against horses, though subsequently he settled to a more rewarding career with an orphans' home in Chicago.

Press, Irina and Tamara (USSR), were sisters who both reached the top in two events. Irina won two Olympic titles – 80 m hurdles (1960) and pentathlon (1964) – and amassed 11 world records. Tamara (the elder by two years) won three Olympic titles – shot (1960, 1964) and discus (1964) – and set 12 world records. Both women suddenly quit international athletics in 1966 just before 'sex tests' became compulsory.

Tamara Press at the 1964 Olympics.

days in Olympic and some other competitions. On the first day come the 100 metres hurdles, shot, and high jump; on the second, the long jump and 200 metres. The events have varied since 1934, when a world record for the event was first recognized. It was another 30 years before it appeared in the Olympics. The Russian Irina Press, then world record holder, beat Britain's Mary Rand for the gold medal, with another British girl, Mary Peters, fourth. And it was Northern Ireland's Mary Peters, Commonwealth champion in 1970, who won Britain's only gold medal in the 1972 Olympics, when she won the pentathlon with a world-record performance.

A men's pentathlon, which featured in three Olympics from 1912, has survived in American competition, the events comprising long jump, javelin, 200 metres, discus, and 1,500 metres. Jim Thorpe won four of the five events in the 1912 Games, as well as coming first in the decathlon, but later lost his gold medals on a technicality.

Long-distance running

We may fairly regard any distance over 10,000 metres as 'long distance'. Such distances are rarely run on the track, as they are boring for runner and spectator alike. More often, long-distance events are run on roads. Typical distances run on the track (and for which there are recognized world records) are 20,000 metres, 10 miles, and 1 hour races. Road runs vary in distance and are often 'point to point' type events: two of the most famous are the London to Brighton race in Britain (50 miles) and the Comrades Marathon in South Africa (54 miles from Pietermaritzburg to Durban in 'even' years and in the reverse direction in 'odd' years). A more extreme kind of running is the ultra-long-distance type of event, which can measure 100 miles or more. In 1973 Britain's Ron Bentley ran a record 161 miles 505 yards in 24 hours.

But the most famous long-distance run is the marathon, which takes its name from Marathon in Greece, from where a messenger – Pheidippides – ran the 24-odd miles to Athens with news of an Athenian victory and promptly dropped dead. This story was revived with the first modern Olympic Games in 1896, and the place of this race was ensured when this first Olympic marathon title

was won by Spyridon Louis, a Greek shepherd. The distance of the marathon varied for many years thereafter, and any long-distance run was in danger of being termed a marathon. But the distance was standardized at 26 miles 385 yards in 1924, this distance being the length of the 1908 race at the London Olympics, from Windsor Castle to the Shepherd's Bush stadium. The 1908 Games also gave the marathon its greatest boost: an Italian candy-maker (and experienced long-distance runner) Dorando Pietri dramatically collapsed in the stadium on the final lap of the race, was helped by anxious officials, and disqualified.

The names of some Olympic champions are soon forgotten. But among those who will always be remembered are the Czech Emil Zatopek, who won his third title of the Games in this event in 1952, and Ethiopia's Abebe Bikila, who ran barefoot to win in 1960, and in 1964 became the first man to win twice. Other prominent marathon runners include England's Jim Peters, who collapsed within sight of the finishing line

Puttemans, Emiel (Belgium), set world records at 3,000 m, 2 and 3 miles, and 5,000 m in 1971 and 1972. Second to Lasse Viren in the Olympic 10,000 m, he was only 5th in the 5,000, but proceeded to break Viren's new world mark later that month with 13 min 13.0 sec, eclipsing Ron Clarke's 6-year-old 3-mile record in the same run.

Rand, Mary (GB), was Britain's first female Olympic athletics champion, winning the 1964 long jump with a world record 22 ft 2¼ in. She also collected a pentathlon silver and a relay bronze. Mary (née Bignal) had a long and varied athletics career, which began internationally in 1957 and included a gold in the 1966 Commonwealth Games long jump.

Ritola, Ville (Finland), a contemporary of Paavo Nurmi, won 8 Olympic medals, 5 of them gold, but was constantly overshadowed by his poker-faced rival. Four golds came in 1924, in the 10,000 m and 3,000 m steeplechase and two team victories; the 5th was the 1928 5,000 m, in which he inflicted a rare defeat on Nurmi. He reduced Nurmi's world 10,000 m record by 17 sec in two runs in 1924, only for Nurmi to slash it by another 17 sec just 8 weeks later.

Above: *Loneliness does not seem to bother South African long-distance runner Wally Haywood on the London–Brighton run in 1953, when he broke the record by 22½ minutes, covering the 52 miles 694 yards in 5 hr 29 min 40 sec at the age of 45. A few weeks later he ran 159 miles 562 yards in 24 hours, a record that lasted 20 years. In South Africa he won five Comrades Marathons.*

Below: *David Bedford (A1) in the 1971 International Cross-Country Championships, which he won. Run over a course of 7½ miles, the Championships were first held in 1903. Doris Brown (USA) won the first five women's titles (1967–71), on a 4-mile course. England have always been a stronghold of the sport, but Finland dominated the Olympic cross-country when it was last held in the 1920s.*

Roelants, Gaston (Belgium), was unbeaten in the steeplechase from 1961 to 1965, winning the Olympic title in 1964 and setting world records in 1963 and 1965 (8 min 26.4 sec). In 1972 he won his 4th International Cross-Country Championship (10 years after his first) and broke his own world records for 20,000 m and 1 hr, having set them in 1966.

Roelants on his way in 1972 to a record-equalling fourth International Cross-Country title.

Rudolph, Wilma (USA), tall, graceful, slender, overcame a serious illness as a child, when she lost the use of her left leg for three years, to become the fastest girl in the world. As a 16-year-old in Melbourne, she won a bronze medal in the relay. But at Rome in 1960, as world 200 m record-holder, she took the world by storm in winning both sprint gold medals plus the relay gold. She retired after setting a world 100 m record of 11.2 sec in 1961.

at the 1954 Commonwealth Games suffering from dehydration; Brian Kilby and Ron Hill, British runners who held European and Commonwealth titles simultaneously; and English-born Australian Derek Clayton, who set a world's best time for the event of 2 hr 8 min 33.6 sec in 1969.

As may be imagined, the training involved in the long-distance events is extreme. Some men are reported to run over 200 miles a week, which is near the body's physiological limit.

Walking

The place of race walking in the athletics calendar is hotly disputed, and moves have been made to have it excluded from the Olympic Games. Walking – athletically speaking – is defined as progressing with unbroken contact with the ground and with a momentary straightening of the knee in every stride. The scope for stretching the rules has long been the bane of judges, and for this reason short walking races – the 3,000 and 10,000 metres events – have been dropped from the Olympic programme and from most other major meetings.

Race walking – generally over extremely long distances – began in Britain in the 19th century, though the balance of power is now tilted in the direction of the USSR and East Germany. Through the 20th century, though, the best walkers have been Britain's George Larner, a Brighton policeman who won two gold

English-born Norman Read (10) of New Zealand leads the field at the start of the 1956 Olympic 50 km walk. He went on to win by over 2 minutes.

medals in 1908, Italy's Ugo Frigerio who won three Olympic titles, two in 1920 and one in 1924, and Russia's Vladimir Golubnichiy, with two golds (1960, 68), a bronze (1964), and a silver (1972).

There is no internationally recognized women's walking, though some of the more emancipated nations promote it. The IAAF do not list any women's world's records, and the men's records are restricted to a few track distances.

Indoor athletics

As a section of athletics in its own right and not simply as an off-season adjunct to the outdoor sport, indoor athletics came of age in the 1960s when the first European Indoor Championships were held, in 1966; they were granted full IAAF international status in 1970. Indoor track and field had flourished for decades in the United States.

As might be expected, the programme is rather simpler than an outdoor meet. Of the throws, only the shot is held; all four jumps are practicable; on the track, short straight sprints of 50 or 60 metres, and then a jump to 400, 800, 1,500, and 3,000 metres. The tracks vary in size, from some which measure 300 yards to others less than 200 yards. And because of the tight bends necessary, such tracks are almost always banked, with the sprint stretch being laid down separately.

The first indoor meets took place in the United States in 1868, and such gatherings have always been popular there, especially since the 1925 tour of Paavo Nurmi. Since World War II, indoor track and field has become more and more widespread in Europe, with income from television making up for the small crowds to which indoor arenas are often restricted.

Indoor performances are hardly comparable from one venue to another, with even the character of the floor affecting the jumps. Most non-track events, however, reach a standard comparable with outdoor performances, but on the track the constricted bends make any approach to outdoor times – except in the 3,000 metres – unlikely.

Professional athletics

Track and field athletes who compete for money have a long history. In the early days of the sport there was no distinction between amateurs and professionals, though it is safe to say that in Britain the

East Germany's world record hurdler Annelie Ehrhardt wins the 60 metres event in a 1973 indoor match against Britain at Cosford.

Orienteering spread to Australia in the 1970s, and the bushland near Sydney (above) *provides an ideal setting for the sport.*

Above left: *Tossing the caber, a traditional event in the Highland Games, which are not only held in Scotland but in places as far away as Australia and America. Other events include throwing heavy weights, for height as well as for distance.*
Above: *An Olympic event up to 1920, the tug-of-war is sometimes included in athletics meetings. There is an international body, and annual European championships.*

harsher areas of the North and Scotland fostered the professional 'pedestrian', whereas the 'effete' South with its universities favoured the amateur approach. In Britain, the last surviving relic of the old days of the professional is to be found in the Powderhall New Year Handicap. The old classic professionals' distance of 130 yards has been honed down to 120 yards, and the small prize and large amount to be won on betting is normally claimed by an athlete who would be pushed to hold his own in the amateur ranks. Another centre of professional sprinting is the small Victorian town of Stawell (pronounced 'stawl'), Australia, where an Easter handicap is run over 130 yards.

Repeated and abortive attempts to start a big professional circus in the United States finally met with a measure of success in the winter of 1972–73, when the International Track Association lured some of the big stars of the late 1960s away from the amateur ranks to chance their luck on a pro circuit. Among the erstwhile Olympians signed up were Kip Keino, Jim Ryun, Lee Evans, and shot putter Brian Oldfield, and the first big European name on their books was that of Scotland's temperamental middle-distance star Ian McCafferty. The professionals' aim was to play for the big TV networks, but they found it difficult to attract the up-and-coming athlete.

Orienteering

The combination of intellectual and physical abilities needed to excell in orienteering is a clue to this relatively new sport's Scandinavian origins. Since its inception, it has spread to many other countries and it presents the participant with a unique challenge to his map-reading ability, stamina in travelling across open country at speed, and appreciation of hitherto unseen terrain.

An orienteering competition – it cannot be termed a race – takes place in hilly or wooded countryside in which map reading and navigation are prerequisites for success. Men's courses are normally between 6 and 9 miles, over which from 8 to 16 check points have to be visited.

Competitors start out at one-minute intervals. First they visit a master map and note the position of the check points on their own large-scale maps (about $2\frac{1}{2}$ inches to the mile). They then have to visit them all in turn, deciding which route will be the quickest, choosing perhaps between a thickly wooded section

Ryun, Jim (USA), a tall and powerful miler, set some remarkable world records in the mid-1960s. He broke 4 minutes for the first time in 1964, and in 1966 – at 19 – he set a new world half-mile record (1 min 44.9 sec) and then hacked 2.3 sec off the world mile record, with 3 min 51.3 sec. Ryun's training schedule was prolific, and he was virtually unbeatable in 1966 and 1967, cutting another fifth of a second off his mile record and crushing his greatest rival Kip Keino in a 1,500 m run that lopped 2.5 sec off Herb Elliott's 7-year-old world mark. But an attack of glandular fever weakened him for the 1968 Olympics, where he ran extremely well to come 2nd to Keino in the 1,500 m. The strain of big-time athletics began to tell on Ryun and he retired for a brief period afterwards, but came back to make his third Olympic team. Sadly, he tripped in his 1,500 m heat and was eliminated. His amateur ambitions ruined, he turned professional.

Shrubb, Alf (GB), one of the great 'kings of distance', set world marks for 2, 3, 6, and 10 miles in 1903–4 that stood for more than 20 years, until the era of Nurmi. It was his misfortune that Britain did not send a team to the St Louis Olympics. He won virtually everything going in Britain between 1901 and 1904, before being declared professional in 1905.

45

Athletics

The 1974 Commonwealth Games at Christchurch, New Zealand, produced some outstanding performances. **Right:** *Kenya's Ben Jipcho, having already won the steeplechase, outsprints England's Brendan Foster in the 5,000 metres, both men getting within 2 seconds of the world record.* **Far right:** *Ian Thompson (England), 24 and running only his second marathon, wins easily in 2 hr 9 min 12 sec, the second fastest time ever.*

Snell, Peter (NZ), possessed all the desirable attributes of the best middle-distance runner in the world — speed, strength, power, an easy style, and a will to win. Success — three Olympic and two Commonwealth golds — and records — five individual world records — came his way in a top-class career lasting from 1960 to 1965. As a raw newcomer he won the 800 m at Rome in 1960, and two years later stamped his class on the sport with world records for 800 m, 880 yd, and 1 mile, as well as winning both half and mile at the Commonwealth Games. Snell timed his preparations well for the 1964 Olympics. He completely dominated his races — 800 and 1,500 m — to win both with apparent ease. Later in 1964 he set world records for 1,000 m and 1 mile (3 min 54.1 sec). After an exhausting tour of Europe and America in 1965, he retired.

Stecher, Renate (E. Germany), stood out as *the* female sprinter of the early 1970s, with 100–200 m doubles in the 1971 European championships and the 1972 Olympic Games. Hailing from Jena, with a smooth, economical sprint style, she continued to break records, with 1973 times of 10.9 sec for 100 m and 22.4 for 200 awaiting ratification.

Thorpe, Jim (USA), was voted the greatest American athlete of the first half of the 20th century — ahead of Babe Ruth and Jack Dempsey. Half American Indian and half Irish, he was brought up in Oklahoma and had a natural aptitude for sports. He won the decathlon and pentathlon at the 1912 Olympics, only to be stripped of his honours when it was discovered he had once been paid for playing baseball. He later played major league baseball for the Boston Braves, and pro football when a league was started in 1920. As an amateur he had been one of the all-time football greats. His remarkable story was made into a film starring Burt Lancaster (*Man of Bronze* or *Jim Thorpe – All American*).

navigated on a compass bearing or a rather longer but more straightforward route along roads or paths. The winner, of course, is the person who visits all the check points in the shortest time, but to finish at all can often be considered an achievement in itself.

Orienteering originated in Sweden in 1918 when a youth leader, Major Ernst Killander, heightened interest in cross-country running by the inclusion of check-points and charts. The sport grew and, with the introduction of a special compass-cum-protractor in the 1930s, it was to rival soccer, athletics, and skiing as a major sport in Scandinavia. In 1961, the International Orienteering Federation was set up. And the world championships – held every two years, for men and women individual and teams – were inaugurated in 1966.

Championships

The centrepiece of world athletics comes round every four years when the IAAF stages the world championships in conjunction with the Olympic Games. By sticking to the quadrennial basis of the Olympics, the Olympic committee have given other celebrations scope to come into existence in the intervening years. These include the European championships, first held in 1934 and normally held every four years; the British Commonwealth Games, first held in 1930 and held in even years between Olympics; and the Pan-American, Balkan, Mediterranean, African, Asian, and Pacific games. All multi-sport Games have athletics as their main sport.

The most competitive team (as opposed to individual) championship in world athletics is the European Cup, separate competitions for which are held for men and women. A measure of the Eastern European hold over Continental athletics

is that the USSR won the men's event on three of the first four occasions it was held – in 1965, 1967, and 1973 – and the women's in 1965 and 1967, with East Germany winning the men's cup in 1970 and the women's in 1970 and 1973.

Such multi-national contests apart, the bread and butter of international athletics is seen in two forms of contest. There is the invitation meeting, in which leading athletes from many countries may compete in a range of events designed to show off their talents. And there is the international match, in which two or more national teams compete in a complete range of events in a two- or three-string match. Walkers and decathletes and pentathletes are catered for in special internationals, which normally involve a number of countries.

TRACK AND FIELD 'MOSTS'

Olympic gold medals

Total	9	P. Nurmi (Fin)
women	4	F. Blankers-Koen (Neth)
	4	B. Cuthbert (Aus)
Individual	8*	R. Ewry (USA)
women	3	F. Blankers-Koen (Neth)
	3	B. Cuthbert (Aus)
	3	T. Press (USSR)
In one Games	5	†P. Nurmi (Fin)
women	4	‡F. Blankers-Koen (Neth)
individual	4	§A. Kraenzlein (USA)
women	3	‡F. Blankers-Koen (Neth)
In one event	4	¶A. Oerter (USA)

Olympic medals

Men	12	P. Nurmi (Fin)
Women	7	S. De La Hunty (Aus)

World records**

Men	19††	P. Nurmi (Fin) 13 events
	18	E. Zatopek (Czech) 9 events
	17	R. Clarke (Aus) 8 events
Women	16‡‡	B. Cuthbert (Aus) 9 events
	14	I. Balas (Rom) 1 event
	12	T. Press (USSR) 2 events

*Plus 2 in the 1906 'Intercalated' Games.
†1924. ‡1948. §1900. ¶Discus (1956–68).
**For events currently recognized.
††Includes 2 relays. ‡‡Includes 5 relays.

WORLD ATHLETICS RECORDS – men

Event	Record	Athlete	Date
100 yards	9.1 s	Bob Hayes (USA)	21.6.63
	9.1 s	Harry Jerome (Canada)	15.7.66
	9.1 s	Jim Hines (USA)	13.5.67
	9.1 s	Charlie Greene (USA)	15.6.67
	9.1 s	John Carlos (USA)	10.5.69
	9.1 s	Steve Williams (USA)	12.5.73
100 metres	9.9 s	Jim Hines (USA)	20.6.68
	9.9 s	Charlie Green (USA)	20.6.68
	9.9 s	Ronnie Ray Smith (USA)	20.6.68
	9.9 s	Jim Hines (USA)	14.10.68
	9.9 s	Eddie Hart (USA)	1.7.72
	9.9 s	Reynaud Robinson (USA)	1.7.72
	9.9 s	Steve Williams (USA)	22.6.74
200 metres (straight)	19.5 s	Tommie Smith (USA)	7.5.66
200 metres (turn)	19.8 s	Tommie Smith (USA)	16.10.68
	19.8 s	Don Quarrie (Jamaica)	3.8.71
220 yards (straight)	19.5 s	Tommie Smith (USA)	7.5.66
220 yards (turn)	20.0 s	Tommie Smith (USA)	11.6.66
400 metres	43.8 s	Lee Evans (USA)	18.10.68
440 yards	44.5 s	John Smith (USA)	26.6.71
800 metres	1 m 43.7 s	Marcello Fiasconaro (Italy)	27.6.73
880 yards	1 m 44.1 s	Rick Wohlhuter (USA)	8.6.74
1,000 metres	2 m 16.0 s	Danie Malan (S. Africa)	24.6.73
1,500 metres	3 m 32.2 s	Filbert Bayi (Tanzania)	1.2.74
1 mile	3 m 51.1 s	Jim Ryun (USA)	23.6.67
2,000 metres	4 m 56.2 s	Michel Jazy (France)	12.10.66
3,000 metres	7 m 35.2 s	Brendan Foster (GB)	3.8.74
2 miles	8 m 13.8 s	Brendan Foster (GB)	27.8.73
3 miles	12 m 47.8 s	Emiel Puttemans (Belgium)	20.9.72
5,000 metres	13 m 13.0 s	Emiel Puttemans (Belgium)	20.9.72
6 miles	26 m 47.0 s	Ron Clarke (Australia)	14.7.65
10,000 metres	27 m 30.8 s	Dave Bedford (GB)	13.7.73
10 miles	46 m 4.2 s	Willy Polleunis (Belgium)	20.9.72
20,000 metres	57 m 44.4 s	Gaston Roelants (Belgium)	20.9.72
1 hour	12 mi 1,610 yd (20,784 m)	Gaston Roelants (Belgium)	20.9.72
15 miles	1 h 12 m 48.2 s	Ron Hill (GB)	21.7.65
25,000 metres	1 h 15 m 22.6 s	Ron Hill (GB)	21.7.65
30,000 metres	1 h 31 m 30.4 s	Jim Alder (GB)	5.9.70
Marathon*	2 h 8 m 33.6 s	Derek Clayton (Australia)	30.5.69
4 × 100 m relay	38.2 s	United States	20.10.68
	38.2 s	United States	10.9.72
4 × 110 yd relay	38.6 s	United States	17.6.67
4 × 200 m relay	1 m 21.5 s	Italy	21.7.72
4 × 220 yd relay	1 m 21.7 s	United States	20.4.70
4 × 400 m relay	2 m 56.1 s	United States	20.10.68
4 × 440 yd relay	3 m 2.8 s	Trinidad & Tobago	13.8.66
4 × 800 m relay	7 m 8.6 s	West Germany	13.8.66
4 × 880 yd relay	7 m 10.4 s	United States	12.5.73
4 × 1,500 m relay	14 m 40.4 s	New Zealand	22.8.73
4 × 1 mile relay	16 m 2.8 s	New Zealand	3.2.72
3,000 m steeplechase	8 m 14.0 s	Ben Jipcho (Kenya)	27.6.73
120 yd hurdles	13.0 s	Rod Milburn (USA)	25.6.71
110 m hurdles	13.1 s	Rod Milburn (USA) (twice)	6 & 22.7.73
200 m hurdles (str)	21.9 s	Don Styron (USA)	2.4.60
220 yd hurdles (str)	21.9 s	Don Styron (USA)	2.4.60
200 m hurdles (turn)	22.5 s	Martin Lauer (Germany)	7.7.59
	22.5 s	Glenn Davis (USA)	20.8.60
400 m hurdles	47.8 s	John Akii-Bua (Uganda)	2.9.72
440 yd hurdles	48.8 s	Ralph Mann (USA)	20.6.70
20,000 m walk	1 h 24 m 45 s	Bernd Kannenberg (W. Germany)	25.5.74
2 hours walk	16 mi 1,535 yd (27,153 m)	Bernd Kannenberg (W. Germany)	11.5.74
30,000 m walk	2 h 12 m 58 s	Bernd Kannenberg (W. Germany)	11.5.74
20 miles walk	2 h 31 m 33.0 s	Anatolyi Vedjakov (USSR)	23.8.58
30 miles walk	3 h 51 m 48.6 s	Gerhard Weidner (W. Germany)	8.4.73
50,000 m walk	3 h 52 m 52.8 s	Christop Höhne (E. Germany)	1.5.74
High jump	7 ft 6½ in (2.30 m)	Dwight Stones (USA)	11.7.73
Pole vault	18 ft 5¾ in (5.63 m)	Bob Seagren (USA)	2.7.72
Long jump	29 ft 2½ in (8.90 m)	Bob Beamon (USA)	18.10.68
Triple jump	57 ft 2¾ in (17.44 m)	Viktor Saneyev (USSR)	17.10.72
Shot	71 ft 7 in (21.82 m)	Al Feuerbach (USA)	5.5.73
Discus	224 ft 5 in (68.40 m)	Jay Silvester (USA)	18.9.68
	224 ft 5 in (68.40 m)	Richard Bruch (Sweden)	5.7.72
Hammer	251 ft 3 in (76.60 m)	Reinhard Theimer (E. Germany)	4.7.74
Javelin	308 ft 8 in (94.08 m)	Klaus Wolfermann (W. Germany)	5.5.73
Decathlon	8,454 points	Nikolai Avilov (USSR)	7/8.9.72

* Hand timing.

Tyus, Wyomia (USA), became the first sprinter to retain an Olympic title. She won the 100 m in 1964 and retained it in 1968 with a world record 11.0 sec. From the same stable as Wilma Rudolph – Tennessee State University – Wyomia won a third gold medal in the 1968 sprint relay, in another world record.

Viren, Lasse (Finland), recalled the glorious days of the 1920s for Finland when he won the 5,000 and 10,000 m titles at the 1972 Olympic Games. His 10,000 m win was most dramatic, as he took a tumble half-way through the race but still came back to win in a world-record time of 27 min 38.4 sec. He played a similar waiting game in the 5,000 m to win again in a sprint finish, from the holder, Mohamed Gammoudi.

Warmerdam, Cornelius (USA), widely regarded as the greatest pole-vaulter ever, made the first 15-ft vault in 1940 and set his third world record in 1942, 15 ft 7¾ in, a mark that lasted 15 years – and all with a bamboo pole. He seemed to be able to vault 15 ft whenever he wanted, and a measure of his complete supremacy over his contemporaries was that when he retired from amateur competition in 1944 with a record of 43 15-footers, it was 7 years before another vaulter reached that mark.

Cornelius Warmerdam, pole vaulter supreme in the era of bamboo poles. It took 15 years and the advent of the steel pole to beat his world record.

Wooderson, Sydney (GB), a small, slight, bespectacled figure, loomed large in world middle-distance running in the 1930s and 1940s. An injury kept him out of the 1936 Olympic 1,500 m final, but the next year he set a world mile record of 4 min 6.4 sec. In 1938 he set world records for the 880 yd and 800 m and won the European 1,500 m title. After the

war, Wooderson, who had a fine sprint finish, turned to longer distances and won the European 5,000 m title in 1946.

Zatopek, Emil (Czechoslovakia), regarded by most experts as the world's greatest ever middle- and long-distance runner, possessed all the attributes of the perfect athlete. He had pace, boundless stamina, judgement, guile, determination, and his own special brand of aggressiveness on the track that stamped him as a true champion. Gold medallist in the 10,000 m and runner-up in the 5,000 at the 1948 Olympics, he won both events in the 1950 European championships and both at the 1952 Olympics at Helsinki, where he added the marathon to complete a unique treble. He was unbeaten over the 10,000 m in 38 races from May 1948 to July 1954, when he retained his European title. Between 1949 and 1955 he set 18 world records over distances from 5,000 to 30,000 m. He bowed out of athletics, after an operation, with 6th place in the 1956 Olympic marathon.

A great hero in his own country, he was nevertheless censured for his active support of the liberal Dubcek government during the tragic political events of 1968 and, sadly, was later humbled by the totalitarian regime. But one thing they could not take away from him was the respect he earned throughout the world as a great sportsman and magnificent athlete.

WORLD ATHLETICS RECORDS — women

Event	Time/Distance	Name	Date
60 metres	7.2 s	Betty Cuthbert (Australia)	27.2.60
	7.2 s	Irina Botchkaryova (USSR)	28.8.60
	7.2 s	Andrea Lynch (GB)	22.6.74
100 yards	10.0 s	Chi Cheng (Taiwan)	13.6.70
100 metres	10.9 s*	Renate Stecher (E. Germany)	7.6.73
200 metres	22.0 s	Irena Szewinska (Poland)	13.6.74
220 yards	22.6 s	Chi Cheng (Taiwan)	3.7.72
400 metres	49.9 s	Irena Szewinska (Poland)	22.6.74
440 yards	52.2 s	Kathy Hammond (USA)	12.8.72
800 metres	1 m 57.5 s	Svetla Zlateva (Bulgaria)	24.8.73
880 yards	2 m 2.0 s	Dixie Willis (Australia)	3.3.62
	2 m 2.0 s	Judy Pollock (Australia)	5.7.67
1,500 metres	4 m 1.4 s	Ludmila Bragina (USSR)	9.9.72
1 mile	4 m 29.5 s	Paola Cacchi (Italy)	8.8.73
3,000 metres	8 m 52.8 s	Ludmila Bragina (USSR)	6.7.74
4 × 100 m relay	42.8 s	United States	20.10.68
	42.8 s	West Germany	10.9.72
4 × 110 yd relay	44.7 s	United States	9.7.71
4 × 200 m relay	1 m 33.8 s	Great Britain	24.8.68
4 × 220 yd relay	1 m 35.8 s	Australia	9.11.69
4 × 400 m relay	3 m 23.0 s	East Germany	10.9.72
4 × 440 yd relay	3 m 33.9 s	United States	12.8.72
4 × 800 m relay	8 m 8.6 s	Bulgaria	12.8.73
100 m hurdles	12.3 s	Annelie Ehrhardt (E. Germany)	22.7.73
200 m hurdles	25.7 s	Pamela Ryan (Australia)	25.11.71
High jump	6 ft 4½ in (1.94 m)	Jordanka Blagoyeva (Bulgaria)	24.9.72
Long jump	22 ft 5¼ in (6.84 m)	Heide Rosendahl (W. Germany)	3.9.70
Shot	70 ft 4½ in (21.45 m)	Nadyezhda Chizhova (USSR)	29.9.73
Discus	229 ft 0 in (69.90 m)	Faina Melnik (USSR)	27.5.74
Javelin	216 ft 10 in (66.10 m)	Ruth Fuchs (E. Germany)	7.9.63
Pentathlon	4,932 points	Burglinde Pollak (E. Germany)	23.9.73

* Hand timing

Ludmila Bragina (USSR) outclasses the rest of the field in the first ever Olympic 1,500 metres for women, at Munich in 1972. An imperturbable front runner, she broke her own world record (4 min 6.9 sec) in her heat (4:6.5), her semi-final (4:5.1), and again in the final (4:1.4).

Badminton

A game of subtlety, of delicacy erupting into a violence of speed; a fusion of power, instant reflexes, and tactical decision – badminton is all of these. At the highest level it is a most spectacular sport . . . yet it also brings enjoyment to countless players all over the world who find as much satisfaction in keeping the shuttlecock in flight as in scoring points.

Like so many sports, badminton began in England, adapted from a centuries old game called battledore and shuttlecock. The name came from Badminton, the country home of the Duke of Beaufort, where guests played the game in the 1870s. The English took the game to India, and it was there that, in 1877, the first rules were drawn up.

That these rules should have been formulated in Asia is most appropriate, for the Asians have virtually made the game their own. Badminton is the national sport in Malaysia, Singapore, and Indonesia, and such names as Wong Peng Soon, Eddie Choong, and Rudi Hartono feature prominently among the All-England Championships winners.

The All-England Championships are to badminton even more than Wimbledon is to tennis. It is *the* tournament all the world's leading players attend, and a glance at the winners' lists shows where the game's strength lies – the United States, Denmark, Sweden, Britain, and of course, the Asian countries, including Japan where the game has experienced rapid growth. The Championships were first held in 1899 and were organized by the Badminton Association, which was formed in 1893.

At international level, the game is administered by the International Badminton Federation (IBF), founded in 1934. Member countries compete for the Thomas Cup (men) and Uber Cup (women), team contests that began in 1948 and 1956 respectively. The trophies were donated by Sir George Thomas, four-time All-England champion (1920–23) and Mrs Betty Uber, who represented England 37 times (1926 to 1951). Indonesia and Malaysia have dominated the Thomas Cup, while first the United States, thanks to Judy Devlin Hashman, and then Japan have held sway in the Uber Cup. In 1966 badminton was included in the Commonwealth Games programme.

How to play

Played as singles or doubles, badminton offers an immense variety of shots from any part of the court. Rallies are won by placing the shuttle in any part of the opponent's court or by forcing errors. A player can play a variety of shots with a similar action. Most shots are played with a supple movement of the wrist, and wrist control is essential to play the deceptive shots that are a major feature of the game. In the *smash*, the shuttle is hit down from an overhead position as hard and steeply as possible over the net. The *drop shot* is a deceptive shot, disguised as a smash, in which the impact is checked so that the shuttle drops closer to the net. The *clear* is a defensive overhead shot which sends the shuttle high and deep to the back line. These strokes can be made forehand or backhand, and shots can also be played underarm or side-arm (the *drive*).

The shuttlecock ('shuttle' or 'bird') is made from goose feathers (14–16) inserted into a kid-covered cork base, although plastic shuttles are adequate substitutes at lower levels. The shuttles

Choong, Ewe Beng (Malaya), known as Eddie, produced from a 5 ft 3 in frame a tremendous hitting power, remarkable stamina and speed, and an entertaining unorthodoxy. Although often using defensive tactics, he was nonetheless a most spectacular player. He won 4 All-England singles (1953–54, 56–57), and 3 doubles with his brother David. He also won the US singles in 1954 and the prestigious All-Malayan singles in 1957 and 1960.

Freeman, David (USA), is for many the greatest badminton player of all time. A master of the court, accurate to a degree of perfection, he won the US singles 7 times (1939–42, 47, 48, and 53), the doubles 5 times, and the mixed 3 times. His only appearance in the All-England (1949) saw him win the singles,

and in the inaugural Thomas Cup contest, in 1948–49, he defeated the great Wong Peng Soon by 15–4, 15–1.

Hartono, Rudi (Indonesia), became, in 1973, the first man to win the All-England singles in 6 successive years, thus claiming the trophy outright for the second time. A mainstay of Indonesia's successful Thomas Cup team of the 1970s, he also won the Olympic Demonstration Tournament at Munich in 1972.

Rudi Hartono in action at Wembley in 1973, when he won his record sixth consecutive All-England singles. In 1974 he won again.

49

Badminton

The Empire Pool, Wembley, venue of the All-England tournament, the virtual world championships of badminton.

Hashman, Judy (née Devlin) (USA), dominated badminton as no other player has. A natural all-rounder with complete control of the court, she helped the United States win the Uber Cup three times. Her personal record is phenomenal: 10 All-England singles (1954, 57–58, 60–64, 66–67), 7 doubles; 12 US singles (1954, 56–63, 65–67), 10 doubles, and 6 mixed.

Kops, Erland (Denmark), a strong, hard-hitting but tremendously accurate player with a full range of strokes, won his first All-England singles title in 1958 and went on to chalk up

a record 7 victories in the event (1958, 60–63, 65, 67). To these he added 5 doubles titles, and he made 5 appearances in Denmark's Thomas Cup sides between 1957 and 1970. By the power and economy of effort of his strokes, Kops has greatly influenced modern thinking on stroke-play.

Wong Peng Soon (Malaya) first appeared on the international scene in 1937. By 1955, when he turned professional, he had won 4 All-England singles (1950–52, 55) and 8 All-Malayan singles (1940–41, 47, 49–53). In 1948–49, 1951–52, and 1954–55 he helped Malaya win the Thomas Cup. On court he always seemed to glide, and his game was memorable for deceptive strokes and beautiful footwork.

The Devlin sisters in 1954, Sue (later Mrs Peard) and Judy (later Mrs Hashman), kneeling. Daughters of Frank Devlin, himself six times All-England singles champion between 1925 and 1931, they won their first All-England doubles title in 1954, and went on to win another five as partners.

are graded by weight (4.73–5.50 gm) for use in varying atmospheric conditions. Rackets are made of either wood, wood with steel shaft, or all steel, and are strung with gut or nylon. They usually weigh between 4 and 5 oz.

A match is decided by the best of three games, each game going to 15 points (occasionally 21) or, in ladies' singles, 11 points. Only the person or pair serving (the side 'in') can score points, so the non-serving side ('out') must first win a rally and gain service before scoring. First service is decided by toss – winner chooses service or ends – and the winner of a game has first service in the next.

If a game reaches 13-all, the player or pair reaching 13 first chooses to play to 15 or 18 ('set to 5'). Similarly, at 14-all, the first to 14 may choose to 'set to 3' (playing to 17). In ladies' singles, the option at 9-all is 'set to 3' (12 pts) and at 10-all, 'set to 2'.

Service, made with both feet still and touching the court inside the service

court, is diagonal. It comes first from the right-hand court and alternates from right to left at each rally until service is lost. The opponent then serves from his right-hand court. In doubles, each pair serves before losing service, except that at the start of the game the serving side

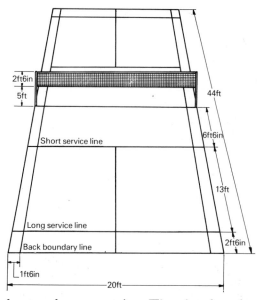

have only one service. The shuttlecock must be struck below waist level with an underarm stroke.

Service made, play continues until the shuttle goes out of play by failing to clear the net, hitting the ground, touching a player, hitting something outside the court, being hit consecutively by the same player or pair, or by being 'slung' (held on the racket). The side in fault loses the rally.

BADMINTON 'MOSTS'

All-England		
Men's singles	7	Erland Kops (Denmark)
	7	Rudi Hartono (Indonesia)
Women's singles	10	Judy Hashman (USA)
Thomas Cup	5	Indonesia
Uber Cup	4	Japan

Baseball

An intrinsically American game, baseball is, nevertheless, played all over the world. Japan is a stronghold of the game, and in Australia it has caught on as a winter sport. An annual European baseball championship was inaugurated in 1954. And an International Baseball Association was formed in 1936. Yet the World Series is a championship played for annually between two American professional clubs, the winner being regarded as the 'world champions'. And who could argue with that claim?

One American claim that is disputed, however, is their assertion that the game was invented by West Point cadet Abner Doubleday in 1839 at Cooperstown, New York. The myth was first perpetrated in 1889, and grew to such proportions that Cooperstown became the shrine of the game, housing the Baseball Museum and Hall of Fame. Yet there is irrefutable evidence that America's No. 1 summer sport developed from the old English game of rounders and similar games such as 'one old cat'.

If the origins of baseball are not to be found in America, though, the beginning of its development into the game we know today is. In 1845, in what is now Madison Square Garden, a team called the Knickerbockers was born, and Alexander Joy Cartwright headed the committee that drew up the first standard baseball rules. The first game was played on 19 June 1846 at Elysian Field, Hoboken, New Jersey, where the New York Club beat the 'Knicks' 23–1.

The National League was formed in 1876, the American League in 1901, and in 1903 the champions of the respective leagues played each other in the first World Series. A second took place in 1905, which was the prototype of the annual best-of-seven championship of today.

The man who influenced baseball most was 'Babe' Ruth, who in the 1920s changed it from a largely defensive to an excitingly attacking game with his cavalier approach to batting. Home runs flowed from Ruth's bat, big money flowed into baseball, and the game has never looked back.

Baseball is played 9-a-side on a 90-ft square 'diamond' infield with a large outfield making a playing area some 400–500 ft across. At one apex of the diamond is *home plate*, where the batter stands, and going anticlockwise along the other corners are 1st, 2nd, and 3rd bases. The pitcher throws the round 5-oz ball (9-inch circumference) from a mound in the middle of the diamond, $60\frac{1}{2}$ ft from home plate. To score a run, the batter must hit the ball initially infield, and run round all the bases. He can do this one base or more at a time.

Babe Ruth watches another of his 714 home runs soar into the crowd.

Cobb, Ty, the 'Georgia Peach', a prolific hitter and base runner, set innumerable records in the early 1920s, many of which still stand today. In 24 seasons (1905–26 Detroit Tigers, 1927–28 Philadelphia Athletics) he had a record lifetime average of .367. His other lifetime records included: 4,191 hits, 2,244 runs scored, 892 stolen bases, 12 times leading league batter. He stole a record 96 bases in 1915.

DiMaggio, Joe, New York Yankees outfielder (1936–51), hit safely in a record 56 consecutive games in 1941. A quiet, modest man. the 8th of 9

children of an Italian-born crab fisherman, he became a national hero, marrying actresses Dorothy Arnold and then Marilyn Monroe. Twice leader of American League batting, he was named its 'Most Valuable Player' 3 times.

Johnson, Walter, the 'Big Train', regarded by many as the best fast-ball pitcher of all time, won 414 games for the Washington Senators (1907–27), struck out a record 3,497 batters, and chalked up a record 113 shutouts. In 1913 he pitched a record 56 consecutive innings without conceding a run.

Koufax, Sandy, left-handed Los Angeles Dodgers pitcher, struck out a record 382 batters in 1965. When he retired in 1966 with arthritis in his pitching arm, he had pitched a record 4 no-hitters in his career, including a perfect game (no batter on base) against the Chicago Cubs in 1965, and won the Cy Young pitching award 3 times.

Baseball is a major spectator sport in Japan, with professional teams operating in the major cities.

Baseball

Mantle, Mickey, like Ruth a New York Yankees outfielder, was the most exciting hitter in baseball since his famous predecessor. A superb all-round player, he could hit right- or left-handed and was a brilliant fielder with a formidable throwing arm. Three times the American League's 'Most Valuable Player', he was 4 times home run champion, hitting 50 in a season twice with a career tally of 536 (a record for a switch-hitter). He played in 12 World Series (1951–64), including 7 on the winning side, for a record 40 rbi (including a record 18 home runs) and a record 42 runs scored.

Ruth, George Herman 'Babe', completely revolutionized baseball in the 1920s and brought the crowds flocking to see his spectacular big hitting. He began as a pitcher with the Boston Red Sox in 1914, winning 65 games in 3 seasons, and pitched 13 consecutive scoreless innings in a marathon World Series game against Brooklyn. He took this to a record 29 in 1918 and his own record to 3 out of 3 wins when Boston won their 3rd World Series in 4 years — but he was pitching less as his batting potential developed, and that season he tied for the American League home run championship with 11. In 1919 he set a major league home run record with 29, went to the Yankees for $125,000 and slugged an incredible 54 in 1920. In 1921 it was 59, and the Yankees won their first pennant. He was AL home run champion 12 times in all, including his famous 60 in 1927. A left-hander, he was a splendid outfielder. He played in 7 World Series for the Yankees (4 won) before finishing his days with the Boston Braves in 1935. He hit a record 714 home runs in his 22-year league career, plus 15 in World Series and 1 for the American League in 1933, in the first All-Star Game.

There are nine innings, each side having nine turns 'at bat'. The fielding side consists of the pitcher, a catcher (behind the batter), four infielders, and three outfielders. Fielders wear a glove on their non-throwing hand. The pitcher tries to throw the ball over the plate (17 inches wide), within the strike zone (batter's shoulders to knees). If he does so, or if the batter swings and misses or fouls out (hits it behind), a *strike* is called. If the batter does not swing and it is not a strike, a *ball* is called. Three strikes and the batter is out (but he cannot foul out on the third strike). Four balls and he 'walks' to first base.

If the batter hits the ball into fair territory, he must drop his bat and run – to 1st base (a *single*), 2nd base (a *double*), 3rd base (a *triple*), or home plate (a *home run*). Any member of his team already on a base can run too – and *must*, to avoid two on a base. Every man that reaches home plate scores a *run*. (So a ball 'hit out of the park' with 'bases loaded' is worth four runs.)

Below: *Roger Maris of the New York Yankees hits one of his record 61 home runs in 1961. This beat Babe Ruth's 34-year-old record by one, but Maris batted in more games.*

Sandy Koufax (above) *and Maury Wills* (below, sliding in to home plate) *were two record breakers for the Los Angeles Dodgers as pitcher and base runner, respectively.*

The batter is out if he hits the ball in the air and is caught by a fielder (in fair territory). A runner is also out if he is forced to run to a base and the fielder on that base collects the ball and has one foot on 'the bag'. He may 'tag' the runner by touching him with the ball without having a foot on the bag. A base runner may *steal a base* even when the batter does not hit the ball. More than one runner may be put out on the same play.

When three batters are out, the half-inning closes and it is the fielding side's turn to bat. Substitutes are allowed at any stage, but a substituted man may not return and the substitute must take his place in the batting order.

Softball developed from baseball, and is played on a smaller field with a larger (12-inch circumference), softer ball. Pitching is underarm. The game is 7-a-side and is popular throughout the world, especially with women and children. *Rounders*, a basic form of which is popular with schoolchildren, is played with five bases, each side having two innings.

BASEBALL 'MOSTS'

The Teams
World series won	20	New York Yankees
AL Pennants	29	New York Yankees
*NL Pennants	16	New York Mets

The Batters
Season			
home runs	61	Roger Maris, 1961	
	60†	Babe Ruth, 1927	
hits	257	George Sisler, 1920	
Career			
home runs	715	Hank Aaron (to 1974)	
	714	Babe Ruth	
hits	4,191	Ty Cobb	
average	367	Ty Cobb	

The Pitchers
Season		
wins	41	Jack Chesboro, 1904
shutouts	16	Grover Alexander, 1916
strikeouts	382	Sandy Koufax, 1965
Career		
wins	511	Cy Young
shutouts	113	Walter Johnson
strikeouts	3,497	Walter Johnson
no hitters	4	Sandy Koufax

The Runners – stolen bases
season	104	Maury Wills, 1962
career	892	Ty Cobb

Attendance
World Series	92,706	Los Angeles (v White Sox) 6.10.59
Double header	84,587	Cleveland (v Yankees) 12.9.54
Single game	78,672	‡Los Angeles (v Giants) 18.4.58

* From 1905.
† In 154-game season (as opposed to 162 games).
‡ At Memorial Coliseum.

Basketball

Wearing the same white strip as their illustrious footballing counterparts, Real Madrid's basketball team clash with TSSKA of Moscow in a European Cup basketball match.

Invented in 1891, basketball had become, by the early 1970s, one of the most popular sports in the world. With some 130 countries playing the game, it has more players than any other team game. And it is claimed that more people watch basketball than any other sport.

The man responsible for inventing basketball, Dr James Naismith, was a student at the International YMCA Training School at Springfield, Mass., in America. At that time, there was no suitable team game for keeping students occupied indoors in the winter months, so Naismith's instructor asked him to devise one. The gymnasium at the college had a balcony round it, and Naismith struck on the idea of hanging boxes from it as goals. There were no suitable boxes available, so he used peach baskets – and that is how the game got its name.

Basketball spread throughout America, and then to other countries, and the world's governing body, the Fédération Internationale de Basketball Amateur (FIBA) was formed in 1932. And in 1936 basketball became an official Olympic sport. The United States won every Olympic tournament without losing a game until their sensational defeat by Russia in the final of the 1972 Games. The world championships were inaugurated in 1950, and Argentina, the hosts, became the first champions. The European Championships were first held in 1935, and the biannual post-war competitions have been largely dominated by the USSR. There are also European club cups for both men and women.

In the United States, basketball is a major spectator sport, and the pro-fessional game is big business. Teams in the big professional leagues might entice the leading college stars with million-dollar contracts. Professional rules differ in some respects from the universally recognized international rules, and a certain amount of physical contact has been allowed to creep into what is essentially a non-contact game.

Less serious, but nonetheless pro-fessional, are the Harlem Globetrotters, the touring 'circus' who mix clowning with remarkable virtuosity. Since 1927 they have been exhibiting their brand of knockabout basketball all over the world, and as ambassadors of the sport have no equal, having been seen by over 75 million people in nearly 90 countries.

How to play

Basketball is a five-a-side game but a team can, and usually does, use up to five substitutes. Normally a team has a centre, two forwards, and two guards, but such is the speed and fluidity of the game that all players must be competent in both defensive and attacking aspects. A game is divided into two periods of 20 minutes actual playing time, with a 10-minute interval. A game cannot end in a draw; extra periods of 5 minutes are played until the tie is broken.

The aim of each team is to throw the $9\frac{1}{2}$–10 inch diameter ball (circumference $29\frac{1}{2}$–$31\frac{1}{2}$ in) into an 18 inch diameter

The Harlem Globetrotters, despite their clowning, are first-rate basketball players and have been wonderful ambassadors for the sport throughout the world for nearly half a century.

basket defended by their opponents. A *field goal*, which is scored during normal play, is worth two points; one point is awarded for a goal from a *free throw*, taken from 15 ft. The basket is fixed, at a height of 10 ft, to a 6 ft wide by 4 ft backboard, 4 ft inside the court.

Play starts with a *jump ball*. The referee throws the ball up between one player from each side, who stand in the centre circle on either side of the centre line. They jump and attempt to tap the ball to one of their team-mates. Players may throw, bounce, tap, or roll the ball to each other, but may not punch or kick it. A player may *dribble* the ball by bouncing it, but once he stops bouncing

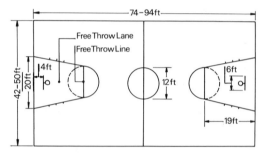

it he must release it. A player may not run with the ball, but may carry the ball for one pace or may pivot with the ball in his hands. He may shoot at goal from any position on the court.

Personal contact is not allowed, neither is the blocking of a man without the ball. The penalty for an unintentional *per-sonal foul* is a *throw-in* to the other side, from the side-line at the point nearest where the offence took place. The penalty for a personal foul that is in-tentional, or is committed when the player fouled is in the act of shooting, or is committed in the last 3 minutes of the game, is two free throws to be taken by the opponent fouled or possession of the ball, whichever the captain chooses. For a *player technical foul* (such as delaying the game, two free throws are awarded and may be taken by any player. A player who has committed five fouls must leave the court. For a *coach tech-nical foul*, occurring when a coach or a substitute breaks the rules, one free throw is awarded, with subsequent possession at mid-court, to the opposing team.

For *violations* of the rules, such as carrying the ball or for remaining in the *restricted area* for more than 3 seconds, the opponents get possession and restart

Women's basketball, France v China. The first women's world championships were held in 1953, in Chile, and were won by the United States. Italy won the first European championships, played in Rome in 1938, and now held every two years. Since the war, Russia have dominated both the world and the European championships.

with a throw-in. When the ball goes out of bounds, play is restarted by a throw-in from the place where the ball went out (taken by the opposing team), or, in cases where it is not clear who put the ball out, by a jump ball.

A game is controlled jointly by a referee and an umpire, who are of equal status. They are assisted by a time-keeper and a scorer. The timekeeper is concerned with recording the playing time, it being up to the senior officials to count the seconds for time limits.

The rules of basketball are framed to keep the game moving, and contain a number of time limits. Apart from the 3-second rule in the restricted area, officials have to apply a 5-second rule, for players putting the ball in play, and a 10-second rule, which stipulates that the attacking team must bring the ball into its front court within 10 seconds of getting possession, and may not pass the ball to its back court. There is also a 30-second rule, which states that the team in possession must make a goal attempt within 30 seconds of gaining control. Depending on the class of game, the time would be counted off by the officials or, in international matches, by a 30-second operator, sometimes with sophisticated electronic scoreboards on court indicating how much time remains. In American pro basketball, this is a 24-second rule.

BASKETBALL 'MOSTS'

Olympic championships	7	United States
World championships – men	2	Brazil
– women	4	Russia

Memorable moments in sport

An American nightmare

Dateline: Munich, 10–11 September 1972. The Americans had never lost an Olympic basketball game, having won every gold medal for the sport since 1936. But they are not such a dominating force in Munich, and are struggling in the final against the Russians. Then, in the last 3 minutes, the Russian team begin to wilt. Some chances are missed and the Americans creep up to within a point with only seconds to go. The Russians miss another basket. From the rebound, 21-year-old Doug Collins races to the other end, but is sent sprawling headlong out of court. Stunned, he finally gets up after an agonizing interlude to take the two free throws that will decide the match.

The first drops in – 49–49. The young Illinois State college star takes aim again. And in it goes – USA 50 USSR 49. There are only 3 seconds to go on the clock as the Russians restart the game; the buzzer goes, but the clock now shows 1 second. The referee asks the table officials why the signal had been sounded. Not satisfied he orders the 1 second to be played. The Russians bring the ball into play again, and the buzzer sounds.

The court is a mass of jubilant American fans and players, with some of the team leaping around in delight, their proud record intact after a fairytale finish – the scene might have come straight out of a 1950s movie. The ending, however, was pure Hitchcock . . .

Over the noise of the celebrations can be heard what at first sounds like an officious announcement to clear the court. But, ominously, the voice is persistent, and it appears that there are still 3 seconds to be played.

The court is eventually cleared and the players take up their positions, the Americans as if in a dream, for they can barely comprehend the situation. From underneath his own basket, Ivan Edeshko throws a court-length pass to 6 ft 7 in Alexander Belov. He catches the ball cleanly as the two Americans guarding him collapse in a heap, and pops it in the basket as the buzzer goes – USSR 51 USA 50, and now it is the Russians' turn to rejoice.

Top: *American players and fans acclaim their 'victory'. They had dramatically closed a 10-point gap and scored the winning basket with seconds to go. But then they are brought back to play another 3 seconds, long enough for Belov (above) to catch a court-length pass and flip the ball in. And now the Russians raise their arms in celebration (below).*

Billiard table games

Davis, Joe (England), supreme at snooker, second only to Walter Lindrum at billiards, was the only man to hold both world titles simultaneously. In the 1920s he introduced revolutionary techniques and tactics into snooker that, combined with his personality and business acumen, turned it into a world game. He won the first world championship in 1927, and proceeded to beat allcomers until he retired from championship play in 1946, having won 15 consecutive titles. He continued to dominate the snooker scene, however, and in 1955 crowned his career with a 'maximum' 147 break. In all, he made 687 'century' breaks. He beat Tom Newman for the world billiards title in 1926 and retained it until Walter Lindrum beat him in 1933. His best championship break was 2,052 in 1930, made without the aid of any repetitive sequences.

Joe's brother **Fred Davis** won the world snooker championship 3 times (1948–49–51), having in 1940 come closest to beating Joe (36–37).

Joe Davis

Ray Reardon won his third snooker world championship in 1974, suddenly emerging as the world's outstanding player. He made five maximum breaks of 147, two of them awaiting ratification.

The origin of billiard games is obscure, but it is thought that they evolved from old forms of bowls. Games were developed in England and France: Mary, Queen of Scots had a table in the 16th century and Louis XIV took up the French version in 1694, becoming very proficient.

Billiards as we know it today took shape in England in the late 1700s, and soon attracted big gamblers. The game became organized in the late 1800s, and the Billiards Association was founded in 1885. In 1919 this became part of a new body, the Billiards Association and Control Council. A world championship was first staged in 1870 and held regularly until 1934, but experts became so good that the game became boring as a spectacle. Snooker, invented in India in the late 1800s by British Army personnel, overtook billiards in popularity, largely owing to the personality and skills of Joe Davis, who won the first world championship, in 1927, and dominated the game until after the war.

Both billiards and snooker are played on a 12×6 ft $1\frac{1}{2}$ in table, with six pockets, standing about 2 ft 10 in from the floor (a half-size table is 6 ft long). The playing surface is less because of the cushion overhang. The hard $2\frac{1}{16}$-in diameter balls are made of a composition material called crystallate. The cue, which is used to strike the balls, must be at least 3 ft long, and is usually about 4 ft 10 in. Made of wood, usually ash, it tapers to a point of about $\frac{1}{3}$-in diameter on which a leather 'tip' is stuck. Chalk is used on the tip during the game to prevent slipping when it comes into contact with the ball. In both games, players (one against one) take turns to play, each continuing until he fails to score. The balls must be stationary before a stroke can be played.

There are many other kinds of billiard table games. American 'pocket billiards' has several versions, and games played on pocketless tables are popular in America and on the Continent. A popular pub game in Britain is bar billiards, played on a small table with eight balls, mushroom-shaped hazards, and numbered holes.

Billiards

There are just three balls in billiards – a red and the two white cue-balls, 'spot' and 'plain'. Players score by potting or going in-off the red (3 points) or the other white (2) or by means of a cannon (2). If a player pots his opponent's white, it stays down for the rest of the break, and his opponent then plays it from the 'D'. When the red ball is potted, it is re-spotted on its spot; if the cue-ball goes in-off, it is played from the 'D'. A ball must be played out of baulk from the 'D'.

The penalty for failing to hit a ball with the cue-ball is 1 point, or 3 if it goes into a pocket (added to opponent's score). The opponent may play the balls as they are or have them spotted (white on centre spot) and play from the 'D'.

Games are played to a fixed number of points (100, 500, etc) or the winner is the player leading at the end of a specified period (1 hr, 2 hr, two 2-hr sessions, etc). The game starts with the red on its spot and the cue-ball in the 'D', the other white being 'in hand', that is, off the table.

As experts mastered the game to such an extent that they were able to stay at the table for hours on end, building up breaks of thousands by repeating the same shot, rules have been introduced to prevent the game developing into a tedious spectacle. (For example, Tom Reece made an unofficial, unfinished break of 499,135 in 1907 mainly by means of the 'cradle' cannon, in which the object balls are manoeuvred into the jaws of a corner pocket.) There are now limits on the number of consecutive cannons or pots and in-offs that may be made.

Snooker

Both players use the same white cue-ball and aim to pot one of the 15 reds (1 point) before taking a colour (black 7, pink 6, blue 5, brown 4, green 3, yellow 2). The reds, which start the game set up in 'pyramid' formation above the pink spot, remain in the pockets when potted; the colours are respotted. When the colour attempted after the last potted red has been played, the colours are taken in turn from yellow to black, and remain in the pockets when fairly potted.

The game starts with the balls on their spots, and the first player breaks off from the 'D'. There are no in-offs, and if the cue-ball goes into a pocket the player is penalized. A player who misses the ball 'on' or nominated (as in the case of a colour after a red) is also penalized. Penalties vary from a minimum 4 points to 7, depending on which ball is hit or

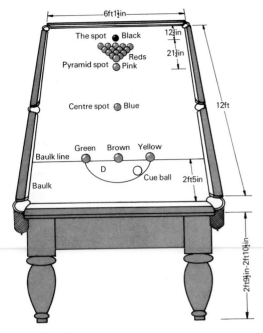

Diagram labels: 6ft1½in · The spot · Black · 12½in · Reds · 21½in · Pyramid spot · Pink · Centre spot · Blue · 12ft · Green · Brown · Yellow · Baulk line · D · Baulk · Cue ball · 2ft5in · 2ft9½in–2ft10½in

missed. Players do not always try to pot a ball – they may play safe or attempt to leave a snooker. If a player is snookered after a foul shot, he may nominate to play any ball, which then assumes the same value as the ball 'on'. More than one red may be potted at once, giving an extra point or points.

Other games

Pool, or *pocket billiards*, a predominantly American game, is played on a $9 \times 4\frac{1}{2}$ ft table with 15 coloured, numbered balls and a white cue-ball. The most popular version is called '14-1', in which a player must nominate ball, pocket, and number of cushions the ball will strike. A point is scored for each ball potted. When 14 balls have been potted they are racked again, and the striker attempts to pot the 15th ball, scattering the others to continue his run. The winner is the first to reach a specified number of points (50, 100, etc). In another version, *rotation*, the balls are potted in numerical order and are worth their numerical value.

BILLIARDS & SNOOKER 'MOSTS'

Billiards

World titles (amat)	4	R. Marshall (Aus)
Break	42,746*	W. Cook (Eng) 1907
	4,137†	W. Lindrum (Aus) 1932
	1,784	J. Davis (Eng) 1936
– amateur	859	M. Lafir (Ind) 1973

Snooker

World titles	15	J. Davis (Eng)
–amateur	2	G. Owen (Eng)
Break	147	J. Davis (Eng) 1955
	147	R. Williams (Eng) 1965
	147	R. Reardon (Eng) 1974

*With anchor cannon. †Pre baulk-line rule.

Billiards and snooker terms

Bottom Applying *bottom* means striking the cue-ball low down to retard its forward motion on contact with the object ball.
Break Sequence of scoring shots.
Break off Start play with the first shot.
Bridge Position of the hand on which the cue rests.
Cannon In billiards, hitting both object balls.
Cue-ball The ball struck with the cue.
Frame A complete game of snooker.
Free ball When a player is snookered after his opponent has fouled, he may play a *free ball*, that is, nominate any ball to play, that ball assuming the same value as the one 'on'. It is a foul to leave a snooker behind the nominated ball except when only pink and black remain.
In hand After an in-off in billiards, a player is *in hand*, and plays his ball from the 'D'.
In-off A scoring stroke in billiards in which the cue-ball goes into the pocket after striking an object ball.
Losing hazard An in-off.
Nursery cannons Cannon play in which a player scores a sequence of cannons with the three balls close to the cushion. A maximum of 75 cannons is allowed, after which a player must score a pot or an in-off.
On In snooker, a ball 'on' is one that may legally be played.
Object ball The ball aimed at.
Pot A scoring stroke in which the object ball is struck into a pocket.
Rest A rod with a metal bridge on which the cue slides, used when the cue-ball is in an inaccessible position.
Screw Applying *screw* means striking the cue-ball low with follow-through to reduce the angle of motion after contact with the object ball.
Screw back Like *screw*, but imparting recoil to the cue-ball on contact with the object ball.
Shot to nothing A shot in snooker by which a player aims to pot a ball and bring his ball back into a favourable position for himself if he is successful, but an unfavourable position for his opponent if he is not.
Side Applying *side* means striking the cue-ball to one side to modify the angle of cue-ball after contact.
Snooker A position in which the cue-ball cannot hit a ball 'on' directly because of an intervening ball or balls.
Spider A rest with a high bridge so that the cue may clear a ball close to the cue-ball.
Stab A sharp, stunning stroke that stops the cue-ball dead after contact with the object ball.
Stun A heavy deadening stroke similar to stab, in which the cue-ball is made to stop near the point of contact with the object ball.
Top Applying *top* means striking the cue-ball high up to make it run on after contact with the object ball.
Winning hazard A pot.

Lindrum, Walter (Australia), indisputably the world's finest billiards player, carried all before him when he arrived in England in 1929, making 67 breaks of 1,000 during his stay. For one reason or another, he did not play in the world championship until 1933, when he beat Joe Davis narrowly in the final, a feat he repeated in 1934 before devoting the rest of his career to exhibitions and charity work. A master of the nursery cannon, he made a world record 4,137 break in 1932 (before the introduction of the 'baulk line' rule), and set countless other records.

His nephew **Horace Lindrum**, renowned for his entertaining exhibition play, won the world snooker title in 1952 and was also a fine billiards player.

Walter Lindrum during his all-conquering tour of England in 1929, in play against Willie Smith.

Cushionless variants of billiards are popular on the Continent and in America. Tables measure 10×5 ft or 8×4 ft. Players score points by means of the cannon, called a 'carion' or 'billiard'. In 'three-cushion' billiards, at least three cushions must be struck by the cue-ball before the second object-ball is hit.

Bowling sports

Bryant, David (England), smoking his inevitable pipe, stamped his personality on bowls in the late 1950s, becoming the sport's first crowd-puller. A Somerset schoolmaster before he gave up teaching in 1972, he won the singles title in the first world championships (1966), and in Commonwealth Games won singles and fours golds in 1962 and the singles again in 1970. Still only 40 years old, he had by 1973 won a record 12 EBA titles (including a record 5 singles) plus 5 British Isles titles (3 singles) and 6 EBA indoors singles. Bryant was awarded the MBE in 1969 and brought further honour to his sport when he carried the flag for the British contingent at the 1974 Commonwealth Games, going on to win his third singles title.

David Bryant

A vital measurement in bowls, the distance between a wood and the jack.

Throwing stones at targets is probably man's oldest recreational activity. There is strong evidence of a form of bowling being played in Egypt over 7,000 years ago, in which the ball was rolled towards a target. A 'target' bowling game called *kegeln* developed in medieval Germany. Priests got their congregants to use their *kegels* (clubs) as pins, representing the devil, who had to be knocked down. The cloisters would have been an ideal place for what was more a ritual than a sport. Eventually it did develop into a pastime and it is Martin Luther who is credited with standardizing the number of pins at nine.

Ninepins spread to other countries, and took hold most strongly in England. Known at first as *kayles* (*kyles* in Scotland), it later became *skittles*, which now exists in countless forms. In the United States, ninepins was transformed into tenpin bowling.

Meanwhile, in England in the Middle Ages, another form of bowling developed in which the target became another, smaller bowl. The oldest green in the world is at Southampton and dates from 1299. The game had its ups and downs, being banned a number of times either because it interfered with archery practice or because of the betting, fighting, and drunkenness often associated with it.

However, the nobility and even royalty fostered the sport. But it was in Scotland in the 19th century that the great forward surge began, with the introduction of sea-washed turf greens and after W. W. Mitchell in 1849 drew up standard rules.

Bowls

Three different codes exist in Britain: Association, Federation, and Crown Green. The world game, also called *lawn bowls*, or *flat green bowls*, is the Association one. The first 'association' was the Border Bowling Association, formed in Scotland in 1872. New Zealand formed the first national association (1886), and this led to the birth of the International Bowling Board (IBB), the world authority, in 1905. The first world championships were staged in 1966. Women have their own, parallel organizations. Indoor bowls, played on carpets, became one of the fastest growing sports in the 1960s.

Until the end of World War II, bowls was primarily a game for member nations of the British Empire. It was included in the first Empire Games, in 1930, when all three events (singles, pairs, fours) were won by England.

Till the arrival of David Bryant as an English title holder in 1957, the game had been far greater than its players. He was to become the world's No. 1 and the first major crowd-drawer. When England introduced a tournament in 1973 with £50 prize vouchers for winners, the shift from pure recreation to the intense competition of squash and tennis was firmly on its way.

The object of bowls is to deliver one's woods, as the bowls are called, so that as many as possible finish nearer to a small, normally white, bowl – the *jack* – than the opponent's best bowl. Each one so doing scores a point – a *shot*. Bowls, now made out of plastic rather than wood, are brown or black, weigh from 3 to $3\frac{1}{2}$ lb, and have a diameter of $4\frac{3}{4}$–$5\frac{1}{8}$ in. They are shaped (biased) so that they follow curved paths when traversing the rink. The bias must not be less than that of a standard bowl held by each official tester, and the bowl must be stamped with the IBB imprint accordingly every 10 years.

There are few differences between the Federation and Association game, which is played on a flat strip of lawn – a *rink* – about 40 yd long and 19 ft wide. A *green* usually has six such rinks side by side, so resulting in an overall size approximately 40 by 40 yd. It is surrounded by a ditch not less than 2 inches in depth and from 8 to 15 inches wide. Bowls that touch the jack on their original journey down the rink remain in play even when they run, or are later cannoned, into the ditch, and the jack also remains *live* when in the ditch.

There is no ditch in the Federation game, and bowls that run off the green or are driven beyond the boundary or into the ditch (in practice, the Federation game is often played on Association greens) are called *dead*. If the jack is driven out of play the *end* is replayed.

Each player's (or team's in the case of pairs, triples, and fours) full complement of bowls is delivered in one direction down the green, the score is recorded, and then the process is repeated from the other end of the rink, hence the term 'ends'. Pairs and fours matches are of 21 ends, triples 18 ends, and in singles the winner is the player first scoring 21 shots. In singles and pairs each player alternates with his adversary in delivering four bowls. Triples is three bowls per player, and in fours each player uses two bowls.

Crown Green bowls relates almost exclusively to the north-west of England. Those who play it claim it is the most skilled of all varieties of bowls. They enumerate many reasons: the green itself rises to a crown in the centre 9 inches high; as well as the bowls, the jack is biased; the game takes place in any direction the players like, and not just up and down a comparatively narrow section of the entire green.

The object is identical, to deliver one's bowls nearer to the jack than the opponent's. Singles is played almost exclusively. Each player uses only two bowls, and matches are normally 41 up. Many greens are attached to public houses, and gambling abounds.

Tenpin bowling

Tenpin bowling was devised in the United States to circumvent a law banning ninepins. The Dutch had introduced lawn bowling to America in the early 1600s, but by the early 1800s the skittles game had superseded it in popularity. There was heavy betting on ninepins, and the game became riddled with gangsters, so much so that a law was passed classifying it as a form of gambling, and thus illegal. So a tenth pin was added, the pins rearranged in a triangle, and a 'new', legal, game was born.

The American Bowling Congress was

Three contrasting faces of bowling sports. Above: Crown green bowls, a working-man's game played in the North of England. *Below:* Bowls on the sedate lawns of Wellington's Khandallah Green, in New Zealand. *Bottom:* Busy tenpin lanes in a Tokyo bowling centre.

established in 1895, the Women's International Bowling Congress in 1916, and by the 1970s America alone had some 30 million bowlers. The advent of automatic 'pinspotters' to replace the boys who formerly set up the pins – and still do at skittles – signalled a mushrooming of the sport in the 1950s. Multi-lane bowling alleys went up all over America, and this ultra-modern sport took hold in other countries, too, Japan boasting a 252-lane bowling centre in Tokyo.

The attraction of the game for many is that even a novice can knock down all 10 pins with one ball. Basically a game consists of 10 *frames* for each player, a frame being two balls – or one, if all the pins are knocked down with the first. This is called a *strike*. If all 10 pins are knocked down with the two balls, it is called a *spare*. A player scores a point for each pin knocked down, but a strike entitles him also to double the score of his next two balls, a spare to double the score of his next one. The 'perfect game' is a maximum score of 300, consisting of strikes in each of the 10 frames plus strikes with the two extra balls earned by a strike in the 10th frame.

The hard rubber ball weighs 10 to 16 lb, with a circumference of 27 in, and is bowled from behind a *foul line* 60 ft from the No. 1 (head) pin. It has two finger-holes and a thumb-hole, and most bowlers use a three-finger grip after a four-step run-up. The 15-inch-high pins are set in a 36-inch triangle.

The orthodox ball for a strike should hit the 'pocket' between Nos. 1 and 3 pins for a right-hander, the No. 1 and No. 2 pins for a left-hander. For experts, the game almost takes on the aspect of target practice, although a 'near miss' can leave an awkward *split*, in which the bowler needs to knock down two or more widely spaced pins to save his spare. Such shots require the greatest skill, and it seems a pity that they become part of the game only after an indifferent first shot. Nevertheless, for the novice and expert alike, a strike is a most satisfying experience, heightened no doubt by the sound of the pins tumbling and the sight of the flashing lights announcing the achievement.

Other bowling games

The first indoor bowling alley was built in London in 1455, and skittles have been played in pubs and hotels up and down the country in a variety of regional forms for hundreds of years. In *West Country skittles*, balls (about 6 lb) are rolled at a diamond-shaped formation of nine heavy wooden pins about 30 ft away. In a Midlands version (*long-alley skittles*), cylindrically shaped 4-lb 'cheeses' are allowed to bounce on the 36-ft pitch before hitting the pins. In *Old English skittles*, played mainly in London under the auspices of the Amateur Skittles Association, 8–12 lb wooden 'cheeses' are projected at $14\frac{1}{2}$-inch-high skittles in a 4 ft 6 in square frame 21 ft away. Players try to knock down the 9 pins in fewer than 5 throws, scoring a point for each 'toss', with the lowest score winning a particular frame.

In *boules*, immensely popular in France, the rules are similar to those of bowls, but iron balls are thrown at the metal jack, often on rough ground. In a similar game, *petanque*, the balls are of wood studded with nails.

Canadian fivepins, a game almost exclusive to Canada and also one of its most popular sports, is played on a regulation tenpin alley with similar rules; the balls are smaller and the pins are the squat duckpins with thick rubber bands round their middle. America also has variations of *duckpins* and tall, narrow *candlepins*.

The French game of boules, in which metal bowls are thrown rather than bowled.

The diagram illustrates the two ends of a tenpin lane, showing the positioning and numbers of the pins (right).

Gutter
Lane
Foul line
3ft6in
1 2 3 4 5 6 7 8 9 10
60ft

BOWLS AND BOWLING 'MOSTS'

Bowls – World and Commonwealth titles
5 David Bryant (England), including 4 individual golds

Tenpin Bowling (official records, all US)

Highest 3-game score	886	Albert Brandt (1939)
Most perfect games	24	Elvin Mesger
Most consecutive strikes	29	Frank Caruana (1924); Max Stein (1939)

Boxing

Ali, Muhammad (USA), the most colourful boxing character of the century, was first known as Cassius Clay. After winning the light-heavyweight gold medal at the 1960 Olympic Games, he turned professional, being sponsored by a group of wealthy businessmen, and won the world heavyweight title at the age of 22, sensationally retiring Sonny Liston after 6 rounds. He defended it successfully on nine occasions, but was stripped of the championship when he refused to join the US Army, having adopted the Muslim faith and changed his name to Muhammad Ali. At that time, he was undefeated in 29 bouts, in which he displayed exceptional boxing ability. Out of the ring for $3\frac{1}{2}$ years, he made a comeback that saw him defeated by Joe Frazier when attempting to regain a title he had never lost.
Record to 1973: W 39 (30 i.d.), L 2.

Armstrong, Henry (USA), known as 'Homicide Hank' because of his non-stop aggressive attacking, was the only man to win and hold three world titles simultaneously — feather (1937), light and welter (1938); he also fought a draw for the middle-weight title (1940). He fought at top speed, smothering an opponent with a ceaseless rain of punches. He successfully defended his welterweight title 19 times.
Record: W 114 (97 i.d.), D 8, L 22, ND 1.

Carpentier, Georges (France), began as a mere boy and boxed at each weight, becoming European champion from welter to heavyweight. Noted for straight right-hand punching to

The popularity of boxing is always enhanced by a colourful and busy world heavyweight champion. Muhammad Ali (above, in typically aggressive mood) was just that, whether in or out of the ring.

Boxing as an amateur sport came into prominence because of the ancient Greek Olympic Games. And when the Romans took it up as a spectacle, professionalism might be considered to have begun. But whereas the Greeks used their bare hands, the Romans introduced the cestus, the original 'knuckle-duster'. Pugilism spread from Athens and Rome to the rest of Europe, and it found a ready home in England, especially on the village fairgrounds.

In 1719, James Figg, who had proved himself champion at many manly sports, opened an amphitheatre in Tottenham Court Road, London, where the noble art was taught, exhibitions provided, and contests staged that aroused the keen interest of all sportsmen, high and low. Figg also visited all the annual fairs across the breadth of England, using a business card drawn for him by William Hogarth. In 1723, by order of George I, a 'Ring' was formed in Hyde Park for the purpose of providing an arena for impromptu contests in which boxing featured predominantly.

John Broughton came next as Champion of England, and in 1745 he drew up the first set of rules for the 'Prize Ring'. He also introduced gloves, which were termed the 'mufflers', in order that his aristocratic patrons should not be disfigured. In fist fighting, a round

the chin, he k.o.'d Battling Levinsky for the world light-heavyweight title in 1919. In 1921 he challenged Jack Dempsey for the heavyweight crown in the first 'million dollar gate'. He lost in four rounds.
Record: W 85 (51 i.d.), D 5, L 15, ND 1.

Boxing

Cooper, Henry (GB), one of twins, was the longest reigning British champion (1959–69 and 1970–71). He won a record three Lonsdale Belts outright, and was in turn British, European, and Commonwealth champion. He fought Muhammad Ali for the world heavyweight title, but lost in six rounds with a badly damaged left eye. A stand-up, classical boxer, he had a devastating left hook, known as "Enery's 'Ammer", which once floored Ali in sensational manner. Record: W 40 (29 i.d.), D 1, L 14.

Corbett, James J. (USA), a San Franciscan bank clerk, became the first world heavyweight champion under Marquis of Queensberry Rules when he k.o.'d the great John L. Sullivan in 21 rounds in 1892. A classical boxer, he mixed well outside the ring, becoming known as 'Gentleman Jim'. He reigned as champion for five years before losing to Bob Fitzsimmons Record: W 20 (9 i.d.), D 6, L 5, ND 2.

Dempsey, Jack (USA), former hobo, miner, and lumberjack, became world heavyweight champion. An aggressive, two-fisted fighter of great durability and immense punching power, he knocked down giant Jess Willard seven times in the 1st round to become champion in the 3rd (1919). He successfully defended his title five times, but lost it on a points decision to Gene Tunney after a reign of seven years. He made a valiant effort to recapture it, putting Tunney down for 14 seconds in the famous Battle of the Long Count. Record: W 60 (49 i.d.), D 8, L 7, ND 6.

Driscoll, Jim (GB), clever Welsh featherweight, known

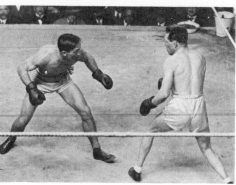

Action through the ages. Top left: *A scene from the golden age of prizefighting, the great Jem Belcher is knocked off his feet by Henry Pearce in 1805.* Top right: *Jack Johnson (right) chased Tommy Burns halfway round the world to get a crack at the heavyweight title. He finally caught up with him in Sydney in 1908, and battered him to defeat in 14 rounds.* Above: *Frenchman Georges Carpentier (left) sizes up Britain's Ted (Kid) Lewis before demolishing him inside a round*

in this 1922 defence of his world light-heavyweight crown. Above right: *'Ferocious Fred' Mills (right) wades in against America's Gus Lesnevich to take his world light-heavyweight title in 1948.* Below left: *Cassius Clay, as he then was, lies stunned by Henry Cooper's left-hook at Wembley in 1963, but forced Cooper to retire in the next round.* Below right: *Bob Foster (USA) successfully defends his light-heavy crown against Britain's Chris Finnegan (left) at Wembley in 1972.*

as 'Peerless Jim' because of his classical boxing, won the first 9-stone Lonsdale Belt outright in 11 months, and was unbeaten in 11 contests in America. He retired as undefeated British champion after holding the title for 13 years, fighting his last contest at 38. Record: W 53 (27 i.d.), D 6, L 2, ND 9.

ended when one of the contestants had been knocked down or thrown to the floor. He was then given 30 seconds to 'toe the line', a mark drawn across the middle of the square. Some battles saw a great many rounds completed that occupied several hours. When an important match was arranged, it was fought in a meadow before thousands of spectators. But these open-air encounters were regarded as breaches of the peace by the forces of law and order, and the site of a contest was usually kept secret until the very last moment.

The end of the Prize Ring came in 1867 when the 8th Marquis of Queensberry was responsible for drawing up an entirely new set of rules. These elimin-

ated all wrestling holds and foul blows, introduced points scoring, limited the duration of rounds to 3 minutes, and compelled the use of gloves. By this time, the commercializing of boxing had become widespread. But it did not become in any way controlled until the formation of the National Sporting Club (NSC) in 1891, with headquarters at Covent Garden in London. This body, with private membership, reframed the rules, which have remained basically the same ever since. The weight divisions were also stabilized from flyweight to heavyweight, and Lonsdale Belts, so named after the president, Lord Lonsdale, were instituted for British championships. The

NSC exercised a powerful influence over the sport and did much to remove from boxing its illegal status. The Club held sway until 1929, when the British Boxing Board of Control was formed, taking over the responsibility of the sport in Britain. The appointment of a single adjudicator has remained, but in most other countries a referee and

two judges render their verdicts on a majority basis.

The greatest advance in professionalism came in the United States, where there were vast resources of talent as well as many cities containing large indoor and outdoor arenas where huge crowds could be accommodated. The first heavyweight championship fight

Memorable moments in sport

The battle of the long count

Dateline: Soldiers' Field, Chicago, 22 September 1927. A year after Gene Tunney had surprisingly taken the world heavyweight title from a ring-rusty Jack Dempsey, 104,943 eager fans paid $2,658,660 to see a return match. What they got for their money was a contest that bristled with incident, and produced a sensational moment that has become a legend in ring history.

For the first six rounds, the pattern of the fight was similar to that of their first meeting, with Tunney making full use of the ring and spearing off the aggressive Dempsey with an accurate left to the face and the occasional right cross. Then, in the 7th round, it happened! Tunney backed hastily into the ropes, reached them sooner than he anticipated, and was hurled back into the Mauler's blazing fists, his guard momentarily down.

In a flash, Dempsey landed four magnificent punches on Tunney's jaw, left and right hooks that thudded onto

the target, causing the champion's knees to buckle. He sank to the canvas, his left glove grasping the nearby bottom rope, a dazed look on his handsome features. Dempsey hovered over him, ready to apply the 'kill'.

Referee Dave Barry, in strict accordance with a recent rule, ordered Dempsey to go to a neutral corner. But several seconds elapsed before the ex-champion complied – too late, for the champion had scrambled to his feet, beating the 'count', even though ringside stopwatches registered that he had been down for 14 seconds. He managed to stay clear of further trouble until the bell, recovered well in the interval, then completely outboxed the tiring Dempsey in the last three rounds to keep his title.

Critical seconds are ticking away as Jack Dempsey hovers over the champion, Gene Tunney, ready to finish him off should he get up. But the referee cannot start his count until Dempsey has moved to a neutral corner, and Tunney recovers to retain his title.

Fitzsimmons, Bob (GB), the only English-born boxer to win the world heavyweight title, was the first man to gain three world crowns – middle, heavy, and light-heavyweight, in that order, the last at the age of 41. Born in Cornwall, he developed his boxing in New Zealand and Australia before proceeding to America. A powerful puncher, he defeated James J. Corbett for the heavyweight title. Weighing little more than a middleweight, he gave away 2¾ inches and 55 lb when losing to James J. Jeffries in 1902. Record: W 28 (23 i.d.), D 1, L 7, ND 5.

Jeffries, James J. (USA), a powerfully built heavyweight, won the world title in his 13th professional bout, at the age of 24. A hard-swinging puncher who attacked with a pronounced crouch, he defended the championship on six occasions during a reign of six years, then retired undefeated. Lured back to the ring five years later in an effort to restore the title to the 'white race', he was heavily punished and beaten in 15 rounds by Jack Johnson. Record: W 20 (16 i.d.), D 2, L 1.

Johnson, Jack (USA), the first coloured heavyweight champion of the world, was a fine defensive boxer, and a destructive hitter, especially with the uppercut. He beat Tommy Burns for the title in Sydney, Australia, but once champion, Johnson made himself unpopular. He reigned as champion for seven years, until at 37 he was knocked out by Jess Willard in 26 rounds. Johnson afterwards declared he had been forced to 'lie down', and the outcome of the contest has been the subject of controversy ever since. Johnson continued to box until his 50th year, and was killed in a car crash in 1946, aged 68. Record: W 78 (44 i.d.), D 14, L 7, ND 14.

Louis, Joe (USA), on his record the greatest of all the heavyweight champions, was also the most popular. Master of the left jab, he was a fine hooker with both hands and speedily finished off a weakened opponent. Born in Alabama, he became famous as the 'Brown Bomber'. World heavyweight champion at 23, he defended his title in the next 12 years against 25 challenges, retiring undefeated. Owing millions of dollars in income tax, Louis returned to the ring at the age of 36, but failed to regain the title from his successor, Ezzard Charles. A k.o. defeat by Rocky Marciano, only the second in his career, ended his comeback attempt. Record: W 68 (54 i.d.), L 3.

Lynch, Benny (GB), Glasgow newsboy who became world flyweight champion, was a compact, versatile puncher with

Joe Louis, in March 1948, three months before he successfully defended his title for the last time. He made an abortive comeback in 1950.

good footwork and keen boxing brains. He won the world title and became British champion by knocking out Jackie Brown in two rounds in 1935. After a sensational title defence against Peter Kane, whom he knocked out in 13 rounds, weight-making difficulties caused a sudden decline, and he died of debilitation at the age of 33. Record: W 57 (i.d. 27), D 9, L 6.

A typical, relentless two-fisted attack from Rocky Marciano has Roland LaStarza wilting on the ropes. The referee stopped the fight in the 11th round. After four more successful title defences, Marciano retired undefeated.

with gloves was the meeting between John L. Sullivan and James J. Corbett at New Orleans in 1892.

The outstanding promoter of commercialized boxing was George (Tex) Rickard. When Jack Dempsey became champion by defeating Jess Willard in 1919, Rickard had the foresight to claim the sole services of the new title holder, and thus secured a monopoly of the heavyweight championship. He then staged the first million dollar gate ($1,626,580), in 1921, for the Dempsey–Carpentier fight. Now, with the use of broadcasting and worldwide television, the receipts from outstanding contests have reached astronomical figures.

The chief governing body is the World Boxing Council (WBC), set up in 1963. Outside the United States, most national organizations are affiliated to the WBC. But a curious situation has existed for some time in America, in which New York and some other states recognize the World Boxing Association, which sometimes sets up its own 'world champions'.

In professional boxing, the ring is between 14 and 20 ft square, with three ropes and padded corner-posts. Contestants are bare-chested, with shorts, socks, and boxing boots. Gloves must weigh at least 6 oz up to welterweights, and 8 oz for middleweights and above. The number of rounds ranges from 4 to 15 (title fights). A referee supervises the fight, with the aid of a timekeeper.

A boxer may win a contest on points (allotted by referee or judges), or if his opponent is counted out (unable to rise after 10 seconds) or disqualified, or cannot continue, or if the referee stops

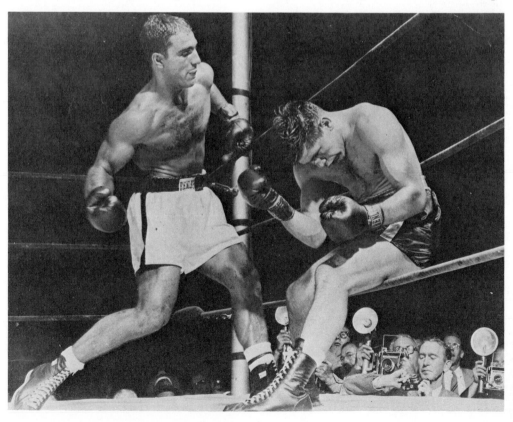

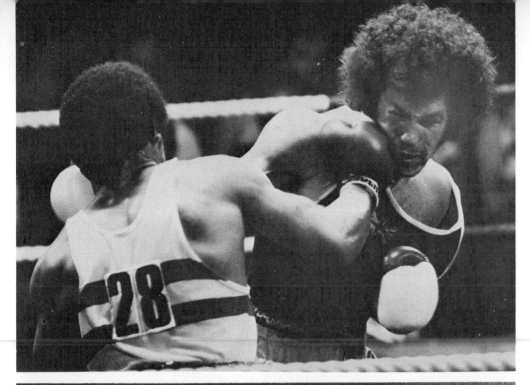

Top: *ABA champion Frankie Lucas was not selected by England for the 1974 Commonwealth Games, but won the gold for St Vincent, beating England's representative (28) in the*

semi-finals. Above: *George Foreman (right) on his way to winning the 1968 Olympic heavy-weight title. He turned professional, and five years later won the world title.*

the fight. The judging of fights, either by the referee in the ring or judges outside, has produced its share of controversy, particularly as neither the fighters nor the spectators are aware of the score until the end of the fight.

Amateur boxing at international level is controlled by the Amateur International Boxing Association (AIBA). Amateur rules provide for three 3-minute rounds in a 12 to 16 ft square ring. Three to five judges award points to a maximum of 20 for each boxer in each round, and the result is determined by majority verdict. Boxing was first staged in the Olympic Games in 1904, and there are now contests at 11 weights.

Fighting weights vary slightly

between amateur and professional boxing. The following table gives the weight divisions recognized by the two leading bodies:

Weight	WBC	AIBA	
	not over	not over	
	st–lb	kg	(st–lb)
Light-Fly	—	48	(7–07)
Fly	8–00	51	(8–00)
Bantam	8–06	54	(8–07)
Feather	9–00	57	(9–00)
Junior Light	9–04	—	
Light	9–09	60	(9–07)
Junior (or light) welter	10–00	63.5	(10–00)
Welter	10–07	67	(10–08)
Junior (or light) middle	11–00	71	(11–02)
Middle	11–06	75	(11–11)
Light-Heavy	12–07	81	(12–10)
Heavy		no limit	

Marciano, Rocky (USA), all-action aggressive fighter, known as the 'Brockton Blockbuster', punched his way in 1952 to the world heavyweight title in his 43rd professional fight, knocking out Jersey Joe Walcott in 13 rounds. After six successful title defences, only one of which went the scheduled distance, he retired undefeated and could never be coaxed back. He was killed in a plane crash the day before his 46th birthday, in 1969. Record: W 49 (43 i.d.).

Mills, Freddie (GB), former milk-round boy, battled his way to world fame in a style that made him known as 'Ferocious Fred'. He loved to wade in with two fists, but could use a straight left to perfection — as he did when winning the world crown at the second attempt from Gus Lesnevich in 1948. He lost it to Joey Maxim in 1950, and retired to become a television entertainer and Chinese restaurant owner. He was 46 when found shot dead in 1965. Record: W 73 (52 i.d.), D 6, L 17.

Moore, Archie (USA), from Benoit, Missouri, was one of the most knowledgeable of all the world light-heavyweight champions. Active for nearly 30 years, during which he got through 8 managers, he won the title at the age of 36 in 1952, and defended it against all-comers on 9 occasions. He never lost the championship. He twice fought for the world heavyweight crown, losing to Rocky Marciano in 9 rounds after flooring him in the 2nd, and to Floyd Patterson in 5 rounds when he was 40. Record: W 193 (140 i.d.), D 8, L 26, NC 1.

Patterson, Floyd (USA), Olympic middleweight champion in 1952 at 17, was the first man to regain the world heavyweight crown. The youngest heavyweight titleholder, he was 21 years 11 months when he beat Archie Moore for the vacant title in 1956. He weighed only 13 stone, but was fast on his feet and boxed in bursts of combination punching coming out of a 'peek-a-boo' defensive cover. He lost the title to Ingemar Johansson in 3 rounds after being floored 7 times, but regained it on a 5th-round k.o. a year later. Eventually defeated by the giant Sonny Liston in 2 min 6 sec of the 1st round, he made three abortive attempts to recapture the crown. Record: W 55 (40 i.d.), D 1, L 8.

Robinson, Sugar Ray (USA), pound for pound the greatest fighter of them all, was a clever boxer, a great ring general, and a precision puncher. As a boy in Detroit, he carried the training bag for his idol, Joe Louis. He reigned as welterweight king for four years and was unbeaten as champion when he won the middleweight crown in 1951. He established a record by winning this title on five separate occasions, once after retiring from the ring for more than two years. He finally lost to Paul Pender in 1960, but in an effort to recapture the crown for the sixth time was held to a draw by Gene Fullmer. At this time, Robinson was a day past his 41st birthday. He had attempted to win a third world title in 1952, and was well ahead against Joey Maxim, the light-heavyweight champion, but the fight took place in a heat-wave and he had to retire at the end of the 13th round with exhaustion. Record: W 175 (109 i.d.), D 6, L 19, ND 1, NC 1.

Sullivan, John L. (USA), known as 'the Boston Strong Boy', was the last of the bare-knuckle champions. A formidable

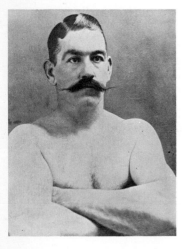

opponent, tremendously strong and a very heavy hitter, he became a national hero. He lost his title to James J. Corbett at New Orleans on 7 September 1892, being knocked out in the 21st round. Both wore 5 oz gloves, and this contest signified the end of the Prize Ring. Record: W 31 (16 i.d.), D 3, L 1, ND 40.

Memorable moments in sport

The Turpin-Robinson return

Dateline: New York Polo Grounds, 12 September 1951. Just 64 days after he had sensationally outpointed the hitherto invincible Sugar Ray Robinson in London, Randolph Turpin defended his title against the ex-champion. A record crowd for a middleweight contest of 61,370 fans paid $767,626 to see what turned out to be one of the most dramatic battles of all time.

For the first half of the contest, a more determined Robinson had the better of the points scoring, but his younger opponent began to assert himself and drove his weighty punches through the challenger's defence in disconcerting manner. By the ninth, the champion had made up a lot of leeway, and as the two fighters emerged from a clinch Robinson was seen to have sustained a nasty cut over his left eye.

During the interval, Robinson's handlers warned him that they could not seal his injury, and that he must do something decisive in the next round. At first, he drew back from the confidently advancing champion and let him toss his punches, while keeping just out of danger range. Then suddenly he stepped in, closed the gap, and banged over a

magnificent right to the chin. It landed flush, and the power behind the punch knocked Turpin clean off his feet. He hit the boards with his back, and lay, arms and legs widespread, like a gigantic starfish.

No one thought he would beat the count, but he did, only to be driven into the ropes under a hail of blows, until he stood, feet apart, his back to the hemp, his body bent over, his arms protecting his chin, elbows covering his ribs. Then began the most systematic barrage of punishing blows ever seen.

The champion was trapped. He did not or could not move away, but took the best the American could give and remained on his feet under the merciless bombardment. Only when he seemed on the point of pitching face down on the canvas did referee Ruby Goldstein intervene. Robinson, from an apparently hopeless position, had recaptured the world's middleweight title with one beautifully timed desperation punch. Had Turpin taken a second count, he might have won, for there were only 8 seconds remaining and Robinson would probably not have been allowed to continue for another round.

Turpin, eyes glazed, guard down, is wide open to Robinson's last desperate, savage assault.

Robinson took his opportunity with both hands, literally, and the referee had to call a halt.

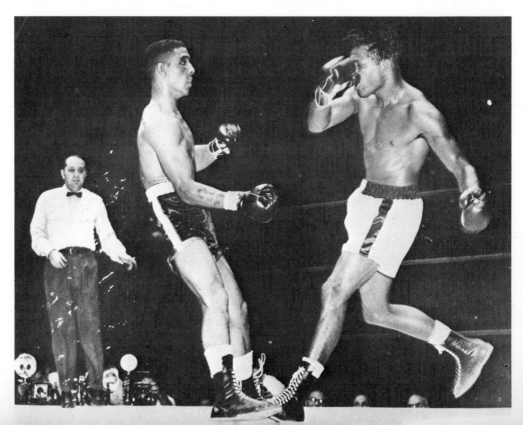

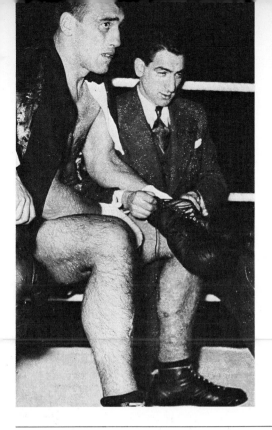

Far left: Primo Carnera, the 'Ambling Alp', was boxing's heaviest champion (1933–34).
Left: Henry Armstrong, the only boxer to hold three titles at once.

Tunney, Gene (USA), the supreme scientist among the heavyweight champions, taught himself to outbox men bigger, heavier, and more powerful-punching than himself. He put brains before brawn so successfully that in 1926 he was able to defeat Jack Dempsey, noted knock-out specialist, who had reigned as world champion for seven years. In a return match he repeated this feat, although having to survive a knock-down that became famous as 'The Long Count'. He retired, having lost only one contest, to the notorious Harry Greb, who took his newly won American light-heavyweight title in 1922. He later outpointed Greb twice for the title. Record: W 56 (41 i.d.), D 1, L 1, ND 17, NC 1.

Turpin, Randolph (GB), hard-hitting middleweight, was a star as an amateur and a box-office draw throughout a 12-year pro career. He created a sensation by outpointing the great Sugar Ray Robinson in London in 1951 to win the world crown, but kept it only 64 days. British middleweight champion for two years, he gave up his crown in 1952 to compete as a light-heavy, a title he won on three separate occasions. He won the European middleweight title in the record time of 48 seconds, beating Luc van Dam of Holland in 1951, but lost it in 1954 to Tiberio Mitri in 65 seconds. He retired as British champion in 1958 and was still boxing in 1962. He died by his own hand at the age of 37. Record: W 64 (43 i.d.), D 1, L 8.

Wilde, Jimmy (GB), the greatest of the world flyweight champions, was known as 'The Mighty Atom', 'The Tylorstown Terror', and 'The Ghost with a Hammer in his Hand'. A physical freak, he never weighed more than 7 st 10 lb, but could knock out men much heavier than himself with a single punch. A Welsh miner, he became British champion at 24. In 1916 he became universally recognized as world champion after defeating Young Zulu Kid of America in London. He retired undefeated as world champion, but at the age of 31 was persuaded to defend his title against Pancho Villa, 9 years his junior, and after he had been out of the ring for 2½ years; he lost in the 7th. Record: W 126 (77 i.d.), D 2, L 4, ND 8.

WORLD TITLES

	Longest held				Most defences	
Heavy	*Joe Louis (USA)	11 yr	8 m	1937–49	Joe Louis (USA)	25
Lt-Heavy	†Archie Moore (USA)	9 yr	1½ m	1952–62	Bob Foster (USA)	12
Middle	‡Tony Zale (USA)	7 yr		1940–47	Harry Greb (USA)	7
					§Sugar Ray Robinson (USA)	7
Welter	‡Freddie Cochrane (USA)	4 yr	6 m	1941–46	Henry Armstrong (USA)	20
Light	*Benny Leonard (USA)	7 yr	7½ m	1917–25	Joe Brown (USA)	12
Feather	Johnny Kilbane (USA)	11 yr	3½ m	1912–23	Abe Attell (USA)	12
Bantam	Al Brown (Panama)	5 yr	11½ m	1929–35	¶Manual Ortiz (USA)	22
Fly	Jimmy Wilde (GB)	6 yr	6 m	1916–23	Pascual Perez (Arg)	18

*Retired.   †Forfeited title.   ‡Frozen during war service.   §5 times champion.   ¶Twice champion.

WORLD TITLE FIGHTS

	Quickest knock-outs			Most knock-downs	
		sec			
Heavy	Tommy Burns bt Jem Roche	88	11	Max Baer v Primo Carnera	
Lt-Heavy	Gus Lesnevich bt Billy Fox	118	8	Archie Moore (4) v Yvon Durelle	
Middle	Al McCoy bt George Chip	45	11	Al McCoy (9) v Mike O'Dowd (2)	
Welter	Henry Armstrong bt Lew Feldman	132	9	Virgil Akins v Vince Martinez	
Light	Tony Canzoneri bt Al Singer	66	10	James Carter v Tommy Collins	
Feather	Freddie Miller bt Jose Girones	150	8	Terry McGovern v George Dixon	
Bantam	Terry McGovern bt Pedlar Palmer	75	14	Vic Toweel v Danny O'Sullivan	
Fly	Emile Pladner bt Frankie Genaro	58	10	Benny Lynch v Jackie Brown	

BOXING FACTS AND FIGURES

Most world titles held simultaneously   3   Henry Armstrong (USA)
Most world titles won   6   Sugar Ray Robinson (USA) 1 welter, 5 middle
Record attendance   120,757 Gene Tunney v Jack Dempsey, Sesquicentennial Stadium, Philadelphia, 23.9.26
Record gate (live) $2,658,660 Gene Tunney v Jack Dempsey, Soldiers' Field, Chicago, 22.9.27
Record individual purse
    from live gate $990,445 Gene Tunney (v Dempsey, 22.9.27)
    incl TV etc $2,500,000 each Joe Frazier & Muhammad Ali, Madison Square Gdn, 8.3.71
Undefeated throughout career   Rocky Marciano 49 wins (rtd as heavyweight champion)
World Heavyweight Champions
    Heaviest Primo Carnera (Italy) 19 st 1 lb   **Lightest** Bob Fitzsimmons (GB) 12 st 4 lb
    Tallest Jess Willard (USA) 6 ft 6¼ in.   **Shortest** Tommy Burns (Canada) 5 ft 7 in
    Oldest Jersey Joe Walcott (USA) 37½ years   **Youngest** Floyd Patterson (USA) 21 yr 11 m
Longest fight   110 rounds, 7 hr 19 min, Andy Bowen v Jack Burke (draw) New Orleans 6.4.1893
Shortest fight   10 sec Teddy Barker (GB) bt Bob Roberts (Nigeria) rsf, Maestag, Wales, 2.9.57; Al Carr (USA) bt Lew Massey (USA) rsf, New Haven, NJ, 3.4.36 (bout stopped after 7 sec but listed as 10-sec win)
Quickest k.o.   10½ sec Al Couture bt Ralph Walton, Lewiston, Maine, USA, 23.9.46
Most k.o.'s in major contests   141 Archie Moore (USA)
Most Olympic Gold Medals   3 Laszlo Papp (Hungary)

Canoeing

Fredriksson, Gert (Sweden), amassed an unprecedented collection of gold medals in Olympic and world championship canoeing, in kayak singles sprints.

His 5 Olympic golds in 1948–52–56 comprised all 3 at 1,000 m and 2 at 10,000 (he came 2nd in 1952). At Rome in 1960 he narrowly missed becoming the first competitor to win 4 consecutive golds in the same event when he came 3rd in the 1,000 m. He took consolation, however, in the pairs, which (in the absence of a 10,000 m singles) he won, gaining his 6th Olympic gold. His world championship record was equally impressive, with 4 K-1 and 3 K-1 relay golds in 4 championships.

Below: *Canoe surfing, a breathtaking sport in which the canoe does not always remain in its orthodox position in relation to the water.* Below right: *Canoe polo is played in swimming pools in special bath canoes.*

Canoeing embraces a variety of competitive and recreational activities involving canoes – the kayak and Canadian paddling canoes, surfing and sailing canoes, and canoes used in slalom racing and canoe polo (a form of free-for-all canoe-handball).

Canoes can be traced back thousands of years, from the 'dugout' made from the trunk of a tree to the bark-covered craft of the North American Indian and the skin-covered kayak of the Eskimo. Competitive canoeing goes back to the 1860s, when a Scot, John MacGregor, designed a 'Rob Roy' kayak canoe and wrote a book in 1865 describing a 1,000-mile journey through Europe in it. The Canoe Club was founded in 1866 and a canoe regatta held on the Thames in 1877. The modern Canadian canoe is an open craft derived from the North American Indian canoes. The kayak is a decked canoe, with a 'cockpit'.

Slalom racing began in Austria in the 1930s. The sport was introduced to the Olympics in 1936 (women's in 1948), and the 1972 Games included five 1,000 metre sprints (kayak singles, pairs, and fours; Canadian singles and pairs) and three slaloms (Canadian singles and pairs; kayak singles) for men, and kayak singles and pairs 500-metre sprints and kayak singles slalom for women. The hold that Eastern European countries have on the sport is reflected in the distribution of gold medals: Russia 6, East Germany 4, and Romania 1. The International Canoe Federation was formed in 1946, and the first world championships held in 1949.

Sprint racing is held on flat water, over 500, 1,000, or 10,000 metres. The boats used are built solely for speed, and the paddlers need enormously strong arms and chests to go flat out for the 3½-4 min needed for men to cover a 1,000 m course.

Slalom racing is a time-trial sport in which crews race down a swirling waterway, usually natural but sometimes specially built. The canoeists have to negotiate 'gates' (pairs of poles suspended over the water) as in skiing, and time penalties are incurred if gates are missed or poles are touched. *Down river racing* takes place over similar courses, but without gates.

The canoe used in *canoe sailing* is the fastest single-handed single-hulled craft, but with its 10 square metres of sail it is far removed from the normal concept of the canoe. British canoe sailors lead the world at this section of the sport, but it is not practised as widely as the paddling side of canoeing.

In *long-distance canoeing*, races vary in length from 10 miles upwards. Such races normally include many 'portages', in which canoes have to be carried round rapids or weirs. There are no world championships, but most leading canoeists compete in the Sella race in northern Spain. *Sea canoeing* and *canoe surfing* are also popular canoe sports.

Above: *A Canadian singles (C1) competitor negotiates a gate at speed. Although slalom racing (both Canadian and kayak) was staged at the first world canoeing championships, in 1949, it was 1972 before it made the Olympics.*

CANOEING 'MOSTS'

Olympic golds	6	G. Fredriksson (Swe)
World titles	7	G. Fredriksson (Swe)
– canoe sailing	3	Alan Emus (GB)

Cricket

Tony Greig, South African-born English all-rounder, emerged from the 1974 MCC tour of the West Indies with a stature to match his 6 ft 7 in physique. Going as vice-captain of England, he made an appalling start to the Test series with the infamous run-out 'incident' in the first Test. This could be put down, however, to his wonderful competitiveness, which was later to shape two Test hundreds and a series-saving 13–156 (8–86 and 5–70) in the last Test. Bowling his newly developed off-cutters rather than his fast-medium stuff, he turned an almost certain defeat into victory over a superior side.

The origins of cricket are like a murky pool. Peering into the depths one can occasionally spot oddments floating about, but its major secrets are obscured.

The archives provide a reference to some prototype of the game being played at the Free School at Guildford, now the city's Royal Grammar School, around the middle of the 16th century. But it seems likely that the first contest between bat and ball took place well before that date.

There is a reference, too, to a party of sailors from the Royal Navy playing the game near Aleppo while on shore leave in 1676, which supposes that cricket had taken a hold in England around that period. History also suggests that pockets of interest developed in the south of England at this time, particularly in Kent, Sussex, and Hampshire. Its rather sophisticated rules and the need for time in which to play it suggests that it was certainly a sport for the privileged at this time. And as with horse racing, betting on the result in large sums

Cricket

Cricket near White Conduit House, Islington, in 1789. The White Conduit Club became the MCC.

Boycott, Geoff (England and Yorks), became, through a patient study of the art, the most technically accomplished opening batsmen in the world. He played for England against Australia in 1964 with less than a season's first-class experience behind him, but has been a regular since, and has scored prolifically against all-comers. Appointed captain of Yorkshire in 1971, he averaged more than 100 per innings in his first season, the first Englishman to do so.

Bradman, Don (Australia, NSW, and S. Australia), arguably the greatest batsman of all time, averaged 99.94 in the 52 Tests he played between 1928 and 1948. His career average almost matched that (95.14), and he reached 100 first-class centuries in only 295 innings. A short man, he scored magnificently off the back foot with the cut and hook, but he possessed every shot. He captained Australia in five Test series, four of them against England. On his retirement, following the 1948 tour, he became one of the most active and knowledgeable administrators in Australian cricket. He was knighted in 1949.

Chandrasekhar, Bhagwat (India and Mysore), superbly overcoming the handicap of a bowling arm withered from a childhood attack of polio, became a medium-pace spin bowler of the highest calibre. Specializing in top-spinners, googlies, and occasional leg-breaks, he has been particularly severe (74 of his 110 Test wickets) against England. He took 35 wickets in the 1973 series between the two countries.

Compton, Denis (England and Middx), swashbuckling and unorthodox, was a popular and most successful run-getter in the years after World War II. He played 78 times in Test matches, scoring 5,807 runs. In 1947, he scored 3,816 runs, including 18 centuries, both records for a season that were still standing more than 25 years later. He also scored the fastest ever triple century, 300 in 181 minutes for MCC against NE Transvaal in 1948–49. His unorthodoxy spread into his bowling, but he took 622 first-class wickets with his chinamen and googlies. A fine footballer with Arsenal, he represented England in a 'Victory' international in 1946.

increased the speed at which cricket developed.

The first county match took place in 1719 at Lamb's Conduit Fields in May of that year, between Kent and London. But it was not until 1744 that the Laws of Cricket were revised into a universally accepted body of rules.

In the 18th century, the game took on a hold that it has never really lost. The universities at Oxford and Cambridge accepted cricket, its patrons abounded amongst the nobility, and the Prince of Wales, the Duke of Cumberland, and the Duke of Richmond followed the game closely.

The Hampshire village of Hambledon then played its part in promoting the game. Inspired by their captain Richard Nyren, the landlord of the Bat and Ball Inn on Broadhalfpenny Down, the village side played and beat the best teams from around the country. The first recorded hundred was 136 by John Small senior, for Hambledon against Surrey in 1775.

The Laws saw a further revision in 1774, with the weight of the ball being raised to $5\frac{3}{4}$ oz and the width of the bat limited to $4\frac{1}{4}$ in. But the main introduction was the leg-before-wicket ruling. Around this time, a third stump was added to the wicket and two bails introduced, and the wicket now bore a

Left: *Australia's run machine Don Bradman about to unleash another scoring stroke.*
Bottom left: *Denis Compton (right) acknowledges his 150 against South Africa at Lord's in 1947, his great season.* Below: *Indian spinner Bhagwat Chandrasekhar sees a chance go begging off Victoria's Bob Cowper in 1967.*

strong resemblance to the wicket as we know it today.

A Yorkshireman called Thomas Lord became that era's most influential figure. A player of considerable ability, he had performed with some success in London, when the Earl of Winchilsea and the Duke of Richmond suggested to him that he started a new ground. Accordingly, on the present site of Dorset Square, Lord's cricket ground took shape, and in 1787 it was opened when Middlesex played Essex.

The ground had a lease of only 21 years, and the centrality of that area marked it down for development. Lord thus found another site, near Regent's Park, where cricket was played for only three years until 1813. The following year he switched to a third site, in St John's Wood, the present headquarters of cricket.

The White Conduit Club had re-emerged as the Marylebone Cricket Club in 1787, and it was this body that made Lord's its home and became responsible for cricket's Laws, a role it retains to the present day.

As England moved sedately into the Victorian era, the appeal of cricket spread throughout the country, and as village teams grew in number so did county clubs. Though, betting apart, competition was only on a friendly basis, standards of play rose sufficiently for an All-England XI to tour the land playing the best of the local sides.

Eminent performers became national figures. Fuller Pilch, a son of Norfolk, became a hero of Kent, and later the massively bearded Dr W. G. Grace was renowned throughout England for his outstanding feats with bat and ball. The game could now support professionals, and soon the best players began to look outside England for greater challenges.

Cricket had proved popular in British colonies. In Australia, inter-state matches began in 1851 with a contest between Tasmania and Victoria. South Africa fostered the game at that time, though its popularity was not far-reaching until the last decade of the century. In the West Indies, the earliest recorded first-class match took place in 1864, whereas New Zealand saw Wellington play Auckland in 1860. With the encouragement of the British Army, cricket in India developed even earlier, and Parsees, Hindus, and Muslims all had clubs by the end of the century.

It was natural then that, in 1859, a group of England's most illustrious performers should set sail for a tour. Surprisingly the destination was Canada and the United States, where cricket was played only by small groups of English settlers. But it was a success, and two years later Australia sponsored the visit of an England side.

Constantine, Learie (West Indies and Trinidad), was among cricket's finest athletes. A tremendous hitter, a fast bowler of genuine pace, and an acrobat in the field, he played 18 Tests for West Indies between 1928 and 1939. For many years he was the most exciting figure in the Lancashire Leagues. On his retirement, he became a leading and most humane figure in West Indian government, knighted in 1962 and being made Lord Constantine in 1969.

Cowdrey, Colin (England and Kent), played more Tests (109 than any other player in the history of the game, scoring 7,459 runs, a total surpassed only by Gary Sobers. An elegant batsman of the highest pedigree and a sharp slip fieldsman, he enjoyed a Test career spanning 17 years, and even at the age of 40 he was still staking a claim for an England place. Captain of England in 27 Tests, he has often, rather unfairly, been a second-choice leader. He toured Australia five times, and there in 1962–63 he made his highest ever score, 307 against South Australia.

Evans, Godfrey (England and Kent), chirpy, extrovert wicket-keeper, claimed a record 219 victims in 91 Tests. Agile and totally tireless, he specialized in athletic catches at full stretch when standing back. An ebullient striker of the ball, he twice reached three figures in Tests. But he could graft when required, and the way he waited 95 minutes to score his first run in a match-saving innings in 1946–47 at Adelaide emphasized his wonderful value to the England side.

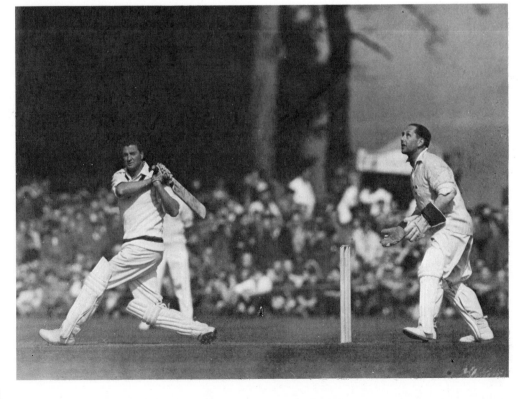

Keith Miller opens up against the Duke of Norfolk's XI during the first match of Australia's 1956 tour, and gives the fans a taste of things to come.

W. G. Grace was still playing first-class cricket in his 60s.

Grace, W. G. (England and Glos), was cricket's most influential figure in the late 19th century. With 54,904 runs and 2,876 wickets to his credit, his exploits are legendary. He played first-class cricket until his sixties, and at 46 made 1,000 in May. He played in 22 Tests, all against Australia, and led England 13 times. Tall, with a long black beard, Grace, a doctor of medicine, was a fearsome competitor. His 126 centuries stood as a record until Jack Hobbs passed it in 1925.

Grimmett, Clarrie (Australia, Wellington, Victoria, and S. Australia), did not play in a Test match until he was 32. A New Zealander who moved to Australia in 1918, he nevertheless became a prolific wicket-taker with his aggressive and extremely accurate leg-spin. Between 1924 and 1936, he played in 37 Tests and ended with a marvellous haul of 216 wickets. On his last tour, in South Africa, he took 44 wickets in 5 Tests, even though he was 43.

Hammond, Wally (England and Glos), would have been remembered for his magnificent close-fielding alone. That he was a batsman of classical style and an astute medium-pace bowler marks him as one of the game's outstanding performers. He made 50,551 runs, 7,249 of them in Tests, took 732 wickets, and held countless catches – his total of 78 in 1928 is still a record. He captained England in the last 20 of his 85 Tests, in which he made 22 centuries, including 336 not out against New Zealand in 1932–33.

Laker's Test

Dateline: Old Trafford, 31 July 1956. Jim Laker had done enough by the close of play on the second day of the Fourth Test against Australia to write himself into the record books. Four days later, he had ensured that he would never be written out of them, with a performance of off-spin bowling that fell right out of children's comics and fairy-tales.

But to begin at the beginning. Laker had been run out for 3 in an England total of 459. By tea on that second day, Laker had dismissed Colin McDonald and seen his spinner-in-crime Tony Lock account for Jim Burke. Australia were 62 for 2. Half an hour after tea, they were 84 all out. Laker had claimed all 8 wickets, 7 of them in 22 balls. He finished with 9 for 37, the best figures in a Test innings for 60 years.

Rain then, as ever at Manchester, came into the act as Australia, having followed on, struggled in their second innings, and play was protracted into the last day. Laker had already had Burke snapped up by Lock, and Neil Harvey caught by Colin Cowdrey, the great little left-hander registering a 'pair'. But the square-shouldered McDonald provided a stumbling block.

By now the pitch had dried out and was beginning to turn again. Laker, always a genuine spinner, made the ball lift and bite, and with athletic catchers of the calibre of Lock, Cowdrey, and Alan Oakman, the Australians had little margin for error. Lock, too, fiercely competitive, was wheeling away at the other end, turning the ball prodigiously the other way with his left-arm spin. Ian Craig helped McDonald for a time, but slowly Laker whittled the Australian

wickets away. Oakman took three catches. Miller, Mackay, and Archer all failed to score. And, remarkably, the wickets were all falling to Laker. McDonald finally perished in the leg trap. Lock got into the act, but only to catch Lindwall. And Laker had another 9 wickets to his name with still one to fall.

Lock, bursting for a wicket after more than 50 overs, could do no more than beat the bat. Then Maddocks, shuffling in front of an off-break, was leg before to give Laker figures of 51.2 overs, 23 maidens, 53 runs, 10 wickets, and match figures of 19 for 90 – a record for any first-class match, let alone a Test. For once it seemed totally irrelevant that England had retained the Ashes.

Incredulous team-mates David Sheppard (left) and Brian Statham (right) applaud Jim Laker as he walks off at the end of the Old Trafford Test in 1956 with a match analysis of 19-90.

The 1870s are perhaps the most significant decade in the growth of the game into its present form. In 1873, rules for the formation of a county championship were laid down, with Derbyshire, Gloucestershire, Kent, Lancashire, Middlesex, Nottinghamshire, Surrey, Sussex, and Yorkshire taking part. And on 15 March 1877 the first 'Test' took place, though the term was not officially adopted for another 15 years.

The venue was Melbourne, and officially the match was billed as an Australian XI versus an England XI. England's Alfred Shaw bowled the first ball; Charles Bannerman, who made 165 not out, scored the first run; and Australia won by 45 runs. England won a second game a fortnight later.

In 1880, Kennington Oval staged the first Test match in England, and there was a regular exchange of tours between the two countries, though on a private

Playing for the Rest of the World against England at Leeds in 1970, South Africa's Barry Richards takes a spectacular catch off fellow-countryman Mike Procter to dismiss Basil d'Oliveira. The 'Rest' won the series 4–1.

basis until the MCC officially organized England's trips from 1903–04.

South Africa played her first Test in 1889, and joined England and Australia as a founder member of the Imperial Cricket Conference in 1909. Almost 20 years elapsed before a fourth nation, the West Indies, joined the fold. England toured New Zealand in 1929–30, so adding a fifth member, and India enjoyed her first Test match in England in 1932, appropriately at Lord's. The new nation of Pakistan began her international career against India in 1952–53. For political reason, South Africa was banished from the Test scene in 1970.

The ICC, now the International Cricket Conference, holds a loose rein over Test cricket; the onus for arranging tours lies with the controlling body in each country. Australia, for example, did not choose to play against New Zealand, after an initial match in 1945–46, until 1973. India and Pakistan have not met since 1960–61. South Africa have only ever played England, Australia, and New Zealand.

Each Test-playing country has its own domestic competition as its breeding ground for international stars. In Australia, the Sheffield Shield, the interstate tournament, has continued since 1892. South African provinces play for the Currie Cup (1889), New Zealand's provinces for the Plunket Shield (1906), the territories of the West Indies for the Shell Shield (1965). India's Ranji Trophy (1934) is played for by states, regions, and even organizations such as the

services, while in Pakistan the major competition is the Quaid-e-Azam Trophy (1953). None of these tournaments is played with the intensity of fixtures that England's County Championship provides. England is the only country in which the game is played professionally seven days a week throughout the season.

In England, the popularity of first-class cricket throughout the first half of the 20th century began to wane in the face of other activities and social change. To combat falling attendances, which threatened the livelihood of cricket's paid performers, a new form of cricket was put on show for the public. Limited-over cricket, with a definite result being achieved in one day, had instant appeal. The Gillette Cup, first at 65 overs a side, now limited to 60, was first played for in 1963. Lord's had a full house for the first final, between Sussex and Worcester.

An even more instant mixture, the John Player League at 40 overs each on a Sunday afternoon, captured further interest. And England saw a third competition, the Benson and Hedges Cup (55 overs) start in 1972. Though purists decry the compromises in style and technique that one-day cricket demands, its popularity has undoubtedly safeguarded the future of the three-day game, which is the bread and butter of the professional sport.

Hanif Mohammed (Pakistan and Karachi) made the highest score in first-class cricket, 499 for Karachi v Bahawalpur in 1958–59. A patient, obdurate opening batsman, he also played the longest innings on record, 16 hours 10 minutes, when he compiled 337 against the West Indies in 1958. One of five cricketing brothers, four of whom played for their country, he made 55 appearances for Pakistan, and his complete, if sometimes boring, dedication served them admirably.

Harvey, Neil (Australia, Victoria, and NSW). Only Bradman made more runs and centuries for Australia than Neil Harvey. A nimble left-hander, and a brilliant fieldsman, especially in the covers, he was a fixture in the side for 17 years. He scored 6,149 runs and made 21 hundreds in his 79 Tests. Always a man for the big occasion, he did not always reproduce his Test match consistency in the Sheffield Shield. He was a particularly skilful player on bad wickets, where his quick footwork and wristy technique stood him in good stead.

Hassett, Lindsay (Australia and Victoria), was a prolific scorer at the highest level, though World War II severely impaired the early years of his career. He was 36 when he took over as captain from Bradman in 1949, but he established a reputation as a fine leader until he retired in 1953 at the end of the England tour. A technically correct batsman of small stature, he made 10 centuries in his 43 Tests, and became only the fifth Australian to reach 3,000 runs at that level.

Hobbs, Jack (England and Surrey), in statistical terms stands unchallenged as cricket's most prolific batsman. In a career that lasted 30 years, he scored 61,237 runs, compiled 197 centuries, 98 of them after his 40th birthday, and scored 1,000 runs or more in 26 seasons. An opener of textbook technique and effortless grace, he aggregated 5,410 runs in 61 Tests which spanned 23 years. In 1925, he made 16 hundreds, and a year later, though 43, he took 316 not out off the Middlesex attack.

Hutton, Len (England and Yorks), was the first modern professional appointed captain of England, and under his command the Ashes were reclaimed in 1953 and retained in Australia two years later. An opening batsman of the highest quality, Hutton had to curb his attacking instincts in the interests of his side. He patiently accumulated 364 against Australia at the Oval in 1938, a record that stood for 20 years. He played 79 times for England, 23 as captain, and he scored 6,971 Test runs, including 19 hundreds.

Kanhai, Rohan (West Indies, Guyana, Trinidad, W. Australia, and Warwicks), was a key batsman in the strong West Indies sides of the 1960s. A brilliant, extravagant stroke-maker, he matured into a controlled run-getter of the highest calibre, maturity that was reflected in his appointment as captain of West Indies in 1973. Though he lost his first series against Australia, he led his team to an outstanding victory over England later that year, and in 1973–74 took his run total to 6,227 in 79 Tests.

Laker, Jim (England, Surrey, and Essex), will always be remembered for his extraordinary return of 19 for 90 (9–37 and 10–53) against Australia at Old Trafford in 1956. This followed his 10–88 in an innings for Surrey against the tourists earlier in the season. An off-spinner who genuinely spun the ball, he finished that series with 46 wickets. In 46 Tests between 1947 and 1959 he took 193 wickets. A useful batsman lower down the order, he twice made hundreds for Surrey and was an integral part of the side that won the championship so regularly throughout the 1950s. He retired in 1959 after a disagreement with his county, and after returning briefly in the early 1960s, for Essex, he became a TV commentator.

Memorable moments in sport

The first tied Test

It's a tie! The West Indians are jubilant as Ian Meckiff fails to beat Joe Solomon's throw.

Dateline: Brisbane, 14 December 1960. Beaten by Victoria and New South Wales, both by an innings, West Indies went into the first Test of the 1960–61 series almost as no-hopers. As always they had plenty to offer on an individual level, with the Gargantuan talents of Gary Sobers, and players of the skills of Conrad Hunte, but collectively they had been slaughtered in England in 1957. Now they had a new leader in Frank Worrell, but to most Australians the home team were strong favourites.

At Brisbane, Worrell won the toss, Sobers effortlessly composed a century, and the visitors made 453. Burly Norman O'Neill launched his own counter-attack, hitting 181, and on the first innings Australia's lead was 52. After some fine bowling from Alan Davidson, the home side needed a comfortable 233 to win with plenty of time to get the runs.

For the first time, Worrell's ability to produce the best from his men began to show. Australia slumped to 92 for 6. But with Richie Benaud and Davidson showing all the composure of front-line batsmen, the crisis was avoided. With half an hour left, only 27 were needed as Wes Hall took the new ball.

Hall's marathon approach to the wicket ate into the time, but the stand advanced to 134, and only 7 runs were needed. Searching a quick single, however, Davidson was run out – a direct throw from Joe Solomon shattering the stumps. Wally Grout took a single off Sobers, so with the 8 balls of the last over to go, Australia still needed 6 to win.

Off the first ball, Grout scampered a leg-bye: 5 to win – 7 balls to go. Off Hall's next delivery, the admirable Benaud was caught at the wicket: 6 balls to go – 5 needed. Ian Meckiff could not score off the next, but from the following ball he and Grout scrambled a bye to the wicket-keeper! 4 to win off 4 deliveries. Grout then slogged the next ball back to Hall, who dropped a chance and gave away a single: 3 now needed off 3 balls.

The sixth ball of the over was cracked by Meckiff into the outfield. They galloped 2 and turned about for a third. But Hunte's arm was equal to the occasion and Grout was run out: 2 balls to go and the scores were level. Hall powered up to the wicket. The ball hit Kline's bat and shot off to square leg. Meckiff sprinted, but Solomon's throw crashed into the stumps again. Meckiff failed by inches to get home, and Australia were all out. Test cricket had seen its first tie.

In 1972, the trend pursued its logical course into one-day international matches, when England met Australia for the Prudential Trophy, a series that is continued between England and the visiting countries each year. Plans are taking shape for a World Cup, a massive jamboree of instant cricket between Test-playing nations, to be staged in England in 1975.

In this respect, the masculine game has been given an example from, of all quarters, women's cricket. A Women's World Cup, the brainchild of the England captain Rachel Heyhoe-Flint, was staged in England in 1973. England beat Australia in the final of a series which showed how skilfully the fairer sex can play cricket. Women's Tests have been played since 1934, and England, South Africa, Australia, and New Zealand have all participated.

The success of one-day cricket has encouraged commercial firms to put their funds into cricket, and those who have done so have invariably reaped reward, not only in England but also in the other cricket-playing countries. The success of this type of game may in the future mean that cricket will have a wider appeal in nations who have found the intricacies of the first-class game beyond them.

Left: *Rachel Heyhoe-Flint, England captain and a fine 'batsman' as well as a prime mover of women's cricket.* Below left: *England fast bowler John Snow beats New Zealand opener Glenn Turner at Headingly in 1973. Turner hit 1,000 runs before the end of May (the first to do so for 35 years) and in 1973–74 scored two 100s in a Test against Australia.* Below: *The great England openers Hobbs (left) and Sutcliffe.*

Larwood, Harold (England and Notts), remains one of cricket's most controversial bowlers. In Australia in 1932–33, his fast bowling at the leg stump was the centre of the 'bodyline' argument. Larwood took 33 wickets, and England, under Douglas Jardine, took the series. Not only was Larwood fast, but his wonderfully smooth action gave him a high standard of accuracy, and that made him the perfect man to carry out the 'leg theory' orders on the tour. After that trip he never played for England again, having captured 78 wickets in his 21 Test matches. Ironically, he later settled happily in Australia.

Lindwall, Ray (Australia, NSW, and Queensland), spearheaded Australia in 61 Tests after World War II, and with Keith Miller formed a redoubtable opening attack. With a smooth, lithe action, he was able to maintain his pace, and he could swing the ball both ways in the air with great control. He made his debut against New Zealand in 1945–46 and left the international scene 14 years later with 228 wickets to his name. A competent batsman who loved to play shots, he made two Test hundreds.

Lock, Tony (England, Surrey, Leics, and W. Australia), a tigerish slow left-arm bowler, was always particularly effective for Surrey and England when in tandem with Jim Laker. A vital cog in the Surrey machine that won seven successive championships in the 1950s, he twice took 200 wickets in a season. After problems with the validity of his action, he changed it completely in 1959, yet resumed where he left off and continued as an England regular until 1963. Recalled for two Tests in the West Indies in 1968, he made a heroic career-best 89 at Georgetown. In all he captured 174 wickets in 49 Tests. His superb catching, particularly in the leg-slip area, was responsible for many more scalps. After a spell with Leicestershire, he emigrated to Perth, where he played a large part in the emergence of Western Australia as a cricketing power, captaining them to only their second Sheffield Shield success.

One-day cricket brings gaiety to Lord's. Kent's triumphant side includes shoulder-high man-of-the-match Asif Iqbal (59, 4–43) and captain Mike Denness, Derek Underwood (left), Colin Cowdrey (3rd right), and Alan Knott (right).

McCabe, Stan (Australia and NSW), was a consistent run-getter for his country in the 1930s, and is best remembered for some great individual innings. He made 232 out of 300 in under 4 hours at Trent Bridge in 1938, and also fashioned a brave 187 not out in the face of 'bodyline' at Sydney in 1932–33 out of 278 added while he was there. He always responded willingly to a crisis, and his brave hooking of Larwood at his fastest was the one counter-attack Australia could muster. He scored 6 Test match hundreds and aggregated 2,748 runs in 39 Tests.

May, Peter (England and Surrey), was perhaps the most technically accomplished batsman in the world during the 1950s. A classic exponent of the drive, he scored his runs with the elegance and timing of a master. As England's captain and premier batsman, he was always under pressure, but he responded calmly and successfully to the responsibility. In 66 Tests, he was captain 41 times, and he compiled 4,537 runs, including 13 centuries. His greatest innings was almost certainly his 285 not out against West Indies in 1957, when in partnership with Colin Cowdrey he saved the Edgbaston Test. Ill-health forced a premature retirement in 1961.

Rules of cricket

Cricket is played by two teams of 11 players on a *pitch* 22 yards long. At each end of the pitch is a *wicket*, comprising three vertical *stumps* each 28 inches high, on top of which rest in grooves two *bails* $4\frac{3}{8}$ inches in length. The wicket must be 9 inches wide. At each wicket, the *bowling crease* is marked, a line 8 ft 8 in long, which runs through the point where the stumps are pitched. At the end of the bowling crease and at right-angles to it runs the *return crease*. Four feet in front of the bowling crease and running parallel to it is the *popping crease*.

To start the game, the two captains toss for the right to bat or field first. The batting side's stay at the wickets is called an *innings*; depending on the nature of the game, each side may have one or two innings. The batting side provides two batsmen at the wicket, and the innings continues until 10 players are dismissed or the captain *declares* the innings closed.

The batting side's aim is to score *runs*. A run is completed when both batsmen cross to opposite ends and make good their ground, by crossing the popping crease. When the ball is struck by the batsman's bat or gloves, any runs that accrue are accredited to his score. Runs also come from *extras* – *byes* when a run is taken though the ball has not touched any part of the batsmen; *leg-byes* when the ball is deflected, but not wilfully, off the person; *wides* when the bowler delivers a ball beyond the batsman's reach; and *no-balls* when the bowler infringes the bowling rules. The bats-

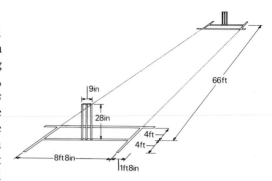

The popping crease, in front of the stumps, is also called the batting crease because a batsman, to be in his ground, must have part of his person or his bat (in hand) grounded behind it. The bowling crease, running through the line of the stumps, is so-called because until the late 1960s the bowler had to have one foot behind this crease at the moment of delivery. A return crease runs at right-angles to the bowling crease at each end of it.

man scores 4 runs when he strikes the ball over the ground's *boundary*, and 6 if it clears the boundary without bouncing. The bat must not exceed $4\frac{1}{4}$ inches in width, and cannot be more than 38 inches long.

The bowling side's aim is to dismiss batsmen and stop runs. Using a leather ball that must weigh $5\frac{1}{2}$–$5\frac{3}{4}$ oz, the bowler must bowl and not throw, and in delivering it some part of his front foot must be behind the popping crease while his back foot lands within the

England's Brian Statham bowls to a typical fast bowler's close field for left-hander Bill Lawry at the beginning of Australia's first innings at Brisbane in 1962 – three slips, a gully, and a point.

Right: *Fielding positions as for a right-handed batsman:*
Wicket-keeper 1
Leg slip 2
Backward short leg 3
Forward short leg 4
Silly mid-on 5
Silly mid-off 6
Gully 7
Third slip 8
Second slip 9
First slip 10
Square leg 11
Mid-wicket 12
Mid-on 13
Mid-off 14
Extra cover 15
Cover point 16
Point 17
Third man 18
Fine leg 19
Deep square leg 20
Deep mid-wicket 21
Long on 22
Long off 23
Deep extra cover 24

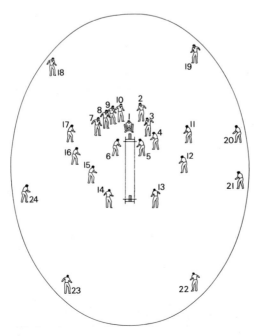

return crease. Six deliveries constitute an *over* (eight in Australia and New Zealand) and no player may bowl two successive overs; overs are bowled from alternate ends. Batsmen may be dismissed in the following ways: *bowled*, when the ball breaks the wicket; *caught*, when a fielder catches the ball off the bat or glove before it touches the ground; *leg before wicket* (lbw), when any part of the batsman's person under certain conditions prevents the ball hitting the wicket; *stumped*, when the wicket-keeper breaks the wicket with the ball, with the batsman out of his ground; *hit-wicket*, when the bat or any part of the person breaks the wicket; *hit the ball twice* (except to guard the wicket); *handled the ball*; *obstructing the field*; and *run out*, when either batsman's wicket is broken by the ball when he is going for a run and is out of his ground.

The fieldsmen are deployed at the captain's discretion for catches and to stop runs. Each side has a wicket-keeper, who wears pads and gloves and whose job it is to stop the ball as it passes the batsman.

The game is won in a two-innings match by the side who score more runs than the opposing side in their two completed innings; otherwise the result is a draw. In one-day limited-over cricket, the side that scores more runs irrespective of the completion of the innings is the winner.

The bowling action of West Indian speed merchant Charlie Griffith was the subject of much controversy in the 1960s. He was called for 'throwing' only twice in his career, yet there seemed little doubt from pictures that his faster ball was illegal.

Miller, Keith (Australia, Victoria, and NSW), was more than a cricketer, he was an entertainer. His natural talent was so boundless that he could, and would, bowl any type of delivery in the middle of a conventional spell of pace bowling. He could slaughter the best attack in the world should the mood take him. And he consistently brought off astonishing catches. In 55 Tests he scored 2,958 runs and captured 170 wickets. But such was his cavalier approach, that figures — impressive though they are — barely do his talent justice.

Oldfield, Bertie (Australia and NSW), captured 130 victims for Australia between 1920–21 and 1937, in 54 Tests. Few wicket-keepers have matched Oldfield's technique. He was deceptively unobtrusive, but his ability to read the direction of the ball meant that he rarely needed to fling himself about. He toured England four times, and 90 of his Test victims were Englishmen. He also proved a stubborn batsman on occasions, once scoring 65 not out during the 1924–25 series between the two countries.

Pollock, Graeme (S. Africa and E. Province), a tall and extremely powerful batsman, is cast in the mould of the great left-handers. With his brother Peter, he formed part of the core of the South African side in the years leading up to their expulsion from international cricket. He made two centuries in his first Test series, in Australia in 1963–64, and scored heavily in his 23 Tests, averaging 60.97. A wonderful upright striker of the ball, he thrashed the Australian attack for 274 at Durban in 1969–70. But, sadly, politics have kept him out of Test matches since that series.

South Africa's Graeme Pollock.

77

Cricket

Australia's Doug Walters is too busy ducking to notice Mike Procter's 'wrong-footed' action in a 1970 Johannesburg Test.

Procter, Mike (S. Africa, Natal, W. Province, Rhodesia, and Glos), is an all-rounder to rival the enormous standards set by Gary Sobers. As a front-line bowler, he achieves genuine pace with an unorthodox 'wrong-footed' action. With the bat, he is a totally equipped stroke-maker, and in 1970–71 scored 6 hundreds in successive first-class innings. He played in 7 Tests before S. Africa were banned from international cricket, and his fast bowling undermined Australia in 1969–70, a series in which he picked up 26 wickets at an average of 13.57.

Reid, John (N. Zealand, Wellington, and Otago), was arguably the greatest and certainly the most consistent cricketer produced by New Zealand. As a broad-shouldered forcing bat and fast-medium bowler, he played in 58 successive Tests, 34 as captain. An athletic fielder, he also kept wicket against England at the Oval in 1949. A prodigious striker of the ball, he hit a record 15 sixes during an innings of 296 in the Plunket Shield. In Test cricket he compiled 3,431 runs and took 85 wickets, and so often stood between his country and total disaster.

Rhodes, Wilfred (England and Yorks), took more wickets than any other player in history. In a career that spanned the last few years of the 19th century up to 1930, Rhodes, bowling slow-left-arm, claimed 4,187 victims. As a watchful batsman,

he worked his way up the order to open the innings for England with success. Twenty-one times he scored 1,000 runs in a season and 23 times he took 100 wickets; on 16 occasions he did the double, a record unlikely to be beaten. In 58 Tests between 1899 and 1930, he scored 2,325 runs and took 127 wickets, playing his last Tests at well over 50 years of age. When one considers that he scored 39,722 runs in first-class cricket, Rhodes could claim to be one of the greatest players the game is ever likely to witness.

Cricket terms

Backward defensive shot Played with the rear foot moved back and across the stumps. The bat comes down straight, and the ball is played down into the ground rather than hit with power.

Bouncer A short-pitched ball delivered with the aim of making the ball bounce up around the batsman's head. Also called a 'bumper', it is a legitimate weapon of the fast bowler provided it is not overused.

Bumper A bouncer.

Byes Runs that are taken when the batsman has not touched the ball with his bat or his person. They usually occur when the wicket-keeper fails to stop the ball.

Chinaman A weapon of an unorthodox slow-left-arm bowler, the ball being spun by the wrist as well as the fingers so that when it pitches it breaks in from the off to the leg to a right-handed batsman.

Drive An extension of the forward defensive shot; the batsman goes forward to a well pitched up ball and places his foot as near as possible to the pitch. He then goes through with his shot letting the bat swing through. Depending where the ball pitches, it may be driven straight (*straight drive*), through mid-off (*off-drive*), through mid-on (*on-drive*), or through the covers (*cover-drive*).

Force off the back foot Begun as for the backward defensive shot, but allowing the bat to swing through to strike the ball in the hope of runs. The top hand must still control the shot, or the ball will be struck into the air.

Forward defensive shot As the batsman picks up his bat, he moves his front foot forward so that it is placed as near as possible to the pitch of the ball. The shot is controlled by the top hand on the bat, which directs the ball into the ground. The batsman's weight is transferred to the front foot, but he must avoid toppling forward or he may be stumped if the wicket-keeper is standing up.

Full toss A delivery that reaches the batsman before it has bounced; a ball that should be scored off as it is easy to hit.

Good length Bowlers aim to bowl a good length. This varies somewhat according to the batsman, but the bowler tries to pitch the ball where the batsman cannot easily decide whether to play forward or back.

Googly A weapon for spin bowlers, aimed to deceive the batsman. A right-arm leg-spinner makes the ball spin to the off after pitching; his googly makes it spin the other way, but from the batsman's point of view the bowler's action seems the same. Instead of the ball being spun out of the side of the hand, the bowler cocks his wrist a little more and delivers it out of the back of the hand, so reversing the spin. For the left-hand spinner, the googly is the reverse of the *chinaman*, an attempt to delude the batsman who is expecting movement in from the off. Instead, the ball moves from leg to off out of the back of the hand once more.

Half-volley A delivery that reaches the batsman just as it bounces; a ball that batsmen should score runs from because it is easy to hit.

Hat-trick A bowler records a hat-trick when he takes three wickets with successive balls. It is still a hat-trick if those three deliveries are in different overs, but only if they are in the same match.

Hook shot The batsman's counter to the bouncer or short-pitched ball. He goes back and across the stumps, ideally so that his head has passed across and outside the line of the ball, and then swings his bat horizontally. Because the ball is bouncing upwards, it is easy to send the ball into the air, but the best hookers roll their wrists over on contact so that they direct the shot downwards behind square leg.

Inswinger A delivery that curves in the air from off to leg to a right-handed batsman. It is bowled by holding the seam vertically but slightly pointing to leg slip, with the shiny side of the ball on the left (see *Shining the ball*).

Late cut A shot played to a short-pitched ball outside the off stump. The batsman goes back and across, and guides the ball behind the wicket with a horizontal bat, taking care to roll the wrists to keep the ball clear of the slips' hands. If the shot takes the ball square with the wicket, it is called a *square cut*.

Leg-break A delivery bowled so that the ball pitches and spins from leg to off. The ball is usually gripped across the seam, and the movement of fingers anticlockwise that imparts the spin is accentuated by the use of the wrist.

Leg-cutter A fast leg-break, but the ball is cut rather than spun. The ball is usually held with the seam almost vertical and the first two fingers cut down the left-hand side of the ball. Usually used by medium-pace bowlers.

Leg-byes Extras when runs are scored by the ball deflecting off the batsman's body. They do not count if the deflection is, in the opinion of the umpire, deliberate or if the batsman attempts no stroke.

Leg-glance A shot played off either front or back foot, the ball being angled behind the wicket on the leg side off a vertical bat.

Long hop A very short-pitched delivery that is inviting to hit.

Maiden over An over during which no runs are scored by the batsmen.

No ball An illegal delivery, which may be called by either umpire. A bowler is no-balled for throwing, for putting his front foot completely over the popping crease, for bowling wide of the return crease, or for having more than two fielders behind the wicket on the leg side. One run is added to the score, unless there is a run (or more) from the bat, which stands. For each no ball the bowler must bowl an extra delivery. The batsman cannot be dismissed by a no ball, but he may be run out off it.

Off-break A ball that spins from the off to the leg on pitching. It is usually bowled by holding the fingers across the seam and imparting spin by moving the first and second fingers in a clockwise direction.

Off-cutter The reverse of the leg-cutter, with the first two fingers cutting down the right-hand side of the ball to move it from off to leg off the pitch.

Outswinger A delivery that curves in the air away from a right-handed batsman. The ball is held in the first two fingers, with the seam angled slightly towards the slips. The left-hand side of the ball should be the dull side (see *Shining the ball*).

Over the wicket A bowler is bowling over the wicket when he delivers the ball with the hand nearer the stumps.

Pull shot Played to a short-pitched ball with a horizontal bat. It is the only shot in which the batsman's weight starts on one foot and ends on the other. He goes back and across, but as he swings into the shot his weight

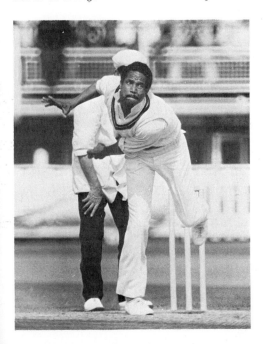

follows the path of the bat and ends up on the front foot. The ball is struck in front of the wicket on the leg side.

Round the wicket A bowler is bowling round the wicket when he delivers the ball with the hand away from the stumps.

Shining the ball Fast bowlers shine one half of the ball, because in theory the shiny half tends to travel through the air faster than the dull half, thus making the ball swing (see *Inswinger, Outswinger*).

Slow-left-arm The orthodox slow-left-arm bowler is the reverse of the right-arm off-spinner. He spins the ball from leg to off, a leg-break.

Square cut See *Late cut*.

Stance The position of the batsman as he waits to receive the ball. He should be side on, with his feet slightly apart and pointing out square on the offside. The stance should be well balanced so that the batsman is equipped to move forwards or backwards as each delivery demands.

Sweep A front-footed shot in which the bat is swung horizontally across the front foot, sending the ball behind the wicket on the leg side.

Top-spinner A weapon for a wrist spinner, with the ball, instead of being spun to break left or right, spun directly towards the batsman. When it bounces, the spin carries it straight forward, but makes it come through quickly so that it might go under an unwary defence.

Wide A delivery that is outside the batsman's reach. It adds one run to the score, and the bowler has to bowl an extra ball. A batsman may be stumped off a wide.

Yorker A delivery that is pitched right up into the batsman's block-hole, designed to go underneath the bat as it is brought down. Difficult to bowl, but very effective.

Gary Sobers, the complete all-rounder, not only the world's supreme batsman and two or three bowlers in one, but a brilliant close-in fielder. He equalled the world catching record for a Test match when he ensnared six England batsmen at Lord's in 1973.

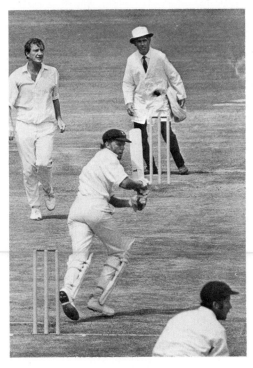

Barry Richards cuts Graham McKenzie for 4 of the 508 runs he scored in his only Test series.

Richards, Barry (S. Africa, Natal, S. Australia, and Hampshire). A perfectly equipped attacking opening batsman, Richards had his career tragically blighted by S. Africa's political problems. In his only Test series, against the Australians in 1969–70, he aggregated 508 runs, with two thrilling centuries. His talents have remained confined to county and provincial levels, where he has been prolific. He was the first batsman to reach 1,000 runs in a Currie Cup series, and in 1970–71 made 356 for S. Australia against W. Australia.

Sobers, Gary (West Indies, Barbados, S. Australia, and Notts), has scored more Test match runs than any other player. He also became the second player to score 2,000 runs and take 200 wickets in Test matches. A wonderfully elegant left-handed bat whose 365 not out against Pakistan beat Len Hutton's 20-year-old Test record by one, he captained West Indies from 1964–65 to 1973, when Rohan Kanhai took over. As a bowler, he is equally effective with left-arm fast-medium, particularly with the new ball, as with orthodox slow-left-arm. On occasions, too, he has taken wickets with googlies and chinamen. At short leg, he is a world-class catcher. His all-round feats are legend, but perhaps the most improbable came in August 1968, when he struck Malcolm Nash of Glamorgan for six sixes in one over. Despite injuries, he remained an extraordinarily great player 20 years after his Test debut against England in 1953–54. In 1973–74, against England, he took his aggregate of runs in 93 Tests to 8,032, his wickets to 235.

Statham, Brian (England and Lancs), bowled fast and with extreme accuracy for England in 70 Test matches between 1951 and 1965, capturing 252 wickets. His unstinting control of line and length almost certainly earned wickets for other bowlers, notably his famous partners Frank Tyson and Fred Trueman, because, tied down by Statham, batsmen took risks at the other end. His best Test haul came against South Africa in 1960, when he captured 27 wickets. A right-arm bowler, he batted left-handed with great gusto at the tail end, and was a brilliant outfield. He captained Lancashire between 1965 and 1967.

Cricket

Trueman, Fred (England and Yorks), arguably the greatest fast bowler of all time, took a world record 307 Test wickets. He burst to prominence in 1952 with 29 wickets in 4 Tests against India as a bowler of sheer pace, but as he matured he cultivated the perfect outswinger. Always a hostile opponent, he was known as 'Fiery Fred', and his Test career had moments of controversy at its outset. But from 1957 he became a regular and played 67 times for England. An outrageous smiter with the bat, he once scored 104 for Yorkshire. His charismatic personality and ready wit have been the instigators of many of cricket's funniest stories.

Trumper, Victor (Australia and NSW), batted majestically and prolifically for Australia in 48 Test matches between 1899 and 1912 for 3,163 runs. His neatness of movement and quickness of foot made him an outstanding stroke-maker, particularly through the covers. He reached three figures 8 times in Tests,

including 214 not out against South Africa in 1910–11 and a memorable 185 not out against England in the 1903–04 series. In England in 1899 he compiled 300 not out against Sussex at the age of 21.

Verity, Hedley (England and Yorks), will always be remembered for the day at Lord's in 1934 when he took 14 Australian wickets to finish with the figures of 15 for 104. As a slow left-arm spinner who was the master of his craft, he became the perfect successor to Wilfred Rhodes for county and country. Like Rhodes, he opened an England innings, though his batting was not quite as eminent as his predecessor's. In 40 Tests in the 1930s, he captured 144 wickets, and might have continued his run had he not tragically been killed in the war. His career best figures were a remarkable 10–10 against Notts in 1932.

CRICKET 'MOSTS', 'BESTS', AND 'LEASTS'

Individual records – batting

Innings – Tests	365*	G. S. Sobers, W. Indies (v Pakistan, Kingston, 1957–58)
– any match	499	Hanif Mohammed, Karachi (v Bahawalpur, Karachi, 1958–59)
Runs – Tests	8,032	G. S. Sobers, W. Indies (93 Tests to 1973–74)
– career	61,237	J. B. Hobbs (England & Surrey)
– Test series	974	D. G. Bradman, Australia (v England, 1930)
– season	3,816	D. C. S. Compton (England & Middx), 1947
Average – Tests	99.94	D. G. Bradman, Australia
– career	95.14	D. G. Bradman, Australia
– Test series	210.50	D. G. Bradman, Australia (v S. Africa, 1931–32)
Hundreds – Tests	29	D. G. Bradman, Australia
– career	197	J. B. Hobbs (England & Surrey)
– Test series	5	C. L. Walcott, W. Indies (v Australia, 1954–55)
– season	18	D. C. S. Compton (England & Middx), 1947
Consec. 100's – Tests	5	E. D. Weekes, W. Indies (v England 1, India 4, 1947–48–49)
– any matches	6	C. B. Fry (1901); D. G. Bradman (1938–39); M. J. Procter (1970–71)
Two 100s in match	7	W. R. Hammond (England & Glos)
Fastest 50 – Tests	28 min	J. T. Brown, England (v Australia, Melbourne, 1894–95)
– any match	8 min	C. Inman, Leics (v Notts, Trent Bridge, 1965)
Fastest 100 – Tests	70 min	J. M. Gregory, Australia (v S. Africa, 1921–22)
– any match	35 min	P. G. H. Fender, Surrey (v Northants, Northampton, 1920)
Fastest 200	120 min	G. L. Jessop, Glos (v Sussex, Hove, 1903)
Fastest 300	181 min	D. C. S. Compton, MCC (v NE Transvaal, Benoni, 1948–49)
Runs in over	36	G. S. Sobers, Notts (v Glamorgan, Swansea, 1968)
Sixes in innings	15	J. R. Reid, Wellington (v N. Districts, Wellington, 1962–63)
Longest innings	970 min	Hanif Mohammed, Pakistan (337 v W. Indies, Bridgetown, 1957–58)
1,000 runs in season	28	W. G. Grace; F. E. Woolley

Individual records – bowling

Analysis – Test Innings	10–53	J. C. Laker, England (v Australia, Old Trafford, 1956)
– any innings	10–10	H. Verity, Yorks (v Notts, Leeds, 1932)
– any match	19–90	J. C. Laker, England (v Australia, Old Trafford, 1956)
Wickets – Tests	307	F. S. Trueman (England)
– career	4,187	W. Rhodes (England & Yorks)
– Test series	49	S. F. Barnes, England (v S. Africa, 1913–14)
– season	304	A. P. Freeman (England & Kent) 1928
Average – Tests	10.75	G. A. Lohmann (England)
200 wickets in season	8	A. P. Freeman (England & Kent) 1928–35
100 wickets in season	23	W. Rhodes (England & Yorks)
5 wkts in Test innings	24	S. F. Barnes (England)
10 wickets in innings	3	A. P. Freeman (Kent) 1929, 30, 31
4 consecutive wickets	2	R. J. Crisp (Western Province)
Hat-tricks	7	D. V. P. Wright (Kent)
Balls bowled – innings	588	S. Ramadhin, W. Indies (v England, Birmingham, 1957)
– match	917	C. S. Nayudu, Holkar (v Bombay, Bombay, 1944–45)
– Test match	774	S. Ramadhin, W. Indies (v England, Birmingham, 1957)
– without runs	137	H. J. Tayfield, S. Africa (v England, Durban, 1956–57)

Wicket-keeping records

Dismissals		
– Test innings	6 (all c)	A. T. W. Grout, Australia (v S. Africa, Jo'burg, 1957–58)
	6 (all c)	D. Lindsay, S. Africa (v Australia, Jo'burg, 1966–67)
	6 (all c)	J. T. Murray, England (v India, Lord's, 1967)
– any innings	8 (all c)	A. T. W. Grout, Queensland (v W. Australia, Brisbane, 1959–60)
– Test match	9 (8c 1s)	G. R. A. Langley, Australia (v England, Lord's, 1956)
– any match	12 (8c 4s)	E. Pooley, Surrey (v Sussex, Oval, 1868)
	12 (9c 3s)	D. Tallon, Queensland (v NSW, Sydney, 1938–39)
	12 (9c 3s)	H. B. Taber, NSW (v S. Australia, Adelaide, 1968–69)
– Test series	26 (23c 3s)	J. H. B. Waite, S. Africa (v NZ, 1961–62)
– season	127 (79c 48s)	L. E. G. Ames (England & Kent) 1929
– Tests	219 (173c 46s)	T. G. Evans (England)
– career	1,493	H. Strudwick (England & Surrey)
Catches – career	1,235	H. Strudwick (England & Surrey)
Stumpings – career	415	L. E. G. Ames (England & Kent)

Fielding records

Catches – Test innings	5	V. Y. Richardson, Australia (v S. Africa, Durban, 1935–36)
– any innings	7	M. J. Stewart, Surrey (v Northants, Northampton, 1957)
	7	A. S. Brown, Glos (v Notts, Trent Bridge, 1966)
– Test match	6	various (10 players up to 1973)
– any match	10	W. R. Hammond (v Surrey, Cheltenham, 1928)
– Test series	15	J. M. Gregory, Australia (v England, 1920–21)
– season	78	W. R. Hammond (England & Glos) 1928
– Tests	117	M. C. Cowdrey (England)
– career	1,011	F. E. Woolley (England & Kent)

All-round cricket records
8,032 runs, 235 wkts,110 catches in Tests	G. S. Sobers (W. Indies)
58,969 runs, 2,068 wkts, 1,011 catches in career	F. E. Woolley (England & Kent)
54,904 runs, 2,876 wkts, 877 catches in career	W. G. Grace (England & Glos)
39,722 runs, 4,187 wkts in career	W. Rhodes (England & Yorks)
2,385 runs, 208 wkts in season	G. H. Hirst (England & Yorks) 1906
3,003 runs, 101 wkts in season	J. H. Parks (England & Sussex) 1937
2,000 runs and 100 wickets in season	4 times F. E. Woolley (England & Kent)
1,000 runs and 200 wickets in season	3 times M. W. Tate (England & Sussex)
1,000 runs and 100 wickets in season	16 times W. Rhodes (England & Yorks)
100 runs & 10 wickets in match	16 times W. G. Grace (England & Glos)
475 runs, 34 wkts in Test series	G. Giffen, Australia (v England, 1894–95)
545 runs, 29 wkts in Test series	G. A. Faulkner, S. Africa (v England, 1909–10)
442 runs, 23 wkts in Test series	J. M. Gregory, Australia (v England, 1920–21)
439 runs, 20 wkts in Test series	K. R. Miller, Australia (v W. Indies, 1954–55)
424 runs, 23 wkts in Test series	G. S. Sobers, W. Indies (v India, 1961–62)
430 runs, 24 wkts in Test series	A. W. Greig, England (v W. Indies, 1973–74)

Record partnerships
Tests			
– 1st	413	V. Mankad (231) & P. Roy (173), India (v NZ, Madras, 1955–56)
– 2nd	451	W. H. Ponsford (266) & D. G. Bradman (244), Australia (v England, Oval, 1934)
– 3rd	370	W. J. Edrich (189) & D. C. S. Compton (208), England (v S. Africa, Lord's, 1947)
– 4th	411	P. B. H. May (285*) & M. C. Cowdrey (154), England (v W. Indies, Birm., 1957)
– 5th	405	S. G. Barnes (234) & D. G. Bradman (234), Australia (v England, Sydney, 1946–47)
– 6th	346	J. H. Fingleton (136) & D. G. Bradman (270), Australia (v England, Melbourne, 1936–37)
– 7th	347	D. Atkinson (219) & C. C. Depeiza (122), W. Indies (v Australia, Bridgetown, 1954–55)
– 8th	246	L. E. G. Ames (137) & G. O. Allen (122), England (v NZ, Lord's, 1931)
– 9th	190	Asif Iqbal (146) & Intikhab Alam (51), Pakistan (v England, Oval, 1967)
– 10th	151	B. F. Hastings (110) & R. O. Collinge (68*), NZ (v Pakistan, Auckland, 1972–73)

All matches			
– 1st	555	P. Holmes (224*) & H. Sutcliffe (313), Yorks (v Essex, Leyton, 1932)
– 2nd	455	B. B. Nimbalkar (443*) & K. V. Bhandarkar (205), Maharashtra (v Kathiawar, Poona, 1948–49)
– 3rd	445	P. E. Whitelaw (195) & W. N. Carson (290), Auckland (v Otago, Dunedin, 1936–37)
– 4th	577	V. S. Hazare (288) & Gul Mahomed (319), Baroda (v Holkar, Baroda, 1946–47)
– 5th	405	*as for Tests*
– 6th	487*	G. A. Headley (344*) & C. C. Passailaigue (261*), Jamaica (v Lord Tennyson's XI, Kingston, 1931–32)
– 7th	347	*as for Tests*
– 8th	433	A. Sims (184*) & V. T. Trumper (293), Australian XI (v Canterbury, Christchurch, 1913–14)
– 9th	283	J. Chapman (165) & A. R. Warren (123), Derbys (v Warwicks, Blackwell, 1910)
– 10th	307	A. F. Kippax (260*) & J. E. H. Hooker (62), NSW (v Victoria, Melbourne, 1928–29)

Team records
Highest total – Tests	903 (for 7)	England (v Australia, Oval, 1938)
– any match	1,107 all out	Victoria (v NSW, Melbourne, 1926–27)
Highest aggregate		
– Tests	1,981 (for 35)	South Africa & England (Durban, 1938–39)
– any match	2,376 (for 38)	Maharashtra & Bombay (Poona, 1948–49)
Lowest total – Tests	26	New Zealand (v England, Auckland, 1954–55)
– any match	12	Northants (v Glos, Gloucester, 1907)
Biggest win – Tests	Inngs & 579	England beat Australia (Oval, 1938)
– any match	Inngs & 851	Railways beat Dera Ismail Khan (Lahore, 1964–65)
Hundreds in innings – Tests	5	Australia, 758–8 dec (v W. Indies, Kingston, 1954–55)
– any match	6	Holkar, 912–8 dec (v Mysore, Indore, 1945–46)

Miscellaneous 'mosts'
Test appearances	109	M. C. Cowdrey (England)
– consecutive	85	G. S. Sobers (West Indies) 1955–72
– as captain	41	P. B. H. May (England) 1955–61
Test attendance	350,534	Melbourne 1936–37, Australia v England
– single day	90,800	Melbourne 1960–61, Australia v W. Indies (2nd day 5th Test)
Test receipts	£87,305	Lord's 1973, England v West Indies
Series attendance	933,513	Australia v England, 1936–37
Series receipts	£261,283	England v Australia, 1972
Highest benefit	£21,109	D. J. Brown (Warwicks) 1973
Youngest Test player	15 yr 124 days	Mushtaq Mohammed (Pakistan) 1958–59
Oldest Test player	52 yr 165 days	W. Rhodes (England) 1929–30
Oldest Test debutant	49 yr 119 days	J. Southerton (England) 1876–77

* Not out.

Left: *Frank Woolley (England).*
Right: *Frank Worrell (W. Indies).*

Weekes, Everton (W. Indies and Barbados), was one of the 'three W's' who played such leading parts in the emergence of West Indian cricket after World War II. A punishing batsman, he scored five successive hundreds in New Zealand in 1955–56, and a record five successive Test centuries against England and India in 1947–48 and 1948–49. He aggregated 4,455 runs in his 48 Tests at the impressive average of 58.61, and most of those he scored quickly.

Woolley, Frank (England and Kent), a tall, upright left-handed batsman, scored 58,969 runs in first-class cricket, an aggregate bettered only by Jack Hobbs. In a career that stretched from 1906 to 1938, he made 64 Test match appearances (scoring 3,283 runs), the last at the age of 47 in 1934, when he was also forced to help out behind the stumps. He made 1,000 runs in a season 28 times, equalling the record of W. G. Grace, and he accumulated 145 hundreds. As a slow left-arm bowler, he took 2,068 first-class wickets, but it is the effortless power of his shots in front of the wicket for which he is best remembered.

Worrell, Frank (W. Indies, Barbados, and Jamaica), one of West Indies' 'three W's' (Clyde Walcott and Everton Weekes were the others), was more than just an outstanding player. His captaincy moulded a set of talented individuals into a winning team, and he led his country to an overwhelming victory in England in the 1963 series. As a prolific run-getter (3,860 in Tests), he always batted with grace. His 9 Test hundreds included a classic 261 at Trent Bridge in 1950. His left-arm medium pace, though often used as a change weapon, nearly always achieved some sort of breakthrough, and he took 69 Test wickets. He led West Indies 15 times in his 51 Tests, always with shrewdness, with success, and with charm. He was knighted in 1964, and his death from leukemia in 1967 was a tragic loss to cricket.

Croquet

John Solomon at Hurlingham in 1962. He took up croquet while still a teenager and with his older partner, Patrick Cotter, had much to do with ridding the sport of its 'vicarage tea party' image.

Solomon, John (England), played for England in the MacRobertson Shield in 1951, before he was 20. By the early 1970s he had won more than 30 major championships, including a record 10 Opens and 10 Open Doubles (with Patrick Cotter).

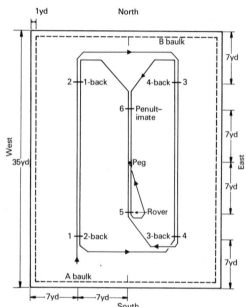

When croquet went to the United States, it became Americanized as roque (above).

shots with each turn. If a player strikes his ball – yellow, say – onto another, say, black, he is said to have made a *roquet*, and earns two immediate bonus shots. He picks up yellow (his ball), places it in contact with black (the roqueted ball), and strikes yellow, moving both balls. This is called a *croquet shot*, and requires a different technique. A *continuation shot* is then played. A player may make a roquet on his other ball (or his partner's in doubles), but he may not make a roquet twice on the same ball in one turn. But if he runs a hoop (in correct sequence), he earns an extra turn. The first player or side to run the 12 hoops and then 'peg out' with both balls wins.

A game of consummate skill, croquet is played on a lawn with mallets, balls, and hoops. The game developed in England in the 1860s, an earlier version called *palle malle* having died out. The name croquet derives from a French word, *croc* (crook or hook).

The first Open Croquet Championship was played at Evesham in 1867, and the All England Croquet Club was founded at Wimbledon. Croquet became popular in America, but was distorted both physically and semantically to *roque*, played on clay courts with rubber-faced mallets and composition balls. Roque, indeed, was an exhibition sport at the 1904 Olympics, in St Louis. Croquet continued to survive in England, where the first international series was played against Australia in 1925, for the MacRobertson Shield. Held every few years, the competition has become a tri-angular tournament, New Zealand having joined in 1963.

Croquet is played on a 35×28 yd lawn by two or four players. There are four balls ($3\frac{5}{8}$-in diameter, weighing 1 lb), blue and black being played by one player or side, red and yellow by the other. The mallets weigh about 3 lb and are about 3 ft long, with a head 9 inches long and 3 inches wide. The object of the game is to 'run' one's own balls through all the hoops twice, in order, and then onto the central peg. The order is 1 to 6, then 1-back to 4-back, penultimate, rover, and peg. The hoops are only $3\frac{3}{4}$ inches wide.

Players take alternate turns, but either ball may be struck at any turn, i.e. black or blue, red or yellow. A turn, basically, is one stroke, the *qualifying shot*. But extra turns may be earned, and extra

All kinds of shots are possible in croquet, follow-through shots, stop shots, even jump shots. And the game has a language of its own, with such terms as 'triple peel' and 'rush'. In tournament play, a system of handicaps called 'bisques' is employed. Women compete on equal terms with men in croquet.

A simpler game, called *golf croquet* (as opposed to association croquet), may also be played. Players take alternate shots, there are no roquets or croquet shots, and the first player to run each hoop wins a point. Another game, *indoor croquet*, was devised in the early 1960s. A kind of mini-croquet, it is played on a carpet with snooker balls.

CROQUET 'MOSTS'

MacRobertson Shield	5	England
Open Championship	10	John Solomon
Women's Championship	15	Dorothy Steel

Cycling sports

Cycling is practised world-wide, both as a pastime and as a competitive sport. The sport has diversified since its beginnings at the end of the last century, so that there is now road racing in a variety of forms; track racing; time trials; and cyclo-cross, a winter activity on cross-country courses equivalent to motor-cycle scrambling.

The sport is governed internationally by the Union Cycliste Internationale (UCI), which has separate sections under the overall umbrella governing the professional and amateur programmes. It is an Olympic sport, and world championships are held every year. Amateurs and professionals can compete together in cyclo-cross, and also in a limited way in other branches, in approved charity meetings, and, since 1972, if the amateurs are national teams nominated by their country's federation.

Outside the UCI competitions, there is also bicycle polo and cycle speedway, both mainly in Britain. The first is self-explanatory; cycle speedway developed after World War II, when youngsters converted bomb-sites in imitation of motorcycle speedway. It is now well established, with permanent stadiums and a national governing body controlling area leagues.

Women's racing on an international basis is a more recent development. Largely through its following in Britain, and to a lesser extent in France, Belgium, and the Netherlands, pressure on the UCI at last succeeded in the establishment of women's world championships in 1958. But women are still excluded from Olympic cycling.

Road racing

Road racing takes several forms. Single-day races can be from place to place or on a circuit covered several times. Stage races are held over a number of days, with each day's competition a self-contained race from place to place with an individual winner and subsidiary prizes. Each rider's time is added from day to day, and the overall winner is the rider with the lowest total time. Bonuses in time are given to top placings each day, and there are subsidiary classifications, such as 'points' and 'mountains', to give

Cycle sport takes many forms, from the grim, all-out effort of the 1,000 metres track time trial to the apparent serenity of a road race through sheep country. Left: Pierre Trentin (France) winning the 1968 Olympic time trial. Below: A stage in an Australian road race.

Anquetil, Jacques (France), time triallist extraordinary, had the ability that many lack – to suffer alone. He was also a great stage-race rider, winning the Tour de France a record 5 times between 1957 and 1964, besides many classics. His record of 9 wins in the classic Continental time trial, the Grand Prix des Nations, must surely stand for all time.

Burton, Beryl (GB), still the supreme British woman cyclist in her mid-30s, in time trials and track pursuiting, multi-champion at all distances since 1958, set all women's competition records. Faster than all but the top men, in 1967 she established a record of 277.25 miles over 12 hr, beating the then men's record, set in the same year, by nearly a mile! World champion on road and track 6 times, she was still fast enough to take the pursuit bronze medal in 1973, when her daughter joined her in the road team.

Coppi, Fausto (Italy), was a legend in his own time, worshipped almost as a god in Italy. It is still debated whether the present-day Eddy Merckx has become the world's greatest ever, or whether Coppi, who died in 1960 of a tropical disease, still reigns supreme in memory. He won the Tour de France only twice (1949 and 1952) and the world road championship once (1953), but he was twice world pursuit champion on the track. The secret of his success was simple – attack, attack, attack.

Harris, Reg (GB), Britain's greatest ever cyclist and possibly the finest track sprinter the world has seen, won 5 world sprint titles, including one as an amateur. He was already Britain's fastest amateur when World War II interrupted his career, but despite serious war wounds he came back to win the world amateur sprint title in 1947. He turned pro after a disappointing 1948 Olympics to win the world professional sprint championship in 1949–50–51–54 as well as many Grand Prix events. He also set many world records, some of which stood for more than 20 years.

Merckx, Eddy (Belgium), has most of his opponents beaten before the start, such is the reputation he has built in his multitude of classic victories, including 4 Tour de France wins in succession (1969–72). Like Anquetil before him, he can recruit top men to his team, men who will work for him; but he has killed any suggestions of being 'nursed' by the manner of his solo victories, when his team support crumbled. A superb climber, he has a finishing sprint too, and above all he can sense the psychological moment to launch his attacks and demoralize the opposition. He was amateur world champion in 1964 and professional in 1967 and 1971, and in 1972 he set a 1-hr world track record.

Belgium's Eddy Merckx.

A motor-paced event in the 1970 world cycling championships at Leicester.

all types of riders equal opportunities. Riders who specialize in sprint finishes, for instance, will concentrate their efforts on the overall points prize, earning points for good placings each day. Good climbers will make their target the overall mountains prize, the route including designated climbs on which points are given.

The most famous stage race is the Tour de France, now spread over three weeks and first run in 1903. It is a professional event sponsored by a variety of commercial concerns who give their name to the various classifications. The competitors ride for trade teams carrying the name of a cycle manufacturer and the 'extra-sportive' sponsor who provides the bulk of the cash to pay them their contract fees plus bonuses for successes. These are firms outside the cycle industry – food firms, refrigerator makers, and so on.

Next to the Tour de France in importance in the professional field are the Italian (the Giro) and the Spanish (the Vuelta) stage races, followed by a number of shorter events in other countries.

Stage races are also run for amateurs, the top one being the Peace Race, which

Dutchman Peter Post (right), 'king of the sixes', hands over to his Belgian partner Patrick Sercu. Possessing abundant strength and stamina and remarkable control, Post became not only the greatest six-day cyclist ever, but a splendid entertainer. By the early 1970s he had well over 60 major victories to his credit, as well as wins in the 1960s in major Derny-paced events and classic road races.

travels through Poland, East Germany, and Czechoslovakia. In Britain there is the Milk Race, originally the professional Tour of Britain and now amateur and sponsored by the Milk Marketing Board.

There are a number of Continental classic one-day races for professionals, the oldest being Bordeaux-Paris, first run as an amateur even in 1891 and won by G. P. Mills of Great Britain. It is now held in two sections, with the riders receiving pace over the second half from Derny machines (motorized pedal cycles).

Track racing

Championship track racing includes sprint, pursuit, kilometre time trial, and motor-paced. Other events seen are handicap races, point-to-point, devil-take-the-hindmost, and Madison.

Sprints for both single bicycles and tandems are timed over the last 200 metres, the earlier part of the 1,000 and 2,000 m being occupied by jockeying for position. A rider usually endeavours to force his opponent to take the lead so that he can get the advantage of pace and the 'edge' in deciding when to attack.

In *pursuiting*, two riders start on opposite sides of the track and chase each other over the distance (3,000 m women, 4,000 m amateur, 5,000 m professional). A rider caught is the loser; otherwise time decides. Team pursuits between teams of four are similar, but the time is taken on the third man to finish.

In the *kilometre time trial*, each rider is

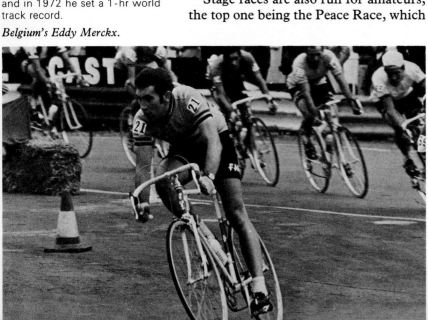

Eric de Vlaeminck (Belgium) dominated the cyclo-cross world professional championships from 1968 to 1973 with six straight wins. A winter sport, held on rugged cross-country courses over total distances of 14 or 15 miles, cyclo-cross is to cycling what moto cross is to motorcycling, except that when the going gets too difficult the cyclists just pick up their machines and carry them.

despatched individually and the fastest time wins. *Motor-paced* riders are paced by specially designed motorcycles, the essential aspect being complete rapport between pacer and rider.

Madison racing is between teams of two riders, one of whom must be racing at any given time while the other takes a breather circling the top of the track. They can change places as they wish, but it must be done by contact, usually the rider 'coming out' giving his partner a push. Hand-slings, practised by professionals, are forbidden for amateurs. The winners are the team finishing a lap or more ahead of the rest. During the race points are awarded for first over the line on specified laps, and these decide the order of finish where teams finish equal on laps covered.

Six-day racing

When cycling was a paramount sport at the turn of the century, endurance track races, often 24 hours, were common. These developed into the 'Six' first seen in New York at Madison Square Garden, hence the term 'Madison' (see *Track Racing*) or 'Americaine' on the Continent.

These races were simply a contest between teams of two (occasionally three) in which one of the team had to be on the track at any time during the six days. In the early hours and at intervals in the day, this would mean one rider of each team dawdling round the track while his partner retired to the trackside cabin to eat and rest.

The object being to lap the rest and gain as many laps lead as possible, frequent 'chases' develop, either at specified times or if a 'prime' of cash is offered from the audience for the first team to gain a lap.

This is still basically the system, but in post-war years it has been found that crowds want more action and variety. And so, on a pattern started by the revived London Six in 1967, the events are now virtually six days of racing, with subsidiary sprints interspersed with the Madison chases and a close-down in the early hours.

Time trials

Time-trialling is a branch of the sport most prevalent in Britain, where it developed at the start of the century when open road racing became the subject of too much police attention.

It was decided to take the sport 'underground' with time trials, in which riders are despatched over a specified out-and-home course at one-minute intervals and the winner is the one with the fastest time. This remained the only official branch of the sport on the open roads in Britain until after World War II.

Time trial championships in Britain are held over various distances from 10 miles for schoolboys to 100 miles and over 12 hours for men and women, and 24 hours for men.

Time trial stages are also included in multistage races, and there are classic time trials on the Continent. Team time trials, for teams of four, gained Olympic recognition in 1960 and world championships in 1962.

Mockridge, Russell (Australia), intelligent and endowed with a remarkable physique, won the Olympic 1,000 m time trial and 2,000 m tandem at Helsinki in 1952, staying on in Europe to shock the cycling world with a victory over all the top professional sprinters in the 1953 open Grand Prix de Paris. Turning professional, he proved his remarkable versatility by switching from sprinting to road-racing, and competing and finishing in the 1955 Tour de France. He returned to Australia to set a long-standing record of 5 hr 47 min 5 sec in the classic Warrnambool-Melbourne race in 1956 and win both the *Sun* and the *Mercury* tours. In 1958 his national titles included the 1,000 m sprint as well as the 125-mile championship. That same year he was killed in a collision with a bus while competing in the Tour of Gippsland.

Porter, Hugh (GB), has followed in the tradition of the great British pursuiters to make his mark in the history of the sport as the first man ever to win the professional world title 4 times (1968–70–72–73). As an amateur, he appeared on the

international scene in 1963, when he won the bronze medal in the world amateur pursuit championship, followed by the Commonwealth title in 1966. He married swimming champion Anita Lonsbrough.

Above left: *One technique in bicycle polo that cannot be practised in polo, rearing up the bicycle to stop the ball.* Left: *Cycle speedway, a sport that grew up on the bomb-sites of post-war Britain.*

Simpson, Tom (GB), was Britain's greatest-ever road-racing cyclist. After a promising amateur career, including a silver-medal ride as a member of the British team in the 1956 Olympic team pursuit, he went to Brittany and joined the cash ranks, taking 4th place in his first-ever world professional road championship in 1959. His victory in the 1961 Tour of Flanders was the first British classic win since 1896. He went on to victories in Bordeaux-Paris (1963) and Milan-San Remo (1964), and in 1965 became the first ever British world professional road champion. Simpson's best Tour de France placing was 6th in the 1962 race, during which he became the first Briton to hold the race leader's yellow jersey. Setting his heart on victory in the 1967 Tour, he collapsed with heat-exhaustion while climbing the Mont Ventoux and died a few hours afterwards, aged 29.

WORLD CYCLING RECORDS (open-air tracks)

	Professional			Amateur	
Standing start					
1 km	1 m 8.6 s	R. Harris (GB) 1952	1 m 4.5 s	N. Fredborg (Den) 1973	
5 km	5 m 51.6 s	O. Ritter (Den) 1968	6 m 0.3 s	J. Lund (Den) 1972	
10 km	11 m 53.2 s	E. Merckx (Bel) 1972	12 m 21.3s	J. Lund (Den) 1972	
20 km	24 m 6.8 s	E. Merckx (Bel) 1972	25 m 0.5 s	M. Frey (Den) 1969	
Hour	49.431 km	E. Merckx (Bel) 1972	47.553 km	M. Rodriguez (Col) 1970	
100 km	2 h 14 m 2.5 s	O. Ritter (Den) 1971	2 h 18 m 43.6 s	J. Lund (Den) 1971	
Flying start					
200 m	10.8s	A. Maspes (It) 1960	10.61 s	O. Phakadze (USSR) 1967	
500 m	28.8 s	M. Morettini (It) 1955	27.85 s	P. Trentin (Fr) 1967	
1 km	1 m 2.4 s	P. Sercu (Bel) 1973	1 m 1.14 s	L. Borghetti (It) 1967	

WOMEN'S RECORDS

	Standing start	
1 km	1 m 15.1 s	I. Kiritschenko (USSR) 1966
3 km	4 m 1.7 s	R. Obdovskaya (USSR) 1969
5 km	7 m 0.1 s	M. Cressari (It) 1972
10 km	14 m 19.9 s	M. Cressari (It) 1972
20 km	28 m 51.4 s	M. Cressari (It) 1972
Hour	41.471 km	M. Cressari (It) 1972
100 km	2 h 44 m 54.8 s	R. Mykkanen (Fin) 1971
Flying start		
200 m	12.3 s	L. Rasuwajewa (USSR) 1955
500 m	32.8 s	L. Rasuwajewa (USSR) 1955
1 km	1 m 12.9 s	G. Browina (USSR) 1955

CYCLING 'MOSTS'

World titles			
— amateur	7*	L. Meredith (GB)	
— professional	7†	J. Scherens (Bel)	
	7†	A. Maspes (It)	
— women	7‡	B. Burton (GB)	
	7§	Y. Reynders (Bel)	
— cyclo-cross	7	E. de Vlaeminck (Bel)	
Olympic titles	4¶	M. Hurley (USA)	
Tours de France	5	J. Anquetil (Fr)	
	5	E. Merckx (Bel)	

*100 km paced. †Sprint. ‡5 pursuits,
2 road. §3 pursuits, 4 road. ¶1904.

Darts

The highspot of the darts year in Britain, the News of the World championships, boisterously supported by thousands of partisan fans and seen by a TV audience of millions. An event for individual competitors, it has not been won more than twice by any one player.

This most English of games, darts probably owes its origins to the close-quarter fighting of medieval archers, in which arrows were thrown rather than shot. Britain now has some 5 million regular players.

The National Darts Association of Great Britain (NDAGB), formed in 1924, unified the rules and introduced the standard 18-inch board numbered in sectors 1–20. The organizing role was taken over by the *News of the World* in 1947, and since 1948 that newspaper has held annual championships. These are virtually world championships, and are now open to overseas competitors.

Darts (11–41 gm) are made of wood, brass, or tungsten with paper, feather, or plastic flights. Dartboard materials include cork, wood, and bristle (sisal tufts), and they are wired with high-tensile galvanized wire. The bull ($\frac{1}{2}$-in diam.), sited in the centre of the board, exactly 5 ft 8 in from the floor, counts 50; the outer bull ($1\frac{1}{4}$-in diam.) 25. A dart in the treble (inner) ring is worth a treble score, and one in the outer ring double. The darts are thrown by players in turn in sets of three from behind a line $7\frac{1}{2}$ or 8 ft from the wall on which the board is hung. The NDAGB use $7\frac{1}{2}$ ft, the *News of the World* and most overseas organizations, 8 ft. Until the distance is standardized efforts to set up a World Darts Council are bound to be hampered.

The championship darts game is '501 down', but the ordinary man is content with '301 down'. The game starts with both or all players needing to score 301 points, starting and finishing with a throw in the double ring. With the first double, scores are subtracted until it is possible to finish exactly on another double. (A bull counts as double 25.) There are also many favourite local games.

Diving

Dibiasi, Klaus (Italy), Europe's most consistent male diver from both boards, gained a surprise highboard silver in the 1964 Olympics, won the gold medal in 1968 by 10 points, retained his title in 1972, and won the inaugural world title in 1973. He was also 2nd in the 1968 springboard, 4th in 1972, and 2nd in 1973. Tall for a diver and blond for an Italian, Dibiasi was in fact born in Austria and trained by his father in Bolzano. In European championships he won the highboard in 1966 and was second in both events in 1970. Dibiasi's Olympic victories were the first by a non-American-trained male diver since 1924.

Krämer, Ingrid (E. Germany), was the dominant figure in world women's diving in the early 1960s. A slim girl with the beauty of the china from her native Dresden, she won both Olympic titles at Rome in 1960 and performed a similar double in the 1962 European championships. At the 1964 Olympics, by now Mrs Engel, she retained her springboard title and was runner-up in the highboard. But at Mexico City in 1968, divorced and remarried as Mrs Gulbin, she could only come 5th in the springboard and did not compete in the highboard.

Ingrid Krämer caught in perfect mid-air pose during the 1960 Olympic highboard event in Rome.

Of all the pastimes involving water, diving is surely the most enjoyed by its casual participants, and – in well run programmes – by spectators and competitors too. Taken to its gymnastic extreme, diving is more than simply plunging into water: it assumes a competitive form in which gracefulness, fitness, and strength are combined.

Competitive diving is a refined form of an energetic pastime; for hundreds of years people in suitable spots dived from cliffs. But for the origins of diving from special stages or boards, we have only

Diving is a graceful and spectacular sport, and American divers have always been to the fore. Top left: Edwin Young, bronze medallist in the 1968 Olympic high diving event.
Top right: Lesley Bush in action at Tokyo, where she won the 1964 high-diving title.
Above: The youngest ever individual Olympic gold medallist at any sport, Marjorie Gestring, winning the 1936 springboard title at Berlin.

to go to the 19th century. It was in Scotland, in 1889, that the first national diving championship was held. Other countries soon followed suit, and the first Olympic events took place in 1904

McCormick, Pat (USA), amassed the most honours by any diver in history. She won the Pan American highboard in 1951 and both springboard and highboard titles at the 1952 Olympics. In 1955 she won both Pan American titles, and in 1956 she repeated her 1952 triumphs in the Olympic Games – the first time such a diving double-double has been achieved. Even more remarkable was that Mrs McCormick's Melbourne successes came only five months after she had given birth to a son. Domestically, she won more than 70 US national titles – another record.

American star Joel O'Connell in the highboard event of a GB v USA match at Crystal Palace in 1967.

High diving, an exotic sport practised by a few dare-devil professionals who perform spectacular dives from 100 ft and more, sometimes into only a few feet of water. Points are given for performance as well as height. Three divers set a world record in Florida in 1974 by diving 133 ft into a 15-ft deep pool.

(springboard) and 1908 (highboard). And because of the common facilities often used, diving and swimming share the same governing bodies – internationally FINA.

Since the early days much has changed, though the two basic events – highboard and springboard – remain. Divers have constantly sought new dives involving more somersaults and twists, and the sport's legislators have had to change their rules accordingly. Not the least change has been that from the rather muscular form of diving of the early 1900s to the more graceful balletic style practised today.

Springboard divers use a sprung board 3 metres from the surface of the water, and some events are held on a 1-metre board. But because of the projection the diver gets from the 3-metre board, the range of dives possible from this height is hardly fewer than that possible from the highboard. Sometimes called a platform or tower, this board is 10 metres high, though less experienced competitors sometimes use alternative boards placed at 5 or 7½ metres. In the early Olympics this event was known as 'fancy high diving' as opposed to the 'plain high diving' event included from 1912 to 1924.

The Olympic Games and world championships (first held in 1973) are the most important diving meetings. In the first Olympics, Sweden and Germany shared the honours, and in 1924 Richmond Eve won Australia's first and only gold medal, in the men's plain diving. But by Eve's time it was apparent that the United States had taken the lead, and American divers won all four events contested at each Olympics from 1928 to 1952. History's most successful diver, Pat McCormick, won both women's titles in 1952 and 1956, but the American stranglehold on women's events was broken by Germany's Ingrid Krämer who won both events in 1960. Three men have won and retained the highboard title since World War II: Sammy Lee (1948 and 1952), Bob Webster (1960 and 1964), and Klaus Dibiasi (1968 and 1972).

Kinds of dives

There are no fewer than six ways to begin a dive. A *standing* dive begins with the diver at the end of the board facing the direction of his dive, and in a *running*

dive he will approach the end of the board running, to get more lift, especially in springboard. A *backward* dive is one in which the diver dives backwards from a standing position, whereas in a *reverse* dive, which begins with the diver on the end of the board facing forwards, he rotates backwards, lifting his feet and dropping his head behind him to enter the water head first. *Inward* dives begin like backward dives but the diver dives in towards the board, not away from it. These five methods are common to both boards, but only from the highboard will a diver begin with the *armstand*, or handstand, on the end of the board, in which any projection has to come from the arms.

A number of movements are possible in the air. *Somersaults* can be done in one of three positions – the *tuck*, with the knees drawn up towards the chest, the *pike*, with the legs straight and the body bent towards the knees, or *straight*, with no bending of the body. *Twists* are movements of the body round its longitudinal axis. Any movements done in the air have to begin and end while the diver is in the air, and finish before he enters the water.

Scoring

Because of the combinations of movements the diver can choose from, each dive is allotted a *tariff*, or degree of difficulty, and better divers choose dives with high tariffs.

Each dive is judged by five or seven judges who award marks out of 10. The highest and lowest marks are discarded and the aggregate (or average) of the remainder is multiplied by the tariff: the product is the score for that dive. This makes scoring complicated, and computers are sometimes used in major competitions. The number of dives (compulsory and optional) varies depending on the competition.

Involved though the scoring method is, it does ensure that the judges have only to judge the dive they see; it blunts the effect of biased judges; and it allows better divers to score according to their ability.

DIVING 'MOSTS'

Olympic Games and World Championships
Gold medals – men   3 Klaus Dibiasi (Italy)
        – women 4 Pat McCormick
                     (USA)

Born in Australia in the 1920s, speedway soon found a home in Britain . . . and Scandinavia and the countries of Eastern Europe.

The spoils of victory: Jackie Stewart (**above**) allows himself a flicker of a smile after winning the 1970 'Race of Champions', yet another triumph in the career of the three-times world champion racing driver who retired in 1973.

Left: John Cooper tears round Brands Hatch on his 348 cc Yamsel. **Below:** The names of two former motorcycle champions, Mike Hailwood (driver) and John Surtees (car), are barely discernible among the welter of advertising at Silverstone.

Women's lib or not, the girls give sport a fresh dimension of grace and beauty: East Germany's Kirstine Gerschau (**above**) on the beam.

Chris Evert (**above**) of the United States and Evonne Goolagong (**right**) of Australia look like gracing the world's tennis courts for many years to come, their precocious talents and cool elegance adding up to a charisma that pulls in the crowds.

Above: *An excited crowd follow the fortunes of Tony Jacklin at Royal Lytham in the 1969 British Open. He won, the first Briton to do so for 18 years.*

Below: *Eddy Merckx of Belgium dominated road racing in the early 1970s. In 1972 he emulated Jacques Anquetil's feat of four consecutive Tour de France wins.*

Equestrian sports

The International Equestrian Federation was formed in 1921 to bring order to a fairly chaotic situation of horse sport. They are now responsible for the international running of show jumping, horse trials, dressage, and, a fairly recent addition to the international agenda, driving. Prince Philip, the Duke of Edinburgh, became president of the FEI (Fédération Equestre Internationale) in 1964.

Of all the equestrian sports, show jumping is the newest, being virtually a 20th-century sport. The first authentically recorded competitions, for 'high' and 'wide' leaping, were held at the Royal Dublin Society's show in 1865, and there were competitions in France and Russia at about the same time.

It was a most haphazard business in those days, but at the Olympic Games in Paris in 1900, three jumping competitions were held. And the following year in Turin, German and Swiss Army officers were invited to test their skill against their Italian counterparts. Count Clarence von Rosen of Sweden suggested to the International Olympic Congress of 1906 that equestrian sports should be included fully in the Olympic programme, and this finally came about when the Games were held in Stockholm in 1912. The three events were, in essence, those that are held at Olympic Games now: dressage, a three-day event, and show jumping.

Show jumping

The competitions that carry the most prestige are the team events known as Nations Cups. These are staged at official internationals, and in Europe

Broome, David (GB), won the 1970 world show jumping championship on Beethoven. A rider for the big occasion, he has won the European championship on the three times he has contested it, in 1961 with Sunsalve, and 1967 and 1969 on

Mister Softee. He won Olympic bronze medals in 1960 on Sunsalve and 1968 on Mister Softee. And he became the fourth man to win the King George V Gold Cup three times, when he triumphed in 1972 on Sportsman.

d'Inzeo, Raimondo (Italy), the younger of two show jumping brothers, won an Olympic team and individual silver medal in 1956 on Merano, a team bronze and individual gold in 1960 with Posillipo, and another team bronze with the same horse in 1964. He won the world championship in 1956 with Merano and retained it in 1960 with Gowran Girl, one of only two men to have won the title twice.

One trophy that eluded him, the King George V Gold Cup, was won three times by his brother **Piero**, who also won the European championship in 1959; and in 1960, on his famous horse The Rock, he won an Olympic silver behind Raimondo.

d'Oriola, Pierre Jonquères (France), is the only man to have won two individual gold medals for show jumping, on Ali Baba in 1952 and Lutteur in 1964, when his team also won the silver. A volatile rider from the Pyrenees, often at odds with his federation, he was the first civilian to ride in their team, in 1946. He won the world championship in Buenos Aires in 1966 with the mare Pomone.

Mary Gordon-Watson takes Cornishman V round clear in the show-jumping stage of the three-day event in the 1972 Olympics to help Britain to the team title and herself to fourth place. The same combination won the 1969 European and 1970 world titles.

Mancinelli, Graziano (Italy), made history when, having been generally regarded as ineligible because he rode for a firm of horse-dealers as a boy, he was admitted to the Olympic Games at the last minute in 1964. Eight years later in Munich he crowned his career by winning the individual show jumping gold with Ambassador. A rider more efficient than elegant, he won the European championship in 1963 with Rockette.

Meade, Richard (GB), became in 1972 Britain's first ever winner of an individual Olympic gold in an equestrian competition when he headed the line-up for the three-day event with Laurieston. The team also won the gold, as they had in Mexico four years earlier when Meade rode Cornishman V. He rode in his first Olympics in 1964, when eighth on Barberry, and was individually second with Barberry in the 1966 world championship. Riding The Poacher, he was in the team that won the world title in 1970, and came second again in the individual, behind team-mate Mary Gordon-Watson.

Ann Moore, on Psalm, the combination that won a silver medal at Munich in the 1972 Olympics.

Moore, Ann (GB), won the European junior show jumping championship on Psalm in 1968, made her senior debut two years later, and won the European ladies title in 1971 — the first rider ever to win both a junior and a senior championship. She retained the title in 1973 in Vienna. In the 1972 Olympics she rode Psalm to take the individual silver, being beaten by Graziano Mancinelli in the jump-off.

Memorable moments in sport

Foxhunter

Dateline: Olympic Stadium, Helsinki, 3 August 1952. Four years earlier in London, Britain had given notice to the world that their days as nonentities among the show jumping nations were over. Then they won a bronze, but now were hopeful of going one, or even two, better. The horses had been flown out, to keep them fresh, and at 8 o'clock on the final morning the competition started.

Duggie Stewart, the least experienced of the British trio, went first on Aherlow, for a reasonable 12 faults, then Wilf White and his great horse Nizefela hit only the final gate. Britain were in with a chance, for last to go were Harry Llewellyn and Foxhunter, a combination that had dominated European competition for years.

But Llewellyn, fearful of overworking his partner, had not given him enough work and their round was disastrous. Refusing to settle, Foxhunter hit the double of parallels, and came into the wall on the wrong stride. For a dreadful moment he nearly stopped, but hurled himself over almost from a standstill, knocking a brick out and landing with his rider sprawling round the underside of his neck. Slowly but surely, Llewellyn

hauled himself back into the saddle, but collected three faults for circling while he did so, and then hit the next.

At halfway, Britain, with $32\frac{3}{4}$ faults, had slumped to sixth place, nearly 10 faults behind the United States, the leaders.

In the heat of the afternoon, before a 70,000 crowd, the battle was resumed. Stewart got the team off to a great start with just 4 faults, and although Chile had overtaken the United States, Britain had pulled up to third. Then Wilf White with Nizefela, calmly, majestically, with his characteristic 'kick-back', sailing over fence after fence, lost a stirrup iron as they came to the last, but were over it clear, when it was seen that one of the two water judges had raised a flag — 4 faults. Chile were still going strong, finishing with $45\frac{3}{4}$ faults.

In came Llewellyn and Foxhunter again. They could afford just one mistake, but not a repetition of the morning. But even that one fence was not needed, as they showed their true form with never a suspicion of a mistake, for Britain's first show jumping gold . . . and for Foxhunter, immortality.

Col. Harry Llewellyn, captain of the British equestrian team, takes Foxhunter through for an unforgettable clear round to clinch the Olympic team gold medal at Helsinki.

Graham Fletcher takes Talk of the North down the spectacular 10 ft 6 in Derby Bank at Hickstead. Horses jump a small fence on top before slithering down the bank.

round; those with one round followed by one or two jump-offs, of which the last is on time; and those in which time is not involved, such as the *puissance*, in which the fences are reduced in number to a minimum of two but get progressively bigger.

Within these generalities, there is considerable scope for variation, including relays for two or three riders, or for one rider with two horses, and, possibly the most popular sort of jumping competition of all, the *derby*. The prototype of this was first run at Hamburg in 1920, and the British Jumping Derby, which is staged at Hickstead, Sussex, was inaugurated in 1961.

The first official FEI show jumping championship was for juniors, in 1952; the men's world championship started in 1953, men's and women's European championships in 1957, and the women's world championship in 1965.

The world championships are now run every four years, alternating biannually with the Olympics, and the European championships every two years, slotting in between the Games and world events. Hans Günter Winkler of Germany and the Italian Raimondo d'Inzeo have both won the world championship twice, and Britain's David Broome, winner in 1970, won three European titles in the 1960s, in three attempts.

The women's world championship, held only twice before 1974, was first won by Mexico silver medallist Marion Coakes (later Mrs Mould), and five years later, in 1970, by Janou Lefebvre (later Mme Tissot) of France. Britain's Pat Smythe won the first running of the women's European championship in 1957 and then scored a hat-trick in 1961–

Mould, Marion (GB), rode her pony Stroller in junior classes, but did not realize their full potential until jumping the bigger fences of adult competition. She won the women's world championship at Hickstead in 1965, the Queen Elizabeth Cup the same year and again in 1971, and the British Jumping Derby in 1967. In Mexico, in 1968, she was the first woman to win an individual medal for show jumping, taking the silver behind Bill Steinkraus.

Roycroft, Bill (Australia), one of the toughest of all three-day event riders, rode Our Solo to victory at Badminton in 1960 *en route* to Rome for the Olympics. There they fell at the drain-pipes, four from home, and Roycroft broke his collarbone. He remounted to finish the course, was taken off to hospital, but next morning walked out to ride a clear in the show jumping and help his team win the gold. In 1965, when he was 51 years old, he rode three horses round Badminton, finished second on Eldorado and sixth on Stoney Crossing, and went on to ride Stoney Crossing to third place in the Cheltenham Gold Cup steeplechase.

Smith, Harvey (GB), a self-taught show jumper, made his mark on horses 'bought for a song'. He made his international debut in Dublin in 1958 on the

£40 buy Farmer's Boy. Often in trouble with the authorities, he won the British Jumping Derby on Mattie Brown in 1970 and 1971, but had to struggle hard to keep it after his notorious 'V' sign. At his best when the cash prize is high, he has never yet won a European title, but was second in 1967 and 1971 and third in 1963, and third also in the world championship in 1970.

Versatile Australian horseman Bill Roycroft makes a good recovery on Our Solo in the cross country.

each country may run only one a year. In the United States and sometimes in Canada, there are often two, to compensate for the difficulty encountered in taking teams of horses over long distances. There must be at least three teams, from different countries, in a Nations Cup. A team consists of four riders and horses, each going round the same course twice, with the best three in each round counting towards the final result. In 1965, the President's Cup was started, based on each country's best six results in Nations Cups during a season, and this is regarded as a world team championship.

Apart from Nations Cups, competitions fall into three categories: those that are decided on time in the first

Equestrian sports

The Royal couple at Badminton, Princess Anne (far right) on Goodwill in 1973 and Mark Phillips on Great Ovation in 1972, the second year in succession that combination won the Three-Day Event. Mark Phillips went on to win a gold medal in the Olympic team event at Munich and chalk up his third Badminton victory in 1974, on Columbus. Princess Anne won the individual European championship in 1971 on Doublet, and came fourth in the Badminton in 1974 on Goodwill.

Smythe, Pat (GB), the most famous woman show jumper of all time, won the women's European championship four times, in 1957 – the first time it was run – and then from 1961 to 1963. In 1956 she was the first woman ever to ride in Olympic show jumping, and on Flanagan won a team bronze. She won the 1962 British Jumping Derby with Flanagan, and the Queen Elizabeth Cup, after many years of near misses, in 1958 with Mr Pollard.

Bill Steinkraus (US) on Fleet Apple at Hickstead in 1971.

Steinkraus, Bill (USA), did much in the 1950s to raise the status of American show jumping. A publisher and an accomplished amateur musician, he rode with great style, made his team debut in 1951, and won a team bronze on Hollandia in the 1952 Olympics. Team captain from 1955 until he retired 17 years later, after Munich, he won a team silver in 1960 on Ksar d'Esprit and America's first individual show jumping gold in 1968 at the Mexico Olympics on Snowbound.

Willcox, Sheila (GB), the finest woman horse trials rider until she broke her back at Tidworth in 1971, achieved the unparalleled feat of a hat-trick at Badminton, in 1957 and 1958 with High and Mighty and in 1959 (as Mrs Waddington) with Airs and Graces. She won the European championship in 1957 with High and Mighty, but was at her peak before women riders were allowed in the Olympic Games.

2–3. And when Ann Moore, silver medal winner in Munich, won in 1971 and retained her title in 1973, Britain had won 9 out of a total of 13 championships.

Horse trials (Three-day event)

Horse trials have their ancestry in the tests that were arranged for officers' chargers, which is why they are often known on the Continent as 'the military' rather than the British term 'three-day event'. Originally these trials were designed to test stamina and were in the form of long-distance rides.

In 1902, the French cavalry staged a championship that included dressage, a steeplechase, show jumping, and a long-distance ride, which approximates to the present-day formula. The vast majority of horse trials in Britain are one-day trials, and these consist of dressage, usually followed by show jumping, with the cross-country phase last. Three-day events start with the dressage. Then follows a 'speed and endurance' phase that comprises roads and tracks, during which the horse is walked or trotted for long periods, sometimes with the rider running alongside to ease the burden, followed by a steeplechase, another roads and tracks, and the cross-country. The show jumping is the final phase, which is logical, since its prime function is to demonstrate that a horse is still fit and ready for action after the previous day's exertions.

Scoring is by a system of penalty points: the dressage marks are given in penalties; in the speed and endurance an optimum time is decided for each section and penalties are given according to the time margin by which a horse fails to reach the standard – a horse finishing within the time allowed is marked zero – and there are penalties for jumping errors, as there are of course in the show jumping.

The penalty system in the speed and

endurance is a new one; previously there was a system of bonuses, but the calculations are now easier.

The oldest three-day event in Britain, Badminton, was started as a result of the Duke of Beaufort's seeing the Olympic event at Aldershot in 1948. Badminton started the following year, and in 1953 was the venue for the first European championship; Britain won the team title – no other team finished – and Lawrence Rook with Starlight and Frank Weldon on Kilbarry filled the first two places. European championships are now held every two years, and Britain, after completing a team hat-trick, were beaten by West Germany in Kiev in 1973. Alexander Evdokimov of the USSR won the individual title.

The world championships are held every four years. The first, in 1966, was held at Burghley, where Ireland won the team title and Carlos Moratorio of Argentina the individual. In 1970, at

Richard Meade on Laurieston in the dressage section of the three-day event, in which they won team and individual Olympic golds.

Punchestown, Britain and Mary Gordon-Watson, with Cornishman V, were victorious.

The courses for the championships are built by officials of the country staging them, but the FEI appoint a technical delegate to examine and approve or alter the fences. There has been so much controversy, however, as for example with the second fence at Kiev which eliminated 14 horses, that the FEI considered appointing a panel of perhaps three technical delegates.

Dressage

Dressage basically means nothing more than training, and this is something from which every horse will benefit whatever his sphere of activity. It is, however, generally accepted that it applies to a fairly specialized branch of equestrian sport, at various standards of accomplishment from that associated with, say, novice horse trials, up to Grand Prix level.

For a long time, dressage has been more widely practised on the Continent than in Britain for mainly climatic reasons – if the winter is so severe that riding indoors is the only possibility, then practising of the movements that can be performed in a restricted space is a natural consequence. As a result, most of the terms used, as well as the word 'dressage' itself, tend to be French – for example, *piaffe, passage, pirouette*.

To a considerable extent the art of dressage is not so much which movements are performed, but the way in which they are executed. The essence of a well trained and ridden dressage horse

Polocrosse, a cross between polo and lacrosse, was developed in Australia in the late 1930s. Teams consist of six players, divided into sections of three who play alternate chukkas.

is lightness; it should do what is wanted freely and as if enjoying it. It is a judge's evaluation of this which results in the marks he gives, as well, of course, as the accuracy with which a movement is performed. Under the FEI ruling, there must be five judges in all international dressage competitions.

Since the early 1960s, the West Germans and Russians have tended to dominate the major international competitions. There is a considerable difference in the two styles, the German horses being accurate but generally heavy and without the gaiety of the better-quality Russians. The Russian team broke the Germans' Olympic domination in Munich in 1972.

EQUESTRIAN 'MOSTS'

Show jumping

Olympic Games		
golds	5	H. G. Winkler (Ger)
individual golds	2	P. J. d'Oriola (France)
team golds	5	Germany
World Championships		
team (President's		
Cup)	5	Great Britain
men's	2	H. G. Winkler (Ger)
	2	R. d'Inzeo (Italy)
European Championships		
men's	3	D. Broome (GB)
women's	4	P. Smythe (GB)
King George V Gold Cup		
rider	3	J. Talbot-Ponsonby (GB), H. Llewellyn (GB), P. d'Inzeo (Italy), D. Broome (GB)
horse	3	Foxhunter

Three-day event

Olympic Games		
golds	4	F. de Mortanges (Neth)
individual golds	2	F. de Mortanges (Neth)
team golds	3	Sweden, Great Britain
European Championships		
team	7	Great Britain
Badminton	3	Sheila Willcox (GB)
	3	Mark Phillips (GB)

Dressage

Olympic Games		
golds	4	H. St Cyr (Sweden)
individual golds	2	H. St Cyr (Sweden)
team golds	4	Germany
High jump*	8 ft 1½ in	A. Larraguibel (Chile) on Huaso (5.2.49)

---

*FEI ratified.

The traditional Argentinian game of pato (the duck) requires expert horsemanship. Four-man teams use only their hands to propel a six-handled leather ball into their opponents' goal. In the 15th century the game was played by Indians with a live duck imprisoned in a leather basket.

Winkler, Hans Günter
(Germany), won a total of five Olympic golds, more than any other horseman. He rode in his first international in 1952, and two years later took the world championship. The son of a

riding instructor, he was taught dressage but not jumping. With Halla, probably the finest show jumping mare ever, he retained his world title in 1955 and won the Olympic individual and team golds in 1956, although riding in great agony from a muscle pulled during his first round. He won team golds in 1960, with Halla, 1964 with Fidelitas, and 1972 with Torphy.

Fencing

A game of chess played at lightning speed is how fencing has been described. The fencer has to think all the time, analysing his opponent's game, always thinking of ways to outwit him. At no moment can he afford to relax or pause. The slightest hesitation can give an irrecoverable advantage to his opponent.

Consequently, fencing requires lengthy practice simply to perfect the techniques. But it is a fascinating sport and one the devotee can enjoy from youth to old age. And provided protective clothing and mask are worn, the danger to the participant is virtually non-existent.

Fencing is practised with three weapons – the foil, épée, and sabre. The foil is the only weapon fenced by women. Swords have been used since the Bronze Age, and even when superseded as a weapon by the gun they continued to be used in close combat and for duelling. Hence fencing – the very word is a shortening of 'defence' – has a long tradition, and all three weapons were included in the modern Olympics from the very first. The world governing body, the Fédération Internationale d'Escrimé (FIE), was founded in 1913. The first European championships (épée only) were held in 1921, and these became the world championships with the 1936 Olympics. World championships at all three weapons are held annually, but are contested concurrently with Olympic

titles every four years. Both individual and team titles are contested, and the Italians, Russians, French, Poles, and Hungarians are usually well to the fore.

The *foil* – and there are two primary kinds, French and Italian – is a light weapon with a tapering quadrangular blade and small, bell-shaped guard. It originally evolved as a practice weapon for the short court sword of the 17th and 18th centuries, and from that time have come the complex rules and conventions that govern foil fencing. Basically, these are based on the principle that the first attack has the right of way until it has been *parried*, when the right of way goes to the opponent's *riposte*. If this in turn is parried, the right of attack passes to the first attacker's *counter-riposte*, and so on until a hit is scored. If, however, an attack is made slowly or with a bent arm, the opponent may score a *stop-hit*, which must arrive a period of *fencing time* before the attack. To be valid, hits with the foil must be made with the point on the trunk of the body.

The *épée*, the duelling sword, is the same length as the foil (about 43 inches), but has a triangular, stiffer, fluted blade and a larger bell guard. It is fenced in conditions as similar to those of a duel

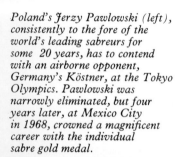

Poland's Jerzy Pawlowski (left), consistently to the fore of the world's leading sabreurs for some 20 years, has to contend with an airborne opponent, Germany's Köstner, at the Tokyo Olympics. Pawlowski was narrowly eliminated, but four years later, at Mexico City in 1968, crowned a magnificent career with the individual sabre gold medal.

d'Oriola, Christian (France), went to his first world championships in 1947 at 19 and won the first of 6 foil titles, including 2 Olympic golds (1952–56). In addition he participated in 6 team titles. A left-hander, d'Oriola was blessed with extremely fast reflexes and remarkable agility, which gave him a fast and penetrating lunge. At his best, he was unbeatable, and he dominated world foil for 10 years.

Elek, Ilona Schacherer- (Hungary), won 5 world championships, including the 1936 and 1948 Olympic titles. She was the only woman to win 2 individual Olympic golds, and these were 12 years apart. She also helped Hungary's foil team to 8 world titles, the first in 1933, the last in 1955, when she was 48. A determined rather than a brilliant fencer, she narrowly missed a third Olympic title in 1952 when she lost in a fight-off.

Giuseppe Delfino (left) of Italy scores a clean hit on Allan Jay (GB) in the 1960 Olympic épée. Delfino won his third team gold and beat Jay in the individual final.

Fencing terms
Barrage A tie or fight-off.
Fencing time The time needed to make one simple fencing movement.
Hit When contact is made with point or edge on an opponent.
On guard The position adopted by a fencer when he is ready for a bout.
Parry A defensive action in which the fencer deflects the attacking blade with his own.
Phrase A sequence of fencing movements leading to a hit.
Riposte An offensive movement made after a successful parry; hence *counter-riposte*.
Stop-hit A counter-offensive action made on an opponent's attack.

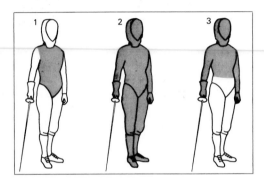

The target area for the three fencing weapons: 1 foil, 2 épée, 3 sabre. All three weapons are fenced by men, but only the foil is fenced by women.

as the protective clothing allows. There are no conventions with regard to the right of attack, and if both épéeists are hit, one of them gains the hit only if his hit arrived more than 1/25th of a second before he himself was hit. Less than that and a hit is scored against each contestant. Hits must be made with the point on any part of the body or protective clothing.

The *sabre*, the cut-and-thrust weapon, has a flattened V-shaped blade and a half-circular guard. Hits must be made to the head, earms, and trunk to just below the waist, and may be made with the whole of the front edge, the back edge nearest the point, or the point itself. The edge hits are known as *cuts*. Attack and counter-attack are governed by rules similar to those of the foil.

Since 1955, the foil and épée have been judged with an electrical apparatus that registers hits. Each fencer is connected to this apparatus by a wire attached to his back and running through a spool at the end of the piste (fencing area). However, because of the conventions governing foil, a president (referee) has to study the *phrase* leading to the hit to ensure that it was according to the rules. At épée, the electrical apparatus is the sole judge. In sabre, bouts are judged by a jury

The 1966 World Fencing Championships, in Moscow. The championships are held annually.

comprising a president, who judges the bout, and four judges, who observe the arrival of the hits.

At all three weapons, a bout lasts until one competitor has scored five hits (for men) or four hits (for women), or until 6 minutes (men) or 5 minutes (women) have elapsed. Competitors are warned when one minute remains. If the time expires with hits level, the bout is drawn.

Irene Camber of Italy (right) competing in the 1948 Olympics, in London. She won the Olympic title four years later, in Helsinki, and the world title in 1953.

FENCING 'MOSTS'

World and Olympic titles		
— men	21	E. Mangiarotti (Italy)
— women	13	I. Elek (Hungary)
Individual titles		
— foil	6	C. d'Oriola (France)
— épée	3	E. Mangiarotti (Italy)
— sabre	4	J. Pawlowski (Poland)
— women's foil	5	I. Elek (Hungary)
Olympic golds (individual and team)		
— overall	6	N. Nedi (Italy); E. Mangiarotti (Italy); R. Karpati (Hungary)
— one Games	5	N. Nedi (Italy) 1920

Hoskyns, Bill (GB), became the first British man to win a world fencing title, at Philadelphia in 1958 — and he had to pay his own expenses to get there! Hoskyns's title came at épée, in which he won silver medals at the Rome (team) and Tokyo (individual) Olympics and in the 1965 world championships (individual and team); but he also excelled at foil and sabre, and won numerous national and Commonwealth Games titles at all three weapons.

Mangiarotti, Edoardo (Italy), was the outstanding technical fencer at both foil and épée of the 1950s. A natural right-hander forced by his father to fence left-handed, Mangiarotti made his international debut at 16 in the 1935 world championships and a year later was winning an Olympic gold in the team épée. He helped the Italians win the same medal in the 1960 Olympics, bringing his medal tally to 21 gold, 14 silver, and 5 bronze at his two weapons. He won 3 individual épée titles — 1951, 52 (Olympic), 54 — and only the great d'Oriola prevented similar success in the foil.

Mayer, Helene (Germany), a powerful fencer, won the 1928 Olympic title and followed this with the first world championship, in 1929. She won the championship again in 1931 before leaving Nazi Germany to settle in the USA. Her return to fence for Germany in the 1936 Berlin Olympics was something of a *cause célèbre* — a Jew in the Nazi team. And some say she deliberately lost to Hungary's Ilona Elek, going down 5—4 in the vital bout, in front of a fuming Fuehrer. A year later she won her third world title — beating Miss Elek 5—3.

Nadi, Nedo (Italy), rates as the most technically excellent fencer of the 20th century. At the 1920 Olympics he won 5 gold medals — the individual and team foil, the team épée, and the individual and team sabre. In the 1912 Olympics he had won the individual foil. He turned professional after the 1920 Olympics.

Pawlowski, Jerzy (Poland), is generally recognized as the finest sabreur of all time. He was the youngest semi-finalist at the 1952 Olympics, and from the 1953 to the 1970 world championships, he collected 21 world and Olympic medals, including 4 individual and 4 team golds. He was Olympic champion in 1968.

Football sports

Sports in which a ball was kicked go back at least to the 2nd or 3rd century BC, when the Chinese are known to have played a game with a stuffed leather ball. The Japanese also played a kind of football, and a text from about 50 BC in the Munich Ethnological Museum mentions games played between the Chinese and the Japanese—the first internationals?

The Ancient Greeks had a ball game called *episkyros*, which the Romans adapted as *harpastum*. Centuries later, men were still chasing a ball, using hands or feet. In Italy, the game of *calcio* developed in Florence, reaching its height in the 1500s. Large wagers were made on the games, between 27-man teams wearing red and green respectively. In Britain things were less organized. The fierce Shrove Tuesday games were more like battles than sport, as players chased the ball through the streets with little regard to person or property. Not surprisingly the game became known as 'mob football', and there were many acts designed to repress it, the first, referring to the 'great noise in the city caused by hustling over large balls', coming in the reign of Edward II, on 13 April 1314. But it was not until 1486 that the term 'football' was first mentioned in such a document.

Despite further attempts to suppress the game because it interfered with archery practice, football survived to be tamed and made respectable in the 1800s, with the public schools to the fore. Each school had its own variation. Some permitted holding and running with the ball, bodily tackling, and hacking of shins, others preferred a dribbling game with little bodily contact. Soccer can be considered to be the ultimate result of the ancient and medieval kicking games, with rugby and the American code derived directly from it (see also *Association football*; *Rugby league*; *Rugby union*). Gaelic football developed separately in Ireland, and had much influence on the Australian rules game.

An 11-a-side game called *speedball*, devised by Elmer Mitchell in 1921 at the University of Michigan, incorporates features of soccer, American football, and even basketball, and resembles Gaelic football. In speedball, a ball that has not bounced may be caught and thrown or kicked, but a ball that has touched the ground may only be kicked and dribbled. It is usually played on an American football pitch, with a round ball. Physical contact is minimal.

Other variations of football are still played in the English public schools, such as Eton, Harrow, and Winchester. In addition to a field game played with a small round ball and small goals, which is a cross between soccer and rugby, Eton also has its famous wall game. This is played on a pitch some 120 yd long but only 6 yd wide, bounded on one side by a 10-ft-high wall. The goals (one a door, the other painted on an elm tree) are outside the pitch, and goals are rarely scored.

American football

Played in some form since early colonial days, football in the United States was organized in the early 1800s by schools and colleges. A 25-a-side 'soccer' match took place between Rutgers and Princeton in 1869, but it was not until the rugby-playing McGill University of Montreal went to play Harvard that the seeds of American football were sown. The match that took place at Cambridge, Massachusetts, in May 1874 was half soccer and half rugby, and so impressed were the Americans by the handling game of the Canadians that they soon adapted their own game. With its heavily padded players, electrifying bursts of action, and remarkably efficient organization, American football owes much to Yale University coach Walter Camp, who laid down many of the rules and in 1891 wrote the first book on the game.

It is played between teams of 11 on a

The unique Eton wall game, an idiosyncrasy that has survived since the early 1800s. The highlight of the year is the match between the scholars (Collegers) and the rest (Oppidans). The game consists of an almost continuous rugby scrum against the wall, but no handling is allowed. The object is to force the ball into the scoring area and then touch it against the wall, scoring one point for a shy. This entitles a shot at goal. But goals (worth 10 points) are hardly ever scored.

New York Jets quarterback Joe Namath takes a cool look at his receivers before releasing another of his precision passes.

Jim Brown scores a typical touchdown. He led the NFL eight times in rushing between 1957 and 1965 before retiring to take up a career on the cinema screen.

field 120 yd by 53 yd 1 ft, with a rugby-type ball about 12 inches long and 7 inches in diameter at the middle, and weighing 14–15 oz. Lines are marked across the pitch at 5-yd intervals between the two goal lines (100 yd apart) and there is a 10-yd end zone beyond each goal line. In college football the H-shaped goal-posts (23 ft 4 in wide) stand on the end line; in the professional game the posts, 18½ ft apart, extend from a single support and overhang the goal line. The crossbar is 10 ft from the ground.

The game is divided into four 15-min quarters, the clock being stopped when the ball is out of play. Free substitution is allowed from up to 40 players in pro football, so that totally different teams are used for defence and offence and a specialist is brought on to kick field goals. A *touchdown* is worth 6 points (taking the ball over the goal line or catching a pass when in the end zone), a *conversion* bringing an extra point. In college football, the ball may be run or passed into the end zone for an extra 2 points. A *field goal*, kicking the ball over the crossbar and between the uprights, is worth 3 points. A *safety*, worth 2 points, is scored when the team not in possession downs the ball-carrier in his own end zone, or if he steps back out of his end zone.

The main characteristics of American football are possession, the forward pass, and blocking. The team in possession of the ball are allowed four *downs* (plays) in which to advance 10 yards. If they advance 10 or more yards in 4 or fewer downs, they start another series; if not, the other side gains possession. Each down starts with a scrimmage line, in which the teams face each other about a yard apart. The offensive side has at least seven players on the line (two ends, two tackles, two guards, and a centre). Behind these *linemen* are the four backs, of which the *quarterback* is the key man of the team, receiving the ball through the centre's legs. Having called one of the many pre-set plays, he might transfer the ball to one of his backs to run, or drop back and throw a spectacular one-handed forward pass for a touchdown. Kicking is usually adopted only on the fourth down. Whatever the play, players will attempt to protect the ball-carrier by *blocking*, using their bodies or forearms. Only the ball-carrier may be tackled rugby-style.

Infringements are punished by territorial losses, from 5 to 15 yd depending on the offence, but play is usually allowed to continue to the end of the down so that the innocent team may gain a greater yardage. Between 4 and 6 officials in black and white striped shirts control the game, depending on the level.

American college football has a vast following, with wide TV coverage. Colleges play in groups called 'conferences', and teams from different conferences play each other in special post-season 'bowl' games. The result of several polls produces an 'All-America Selection'. The top college stars turn professional for astronomical sums.

The first professional league, the US Professional Football Association, was

Brown, Jim, before retiring from football for a lucrative screen career, won the coveted Jim Thorpe Trophy for the most valuable NFL player in 1958, '63 (shared), and '65. Probably the greatest running back of all time, he rushed a record 12,312 yd in his career (1957–65) with the Cleveland Browns, gaining 1,863 yd in one season (1963) and 100 yd or more in 58 games. He scored a record 126 touchdowns, including 106 rushing.

Grange, Harold 'Red', was the man who first brought the crowds to pro football in America. A star with the University of Illinois, he scored 31 touchdowns in 3 seasons of college football, including 5 against Michigan in 1924 from the first 5 times he carried the ball – a feat that earned him the nickname 'the Galloping Ghost'. He turned pro in 1925, and played for the New York Yankees and the Chicago Bears.

Namath, Joe, controversial quarterback of the New York Jets, took them to Super Bowl triumph in 1969, and passed for a record 4,007 yd in 1967. Namath's playboy escapades off the field frequently made the headlines, but these could not eclipse his on-field performances. Cool, courageous, always in control, he had the rare gift of being able to inspire his team to play above themselves. A brilliant analytical football brain and a remarkably quick release and accurate arm combined to make him the best quarterback of his day, if not of all time. Drafted from Alabama University in 1965 for a $400,000-plus contract, he eventually curbed his wild night-life, and despite two brittle knees was still timing his touchdown passes to perfection in the 1970s.

Football sports

'The Juice' (O.J.) Simpson squeezed through all the NFL defences in his remarkable 1973 season.

Simpson, O. J., in 1973 became the first footballer to carry the ball 2,000 yd in the 14-game NFL season. He rushed 2,003 yd to beat Jim Brown's 10-year-old record by 140 yd. The 1968 winner of the Heisman Trophy (voted America's best college player), the 26-year-old Orenthal James Simpson – 'the Juice' to the fans – helped the Buffalo Bills become the game's first 3,000-yd rushing team. The 210-lb 'escape artist' also broke a number of other rushing records: 250 yd in one game (equalled), 39 carries in one game, 332 carries in a season, and 3 of over 200 yd.

Unitas, Johnny, legendary quarterback for the Baltimore Colts, threw a touchdown pass in his first game for them, in 1956, and built up a record streak of touchdown passes in 47 consecutive NFL games over $4\frac{1}{2}$ years. The previous record had been 22. During this time he took them to two NFL Championships (1958, '59). Unitas always knew exactly what he wanted to do. He could throw long or short passes, he knew exactly when to let go, and he never flinched from a hard tackle. He threw a record 287 touchdown passes in his career, and gained a record 39,768 yd passing. He was elected Most Valuable Player in the NFL (Jim Thorpe Trophy) in 1957 and '67.

Canadian football – an Eastern Conference game between Ottawa Rough Riders and Hamilton Tiger-Cats at Lansdowne Park, Ottawa.

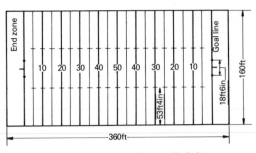

American football is sometimes called the gridiron game, from the pitch markings.

AMERICAN FOOTBALL 'MOSTS'

The Teams

Super Bowl	2	Green Bay Packers; Miami Dolphins
NFC (NFL)	8	Green Bay Packers
AFC (AFL)	3	Miami Dolphins

The Players

Season		
rushing	2,003 yd	O. J. Simpson, 1973
passing	4,007 yd	Joe Namath, 1967
points	176	Paul Hornung, 1960
touchdowns	22	Gale Sayers, 1965
Game		
rushing	250 yd	Orban Sanders, 1947
		O. J. Simpson, 1973
passing	554 yd	Norm Van Brocklin, 1951
points	40	Ernie Nevers, 1929
touchdowns	6	Ernie Nevers, 1929
		Dub Jones, 1951
		Gale Sayers, 1965
Career		
rushing	12,312 yd	Jim Brown
passing	39,768 yd	Johnny Unitas
points	1,742	George Blanda
touchdowns	126	Jim Brown

formed in 1920 with Jim Thorpe as president and star performer (see *Athletics* pen-pictures). A year later it became the National Football League (NFL) and by the 1960s, having absorbed the All America Conference (1946–50), was hugely successful, football having become America's No. 1 sport. Another league, the American Football League (later the National Football Conference) was set up in 1960, and by the end of the 1960s was rivalling the NFL. The respective champions met for the first time in 1967, in a 'Super Bowl' game. The two leagues conduct a joint draft of college stars, maintaining the balance between the leagues and between teams.

Canadian football, which evolved separately from American football, developed on similar lines. The main differences are the field (65 × 110 yd, plus 25-yd end zones); it is played 12-a-side; and there are only three downs in which to gain 10 yd. The professional season lasts from July to November, and is climaxed by the Grey Cup, a play-off between the winners of the small Eastern and Western Conferences.

Australian rules

Played almost exclusively in only four states, but with an intensity unrivalled in any sport anywhere else, Australian rules has a fanatical following. It developed in the 1840s as a mixture of rugby and Gaelic football, and a 40-a-side game was played between Scotch College and Melbourne Grammar School in 1858 in Melbourne, which was abandoned after three weeks. The first code of rules was drawn up by H.C.A. Harrison and Tom Wills in 1860. The Football Associations of Victoria and South Australia were both formed in 1877, Western Australia in 1885, and Tasmania in 1906, the year the Australian National Football Council came into being. The first Australian Football Championships (inter-state) were held in 1908, and have usually been held every three years.

Inter-state games are held every year, but are not popular in Victoria because of the intense club loyalty. Melbourne is the centre of the game, the Victorian Football League consisting of 11 suburban sides plus Geelong. The season is climaxed in September when the top four meet, and the Grand Final regularly attracts crowds of over 100,000.

In the major state competitions, the central umpire awards points (3, 2, 1) to the three 'fairest and best' players. The leading points scorer at the end of the season in each league is awarded that league's medal.

Canberra, Queensland, and New South Wales, and even Papua and New Guinea also play 'rules'. Teams from the weak

A feature of Australian rules football, the spectacular high 'marks'.

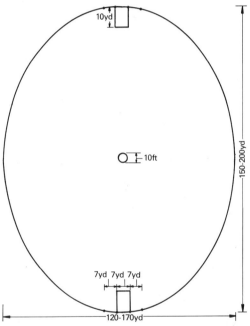

Above: *Carlton play Hawthorn in the huge oval of the Melbourne Cricket Ground. Australian rules draws a large, fanatical following.*

states compete in Section 2 of the Australian Football Championships, but are usually beaten by a team of Australian Amateurs from the 'big four' states.

Rules is played on a huge oval field, with dimensions of the order 150–200 yd by 120–170 yd. The goals consist of two 50-ft-high goal-posts 7 yd apart, flanked each side by shorter 'behind' posts another 7 yd away. A *goal* is scored with a clean kick between the goal-posts and is worth 6 points. A *behind*, worth 1 point, is scored if the ball is touched before it passes between the goal-posts, if it hits a goal-post, or if it passes between a goal-post and a behind post. The game is divided into four quarters of 25 min actual play, with a 20 min interval at half time, and 3 and 5 min intervals at quarter

Bunton, Hayden, widely accepted as the best rules player of all time, played with the graceful elegance that made him the game's greatest attraction between the wars. He was blessed with the perfect gifts for a rover — speed and stamina. He won an unprecedented 6 'best and fairest' medals in his career, 3 'Brownlows' with Fitzroy in the Victorian Football League and 3 'Sandovers' with Subiaco in Western Australia.

Dyer, Jack, a colourful, dynamic giant of a ruckman who earned the title 'Captain Blood', played 310 games in 19 years for Richmond in the Victorian League. Powerful and aggressive, he was virtually indestructible, but he was also fast and possessed a keen tactical brain. In his last years he played more in attack, becoming a formidable goal-kicker and introducing the end-over-end 'drop-punt' kick that soon became an accepted wet-weather weapon.

Farmer, Ken, a prolific points-scoring full forward, kicked 1,419 goals in his 12-year career. He scored more than 100 goals in 11 consecutive seasons (1930–40), in each of which he was South Australia's leading scorer. Predominantly right-footed, Farmer played for North Adelaide.

A capacity crowd watch the 1972 Grand Final between Richmond and Carlton at Melbourne, the centre of Australian rules.

O'Keeffe, Dan, Kerry's stalwart goalkeeper, made a record 10 appearances in All-Ireland finals, in which he won a record 7 winners medals. His first came in 1931, in his championship debut. He retired in 1948 as the longest-serving player in the All-Ireland game.

Gaelic football – Kerry play Down at Wembley Stadium.

and three-quarter time respectively. The ball is shaped like a rugby ball, but is slimmer round the middle.

There are 18 players in a team plus two substitutes, or reserves. They usually line up as six backs, a centre and two wings, and six forwards, with three all-purpose players (a rover and two rucks) who follow the ball. A player may run with the ball as long as he bounces it or touches it on the ground every 10 yd. He may kick, palm, or punch the ball, but not throw it. In *handballing*, as it is known, a player holds the ball in one hand and hits it with the other. Another feature of rules is the *mark*, in which a clean catch is rewarded by a free-kick. Free-kicks are also awarded if a player is fouled. Flying-tackles are not allowed, but the ball-carrier may be tackled around the waist from behind, in which case he must try to kick or punch the ball away. The ball-carrier may also be body-charged between the shoulder and the hips. Players may *shepherd* a team-mate carrying the ball by spreading their arms and even pushing or shouldering an opponent in the chest (only within 5 yd of the ball).

The game is controlled by a chief, central, umpire, two boundary umpires, and two goal umpires. The central umpire starts each quarter and restarts the game after a goal with a high bounce in the centre circle. After a behind, a defender kicks off from the 10 × 7 yd rectangle in front of the goal-posts. When the ball goes out of bounds, the boundary umpires bring it back into play by throwing it backwards over their heads.

Gaelic football

Gaelic football resembles Australian rules in its play, but it uses a round ball, rugby-type goal-posts, with a soccer-type net. The game grew from the medieval parish-to-parish free-for-alls that became a traditional part of Irish culture. Administered by the Gaelic Athletic Association (formed in 1884), it is played almost exclusively in Ireland.

The All-Ireland Championship, instituted in 1887 and held annually, is a competition between counties (from the Republic and Ulster) for the Sam Maguire trophy. The final, held at Dublin's Croke Park in late September, attracts huge crowds (a record 90,556 saw Down beat Offaly in 1961) and is watched by millions on television.

The game is played between teams of 15 (and 3 substitutes) on a pitch measuring 140–160 by 84–100 yd. Goal-posts 16 ft high and 21 ft apart stand in the middle of each goal line, with a crossbar 8 ft from the ground. The game lasts for 60 min, with a half-time interval, although All-Ireland semi-finals and finals last 80 min.

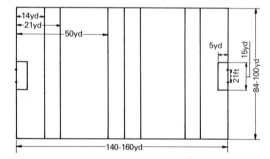

The ball is projected by kicking or fisting, but not throwing, and points are scored by propelling it between the uprights – 3 points for a goal (under the crossbar) and 1 point for placing it over the crossbar.

The ball may be caught in the air, but only the goalkeeper is allowed to pick it up off the ground. Outfield players may kick or scoop it into their hands with the foot. Players may carry the ball with a toe-to-hand movement unique to the game.

When one side puts the ball out of play over the side lines, the other side gets a free-kick. A ball going out of play over the end lines results in a goal-kick to the defending side or a free-kick on the 50-yard line to the attacking side, depending on who put the ball out.

Golf

Few games have had the sudden surge in popularity equal to that experienced by golf in the 1960s. As if by magic, but in fact as the result of much hard work by administrators and public relations men, golf became big business. Its therapeutic effects on the underexercised middle-aged were extolled; the strength, skill, and character of its top performers were held up as an example to all. The sport bloomed; professional golf was a career which, if hard work, was also lucrative. And the game as a popular pastime could be seen growing almost daily in the rash of new driving ranges and fresh courses that sprouted in and around urban areas all over the world.

Golf the competitive sport is world wide. Five different circuits are toured by the world's leading professional players, and in other areas of the world the competitive game flourishes on a lesser scale. And for every regular tournament player there are a hundred 'rabbits', casual weekend or early morning players whose interest in golf is financial only in terms of the money they pay out to play. But the challenge they face is the same as that of the Nicklauses and Players of this world – to get the ball into the cup in as few strokes as possible.

The origins of golf are lost in the Scottish mists, but no true Caledonian will tire of telling how the game began in his country. As early as 1457 a statute was passed which forbade the game on the grounds that it was interfering with the practice of archery. In 1471 the Scottish parliament decreed against both football and golf. Games similar to golf were no doubt played by the ancient Romans (*paganica*), the Dutch (*kolven*), and the Flemish (*chole*), but it is equally certain that it is the Scots who developed the game of golf as we know it today.

Mary Queen of Scots – the first woman golfer – and the Jameses IV, V, and VI are known to have played the game, and it was James VI of Scotland and I of England who brought the game to London, where it was played on Blackheath. Golf was at this time, and for almost another 300 years, a mere pastime, played for pleasure by gentlemen in their parks and by *hoi polloi* on the common links, those salty heath areas by the sea rife with rabbits that kept the grass close cropped.

By the early 19th century, clubs were being formed and tournaments inaugurated, and in 1860 the first (British) Open Championship was contested, at Prestwick. Golf soon took hold in the United States, and the first US Open was held in 1894.

The world's best players and the richest tournaments are now to be found in the United States, though the richest Japanese competitions are beginning to rival the American ones in terms of financial rewards. The US circuit is a series of weekly tournaments that go on effectively all the year round. Only the talented few get their tournament 'card', which entitles them to play, while others have to pre-qualify for every tournament.

Rival, and well sponsored, circuits

Charles, Bob (NZ), was the premier left-handed golfer of the 1960s and early 1970s. His first big win was the 1963 British Open, the year of his first US win, the Houston tournament.

A deadly artist on the putting green, he had his most consistent successes on the European and Australasian circuits, and in 1972 his four tournament victories included Europe's richest prize, the £15,000 John Player Classic.

Crampton, Bruce (Australia), came of age on the US circuit in 1965 when he won three successive tournaments – the Bing Crosby National, the Colonial National, and the '500' Festival Open – a feat unmatched in contemporary American golf. The youthful Crampton had won the 1956 Australian Open, and went to the USA in 1957, having to wait until 1961 for his first circuit win, the Milwaukee Open. In 1973 he became only the second overseas winner of the Vardon Trophy.

Cotton, Henry (GB), had an illustrious career spanning World War II in which he won the British Open 3 times (1934, 37, 48) at a time when no other British player won it more than once. He won at least 30 other tournaments, including three wins in the PGA match-play event, in addition to meeting and beating contemporary leading players in private challenge matches.

A 'Royal and Ancient' scene – Mary Queen of Scots playing golf at St Andrews in 1563.

Hagen, Walter (USA), had a brilliant record in tournaments and his major wins alone included 4 British Opens, 2 US Opens, and 5 US PGA match-play titles. A consummate showman and an inveterate gamesman, he was the first professional golfer to get treatment equal with the gentlemen amateurs. His playing career, which lasted from 1914 to 1933 at the top level, also included 6 appearances for the USA against Britain.

Left: *Walter Hagen in 1928 at Sandwich, where he won his third British Open Championship.* Right: *Ben Hogan in 1956 at Wentworth, where he won individual and team Canada Cup honours.*

Hogan, Ben (USA), entered 5 tournaments in 1953 and won them all, including the US and British Opens and the US Masters. It was the culmination of a career that started with his first pro win at the age of 27 in 1940, included 62 PGA-sponsored victories in the USA, and 4 US Opens and 2 US Masters and PGAs. It also included a fight-back after a dreadful motor accident which, medical opinion claimed, should have ended his career in 1949. As late as 1967 – his 55th year – Hogan could match the best with a back nine 30 in the Masters.

Jacklin, Tony (GB), was assured of fame and fortune in 1969 when he became the first Briton since 1951 to win the Open championship. A year later he augmented his fame with a win in the US Open, all four of his rounds being below par figures. It was also in 1969 that Jacklin had spearheaded Britain's challenge in the tied Ryder Cup match. After his epic 1970 season, Jacklin seemed to go off the boil in 1971, but 1972 saw him win four tournaments, including the Greater Jacksonville Open for the second time.

Memorable moments in sport

The perfect result

Dateline: Royal Birkdale Golf Club, 20 August 1969. Every two years, teams of golfers from the British Isles and the United States do battle in the Ryder Cup, and almost invariably since World War II the Americans have remorselessly come out on top. The first match played for Sam Ryder's gold trophy was at Worcester, Massachussetts, in 1927, and then, and in the following matches in 1929, 1931, 1933, and 1935, the home side won. America's 1937 win at Southport was the first away win, and they were unbeaten in subsequent matches until 1957, when Britain won at Lindrick.

Prominent in Britain's 1957 win was Eric Brown, a determined Scot who had something of a battle royal with the American Tommy 'Thunder' Bolt. He was appointed non-playing captain of Britain's 1969 team, which was spearheaded by the new young lion of British golf, Tony Jacklin. These factors, and the advantage of the home course, gave Britain, who had suffered five consecutive crushing defeats since 1957, a better than usual chance.

Two days of foursomes – eight foursomes and eight four-ball foursomes – ended with no advantage to either side: each had won six matches, with four halved.

This meant that the final day's singles, 16 in all, would decide the contest, and it was a tooth-and-nail fight all the way. The morning session gave Britain a 5–3 lead, and now they needed only $3\frac{1}{2}$ points out of a possible 8 to clinch victory. But the first two matches went to America to level the score. The middle four matches were shared.

In the remaining matches Brian Huggett (GB) and Billy Casper were on the 16th, which Huggett won to level his match, and Jacklin and Nicklaus were level after 15 holes. Huggett and Casper halved the 17th, and when they were playing the 18th Huggett heard a great roar from behind which signalled, he thought, a win for Jacklin. Amid great tension, Huggett holed an eminently missable putt to halve the 18th, in the belief that this was enough to win the cup for the British.

But the cheer he had heard was hailing Jacklin's 55-ft putt on the 17th, to square his match after losing the 16th. And now the outcome of the entire contest depended on the last hole of the last match, between the top golfers of the respective teams. Jacklin putted 3 feet short from some 20 feet; Nicklaus shot 4 feet past the hole. But with cool nerves Nicklaus holed the return, despite large numbers of the partisan crowd willing the ball out. For a second it seemed that Jacklin would have to hole what was in this situation a missable putt to save the whole contest for the British Isles. But in an instant, Nicklaus had scooped up his ball, and conceded the putt. This act of the finest sportsmanship let his friend and rival Jacklin off the hook, put to shame those who had felt antagonism to Nicklaus (because he always tried so hard to win?), and provided the perfect result for one of the closest fought matches in any sport – the first tie in the history of the Ryder Cup.

Above: *Brown (left) congratulates Jacklin and Nicklaus after their great match, and,* below, *with Sam Snead (left) and the cup.*

From the tee, the seventh green at Augusta, permanent venue of the US Masters, seems to be all bunkers, or sand traps as they are called in America. This beautiful course was the brainchild of Bobby Jones, and the Masters is one of the 'big four' tournaments.

Jones, Bobby (USA), had a career as an amateur golfer that will almost certainly remain unmatched in the changed conditions of modern golf. Before retiring from the game at the age of 28 — believing he had professionalized himself by making a series of instructional films — Jones had achieved everything a man could wish for: 13 major titles came his way — 5 US amateur championships, 4 US Opens, 3 British Opens, and 1 British amateur, then the 'big four' tournaments of golf. This single British amateur win gave Jones his unique 'grand slam' of British and American Open and amateur titles in one season, 1930. Handsome and debonair, Jones founded the Augusta National Course, scene of the annual Masters tournament, and was so popular at St Andrews that he was awarded the town's freedom in 1958.

Locke, Bobby (South Africa), with his plus-fours and white cap, was a familiar figure on the world's golf courses in the 1940s and 1950s. His impeccable demeanour and apparent unflappability were a feature of his play, as was his rigid putting procedure, unchanged for long or short putts. Locke's marvellous putting helped him to 43 major tournament wins in four continents, including 4 British Opens, between 1935 and 1957.

Miller, Johnny (USA), was responsible for one of the finest 'charges' in golf history when his last round 63 in the 1973 US Open took him into a winning position by one stroke. The young, blond Miller had made his first impact on the US tour in 1971, when his $91,000 prize money included a win in the Southern Open; the 1972 tour saw him win the Heritage Golf Classic as well as the Otago Classic in New Zealand. Miller was clearly one of American golf's greatest prospects, a fact he emphasized in 1973 when he came 2nd in the British Open and won both team and individual honours in the World Cup.

Johnny Miller at the 1973 British Open. He made an unprecedented start to the 1974 US season by winning the first three events.

have developed elsewhere. The South African circuit lasts from November to March and is a happy hunting ground for many South African and British golfers. The Asian circuit is dominated by the Japanese and Australians, its tournaments going on from April to October. A short Australasian circuit flourishes around the Australian and New Zealand Open championships, roughly from October to January. The British and European tournament round really got off the ground only in the 1970s, but by then the prize money could equal that of the Americans. The British Open has always been the European event with the most prestige, but with additional prize money being drummed up by the European PGAs the circuit as a whole now contains some of the world's richest events.

With the weight of golfing talent being concentrated in the United States, it is not surprising that three of the world's four acknowledged major tournaments are contested on the US tour. The US Open and the US PGA tournaments are played on a different course each year, but the third big American event, the Masters, is played each year at Augusta in Georgia. The fourth side of this so-called 'quadrilateral' or 'big four' is the British Open championship, which is often the world's greatest test of golf played on seaside links courses.

The winning of even one of these four great tournaments is enough to provide a golfer with sufficient income from advertising and endorsements to make it unnecessary for him to play again, though few golfers do in fact retire on their laurels. The prize money for the World Cup (formerly Canada Cup), however, is meagre, but this has not stopped most of the world's top golfers from competing, largely for the honour, and the Americans have excelled in this team (of two) event, which has been held annually since 1953 and also produces an individual winner. The corresponding

Golf

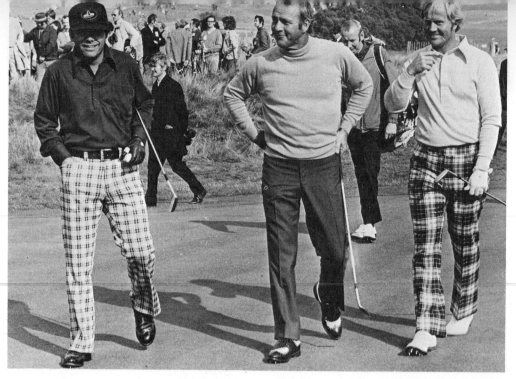

Three happy members of the victorious American Ryder Cup team at Muirfield in 1973, left to right: Lee Trevino, Arnold Palmer, and Jack Nicklaus.

Nicklaus, Jack (USA), golf's 'Golden Bear', so called from his pudgy youthful appearance, has been the constant hero of world golf during the 1960s and early 1970s. A mere record of his 'big four' victories – US PGA in 1963 and 1971; US Masters in 1963, 1965, 1966, and 1972; US Open in 1962, 1967, and 1972; and British Open in 1966 and 1970 – is sufficient to rank him as a modern parallel to Bobby Jones, especially when his US amateur victories in 1959 and 1961 are included. Famed in his early years for his mammoth power off the tee, Nicklaus combines this with tremendous finesse at the short game and on the greens, so that not only was no tournament safe from his prodigious talent but it also seemed that he would collect every record open to him in the game.

Palmer, Arnold (USA). At the end of the 1973 US tour, Arnold Palmer's most recent big win was the 1964 US Masters, his fourth in that event. But Palmer still attracted the crowds – his own massive following was known as Arnie's Army – who were drawn by Palmer's flair and style which had helped make golf the growth sport of the 1960s. His election as 'Athlete of the Decade' in 1970 was no surprise: he was the archetypal American hero – a clean-cut winner. Even when he was in his mid-40s, Palmer, whose 80-odd tournament wins included a US Open (1960), 2 British Opens (1961–62), and 6 team and an individual World Cup, was still regularly among the money-winners.

Player, Gary (South Africa), with Nicklaus and Palmer made up the 'Big Three' on the US courses in the 1960s. And his dramatic win in the 1973 Piccadilly World Match Play Championship was a welcome return to the form of the man who had first won the British Open in 1959. Normally dressed all in black, Player is perhaps the most dedicated golfer in the world, and his hard work has paid off not only in terms of financial winnings, but has enabled him to become the first non-American to complete the 'quadrilateral'.

Right: Gary Player, who showed in 1974 that he was still a great force in world golf with his second US masters victory.

competition in amateur golf is the bi-annual Eisenhower Trophy for teams of four, first held in 1958.

International golf is very much a male preserve, and women's events are given little attention by the press. There is a strong amateur tradition in European ladies golf, but once again the centre of the professional game is in the United States, where there is a fair living to be made by the successful.

Rules of golf

Golf is one of the simplest games, but conversely its rules are among the most complex in all sports. And despite the thick rule book, almost every rule can be broken by the unscrupulous player. It thus turns out that despite the good offices of the Royal and Ancient Golf Club of St Andrews, who are responsible for the rules, the only way to ensure that one's opponents are honest is not to play with known cheats. Yet very rarely does a match official have to step in to reprimand – still less disqualify – a competitor.

The basic rules are: the ball is played from the teeing ground into the hole by successive strokes in accordance with the rules; a maximum of 14 clubs is allowed; and all clubs must consist of a shaft and a head and be rigidly made in one piece. The method of propelling the ball is defined: the ball 'shall be fairly struck at with the head of the club and must not be pushed, scraped, or spooned'. The hole itself must be $4\frac{1}{4}$ inches across and at least 4 inches deep.

Course architects design courses to hamper the golfer to differing degrees with bunkers (sand traps) and water hazards, and players must play their way out of these obstacles according to the rules, with the penalties varying according to whether stroke play or match play rules are in use. And if a player hits his ball out of bounds, he has to play his shot again and add a penalty stroke to his score.

Various rules determine what to do if a ball is unplayable or lost, or whether a particular obstruction may be regarded as a 'loose impediment' and removed without penalty, and so on. Some of the world's leading golfers at times break the rules inadvertantly, so the 'fun' golfer may be excused if he does not have a complete grasp of the finer points of the game's complexities. The basic aim is to get round in as few strokes as possible, while at the same time observing the most important feature of the rule book –course etiquette, i.e. consideration for other players.

Golf terms

Albatross Three under par for a hole.
Approach shot An iron shot or long putt to the hole.
Apron The low grass surround of the green.
Birdie One under par for a hole.
Bogey One over par for a hole.
Borrow Allowance made, in putting, for a slope.
Brassey Old name for wooden club, after the brass plate on its sole for protection.
Bunker A hazard, usually a depression filled with sand.
Caddie One who carries or handles a player's clubs.
Carry Distance from where a shot is played to the spot where it first lands.
Casual water Temporary accumulation of water.
Chip Short, lofted approach shot.
Dog-leg A hole with a sharp turn, at which the second shot is usually played at right-angles to the first.
Dormie In match play, leading by as many holes as there are left.
Double bogey Two over par for a hole.
Draw Bending the ball in flight from right to left.
Driver The club usually used for driving off.
Eagle Two under par for a hole.
Fade Bending the ball in flight from left to right.
Fairway The smooth turf between tee and green.
Fore! Warning shouted to anyone in danger of being hit by the ball.
Fourball Match in which one pair play their better ball against better ball of opponents.
Foursome Match in which each pair plays one ball, striking it alternately.
Green Surface around the hole specially prepared for putting.
Hazard Any bunker or water hazard.
Honour The player or side playing first from the tee has the 'honour'.

Hook Unintentional *draw*; more pronounced.
Irons Clubs with metal heads.
Mashie Old term for No. 5 iron.
Match play The form of golf in which the winner is determined by holes won, not strokes.
Medal play The form of golf in which the number of strokes taken determines the placings.
Niblick Club, corresponding to No. 10 iron, used for lofting.
Out of bounds Ground on which play is prohibited, incurring one-stroke penalty.
Par Score in which first class player should play a hole or holes.
Pitch Lofted approach shot to the green, tending to stop the ball nearly dead.
Pitch and run Approach shot pitched short to run up to the hole.
Play through To pass slower players in front by playing a hole before them.
Plugged ball A ball that stays in the hole it makes on landing.
Pull A shot pulled by the action of the club to the left of the line of flight.
Push A shot pushed by the action of the club to the right of the line of flight.
Rough Unprepared ground.
Slice Unintentional *fade*; more pronounced.
Spoon Club approximating to modern No. 3 or 4 wood.
Stroke play Same as *medal play*.
Stymie Situation on green when opponent's ball lay directly on line between a player's ball and hole in match play; no longer operational.
Tee Teeing ground, the starting place for a hole to be played; the peg on which the ball is placed.
Trap American term for a *bunker*.
Wedge Wedge-shaped club used for lofting, especially out of sand.
Woods The wooden clubs, used for the longer shots.

Snead, Sam (USA), was still rivalling the best golfers when he was over 60, competing with distinction in a number of tournaments. His smooth swing, which had earned him the misapplied nickname of 'Slammin' Sam', served him well through 40 years of competition. Only one major distinction eluded him, victory in the US Open, but he did win 3 US Masters, 3 US PGAs, and 1 British Open. In 1956 and 1960–62 he won Canada Cup team honours, including a record 272 in 1961 to take the individual trophy, and, remarkable to relate, was old enough to follow these triumphs with the world seniors championship in 1964 and 1965, and again in 1970.

Thomson, Peter (Australia), is best known for his hat-trick of wins in the British Open in

1954–56 to which he added subsequent wins in 1958 and 1965. He never took to the US circuit, but had dominating periods in the 1960s and 1970s in Britain, Australasia, and the rich Asian circuits. Thomson was also a strong match-player, and in Britain won the News of the World Match Play four times between 1954 and 1967.

Trevino, Lee (USA), possesses one of sport's most equable temperaments, which enables him to clown and play to the gallery one minute and hit minutely judged shots the next. An erstwhile caddy from El Paso, Trevino won his first big tournament, the US Open, in 1968, and in 1971 he amazed the golfing world by winning, within a few weeks, the US, Canadian, and British Opens. In 1972 he retained his British title. With his wide shoulders, Trevino has enormous power and seems to lack the technical refinements of his rivals. But his judgement is superb, as anyone who saw him on his second Open victory would affirm.

Right: *Out comes the rule book and the two protagonists, Billy Casper (centre) and Bob Charles (obscured), check a point.* **Below:** *Tony Jacklin gets a free 'drop' after his ball had lodged in a rabbit-hole.* **Below right:** *'Babe' Zaharias (formerly Didrikson) dominated women's golf in the late 1940s and early 1950s after an equally remarkable athletics career.*

Golf

Vardon, Harry (GB), was one of the great Vardon-Braid-Taylor 'triumvirate' who dominated British golf in the early 1900s. He won the British Open six times — 1896–98–99, 1903–11–14 — and the US Open in 1903. But it is not Vardon's record, more his reputation and influence on the young game — the overlapping 'Vardon' grip is named after him — that has made his name so well remembered.

Harry Vardon in 1921.

Weiskopf, Tom (USA), made it to the top with a masterful victory in the 1973 British Open — only his second victory outside the USA. By then 32, Weiskopf had come good rather late, but his win was built on a solid foundation of success, including the 1972 Piccadilly World Match Play title and equal-runner-up in the 1972 US Masters.

GOLF 'MOSTS' AND 'LOWESTS'

'Big four' titles	12*	Jack Nicklaus (US)
British Open		
wins	6	Harry Vardon (GB) 1896–98–99–1903–11–14
lowest total	276	Arnold Palmer (US) 71, 69, 67, 69, Troon, 1962
	276	Tom Weiskopf (US) 68, 67, 71, 70, Troon, 1973
lowest round	65	Henry Cotton (GB), Sandwich, 1934
	65	Leopoldo Ruiz (Argentina), Lytham, 1958
	65	Eric Brown (GB), Lytham, 1958
	65	Peter Butler (GB), Muirfield, 1966
	65	Christy O'Connor (GB), Lytham, 1969
	65	Neil Coles (GB), St Andrews (Old Course), 1970
	65	Jack Nicklaus (US), Troon, 1973
US Open		
wins	4	Willie Anderson (US) 1901–03–04–05
	4	Bobby Jones (US) 1923–26–29–30
	4	Ben Hogan (US) 1948–50–51–53
lowest total	275	Jack Nicklaus (US) 71, 67, 72, 65, Baltusrol, 1967
	275	Lee Trevino (US) 69, 68, 69, 69, Oak Hill, 1968
lowest round	63	Johnny Miller (US), Oakmont, 1973
US Masters		
wins	4	Arnold Palmer (US) 1958–60–62–64
	4	Jack Nicklaus (US) 1963–65–66–72
lowest total	271	Jack Nicklaus (US) 67, 71, 64, 69, 1965
lowest round	64	Lloyd Mangrum (US) 1940
	64	Jack Nicklaus (US) 1965
	64	Maurice Bembridge (GB) 1974
US PGA – wins	5	Walter Hagen (US) 1921–24–25–26–27
World Cup		
wins	12	United States 1955–56–60–61–62–63–64–66–67–69–71–73
individual	3	Jack Nicklaus (US) 1963–64–71
lowest aggregate	545	Australia (B. Devlin and D. Graham) 1970
individual	269	Roberto de Vicenzo (Argentina) 1970
Ryder Cup		
singles won	6	Sam Snead (US) 1937–59 (lost 1)
	6	Arnold Palmer (US) 1961–73 (halved 2, lost 3)
matches won	22	Arnold Palmer (US) 1961–73 (halved 2, lost 8)
World Match-Play		
wins	5	Gary Player (S. Africa) 1965–66–68–71–73
World Amateur		
wins	5	United States 1960–62–68–70–72
lowest aggregate	834	United States 1960
individual	269	Jack Nicklaus (US) 1960
US Women's Open		
wins	4	Betsy Rawls (US) 1951–53–57–60
	4	Mickey Wright (US) 1958–59–61–64
lowest total	284	Louise Suggs (US) 1952
Season's winnings	$320,542 (£128,000)	Jack Nicklaus (US) 1972
women	$82,854 (£34,500)	Kathy Whitworth (US) 1973
Biggest prize	$60,000 (£25,000)	Bobby Nichols (US), Dow Jones, 1970
	£25,000 ($60,000)	Christy O'Connor (GB), John Player Classic, 1970
Tournaments won		
season	17	Byron Nelson (US) 1945
consecutive	11	Byron Nelson (US) 1945
Lowest scores		
tournament round	55	Homero Blancas (US), Longview, Texas, 1962
women	62	Mickey Wright (US), Midland, Texas, 1964
nine holes	25	Bill Burke (US) 1970
36 holes	122	Sam Snead (US) 59 + 63, 1959
72 holes	257	Mike Souchak (US) 60, 68, 64, 65, Texas Open, 1955

* 2 British Opens, 3 US opens, 4 US Masters, 3 US PGAs.

Greyhound racing

The first greyhound races, on a straight course, took place in London at Hendon in 1876, but it was not until 1919 that the now familiar oval track and mechanically powered 'hare' were first used – in the United States. England followed in 1926 and Australia in 1927. The name 'greyhound' is misleading: it comes from the old Norse *greyhundr*, of obscure etymology, and greyhounds come in many colours but not grey. It is a breed whose major features have remained unchanged for thousands of years. Characterized by long legs and a slender body, it has superlative vision and hearing and, of course, speed. It was used for hundreds of years in the sport of coursing for hares.

Modern greyhound races take two main forms – graded events and open races. Graded races are between fields of picked dogs, attached to a particular track, which should theoretically finish equal. Known 'wide' runners are given the outside traps, and the others are drawn. Though only modest prize money is offered, these races are the backbone of the sport. Open races are just that, and all dogs are eligible whether attached to a track or privately trained. Entry fees are charged, and the prize money may be quite lucrative.

Alternative forms of racing are handicap races, particularly popular in Scotland and the North of England but not favoured elsewhere, and hurdle races, which are a thrilling sight as the dogs fly over the obstacles.

Because greyhounds run flat out after the electric hare, the races tend to be short affairs, ranging only from 230 yards to 1,200 yards. The standard distance in England is 525 yards. The traps are opened automatically by the hare as it passes them. Six dogs race on British tracks, on grass; eight in Australia and America, on sand tracks.

Greyhound racing has always been a prey to doping from its earliest days, but now special chemical analyses enable dope tests to be made and declared within an hour. Feeding a dog to slow it down was a common ploy, but stringent weight checks have ruled this trick out, too. A third method of deceit was to switch one greyhound with another, but a simple but thorough identity card, which lists a dog's characteristics right down to the marks on its nails, has eliminated this as well.

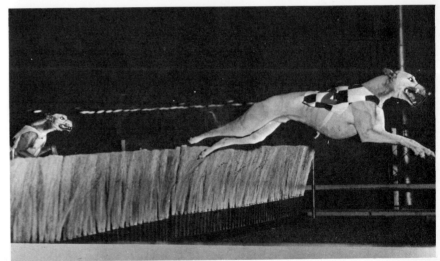

Top: *The tremendous stress on a greyhound's delicately tuned muscles is evident as it takes a bend at upwards of* 35 mph. Above: *Hurdling, a spectacular variation of the sport that is popular in Britain and Australia.*

FASTEST GREYHOUNDS

Highest speed	41.72 mph	The Shoe (410 yd straight, Richmond, NSW, 1968)
– circuit	38.12 mph	Easy Investment (525 yd, 1973)
– hurdles	36.90 mph	Sherry's Prince (525 yd, 1971)

Gymnastics

Caslavska, Vera (Czechoslovakia), attractive blonde with a faultless mature style, won 7 Olympic gold medals, including the combined in 1964 and 1968. In 1964 she eclipsed her great rival, Russia's Larissa Latynina, winning the vault and beam as well as the combined. Her support for the Dubcek regime in 1968 meant that she was the sporting symbol of her country's political resistance when she beat Russia's top competitors for the overall gold medal and won the vault, the asymmetrical bars, and the floor exercises (jointly). She also won 4 world and 11 European championships.

Chukharin, Viktor (USSR), the first of the great Russian gymnasts, took 7 Olympic gold medals, including the combined in both 1952 and 1956. Using rugged power and unflurried technique, he was in the forefront of his country's domination of gymnastics during the 1950s, when Russia re-entered international sport at the Helsinki Olympics.

Endo, Yukio (Japan), an immaculate performer, spearheaded his country's take-over of the leadership of gymnastics from Russia during the 1960s. Endo was a member of the Japanese teams that won 3 Olympic and 2 world team titles during the decade. In addition, his talent for improvization allied to his excellent technique enabled him to win the combined and the parallel bars gold medals at the 1964 Olympics.

Latynina, Larissa (USSR), the most successful Olympic competitor of all time, won 9 gold medals in 3 Games. Between 1956 and 1966 she collected 24 Olympic, world, and European titles with her peerless technique and unemotional temperament. Although soundly beaten by Vera Caslavska at the 1964 Olympics and 1966 world championships, Latynina, who interrupted her long career to have two children, is regarded with the Czech girl as one of the two outstanding female gymnasts of all time.

In international competitions there are six men's events, the floor exercises, rings (1), parallel bars (2), pommel horse (3), vault (lengthwise, 4), and horizontal bar (5). Women have four events, the floor exercises (to music), vault (6), asymmetrical bars (7), and beam (8).

Gymnastics is perhaps the most graceful and artistic of all sports. It is popular throughout the world, but particularly in the Communist countries and in Japan. Its picturesque qualities have made it enormously popular with spectators, who admire the dexterity, skill, and beauty of many of the moves, particularly those in the women's events.

Gymnastics formed part of the sporting tradition of the ancient civilizations of China, Persia, India, and Greece. But modern gymnastics is based on the amalgamation of the theories of two Europeans – the German Johan Ludwig Jahn and the Swede Pehr Ling.

The first modern Olympic Games, in 1896, provided the initial major international competition, which Germany dominated, winning all five gold medals. Germany and Italy were in the forefront of the sport's development before World War II. But the balance of gymnastics changed dramatically at the 1952 Olympics with the appearance of the Russian team, who dominated men's gymnastics until the emergence of the Japanese in the 1960s. The Russian women have been even more successful than the men, winning every Olympic team title from 1952 to 1972.

World championships have been held every four years since 1950. European championships, in which there are no team titles, are held in odd years between World and Olympic championships.

Gymnasts are awarded points by a team of four judges. Their score is obtained by averaging the two intermediate scores contained on the cards the judges display. The highest and lowest scores are discarded. Officials mark out of 10 on the difficulty of the routine, its aesthetic appeal, and its execution.

In Olympics or world championships, competitors must do two sets of exercises on each apparatus – a compulsory (predetermined) set and a voluntary routine of the individual's own choice. The contestant with the highest accumulated score is awarded the first place in the all-round individual

Japan's Sawao Kato at Munich, where he won the combined, parallel bars, and team golds.

Vera Caslavska won two Olympic vault golds.

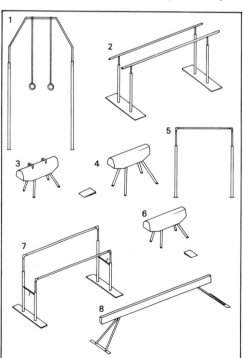

108

Far left: *Larissa Latynina, high priestess of gymnastics in the Soviet Union.* Left: *Miroslav Cerar, who reigned supreme on the pommel horse from 1962 to 1970.*

Shakhlin, Boris (USSR), a masterly gymnast, won 10 individual and 3 team titles in world and Olympic events between 1954 and 1964. His considerable strength allowed him to dominate apparatus requiring power, and he secured the combined exercises title at the 1960 Olympics. Altogether he collected 19 gold, 10 silver, and 4 bronze medals in Olympic, world, and European events.

Turistcheva, Ludmila (USSR), won the fascinating struggle for the 1972 combined exercises title at the Munich Olympics. Despite losing the limelight to her compatriot Olga Korbut, Miss Turistcheva demonstrated all the skill and originality that had brought her the world and European titles in the two previous years. In 1973, she won the 5 individual gold medals (one jointly) in the European championships.

classification. The team competition is decided by aggregating the five highest scores of the six members of the group in each of the exercises.

The top six competitors of the individual event then take part in the finals of the individual apparatus, and are registered with the average of the two initial scores (compulsory and voluntary). Each competitor then does another voluntary exercise and scores anew to settle the order for the individual apparatus.

WORLD & OLYMPIC GOLDS

Total — men	13	B. Shakhlin (USSR)	
— women	17	L. Latynina (USSR)	
Individual — men	10	B. Shakhlin (USSR)	
— women	12	L. Latynina (USSR)	
Olympic — men	6	B. Shakhlin (USSR)	
— women	7	V. Caslavska (Cz)	
Combined title			
— men	3	V. Chukharin (USSR)	
— women	4	L. Latynina (USSR)	
In one year — men	5	*B. Shakhlin (USSR)	
— women	5	*L. Latynina (USSR)	
In one event	5	†M. Cerar (Yug)	

*1958.   †Pommel horse (1962–70).

Memorable moments in sport

The magic of Olga

Dateline: Munich, 30 August to 1 September 1972. Russia's Ludmila Turistcheva won the combined exercises gold medal for women at the 1972 Olympics. But for the crowd in the Sportshalle and millions of television viewers, the darling of the Games was Turistcheva's compatriot Olga Korbut, who finished only seventh in the overall classification.

Just 17, Olga came to the Games with little international reputation, and few had seen her perform before. But she soon captivated the audiences with her elf-like displays of superb skill and balletic beauty. Those lucky enough to be present knew they were witnessing a truly memorable event – the birth of a star.

The tiny Olga, who weighed only 6 st 4 lb, spun through her routines to the enchantment of the spectators. But in the asymmetrical bars, she slipped at the crucial point of her brilliant and daring routine, losing points that she could never make up during the tight competition of an Olympic Games. The crowd sighed in disappointment – and the consistent Ludmila went on to take the combined exercises gold medal. Olga's consolation was a bouquet of flowers from a sympathetic spectator, the applause of the world, and a gold medal in the team competition.

Two days later, Olga stole the thunder once more, and this time she made no mistake. She gave a faultless, breathtaking display on the asymmetrical bars, and there was almost a riot when she was marked down to joint second. Then she won a gold on the beam, there being this time a suggestion of the judges' being swayed in her favour; but who could forget that backward somersault? And finally she brought the house down with an impish, lyrical performance in the floor exercises that won her the gold in front of Turistcheva.

Both her individual golds were won by a mere fortieth of a point, a margin due in no small part to that indefinable magic she radiated called star quality.

Handball sports

Indoor handball, the team game, featured in the 1972 Olympic Games at Munich.

Eton fives, with its upper and lower court and its buttress (to the left) would appear, to the casual observer, an eccentric game – an observation confirmed, moreover, by a glance at the rules.

by Yugoslavia). There is a World Cup run on similar lines to that of soccer, and there are women's world championships. In Britain, a mini-version is also played – 5-a-side on a smaller court.

Adherents of handball claim it is the second fastest team game to ice hockey. The play resembles that of basketball, with end-to-end movements, innumerable goal attempts, and little centre-court action. The game is played on a 38–44 × 18–22 metre court, with goals (3 metres wide, 2 metres high) at each end. The soccer-type ball weighs 15–17 oz, with a circumference of 23–24 inches (smaller and lighter for women and juniors). There are two halves, 30 min each for men, 25 min for juniors, and 20 min for women. Shorter periods are usually played in tournaments. There is free substitution to a maximum of five (one of which is a substitute goalkeeper).

Goals are scored by throwing the ball into the opponent's goal. The game starts

The name 'handball' is used for several games, most of them in some way related but one of them entirely different. The basic similarity of the majority of handball games is that a ball is hit against a wall with the hand; the exception is the team game often referred to as 'indoor handball'.

Team handball was played out-of-doors before World War II, 11-a-side on a soccer-type pitch. Originating in Germany in the late 1800s, it had a chequered development, and it was not until the formation of the International Amateur Handball Federation in 1928 that it emerged as an organized sport. It was included in the 1936 Olympics (Germany winning), and the first world championships were held in 1938.

After the war, however, international handball stagnated; the IAHF was dissolved, and superseded by the International Handball Federation. More significant, though, were the radical changes that were taking place in Northern Europe. The game went indoors and was played 7-a-side on a much smaller arena. This form of the sport spread like wildfire, and although the 11-a-side game is still played in Central Europe, *indoor handball*, as it is known (although it may be played outdoors), has become a world sport. Now played by some 5 million people in more than 40 countries, it was included in the 1972 Olympics (won

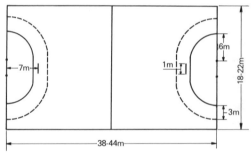

The court for team handball. The goals, which are 3 metres wide, stand 2 metres high. Two 6-metre radius quarter circles joined by a straight line (unbroken line) form the goal area, in which only the goalkeeper is allowed. The broken line, a constant 3 metres away from the goal-area line is called the free throw line. When a defender commits an infringement between the two lines, a free throw is awarded to the attacking side to be taken from the nearest point outside the free throw line. The 1-metre line between the two lines and directly in front of the goal is the penalty throw line, 7 metres from the goal.

with a *throw off* from the centre, the usual pattern being for the attacking side to build for an attempt at goal, with the defending side protecting their goal until either a goal is scored or they get possession. Players may stop, catch, throw, bounce, or strike the ball with their hands, arms, head, body, thighs, or knees. (Only the goalkeeper may use his feet, and then only to stop a ball travelling goalwards.) Players may hold the ball for a maximum of 3 sec, and take a maximum three steps while holding the ball. They may bounce the ball once and catch it, or dribble one-handed, basket-ball-style. The flat of the hand may be used to play the ball from an opponent, and obstruction with the body is per-mitted. Only the goalkeeper may be in the goal area, and he may defend his goal and move about without restrictions to steps and time. There are goal throws, corner throws, throw ins, free throws, and penalty throws (taken from 7 metres). The game is controlled by two referees, assisted by a timekeeper and a scorer.

Excluding the English variations of fives, there are three major forms of 'wall' handball – *soft-ball four-wall, soft-ball one-wall*, and *hard-ball four-wall Irish handball*. They can be played as singles or doubles. In the Irish game, players can kick the ball and hit it with either hand, whereas the soft-ball games allow the use of one hand only. In all three, the first player or pair to 21 is the winner. Only the server or side serving can win points.

The wall handball games probably originated in Ireland. The one-wall game caught on in America, where it is still popular in New York. But it has largely been superseded by four-wall handball, played in North America on a 40×20 ft court and in Ireland and Australia on a 60×30 ft court. World championships, held every three years, were first staged in 1964.

Eton, Rugby, and Winchester fives come from the English public schools after which they are named, although these are more developments of hand-ball of earlier eras than pure innovations. The players hit a small cork-and-rubber ball with the hands covered to the wrists with padded gloves.

Eton fives was developed in the early 19th century by Eton boys hitting a ball against their chapel wall. And when courts were built, they incorporated all the special features, such as step and buttress, of the original playing area. There is a front wall plus two sides, and a shallow step divides the court into an upper and lower section. The game is played by two pairs. The server stands in the upper court – his side is *up* – and the receiver in the lower court – his side is *down*. The other two also stand in the lower court. The ball must be served above a ledge $4\frac{1}{2}$ ft from the floor, bounce off the right-hand wall, and land in the

One of the many variations of handball, a three-wall version popular in Australia, where it was introduced and fostered over the years by Catholic teaching orders from Ireland.

lower court. The return – the *first cut* – must hit either the right-hand wall and then the front wall above the line (ledge), or the front wall above the line and be-tween the right-hand wall and a vertical line 3 ft 8 in from it. When the receiver decides to make the first cut (he 'need not return the first or any service until he gets one to his mind') and it does not fulfil the requirements, the return is called a *blackguard* and may be played by the side 'up'. Only the serving side wins points. The first side to 12 points wins the game (although it may be 'set' as in badminton, at 10- or 11-all); the first to three games wins the match.

Rugby fives can be played either singles or doubles. The court has four walls, and the front wall (15 ft high by 18 ft) has a board across it $2\frac{1}{2}$ ft from the floor above which the ball must be hit. The court is 28 ft long, the back wall 6 ft high. Unique to Rugby fives is the scoring system whereby only the person receiving the service may score. A serve that hits the front wall without hitting the side wall first is a *blackguard*, which the receiver may return if he calls his intention to do so. The game is 15-up (setting to 2 at 14-all).

Winchester fives is like Rugby fives, but has a small buttress along the left-hand wall, and only the serving side can score. It is played singles or doubles, 15-up.

Hockey sports

Men have played team games with sticks and a ball for thousands of years. They probably originated in Persia, from where they were introduced to ancient Greece and then in Roman times to the extremities of the empire, in particular the British Isles.

The sport that evolved in the Scottish Highlands was called *shinty*; that in Ireland, *hurling*. It is generally accepted that hurling was the true ancestor of the game that was played in England and Wales called first 'bandy' or 'bandy ball' and later *hockey*.

Hockey

The derivation of the word 'hockey' is uncertain, one theory being that it came from an old French word 'hoquet' meaning 'shepherd's crook'. Like early football, the game was frequently suppressed, but it also survived.

The game began to be organized in the mid-1800s, and the Hockey Association, formed in 1886, formulated the first set of rules. The game spread from England to other countries, and the International Hockey Board was set up in Britain in 1900. England beat Ireland 8-1 in the final of the first Olympic hockey tournament, in 1908, Scotland and Wales sharing the bronze. The event was next held in 1920, when Great Britain beat Denmark and Belgium to win the gold medals. But hockey was dropped for 1924, precipitating the setting up of a truly international governing body, the Fédération Internationale de Hockey (FIH), which

gradually began to exercise control over all aspects of the international game.

Hockey returned to the Olympic scene permanently in 1928, and India began her long domination of the sport. The game was introduced there by British servicemen in the early 1900s, and India and later Pakistan won every Olympic hockey title from 1928 to 1968, until West Germany broke their hold before a partisan crowd in 1972. The game also flourished in other countries in Western Europe and in Australia and New Zealand. The first World Cup tournament, played in Spain in 1971, was won by Pakistan.

Women first played hockey in 1887 at East Molesey, the Irish Ladies' Hockey Union was set up in 1894, and the All-England Women's Hockey Association in 1895. The latter body was to exert a great influence on the game. The International Federation of Women's Hockey Associations was founded in 1927, but it was another 40 years before the Women's International Hockey Rules Board was formed to try to unify rules throughout the world. Closer co-operation between the men's and women's administrative bodies was established, and in the early 1970s women were experimenting with the rules used in men's hockey.

Women's hockey emphasizes sportsmanship above all, and little international hockey has been played. England are traditionally strong, and it is common to find Wembley invaded by 50,000 shrieking schoolgirls for their internationals.

Hockey is played 11-a-side (with up to two substitutes in the men's game) over 70 minutes divided into two halves. The players usually line up in the old soccer-style 2-3-5 formation in front of the goalkeeper. They may use only the flat side of the stick for striking the ball. Sticks must weigh 12–28 oz (23-oz maximum for women) and be able to pass through a

Top: *Women's hockey – the England defence lines up behind the goal line as a German opponent prepares to take a short corner in an international at Wembley.* Above: *Men's hockey – a defender rushes out after a corner to try to block a shot.*

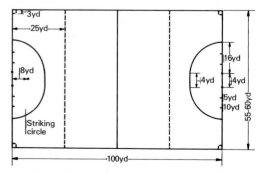

Pitch markings and measurements for men's hockey. For women's hockey, a dotted line is marked 5 yards in from each side line.

2-in-diameter ring. The white ball is leather-covered, has a cork and twine core, and weighs $5\frac{1}{2}$–$5\frac{3}{4}$ oz with a circumference of $8\frac{13}{16}$–$9\frac{1}{4}$ in. The goals are 4 yd wide and 7 ft high, with nets. Goals may be scored only from the striking circles, 16-yd-radius 'flattened' semi-circles around each goal. The game is controlled by two umpires.

A feature of hockey is the *bully*, which is used to start the game at the beginning of each half, after goals have been scored, and in certain other instances. Two opposing players stand opposite each other, over the ball and facing the side lines. They tap the ground and each other's stick three times and then play the ball.

The rules of hockey are similar in many ways to those of soccer. When the ball goes out over the side lines, it is brought back into play with a *push-in* (women still use the *roll-in*). Balls hit over the goal lines are brought back with a *free hit*, a *long corner*, or a *penalty*, or *short, corner*, depending on how the ball went out of play. Offences include raising the stick above shoulder height when striking the ball (called 'sticks'), touching the ball with the back of the stick, stopping the ball with any part of the body but the hand (the goalkeeper may use any part of the body or pad in his own circle), hooking an opponent's stick, obstruction, dangerous or rough play, and offside (as in soccer, but three defenders instead of two in women's hockey).

Offences committed outside the shooting circle are punished with a *free hit* to the other side. For offences inside the circle, either a *penalty corner* or a *penalty stroke* (*penalty bully* in women's hockey) is awarded. A penalty corner is a free hit on the goal line at least 10 yd from a goal post. Defenders (a maximum of six) must stand behind the goal line, and the ball is played out to attackers, standing initially

outside the circle, who must stop the ball with stick or hand before shooting. The penalty stroke, which is awarded for intentional offences or infringements preventing a goal, is a free hit 8 yd in front of goal, with only the goalkeeper defending it. The women's penalty bully is a bully, between one player from each side, 5 yd in front of goal, with all other players standing beyond the 25-yd line.

Hurling and shinty

Hurling, a sport almost exclusive to Ireland, is played 15-a-side on a large pitch (maximum 160×100 yd) with goals 7 yd wide, posts 16 ft high, and a crossbar 8 ft from the ground. Players use their *hurleys* (sticks) to hurl the ball 70 or 80 yards or carry it in solo runs, or fight for possession. They can strike the ball in the air or pull it down with a hand. A goal (under the crossbar) is worth 3 points; a shot over the bar, 1 point. The game, controlled by the Gaelic Athletic Association, is fast and furious, and the final of the All-Ireland Championship has attracted crowds of 80,000 to Croke Park, Dublin.

Shinty, confined mainly to Scotland, is 90 minutes of hard hitting, fast running, and quick interceptions. Controlled by the Camanachd Association (founded in 1893), it is also called 'Camanachd'. Shinty is played 12-a-side on a pitch as large as 200×100 yd, with *hails* (goals) 12 ft wide and 10 ft high. The rules are similar to those of hockey, but players may use both sides of the *caman* (stick) and only the goalkeeper may handle the ball.

Below: *Bandy, a world championship match between Norway and Sweden in Moscow. An 11-a-side game with rules similar to those of soccer, it has been largely superseded by ice hockey.*

Hurling, a fast and furious game in which flying sticks are commonplace.

Shinty, a game for the hardy as depicted in this 1920s photograph of a counties match.

HOCKEY AND HURLING 'MOSTS'

Hockey
Olympic golds – 7 India
Highest score – India 24 USA 1 (1932 Olympics)
Individual – 10 Rup Singh (India v USA, 1932)
Women – England 23 France 0 (Surrey, 1923)
Attendance – 60,707 women's international
   (England v Wales, Wembley, 1969)

Hurling
All-Ireland Championship – 22 Tipperary
Attendance – 84,856 (Cork v Wexford, Croke
   Park, 1954)

Horse racing

Horse racing, which had its origins in sporting challenge matches between members of the aristocracy, is now big business in almost every country in the world.

The sporting instinct, happily, is not dead. But when a single horse can be valued at over $6 million (as the American colt Secretariat was in 1973), clearly the breeding and racing of the Thoroughbred represent vital commercial factors to countless states and individuals.

As international traffic in horses, for racing and breeding purposes, is now so widespread, the struggle for dominance is in deadly earnest. Those countries that lead in the production of class Thoroughbreds can look upon the horse as a contributor for the good in the balance of payments situation.

Although most nations seem to have their economic troubles, racing and breeding continue to survive and thrive everywhere. There has never been greater world-wide demand for horses – so much so, in fact, that the purchase price of any young horse before he goes into training is almost invariably out of all proportion to his earning capacity.

For those who strike it lucky, the pickings can be very rich. For instance, the Austrian-born club owner Henry Zeisel gave 3,000 guineas for Rheingold as a yearling, watched him carry his colours to victories worth over £300,000, then retained a couple of the 40 shares when the colt was syndicated for stud duty for over £1 million. That experience acts as a spur to hundreds of hopeful new owners, the vast majority of whom will end as losers.

The practice of partnerships and syndicate ownership of racehorses is now becoming more prevalent all over the world. This is the result of inflationary tendencies, and spreads the risk of loss in what may be a very expensive animal. Of course, the communist bloc long ago carried this idea to its extreme, for all racehorses there are the property of the state. The sport is carried on more for prestige than any ideas of profit or pleasure.

In most countries the racehorse is basically a medium for gambling. The purists maintain that the purpose of racing is the improvement of the breed; in practice, however, precious few people care whether this year's Derby winner is better than last year's – particularly if they have not backed him.

Indeed, it is arguable that the breed is not improving (on the score of soundness it has surely deteriorated). But people want something to bet on, and racing provides a colourful and often pleasurable method of gambling. The quality of the contestants need not concern the backer, bookmaker, totalisator authority, or government; all that any of them really worry about is the revenue they can make from betting.

Most nations derive considerable funds from the operation of the totalisator (*pari mutuel*), permitting only this type of wagering. Other countries, including Britain, still sanction bookmaking as well, collecting taxes from that sector of the industry.

There have been frequent attempts to outlaw bookmakers in the British Isles, but all have been doomed to failure. The British backer has frequently demonstrated his preference for a personal battle with the 'bookie' rather than a dull encounter with the mindless machine. And the abortive 'Roll-up' bet, in which the punter was required to forecast the first six, in correct finishing order, in a specially arranged handicap of 16 runners, should have been sufficient indication to the authorities that such lotteries have no place in horse racing. Bookmakers, however, have undoubtedly slowed the progress of racing in Britain. Had they been banned at the turn of the century, when the United States and France were already operating only *pari mutuel* betting, the collection and administration of revenue from wagering would now be far simpler, more efficient, and more beneficial to the industry.

While the United States offers splendid spectator facilities and the French prize-money structure is the envy of the world, the British Betting Levy Board gathers insufficient funds to make significant improvements at antediluvian racecourses or to provide adequate purses. It is a sorry situation for England, which evolved the Thoroughbred and gave racing to the world. In recent years it has been forced to rely increasingly on commercial sponsorships from big companies to improve the prize-money structure.

The Thoroughbred was developed in England in the early 18th century as the result of crossing imported Eastern stallions on native-bred (or possibly earlier-imported) mares. The Eastern horses were noted for their powers of

Archer, Fred (GB), was the outstanding jockey of the late 19th century. A dashing, fearless competitor, he was champion for 13 consecutive seasons, until his suicide at the age of 29 during an attack of typhoid. His tally of 21 classic victories (including 5 Derbies) has been

beaten only twice, and his score of 2,748 winners remained a record until Gordon Richards surpassed it in 1943.

Breasley, Scobie (Australia), had a long and successful career as a jockey, both in his native land and in England, retaining his cunning and judgement of pace until the last. He rode his first winner in 1928, but his greatest achievements were reserved for the 1950s and 60s in England, when he was 4 times champion and won Derbies on Santa Claus and Charlottown, the latter at the age of 52.

Donoghue, Steve (GB), a consummate horseman, fearless and with wonderful judgement of pace, rapidly became a public idol and was champion from 1914 to 1923. He was particularly formidable at Epsom, where he won 4 Derbies in 5 years, including a unique hat-trick (1921–23). Towards the end of his career he was identified with the successes of the magnificent stayer Brown Jack.

Opposite page: *The finish of the 1922 Epsom Derby. Steve Donoghue brings Captain Cuttle home by 4 lengths. He rode 6 Derby winners in 11 years.* Left: *Joy for 6-time Derby winner Lester Piggott and owner Henry Zeisel after their 1973 'Arc' triumph with Rheingold.*

Horse racing

O'Brien, Vincent (Ireland), has proved himself one of the most brilliant and versatile racehorse trainers of all time. He first made his name with jumpers, saddling the winners of 4 Cheltenham Gold Cups, 3 Champion Hurdles, and 3 Grand Nationals between 1948 and 1955. When he switched to flat racing, O'Brien soon had a pair of champions in Ballymoss (St Leger, Prix de l'Arc de Triomphe, Irish Derby, Eclipse Stakes, King George VI and Queen Elizabeth Stakes) and Gladness (Ascot Gold Cup, Ebor Handicap). In the following years O'Brien gathered together the most formidable stable in the British Isles, his classic victories including the Epsom Derby with Sir Ivor, Nijinsky, and Roberto.

Piggott, Lester (GB), is regarded by many good judges as the best jockey of all time. An infant prodigy, he rode his first winner at the age of 12, and 6 years later won his first Derby on Never Say Die (1954). There were periodic brushes with the Stewards, who sometimes considered his fearless style a menace to his colleagues, but experience taught him to temper fearlessness with safety. By the end of the 1960s Piggott had perfected a style which looked ungainly, but which none of his rivals could match for effectiveness. With short stirrups and his behind high in the air, he appears to have little control over his mounts. But remarkable strength, uncanny judgement of pace, and an astonishing intuition that tells him how all his rivals are going are the attributes that make him outstanding. Nine times champion jockey and partner of 20 English classic winners, he has been associated with many of the best horses of his time — notably Nijinsky, Sir Ivor, Crepello, Park Top, Petite Etoile, Karabas, St Paddy, and Rheingold.

endurance, and their union with the speedy English mares produced a horse that soon outstripped all other breeds for racing purposes. Three imported stallions were particularly influential in this development process – the Byerly Turk, the Darley Arabian, and the Godolphin Arabian.

There is not a racehorse in the world today that does not trace in the direct male line to one of these great orientals. Indeed, the lines may be traced to just three great English-bred racehorses – Matchem (foaled in 1748), grandson of the Godolphin Arabian; Herod (1758), great-great-grandson of the Byerly Turk; and Eclipse (1764), great-great-grandson of the Darley Arabian. Of the trio, the Eclipse line is easily dominant.

In the early days, races were run over long distances – sometimes as much as 12 miles, but as the Thoroughbred became more precocious, shorter events were introduced. Today, the principal flat races throughout the world are generally for 2- and 3-year-olds, and few are of more than 2 miles.

Hurdlers and steeplechasers cover longer journeys at their more leisurely pace, and arguably give the spectator better value for money with the added excitement of jumping. This branch of

the sport grew out of hunting, and originated in Ireland in 1752. Its popularity continues to grow in Britain, though it has fallen out of favour in many other countries, where people tend to bet less on jumpers and revenue from betting is the sole reason for racing.

The English Jockey Club, formed in about 1750, is generally regarded as the original governing body of the sport. Similar committees of dedicated men wield the power in racing in most countries of the world, though in some cases the Ministries of Agriculture take responsibility.

Over the years, the British Isles, the United States, and France have been regarded as the principal producers of top-grade stock. However, in recent years many other nations, most particularly Australia and New Zealand, have been demonstrating that their best can compare with the best from anywhere. The modern top-class Thoroughbred is almost invariably an international product. The pick of the Americans trace to British imports of the 1940–50 period, while many top European campaigners descend from American stock, a remarkable situation considering the vast disparity in conditions between North America and Europe.

Tattenham Corner, where Derbies are won and lost, and Gordon Richards is perfectly positioned in second place to take Pinza on to a 4-length victory, and crown his career at last with a win in the Derby.

Memorable moments in sport

The gallant Crisp

Dateline: Aintree, 31 March 1973. The Grand National course of 4 miles 856 yd, over 30 tough fences, is among the most demanding in the world. It is rare for more than half the field to complete it. So, when a horse is asked to tackle it with 12 stone on his back, and the prospect of having to concede up to 28 lb to a field of 37 rivals, his task can only be described as monumental. This was the question asked of Crisp in 1973.

With the going very fast, it was obvious that the pace would be good. Crisp, bred in Australia, had come to England with the reputation of being a 2-mile specialist, so his stamina would clearly be put to the test.

Right from the start, Dick Pitman had Crisp with the leaders, and for the first six fences he matched strides with Grey Sombrero, who then made a mistake. The Australian was left in front. It was to be another 3½ miles before Crisp and Pitman saw another horse.

At the end of the first circuit, Crisp had a lead of 20 lengths and was jumping like a stag, foot-perfect at every leap. He came to the 20th fence just as the

Crisp (right) fails by just three-quarters of a length to hold off Red Rum.

second, Red Rum, landed over the 19th.

Brian Fletcher, on Red Rum, had intended to wait longer, but Crisp's relentless gallop forced him into making an earlier move. At the final turn, with two fences to jump, Crisp was still well clear, but Red Rum was marginally closing the gap. As they approached the final fence, the difference was 15 lengths. Pitman glanced back and it was a look which must have given Fletcher hope.

On the 484 yards run-in it became obvious that Crisp had given his all. Pitman drew his whip, but the gallant 10-year-old swerved away from it and Red Rum came ominously closer. Red Rum was really running on to some purpose now, while Crisp, the prize within his grasp for so long, was stopping fast, anchored by his weight, 23 lb more than his challenger.

Just 10 yards from the goal, Crisp had to concede defeat. He had treated the world's most formidable fences with contempt, but he could not beat the handicapper as well.

Only then did the magnificence of Crisp's achievement become apparent. He had forced Red Rum to complete the journey in 9 min 1.9 sec, no less than 18½ sec faster than the record set by Golden Miller 39 years before and which many had thought invulnerable.

Richards, Gordon (GB), established riding records on the British Turf which may stand for all time. He was champion jockey 26 times (in a 29-year period); rode 4,870 winners in his career; rode 12 consecutive winners in 1933; amassed 269 successes in 1947. British racing has never known a more popular figure, a fact recognized by the award of a knighthood in 1953, which Richards celebrated by winning his only Derby, on Pinza. Short, stocky, but very strong, Richards was invariably fast away from the tapes, and he always seemed to have his mounts perfectly balanced and in the right place at the right time.

Saint-Martin, Yves (France), has proved the outstanding French jockey of the post-war period. His career started inauspiciously when he fell off his very first mount in public, but by the age of 19 he was champion jockey. Riding as first jockey to the powerful François Mathet stable, he chalked up several classic victories, including an Epsom Derby with Relko and four wins in the French equivalent, the Prix du Jockey-Club. In 1973 he was associated with the great filly Allez France and notched his 10th jockeys' title.

Shoemaker, Willie (US), is the most successful jockey in history. To the end of 1972 he had ridden the winners of 6,439 races worth almost $50,000,000. Three Kentucky Derbys, 2 Preakness Stakes, and 4 Belmont Stakes highlight the career of the midget millionaire who set a world standard with 485 wins in a season in 1953. His most famous mounts include Swaps, Damascus, and Gallant Man.

Winter, Fred (GB), has enjoyed two highly successful careers in jump racing. After proving himself the outstanding jockey in the post-war era, he turned to training and saddled the Grand National winner in each of his first two seasons. As a jockey he won 2 Grand Nationals, 2 Cheltenham Gold Cups, and 3 Champion Hurdles, as well as a memorable Grand Steeplechase de Paris on Mandarin. In the 1972–73 season he saddled the winners of a record £78,927.

117

Arkle (right), trained by Tom Dreaper and with Pat Taaffe up as always, jumps a fence with Mill House in the 1965 Cheltenham Gold Cup. He beat the English champion by 20 lengths. In 1964 he had beaten 1963 winner Mill House by 5 lengths, and in 1966 he chalked up his third victory in the jumping classic.

Arkle (Ireland) was probably the most popular horse to race in the British Isles. From 1962 to 1966 he ran 26 times over fences, won 22, and proved himself the greatest steeplechaser of all time. He took on top class rivals, often at what seemed impossible handicap terms, but almost invariably came out on top. His wins included 3 Cheltenham Gold Cups, a Hennessy Gold Cup, King George VI 'Chase, and 3 Leopardstown 'Chases. A broken bone in a foot caused his retirement in December 1966, and 'get well' cards flooded into his Irish stable from all over the world.

Brigadier Gerard (England) compiled an outstanding record of 17 wins from 18 starts between 1970 and 1972, and earned for himself the title of the best miler ever produced in England. He scored a marvellous victory over Mill Reef in the 2,000 Guineas, then showed that his talents were not limited to short distances by two victories in the 1¼ miles Champion Stakes and a win in the 1½ miles King George VI & Queen Elizabeth Stakes.

Eclipse (England) was the first great horse in Turf history. Never beaten, nor even extended, in 18 starts in the 1769 and 1770 seasons, he naturally captured the imagination of the sporting public. He subsequently became an important stallion and though he was overshadowed in his own lifetime by a near-contemporary sire in Highflyer, it is the Eclipse male line that has stood the test of time, and some 75% of the world's Thoroughbred population traces directly to him.

Golden Miller (England) landed 5 consecutive Cheltenham Gold Cups in the 1930s, establishing himself as the greatest 'chaser of his era. In 1934 he became the only horse ever to complete the double of Cheltenham Gold Cup and Grand National. His record reads all the better for the fact that he retained his form despite an eccentric owner who made a habit of changing the gelding's trainers and jockeys.

Memorable moments in sport

Secretariat superhorse

Dateline: Belmont Park, New York, 9 June 1973. A crowd of 69,138 turned up for the prospect of seeing the completion of the first Triple Crown in American racing for 25 years. On 6 occasions in the last 15 years there had been a similar situation, but the third leg, the 1½-mile Belmont Stakes, had always proved too much. This time it would be different; this time the contender was Secretariat.

The bright-red chestnut had already lowered the track record in the Kentucky Derby and had come very close to repeating the feat when landing the Preakness Stakes. This time he apparently had only one worthy rival – his Derby and Preakness runner-up Sham – but the distance would surely test him. His

pedigree suggested that he would not be capable of comparable performance over 12 furlongs.

When the stalls opened, Secretariat and Sham at once fought for the lead and after the first half-mile had been completed in 46.2 sec they were separated by a head. Secretariat's trainer, Lucien Laurin, was distinctly worried. 'They're going too fast', he told owner Penny Tweedy.

One, or both, must crack. The pace was suicidal. After another furlong it happened; Sham, a great horse, had to give way to Secretariat, the 'superhorse'.

Secretariat completed a mile in 1 min 34.2 sec, just three-fifths of a second off the track record for that distance, and he was still drawing away. It was not that his rivals were stopping; it was Secretariat's relentless drive that was carrying him clear. This took him through 10 furlongs in 1 min 59 sec, a second inside the track record, and by now his lead was 20 lengths.

His last quarter-mile was, understandably, his slowest, but he was still going faster than his weary opponents and he reached the post an incredible 31 lengths clear in 2 min 24 sec, breaking the American dirt-track record by 2.2 sec. Such was his momentum that jockey Ron Turcotte had great difficulty in pulling Secretariat up; indeed, the colt was clocked a second inside the world record for 13 furlongs as he came to a halt.

Secretariat was not invincible; he was beaten a few times. But on Belmont Day he ran the greatest race in history.

RACING RECORDS

Times

5 furlongs	53.6 sec	Indigenous	Epsom, England (1960)
6 furlongs	1 min 6.2 sec	gelding by Blink/Broken Tendril	Brighton, England (1929)
7 furlongs	1 min 19.8 sec	Last Case	Brighton, England (1966)
	1 min 19.8 sec	Triple Bend	Hollywood Park, USA (1972)
1 mile	1 min 31.8 sec	Soueida	Brighton, England (1963)
	1 min 31.8 sec	Loose Cover	Brighton, England (1966)
1¼ miles	1 min 58.0 sec	Quilche	Santa Anita Park, USA (1970)
1½ miles	2 min 23.0 sec	Fiddle Isle	Santa Anita Park, USA (1970)
1¾ miles	2 min 50.8 sec	Swartz Pete	Alexandra Park, NZ (1966)
2 miles	3 min 15.0 sec	Polazel	Salisbury, England (1924)

Jockeys

Winners – career	6,439*	W. Shoemaker, US (GB 4,870 G. Richards)
– in year	515	S. Hawley (Canada), US, 1973 (GB 269 G. Richards, 1947)
– consecutive	12	G. Richards (GB, 1933); P. Stroebel (Rhodesia, 1958)
Championships	26	G. Richards (1925–53)
Classics	27	F. Buckle (1792–1823)
Derbies	6	J. Robinson (1817–36); S. Donoghue (1915–25); L. Piggott (1954–72)

Trainers

Winners – career	3,596	H. Jacobs, US
– in year	305	D Baird, US, 1973 (GB 146 J. Day, 1867)
Money in year	$2,456,250	E. A. Neloy, US, 1966 (GB £256,899 N. Murless, 1967)
Classics	41	J. Scott (1827–62)
Derbies	7	R. Robson (1793–1823); J. Porter (1868–99); F. Darling (1922–41)

Owners

Winners in year	393	M. H. Van Berg, US, 1969 (GB 115 D. Robinson, 1973)
Money in year	$1,605,896	S. Sommer, US, 1972 (GB £182,059 C. W. Engelhard, 1970)

Horses

Wins	89	Kingston, US, 1885–94 (Europe 80 Catherina, GB, 1833–41)
Consecutive wins	56	Camarero, Puerto Rico, 1953–5 (Europe 54 Kincsem, Hung, 1877–80)
Money	$1,977,896	Kelso, US, 1959–66 /Europe $933,291 Rheingold, GB, 1971–73)
– in year	$860,404	Secretariat, US, 1973
Champion sire	16	Lexington, US, 1861–81 (GB 12 Highflyer, 1785–98)

Sale prices

Syndication	$6,080,000 Secretariat, US, 1973
In training	$725,000 Typecast, US, 1973 (Europe 136,000 gns Vaguely Noble, 1967)
Yearling	$600,000 colt by Bold Ruler ex Iskra, US, 1973 (Europe 117,000 gns Princely Review, 1971)
Broodmare	$450,000 What a Treat, US, 1972 (Europe 1,020,000Fr Hula Dancer, 1968)

Most runners

Most runners	66	Grand National (Aintree, England) 1929
– flat	58	Lincolnshire Handicap (Lincoln, England) 1948

* To end of 1972.

Man o' War (USA), the most brilliant American racehorse of his time, could seemingly beat time records and all opposition at any distance, and for two years (1919–20) carried all before him. Always odds-on favourite, his solitary defeat in 21 starts came when a colt called Upset held him off by half a length, thanks to a 15 lb weight concession and the poor riding of Man o' War's jockey. As a 3-year-old, Man 'o War won all his 11 races and in three of them he started at 100–1 on.

Ormonde (England) was probably the best horse ever trained in England. He raced for three seasons, in an era of thoroughly top-class performers, and he always beat them hollow. From 6 furlongs to 1¾ miles he was unbeatable, his successes including the Triple Crown of 2,000 Guineas, Derby, and St Leger in 1886. Long before the end of his 16-race career, he was suffering from roaring (a wind infirmity), but not even that could stop him.

Phar Lap (NZ) is generally regarded as the best horse ever to race in Australia, where he was imported from his native New Zealand. From 51 races, he won 37 times, including 2 Derbies, 2 St Legers, and a memorable Melbourne Cup. He went to America in 1933 to run in the Agua Caliente Handicap in Mexico and won easily in track record time, taking him within a few thousand dollars of becoming the world's leading stakes-winner. But a fortnight later Phar Lap was dead, poisoned in California.

Ribot (Italy) compiled a perfect record of 16 wins in 16 starts, beating the best that Europe could put against him in the mid-1950s. His performances in his own country made him easily the best horse there, but it was not until his victory in the 1955 Prix de l'Arc de Triomphe that his brilliance was fully appreciated. The next year, when he won the King George VI & Queen Elizabeth Stakes by 5 lengths and a second Arc de Triomphe by 6 lengths, he set the seal on his greatness. Ribot was later to become the world's outstanding sire of classic horses, dying in America in 1972.

Ridden in all his 16 races by Enrico Camici, Ribot climaxed his unbeaten career with a 6-length victory in the 1956 Prix de l'Arc de Triomphe, his second consecutive win in the Longchamp classic.

In Britain, 'women only' races were held for the first time in 1972, with 'mixed' races appearing in 1974. In America, however, jockettes, as they are called, have been competing against men since the late 1960s. Former Hollywood starlet Robyn Smith (left) has been one of the most successful.

Horse racing terms

Accumulator A single bet attempting to name the winners of 4 or more races.
Aged Describing a horse 6 or more years old.
Bay Lightish-brown horse.
Bit Bridle mouthpiece; hence *on the bit*, being restrained.
Blaze White broad mark on face extending over the bones of the nose.
Blinkers Mask limiting a horse's sideways vision.
Brood Mare Mare used for breeding.
Classics The most important races in a particular country; in England, the 5 main 3-year-old races (2,000 and 1,000 Guineas, Derby, Oaks, and St Leger).
Colt Male racehorse under 5 years old.
Dam Brood mare with offspring.
Distance Winning margin of 240 yd or more.
Double A bet attempting to name the winners of 2 races; both horses must win.
Each way In betting, backing a horse both to win and to be placed (finish in first 2, 3, or 4, depending on number of runners and type of race).
Foal Horse under a year old.
Field The runners in a race.
Filly Female horse under 5 years old.
Gelding Castrated horse.
Going State of the ground.
Hand Unit for measuring horses (from ground to withers), equals 4 inches.
Handicap Races in which horses are allotted weights according to an assessment of their chances, in order to equalize their prospects of winning.
Horse Male racehorse 5 or more years old.
Leather Strap connecting stirrup to saddle.
Maiden Horse without a win.
Mare Female horse 5 or more years old.
Match A race arranged between two horses.
Nursery Handicap for 2-year-olds.
Plate Horse's shoe; race with prize money guaranteed by the course.
Selling race Race, for lowest-class of horses, in which the winner must be offered for auction and any other runner may be claimed for a set sum.
Sire Stallion with offspring.
Stallion Horse at stud for breeding.
Starting price The last price quoted on course by leading bookmakers, established by officials; off-course bets are usually settled at these odds.
Stirrups Supports for jockey's feet, suspended from saddle.
Sweepstake Race in which prize money is made up of owners' contributions (such as entry fees and forfeits), sometimes with added money.
Thoroughbred Racehorse with pedigree recorded in stud-book.
Treble A bet attempting to name the winners of 3 races.
Walk-over A race in which there is only one runner, which must walk past judge's box to win.
Weight-for-age A scale of weighting used for races open to all ages.
Yearling Horse between 1 and 2 years old.

Sceptre (England) ranks as perhaps the finest filly ever to race in England. She remains the only filly ever to win 4 of the 5 classic races outright, a feat she achieved in 1902. For much of her career she was owned and trained by the reckless gambler Bob Sievier, who subjected her to a rigorous programme. In June 1902 she had 5 races in 15 days, but she won 3 of them, including the Oaks. Racing until she was 5, Sceptre won 13 of her 25 races and was placed 8 times.

Sea-Bird (France) beat what most observers regarded as the greatest field ever to line up for a classic race when he won the 1965 Prix de l'Arc de Triomphe in a canter by 6 lengths. On that performance alone, he must take rank as one of the all-time greats. He had also won the Epsom Derby and 5 of his other 6 starts. In his Arc de Triomphe victory he had behind him the winners of the French, Irish, American, and Russian Derbies, besides a host of other brilliant runners.

Secretariat (USA) became in 1973 the first horse for 25 years to complete the American Triple Crown of Kentucky Derby, Preakness Stakes, and Belmont Stakes. Before these successes, he had been the champion 2-year-old and was already syndicated for stud purposes for a world-record $6,080,000. The Triple Crown – most especially his crushing 31 lengths victory in the Belmont – clinched his place in history. Perfect in conformation and performance, he may have been the greatest racehorse of all time.

Harness racing

Enthusiastically supported in the United States, Australia, and New Zealand, and to a lesser extent in Europe, harness racing traces its origins to the late 18th century. It was then, following the import of the English thoroughbred Messenger to the United States in 1788, that the standardbred horse had its beginnings. And it is the standardbred that is used in the two methods of harness racing – pacing and trotting.

Standardbred horses are so called because they have to attain a set standard of speed before they are registered. Pacers and trotters are similar in that both are required to travel around an oval track at a specified gait while pulling the driver sitting in a two-wheeled sulky. Frequently they receive handicaps of distance according to their record.

It is in their gait that they differ. Trotters move their left front leg and right back leg forward simultaneously, whereas pacers move both left (or right) legs forward in what is known as a lateral gait. In addition, pacers wear straps called hopples to ensure they do not change their gait or break into a gallop. The unhoppled trotter is more likely to do this, and as a result requires much more schooling than his fellow standardbred.

It is not surprising, therefore, that many trainers prefer to school pacers, and, especially in Australia and New Zealand, pacing, which is the faster of the two, is by far the more popular. In

New Zealand pacer Caduceus raced successfully in Australia, America, and Canada.

most of Europe, however, pacing is banned and trotting thrives, though in Wales, where harness racing was boosted by the opening of the Prestatyn Raceway in the early 1960s, pacing is dominant.

Although harness racing was active in Australia and the United States from the mid-1800s, it was not until the advent of evening meetings and mobile starting gates in the post-World War II era that the sport enjoyed the enormous support it has today. Prize money for the major races often rivals and exceeds that of horse racing.

For example, the Hambletonian – America's 3-year-old trotting classic – offers prize money in the region of $US 125,000, while the Inter-Dominion Pacing Championships for Australian and New Zealand pacers is worth prize money of some $A 100,000. Yet even such sums are minute when compared with the amount that harness racing draws in betting. Australia's rich Miracle Mile, held in Sydney, attracts well over $A 1 million of the punters' money every year.

The 1960s saw an increasing interest being taken by American reinsmen in Australian and New Zealand horses. The first target was the New Zealand gelding Cardigan Bay, who was to become the first standardbred horse to win a million dollars and at the time of his retirement was the seventh money-winning horse of all time – the first six were thoroughbreds.

Top left: *Trotters race neck and neck at an evening meeting in the United States.* Top right: *Perhaps the earliest form of harness racing was the chariot races held in the ancient Greek Olympics. This race was staged in 1970 to mark the opening of a newly excavated Roman Hippodrome at Tyre, in the Lebanon.* Above left: *Troika races are held at the end of winter in the Moscow Hippodrome.* Above: *Trotting at Addington, the headquarters of the sport in New Zealand.*

PACING AND TROTTING 'MOSTS'

Highest price		
Trotter	$US 3,000,000	Nevele Pride (US) 1969
Pacer	$US 2,500,000	Albatross (US) 1972
Most won		
Trotter	$US 1,764,802	Une de Mai (US) (to 1973)
Pacer	$US 1,201,470	Albatross (US)
World mile record		
Trotter	1 min 55.6 sec	Noble Victory (US) 1966
Pacer	1 min 54.6 sec	Albatross (US) 1972
Drivers		
Wins	4,065	H. Filion (Canada)
Best season	605	H. Filion (Canada) 1972 (US)

Ice hockey

Anatoli Firsov at the 1968 Olympics, in which he was leading points scorer with 16.

The evergreen Gordie Howe, watched by one of his sons, Mark (right), playing for the Houston Aeros in the WHA, after a record NHL career.

Often described as the world's fastest team game, ice hockey is played six-a-side on skates, with laminated wood sticks and a vulcanized rubber puck. Amateur matches are controlled by two referees. A game is divided into three periods, each of 20 minutes actual play while the puck is in motion, measured by stop-watch. The normal line-up is a goalminder, two defencemen and three forwards, but substitutes are allowed at any time and most teams carry between 11 and 18 players.

The ideal ice rink area measures 200 × 85 ft. Barrier boards (3 ft 4 in to 4 ft high) surround the rink, which is curved at the four corners. Red goal lines are 11–15 ft from each end of the rink. In the centre of these are the goals, 4 ft high and 6 ft wide, with nets at least 2 ft deep. Two blue lines divide the rink equally into three zones (attacking, neutral, and defending), and a centre red line bisects the rink. The centre is marked by a blue spot.

Play begins with a face-off, when the puck is dropped between two opposing players, and is restarted by a face-off on the nearest of the marked spots at which a misplay occurred. Goal judges indicate a score with a red light from behind the net. Goals must be scored from the stick and not by foot or hand. But the hand may be used to drop the puck to the ice. Players are penalized for infringements by being sent off to sit on the penalty bench ('sin bin') for two or more minutes,

according to the severity of the offence.

Sticks are limited to 53 inches, but the goalminder's is wider and heavier. The puck is circular, 3 inches in diameter and 1 inch thick, weighing between $5\frac{1}{2}$ and 6 oz. The hockey skate blade is shorter than the speed skate, and only 1/16th inch wide, reinforced by hollow tubing. Protective padding is essential, with extra thick guards for the goalminder.

Roughly adapted from field hockey, the first game using a puck is claimed to have been played by Crimean War veterans in a Royal Canadian Rifles regiment when Kingston Harbour, Ontario, froze round about 1860. Montreal, and later Canada as a whole, became the

The goal lines and the centre line of an ice hockey rink are marked in red, the two lines bounding the neutral zone and dividing the rink into three equal sections, in blue. Face-offs take place at the various marked spots.

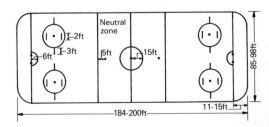

Bobby Orr of the Boston Bruins shows his precocious talents to the Toronto Maple Leafs in 1967. He fulfilled his early promise to become the most exciting player in professional hockey.

Below: *Ice hockey came back to Wembley in 1973 when the newly formed London Lions (in light jerseys) staged a number of matches against foreign opposition and then went on a highly successful European tour.*

centre of early development. The first recognized team, McGill University, was formed in 1880, playing to rules devised by two students, W. F. Robertson and R. F. Smith, in 1879. It spread to the United States in 1893, catching on in Europe around the turn of the century. A five-team league began in Britain in 1903, and the International Ice Hockey Federation was founded in 1908.

The first European championship was won by Britain in 1910. The first world and Olympic titles were decided concurrently in 1920. Canada won every Olympic event until defeated by Britain in 1936. Russia has dominated since 1964, with Czechoslovakia and Sweden the most consistent challengers. Britain's peak years dated from 1934 until the mid-1950s, when some of the big ice stadiums became too vulnerable to property developers. Meantime, the sport has expanded almost everywhere else it is played.

Professional ice hockey is controlled by a referee and two linesmen, with basically similar rules to the amateur game, slightly varied in interpretation. The National Hockey League (NHL) of North America, contested between foremost American and Canadian clubs, is the world's major professional competition. Inaugurated in 1917, it now comprises 16 teams in two sections, from which emerge contenders for the Stanley Cup, symbolic of ice hockey supremacy and won by Montreal Canadiens in 1973 for the 18th time. Toronto Maple Leafs, next most successful, had recorded 11 victories. For years, the NHL and Stanley Cup have been unquestionably the top professional tournaments, but new big-time leagues, one including European participation, may soon cause some changes to the traditional structure.

Ice hockey terms

Assist Credit to player making a pass to help a goalscorer.
Board-checking Pushing an opponent onto the boards.
Face-off Means of starting play, the referee dropping the puck between two opponents.
High-sticking Carrying the stick above shoulder level.
Hooking Impeding a player with the stick from behind.
Offside When a player precedes the puck into his attacking zone or when a loose puck travels over more than one line.
Penalty shot A free shot at goal, awarded when an attacker is fouled in a blatant scoring position.
Shut-out Achievement of a goalminder who survives a match or period without conceding a goal.
Stickhandling Retaining possession while keeping the puck moving.

ICE HOCKEY 'MOSTS'

World titles	19	Canada
Olympic titles	6	Canada
Stanley Cup wins	18	Montreal Canadiens

National Hockey League Records

Career goals	786	Gordie Howe
Season goals	76	Phil Esposito (1970-71)
Season points	152	Phil Esposito (1970-71)
Shut-outs	103	Terry Sawchuk
Games played	1,687	Gordie Howe

Hull, Bobby, reputed to have the game's fastest shot, more than 100 mph, exhibited full puck control at fast speeds. With Chicago Black Hawks, he became the first NHL player to score 50 goals in a season more than once, achieving in 1965–66 a record points score of 97 (54 goals and 43 assists). He became player-coach of Winnipeg Jets (WHA) in 1972.

Orr, Bobby, husky Boston Bruins defenceman, is widely regarded as the best all-round player the game has known. He won 4 NHL trophies in 1970 when only 22 and in his fourth professional season: best defender, outstanding Stanley Cup player, leading scorer, and most valuable player. He amply fulfilled great early promise when a child prodigy.

Sawchuck, Terry, perhaps the greatest goalminder ice hockey has had, spent most of his 18-year career with Detroit Red Wings, also playing more briefly for Boston Bruins, Toronto Maple Leafs, and Los Angeles Kings. He achieved a record 100th shut-out for the NHL in 1967 and was the pioneer of the now conventional crouching stance.

Lacrosse

Lacrosse, played mainly in North America, England, and Australia, is the direct descendant of the North American Indian pastime 'baggataway', which fascinated early adventurers in that part of the world in the 18th century.

A popular spectator sport, with brilliant running and throwing, lacrosse is played on a field measuring 110 by 70 yd maximum, with the goals, 6 ft square, placed 80–90 yd apart. Teams consist of 10 players. In the United States and Australia, up to 9 substitutes are allowed; in England, only one, in cases of injury. The object of the game is to score goals by moving the hard rubber ball ($4\frac{1}{2}$–5 oz and $7\frac{3}{4}$–8 in diameter) with the *crosse* or stick. The game took its name from the crosse, which the French travellers in eastern America saw and likened to a bishop's crozier – in French *la crosse*. The crosse is between 3 and 6 ft in length, curved at one end to accommodate a loose woven net in which the ball is carried.

A lacrosse match, played under international rules, has a duration of four periods of 15 minutes actual play. In the 10-man game, the team is made up of a goalkeeper, three defenders, three midfield players, and three attackers, and under international rules four players must remain in the defensive zone and three in the attacking zone at all times. The strain this places on the three midfield players means that these are most frequently substituted.

The Midlands (dark shirts) take on an American touring side. Women's lacrosse is widely played in Britain, which is the stronghold of the sport.

Eighty years after the first Iroquois Cup match, Lee play South Manchester (light strip) for the 1970 trophy.

The game is controlled by a referee, who rules on fouls for which the penalties range from 'free positions', 'penalty positions', and various periods of exclusion from the game. Technical fouls include offside, crease infringements (staying close to goal for too long or entering the opposition's goal area), and illegal screening. Personal fouls, more serious, include striking an opponent with the crosse, tripping, illegal body-checks, and persistent bad conduct.

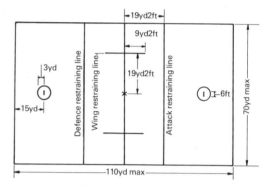

However, it is legal to *check* a man running with the ball by attempting to knock the ball from his crosse, to *shoulder charge*, or to impede his progress by means of a *body-check*.

There are two other main forms of lacrosse. *Women's lacrosse*, which bans bodily contact and checking, has two 25-minute halves and is always between teams of 12 players. And *Canadian box lacrosse* is a 6-a-side game played on a small (54×20 yd) pitch bounded by a fence to keep the ball in play.

The fragmented popularity of lacrosse in the world means that there are few international matches. Lacrosse was included in the Olympics of 1904 and 1908 (both won by Canada), and later as an exhibition sport. And a world field lacrosse tournament was held in Canada in 1967 (won by the United States) and another scheduled for Australia in 1974.

In Australia, lacrosse is played in Victoria, South Australia, and Western Australia, organized in state leagues. Canadian lacrosse is mainly box lacrosse, being popular in Ontario and British Columbia. In Britain, the main strength of the sport is in Lancashire, Cheshire, London, and the universities. The annual national championship, for the Iroquois Cup, first held in 1890, is played between the champion clubs of the North and South.

Martial arts

The 'martial arts' of unarmed combat have always featured in a soldier's preparation for war. Throughout the world, knowledge of self-defence has been a part of military training. This has naturally led to the practice of having competitions in the numerous combat sports. The ancient Olympic Games included an event called *pankration* in its programme. Contestants were allowed to throw, punch, kick, knee, elbow, strangle, gouge, or armlock their opponents. The winner was the competitor left standing. It was a savage sport in which fighters often ended up either maimed or dead.

From pankration, the different styles of unarmed combat sports were developed. The striking skills of punching and kicking and the grappling techniques involving throwing, strangling, and armlocking gradually became regularized into modern sports. Europe was where boxing and wrestling were primarily developed. In the East, the conquests of Alexander the Great led to the spread of other elements of pankration. Each region in the world added its own characteristics to evolve its particular style.

The most widespread form of grappling sport in the Orient has been *judo*, a form of jacket wrestling. This was developed from the ancient art of *ju-jitsu*, a combination of violent tricks used to hurt, often fatally, an opponent in battle. Ju-jitsu was learned by the Japanese samurai (knights) for use when they were disarmed. There were different styles of ju-jitsu, and judo (literally 'easy way') was originally only the most successful of them.

The striking skills of kicking and punching received different emphasis in different parts of the Orient. *Karate* (literally 'empty handed') was brought into Japan from the island of Okinawa by Funakoshi Gichin in 1919. It has spread throughout the world and has proved the most popular of the Oriental martial arts.

Another sport derived from ju-jitsu is *aikido*, in which little physical force is used. *Tae-kwon-do* (literally 'the way of hand and foot') developed in Korea. Its outstanding feature is when a participant jumps to a height from which he can kick at an opponent's head. *Kung-fu*, a form of Chinese fighting, has also been successful. *Thai boxing* is a formalized fighting method in which competitors in

boxing gloves and bare feet do battle in a ring similar to that of boxing. *Sumo wrestling*, popular in Japan, is a sport with considerable ceremony in which massive, almost naked, men try to push each other out of the ring (see *Wrestling*). In *kendo*, contestants wear padded armour and fight with swords.

Judo

Whereas ju-jitsu was purely a method of self-defence, judo became a sport and eventually earned Olympic recognition at the 1964 Games in Tokyo. Much of the successful development of judo is owed to the efforts of its founder, Dr Jigoro Kano, who had studied different styles of ju-jitsu before opening the Kodokan Judo School in 1882. Judo proved itself the most efficient style of ju-jitsu in a series of contests with other styles. From then on, judo expanded, first in Japan and then throughout the world, and the other schools of ju-jitsu diminished.

But it was not until after World War II that judo became truly competitive

Daigo, All Japan judo champion in 1951 and 1954, throws an opponent with a spectacular harai goshi, a sweeping left-handed loin throw.

Originating probably in the 1500s, Thai boxing is a popular professional sport in Thailand, with a large following also in Japan. Contestants are allowed to kick, knee, elbow, and use leg throws as well as punch.

Karate contestants grapple for an opening.

The massive Dutchman Anton Geesink almost disdainfully throws an opponent at the Tokyo Olympics in 1964, when he shattered the myth of Japanese invincibility by winning the open gold medal in the judo – a feat emulated in 1972 by his compatriot Willem Ruska, who won both heavyweight and open titles.

internationally. The European Judo Union was founded in 1948 and the International Judo Federation three years later. The European championships were first held in 1951 and have been staged annually ever since except for 1956.

The first world championships were held in 1956 and were dominated by the Japanese, who as inventors of the sport were still pre-eminent. But their stranglehold was broken at the 1961 Championships, when a 19-stone Dutchman, Anton Geesink, defeated the three Japanese representatives for the title. Geesink not only exposed the myth of the Japanese invincibility, but also emphasized the need for weight categories. Judo had always believed that it was possible for a skilled small man to compete on level terms with a skilled big man.

When judo was introduced to the Olympic programme in 1964 there were three weight classes plus the Open (unlimited weight) category. The Japanese representatives took the gold medals in the three weight divisions, but Geesink triumphed again in the Open category. By 1967, two other weight classes were added to the list to make five in all: lightweight (under 9 st 12 lb), welterweight (under 11 st), middleweight (under 12 st 8 lb), light-heavyweight (under 14 st 9 lb), and heavyweight (over 14 st 9 lb).

Judo competitors wear a judogi (judo suit) which is kept in place by a belt, the colour of which denotes the expertise of the exponent. A competitor attempts to win with either a clean throw, a 30-second hold-down immobilizing one limb, or by obtaining a submission from a strangle or armlock. These all end a bout immediately. But in closely fought contests, a referee and two judges give their decision as to which fighter has been the more aggressive and scored

more knock-downs on his opponent. There are no rounds in judo. The scheduled duration of a contest is usually from 3 to 10 minutes, depending on the importance of the event.

In major competitions a repechage system is employed. All the fighters in the class are divided into two pools, which are conducted on a knock-out system until there are two winners, who make up two of the semi-finalists. Any competitors who have lost to either of these pool winners then fight off between themselves to provide the other two semi-finalists. From then on the straightforward knock-out system is employed.

Women also participate in competitions, although the weight categories are lighter than for the men and there are no major international tournaments.

One attractive feature of the sport is the grading system in which all judoka (people who practise the sport) are divided into kyu (pupil) or dan (degree) grades. Both fighting ability and technical knowledge are needed before a person can be promoted. The main target of any judoka is a black belt (1st dan). After that he can proceed up the dan grades. It is possible for a judoka to reach 12th dan, but no one has been granted this honour by the Kodokan grading panel, 10th dan being the highest.

JUDO 'MOSTS'

Olympic titles	2	W. Ruska (Neth)
World titles	3	H. Minatoya (Jap)
World and Olympic	4	W. Ruska (Neth)

Karate
When Funakoshi Gichin introduced karate to the Kodokan after World War I, he excited the Japanese with the potential of this method of unarmed combat. The Okinawans had evolved a system of blows with feet, fists, elbows, knees, and even head that was both devastating in its power and versatile in its use.

Gichin founded the *shotokan* style of karate in 1936. This was the conventional system of the Okinawans but modernized by Gichin. The Japan Karate Association, the controlling body of the shotokan style, was established in 1955, and two years later they held the first All Japan Championships. This orthodox style lies between the fast-moving *shito-ryu* and the powerful *goju-*

ryu schools. It is the most popular style both in Japan and throughout the world.

The other two major schools of karate are *wado-ryu* (way of peace) and *kyoku-shinkai*, founded by the Korean Mas Oyama, and based on tremendous strength. Oyama popularized his style by fighting wild bulls, and he killed three with his bare hands.

Instructors in these styles travelled all over the world teaching their own special methods. France in the late 1950s was the first European country to take up karate seriously. The first British championships were held in 1964. By the end of the 1960s a European Karate Union was running annual European championships and a World Karate Union had staged world championships.

There are two kinds of karate contests – *kumite* (sparring) and *kata* (forms). In kumite, a contestant attempts to pierce an opponent's guard with a blow, but withdraws it before striking his opponent. The success of the effort is considered by the referee and four judges who sit in the corners of the 9-metre-square fighting area.

If any of the officials think that an *ippon* (point) or *waza-ari* (almost a point) has been scored, he blows his whistle and indicates with his red or white flag, the colour of which approximates to the belt of the successful fighter. If the referee agrees, he declares the point. Usually just one point – which if the blow had been continued might have been fatal or disabling – is needed for victory. There are no rounds, and contests usually last one minute.

In kata, competitors perform a series of set movements of attack and defence, and are marked on their precision and correct posture. The preliminary rounds are conducted on a knock-out basis. In the final pool, seven judges with numbered cards award marks. The highest and lowest marks are discarded, and the remaining five totalled.

Aikido

Aikido is a martial art that lies between judo and karate. Many of its techniques come from ju-jitsu, and it requires an exactness of movement and precision to an even greater extent than either judo or karate. Unlike the other two, very little physical force is required, and there is little body contact between the contestants. Most of the aikido moves involve locks against the wrist or elbow joints, and a competitor uses an opponent's moves in order to defeat him.

There are two chief styles of aikido – *Uyeshiba* and *Tomiki*. Uyeshiba is the founder of aikido – literally 'the way of accumulated force and unity of action' – which was evolved from a number of the other martial arts but chiefly from ju-jitsu. In the Uyeshiba style there are no competitions. The Tomiki style is less formalized and has been accepted as a method of physical education by Japanese schools and universities. It stages competitions, which involve both free aikido contests – without weapons – and also contests with knives. There are no weight categories. National championships are staged annually, but world championships have yet to be held.

Kendo

Kendo (sword way) is a development from the ancient samurai system of Japanese sword fighting. It evolved from *kenjutsu*, the techniques of fighting in which the medieval knights were skilled.

A kendoka (a person who practises the sport) wears padded armour and a helmet, and fights with a bamboo sword. A metal sword is used for kata (forms), a series of set moves. Of all the martial arts, kendo probably keeps more closely to the original ideas and philosophy of the samurai. The ceremony of bowing before and after practice and the etiquette of the samurai are rigidly adhered to. A kendoka always follows a parry with a riposte, since the aim of the samurai was always to destroy his opponent. Short steps are taken to give the attack impetus, but sometimes a jump is employed in a counter-attack. The object is to land an effective blow on the opponent's body or head.

The World Kendo Federation administers the sport, and organized the first world championships in 1970. Seventeen countries entered, but Japan provided the four semi-finalists, with Mitsui Kobayashi taking the title.

Top: *Naginata, a sport in which contestants fight with long wooden staves, is practised mainly by women in Japan.* Above: *Kendo, in which bamboo or metal swords are used, is the closest of the martial arts to the traditions of the ancient Japanese samurai.*

The white-robed venerable founder of aikido, Professor Morihei Uyeshiba himself, demonstrates the art with one of his followers.

Miscellany

Sport offers infinite possibilities, and over the years man has invented all sorts of ball games, target games, races involving animals or machines, combat sports, and sports involving the practise of special skills and techniques. Above: *Pigeon racing,* which in Britain alone boasts some 100,000 pigeon 'fanciers' who breed and race homing pigeons. The birds average about 40 mph and are timed on special clocks by means of coded rings on their legs. Top right: *Reindeer racing,* a popular sport in the Arctic regions of Russia. Above right: *Broomball,* an example of improvization in sport. Above far right: *Stool-ball,* an ancient game still played by women in Britain, possibly a forerunner of cricket. Right: *Soap-box derby,* a downhill coasting race for children in home-built motorless racing carts, which attracts crowds of some 70,000 to the Akron classic. Below: *World marbles championship* at Tinsley Green, Sussex, where the Toucan Terribles reign supreme. Below right: *Rugby netball,* a cross between two sports.

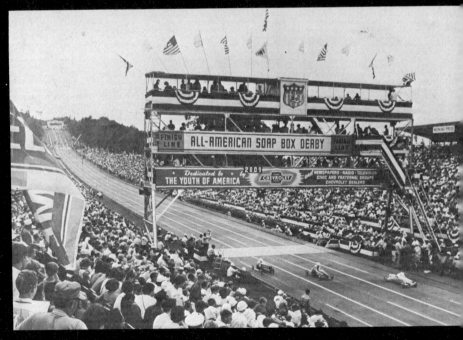

Top: *The barbaric sport of cockfighting as depicted in 1908 at the Royal Cockpit, Birdcage Walk, in London. Originating at least 3,000 years ago in southern Asia, it became a popular gambling sport. It is still legal in some countries of the Far East and Latin America and is practised illegally elsewhere.* Above: *Jousting, another ancient sport, still revived from time to time at fêtes.* Below: *Buck-jumping at a rodeo. Popular in North America and Australia, rodeo sports include calf roping, bareback riding, steer* wrestling, saddle bronc riding, bull riding, and even wild-cow milking. Above right: *Tree-felling at a woodchopping carnival in Australia. Lumberjack championships in North America include such events as birling (performing or racing on floating logs), tree-climbing, sawing, and axe-throwing.* Right and below right: *In a good cause, people will race anything – from snails to elephants.* Bottom right: *The traditional English game of quoits, in which a metal ring is tossed onto a fixed peg.*

Modern pentathlon

The all-rounder is today an obsolete animal except in one single sport – the modern pentathlon, in which versatility and adaptability are essential. There is a legend that explains the origin and sequence of the sport. A messenger is charged with carrying a message by horseback through hostile country; he sets off on a horse, has to beat off attackers with sword and pistol, swim across rivers, and run across country to his destination. In brief, the origin of the event is military, and the order of the five constituent events is cross-country riding, fencing, pistol shooting, swimming, and cross-country running.

The modern pentathlon was a pet scheme of Baron Pierre de Coubertin, the founder of the modern Olympic Games. Against some opposition, he managed to have it included in the 1912 Olympics, since when it has continued to feature as an Olympic sport for men. World championships were first held in 1949, and since then have been held in non-Olympic years. Because of the taxing nature of the organization of the sport, for both practice and competition, it has always been dominated by the military forces, mainly in Eastern Europe and Sweden.

The modern pentathlon competition is run on a points basis, each sport being judged on an objective standard. The *riding* is done on horses supplied by the organizers and drawn for by lot, and each competitor is allowed 20 minutes to get to know his horse. He then rides over an 800-metre course with 15 obstacles designed to test the rider rather than the horse. The 'standard' is 2 minutes/1,000 points. The maximum score is limited to 1,100 points.

The *fencing*, on an all-fight-all basis, is done with the épée, and a bout is decided on the first hit. The basic score of 1,000 points is awarded for winning some 70% of the bouts (scoring tables are used to give the precise score). Each competitor has to fight at least 20 bouts, so if there are fewer than 21 competitors each fights the other twice.

The *shooting* is done with a .22 pistol at a 25-metre 'snap' target. Twenty scoring shots are fired in four series of five, each shot being worth a maximum 10 target points. A total of 194 target points is worth 1,000 pentathlon points, with each target point above or below this mark counting plus or minus 22 points.

The *swimming* is 300 metres freestyle: a time of 3 min 54 sec is worth 1,000 points, with each $\frac{1}{2}$ sec below or above counting plus or minus 4 points.

The *running* is over 4,000 metres cross-country. A time of 14 min 15 sec realizes 1,000 points, each second above or below this par counting as a penalty or bonus of 3 points.

Left: Igor Novikov (USSR) on the way to the world modern pentathlon title at Aldershot in 1958. In all, he won five individual titles. In the Olympics he won team golds in 1956 and 1964, but individually had to be content with a silver and two 4th places. Below: Pistol shooting has caused frequent controversy because of the habit of some competitors of taking tranquillizing drugs.

Hungary's Andras Balczo in Melbourne during the 1966 world championships, in which he won individual and team honours. Five times world champion, it looked as though he had lost his chance of an individual Olympic gold when he came second by only 11 points in 1968, but he was a most popular winner at Munich.

MODERN PENTATHLON 'MOSTS'

World championship and Olympic Games

Individual	6	Andras Balczo (Hungary)
Team	11	USSR

Olympic Games

Total golds	3	Andras Balczo (Hungary)
Individual golds	2	Lars Hall (Sweden)

Motor sport

It seems to be a human characteristic that if two or more drivers set off down a stretch of road at the same time, and if there are no restrictions, the outcome will be a race. This urge to be fastest has existed ever since the motor-car was invented. Indeed, the first event took place as early as 1895, when a party of hardy pioneers raced one another from Paris to Bordeaux and back – a distance of 732 miles.

Since this initial race, the shape of motor sport has changed continually – partly to keep pace with technical developments, and partly to protect the drivers (and, come to that, the public) from the perils of speed. For example, there was a fearful carnage on what should have been the Paris–Madrid race of 1903. A number of drivers were killed, but what really worried the authorities was the toll of spectators mown down by vehicles out of control.

After that, racing on public highways was forbidden unless special arrangements were made. Even so, the problem of safeguarding onlookers was far from

over. As recently as 1955, the rules of the Le Mans 24-Hour Race had to be modified after a Mercedes had catapulted into the crowd. Eighty spectators were killed.

Nowadays, international motor sport is run by the International Sporting Commission of the Fédération Internationale de l'Automobile (FIA), the organization that governs world motoring. National clubs are responsible to this body, and most local clubs are affiliated to their national clubs.

Motor sport covers an almost infinite variety of forms, and it is possible for almost anybody who feels the urge to have a go. It ranges from grand prix events in which the ultimate in speed and skill compete for large sums of money before an audience of tens of thousands; to club events, in which weekend enthusiasts pit their Minis against one another. It requires something in the order of £100,000 to build a Formula One car, while it would be possible to go out on the track in a race sponsored by a local club for an investment of a few hundred pounds.

Emerson Fittipaldi takes his JPS-Ford up Pilgrims Rise and into Druids Bend on his way to winning the Daily Mail Race of Champions at Brands Hatch in 1972 – a sign of things to come, for he went on to become the youngest ever world champion that year.

Ascari, Alberto (Italy), son of the famous driver Antonio Ascari, gained his early successes on motor-cycles. He switched to four wheels in 1940, and after the war rapidly became one of the leaders in the Ferrari team. He won the World Championship in 1952 and 1953, with 6 and 5 GP wins respectively. He was unaccountably killed at Monza in 1955 while trying out a Ferrari sports car.

131

Brabham, Jack (Australia), one of the few motor-racing aces who lived to enjoy retirement, won fame as a manufacturer as well as on the track. A skilled motor mechanic at the age of 16, he went into motor-racing as a midget-car driver on dirt tracks. He switched to road racing in 1952 and went to England in 1955, joining the Cooper works

team the next year. After winning the World Championship driving Coopers in 1959 and 1960, he set about designing his own car. And in 1966 he gained the singular honour of being the first man to win both drivers' and constructors' championships. He retired from driving in 1970, having taken part in a record 127 championship races.

Clark, Jim (Great Britain), son of a Scottish sheep farmer, drove his father's Austin Seven at the age of 9. He joined Lotus in early 1960, and in 1961 began a string of successes that elevated him to the ranks of such as Fangio and Nuvolari. He won the World Championship twice, in 1963 with 7 GP victories and with 6 in 1965, when he also won the Indianapolis 500.

Quiet and likeable, Clark was one of the most consistent drivers on the track; the conditions of a race never seemed to affect him. Bad luck robbed him of the 1967 Championship, but he took the first 1968 GP, at Kyalami, South Africa, in his Lotus-Ford to chalk up his 25th GP and break Fangio's record. He looked

set for another Championship, but in April, in a Formula Two race at Hockenheim in Germany, he slid off the track on an easy right-hand turn, collided with a tree, and died minutes afterwards.

The cars are on the starting grid at Silverstone for the 1963 British GP. No. 4 is Jim Clark in a Lotus, No. 9 Dan Gurney (Brabham), No. 1 Graham Hill (BRM), No. 8 Jack Brabham (Brabham). Clark, the 1962 winner, won it again, and then won it in 1964, '65, and '67.

A competition can be worthy of the name only when like is matched against like. Consequently, motor sport is sub-divided into a number of groups – and then, according to the sizes of engines, into categories within these groups. Groups 1 and 2 are for ordinary production cars – though those in Group 2 are less ordinary than those in Group 1, for modifications are allowed. Groups 3 and 4 are for sports cars; Groups 5, 6, and 7 are for sports racing cars; and Group 8 covers the single-seater racing cars. Finally, Group 9 is the so-called *Formula Libre*, in which anything goes.

Grand prix racing

The most powerful and technically sophisticated vehicle in motor sport is the Formula One car – or, to give it another name, the grand prix vehicle. The French more or less invented motor racing; and it was in France, in 1906, that the first grand prix race took place. A triangular course was selected in the area of Le Mans, and 12 laps, a distance of nearly 770 miles, was decided upon for the event – which took place over two days. The going, which was over rough roads, was terrible. One driver came off the road from sheer exhaustion; another nearly went blind. When it was all over, it was won by a Hungarian driver named François (Ferenc) Szisz at the wheel of

a Renault. His average speed was nearly 63 mph.

Over the years, the grand prix races multiplied and became a source of national pride. The first closed circuit for grand prix racing was built in Italy at Monza in 1922. The idea originated in the mind of Mussolini, who had a liking for fast cars and racing. At one time, both his son and his chauffeur were upholding his country's honour in the sport – an honour which he took very seriously indeed.

Germany followed the lead set by the building of Monza by constructing the colossal (14 miles to a lap) circuit at Nürburgring in 1927. In this case, the scheme was endorsed by the mayor of Cologne, Konrad Adenauer, who saw the building of it as a partial solution to the unemployment problem of the Cologne-Coblenz region. Dr Adenauer's purpose was also to increase the tourist appeal of the Eifel district.

During the years leading up to World War II, Italy and Germany were far out ahead in the struggle for grand prix victories – with Germany having the edge on Italy. The Alfa-Romeos from Milan had shown themselves to be extremely competitive, but they were gradually overhauled by the massive Mercedes and Auto-Unions. The latter, which were designed by Dr Ferdinand Porsche (who also produced the prototype Volkswagen), were the first grand prix cars to have their engine mounted at the rear.

At the outbreak of World War II, Britain was about the only major European power that did not run an annual

Memorable moments in sport

Fangio's finest hour

Dateline: Nürburgring, 4 August 1957. Four-times World Champion, Juan Manuel Fangio had already won three of the four grands prix that year. And in practice for the German event, he had won pole position with a 9 min 25·6 sec lap, 16 seconds better than his record in 1956. There was one snag, however; for the tortuous 312-mile race on Europe's most arduous circuit, Fangio's Maserati would need a rear tyre change.

On the front line of the starting grid with Fangio were his team-mate Behra and the two British drivers Mike Hawthorn (less than 3 seconds behind Fangio in practice) and Peter Collins, both in Ferrari's. Fangio took the lead on lap 3, increasing it with a remarkable exhibition of driving to over 30 seconds on lap 12, when he swung into the pits for his tyre change.

The stop unaccountably took nearly a minute, and the champion found himself more than half a minute down on the two Ferraris with 10 laps to go. And with a heavier tank (the Maseratis also took on petrol during their pit stop), this was soon nearly 50 seconds. Then, on lap 15, Fangio started to 'go'. He took 12 seconds off the unsuspecting Ferraris, and another 5 on lap 16. Lap after lap he reduced the lead – and the lap record – until an incredible 9 min 17·4 sec 20th lap took him within 3 seconds of his rivals. First he took Collins – twice – then Hawthorn, and on the last lap increased his lead to 3·6 seconds. In winning his greatest race, he had reduced the lap record 10 times and clinched his fifth World Drivers Championship.

Juan Manuel Fangio hurls his Maserati across the finishing line to win the 1957 German GP after a breathtaking race in which he gained 50 seconds on his rivals in the last 8 laps.

Fangio, Juan Manuel (Argentina), arguably the greatest racing driver of all time, an opinion supported by his record 5 World Championships – in 1951 and 1954–57 – and his 24 major GP wins. Fangio shot to fame in Europe in 1949 with 6 wins in 10 races, which won him a contract with Alfa-Romeo. He was then 38, and his sudden rise followed years of only sporadic success at home and an unimpressive appearance in Europe in 1948. He won his first Championship in an Alfa, and when they withdrew from racing switched to Maserati, coming second to Ascari in 1953. After successes in the Argentine and Belgian GPs of 1954, he was signed up by Mercedes and proceeded to win four more and the title. He retained it in 1955, and when Mercedes withdrew from the sport won his next two Championships with a Ferrari and then a Maserati.

A big, powerful man, Fangio had a mind that functioned with

the precision of a computer. He also knew when to call it a day, retiring in 1959 at the age of 48.

Fittipaldi, Emerson (Brazil), the younger of two motor-racing brothers, shook the sport in the early 1970s with his remarkable rise to the top, culminating with the World Championship in 1972.

A protégé of Jim Russell, he was soon driving a Formula One Lotus for Colin Chapman, and became, at 25, the sport's youngest ever champion.

grand prix. One had been held at Brooklands in 1926 and 1927, and in the mid-1930s Donington Park in the Midlands was the venue. But it was not until a former airfield at Silverstone was converted into a race track in 1948, that the British Grand Prix became a regular event in the calendar. Silverstone shared the event with Aintree from 1955 and then with Brands Hatch from 1964.

Some grand prix events, such as the Monaco race, are held on much the same circuits as those on which they began – in this instance, a devious round-the-houses stampede along the streets of the Principality. Others have changed their venues from year to year. France, for example, has held its grand prix at more than a

Brooklands in the 1930s. Above: *John Cobb all out on the Railway Banking.* Above right: *An artist's impression of the track.*

Hawthorn, Mike (Great Britain), drove for BRM and Vanwall, but for want of a competitive British car accepted Ferrari's offer to drive for the Italian team in 1953, winning the French GP in a classic battle with Fangio. In 1955, he won the Le Mans 24-Hour Race – though

the Continental press wrongly blamed him for the catastrophe. In 1958 he won the World Championship by a single point from Stirling Moss, but was killed in a road accident in January 1959 after he had announced his retirement from motor racing.

Hill, Graham (Great Britain), determined, courageous, with a wit as quick as his cars, made his grand prix debut at the wheel of a Lotus in 1957 after years of early struggles. He joined BRM in 1960, and in 1962 became the first British driver to win the World Championship in a British car. In 1967, he rejoined Team Lotus after winning the Indianapolis 500 for them the previous year, and became World Champion again in 1968. He made a remarkable, yet characteristic, recovery from serious leg injuries sustained in a crash at Watkins Glen in 1969. In 1972 he won the Le Mans 24-Hour Race and in 1973 built his own Formula One car.

dozen venues, including the Bugatti circuit at Le Mans – once described by Graham Hill as 'a Micky Mouse affair'. Its chief venues are now the spectacular Clermont-Ferrand and the ultra-modern Le Castellet, near Marseille.

A number of countries, such as Spain and Argentina, have allowed their grands prix to lapse over a period of years, and have then resumed them. Others have given them up altogether. After the disaster at Le Mans in 1955, several nations prohibited motor racing for a short period. In the case of Switzerland, the ban turned out to be permanent.

One feature of grand prix racing has been the way in which a particular country has held the ascendency for several years. First, it was France; then Italy

and then Germany. Britain's turn came with the advent of the rear-engined racing car, which was pioneered by Charles Cooper of 500 cc racing-car fame; the first victory was won by Stirling Moss at Buenos Aires in 1958. Since then, the names of Lotus, Brabham, and McLaren have been well to the fore in grand prix racing.

In 1950, an Italian count named Antonio Brivio conceived the idea of organizing a World Drivers Championship based on a points system. In its first four years, the championship was won by drivers of Italian cars – in all but one instance by Italian drivers. Between 1951 and 1957, the Argentinian driver Juan Manuel Fangio won it five times (four of them in a row), setting up a record

Left: *Antonio Ascari in an Alfa Romeo in 1925.* Centre left: *Stirling Moss in a Maserati at Silverstone in 1956.* Bottom left: *Graham Hill in a BRM in 1962, when he became the first British driver to win the World Championship in a British car.* Below: *The 1972 South African GP at Kyalami.*

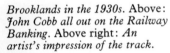

Above: François Cevert (right) casts an anxious glance towards stunned team-mate Jackie Stewart as they survey the scene, right, after Jo Siffert's fatal crash at Brands Hatch in 1971. Two years later Cevert himself was killed, at Watkins Glen.

still unapproached nearly 20 years later. Since 1958, however, it had been largely dominated by British or Commonwealth drivers, with names such as Jack Brabham, Jim Clark, Graham Hill, and Jackie Stewart to the fore.

The early grand prix cars had two men aboard them. One was the driver; the other, his mechanic. Races were over long distances, and they frequently had to make repairs *en route*. Today's events are over much shorter distances – a maximum of 400 km (250 miles) is stipulated in races counting towards the World Drivers Championship – and seldom last for longer than two hours. There should be no necessity to refuel. Any driver who has to make a pit-stop for whatever reason can count the race lost.

When the World Drivers Championship was instituted in 1950, the regulations for Formula One cars stipulated a maximum engine size of $4\frac{1}{2}$ litres (or $1\frac{1}{2}$ litres if they were supercharged). Various modifications took place until 1966, when the formula still in force in the early 1970s was produced. The limit on unsupercharged engines is 3 litres. In the unlikely event of anybody producing a supercharged version (the technical difficulties due to the rules governing fuel would be enormous), the limit would be $1\frac{1}{2}$ litres.

Only certain races are permitted by the FIA to count towards the World Championship. The circuit owners have to satisfy the FIA and, more recently, the drivers themselves – the Grand Prix Drivers' Association has become a powerful body – that they comply with reasonable standards of safety. Scoring for the first six places is 9 points, 6, 4, 3, 2, and 1.

In the Dutch Grand Prix of 1967, a Lotus driven by Jim Clark scored an unexpected victory – and one which was to have a profound effect on the championship for a number of years. Clark's car had a new engine in it. Built by a Northampton firm named Cosworth, with a good deal of financial assistance from Ford, it had not been run in when it reached the Netherlands. And yet there

Moss, Stirling (Great Britain), one of the most brilliant drivers of his time who, largely through bad luck, never won the World Championship. A dynamic personality, with abundant natural gifts, he showed early promise, and at 19 won his first Formula Three race at Goodwood in 1948. He was determined to win his fortune as a driver in a British-built car, but nothing competitive was available. After turning down an offer from Ferrari, he eventually had to settle for a Maserati. His first grand prix victory was in the British event of 1955 at the wheel of a Mercedes, and he went on to win a total of 16 GPs, finishing second 4 times and third 3 times in the World Championship.

He heralded British motor-racing supremacy in 1958 when he won the Argentine Grand Prix in a Cooper, the first success of the rear-engined epoch. But he switched to Vanwall and lost the Championship by a point to Mike Hawthorn. He later drove for BRM and Lotus before retiring from the sport after a serious crash at Goodwood on Easter Monday 1962. His name remained synonymous with motor racing in Britain.

Nuvolari, Tazio (Italy), variously nicknamed 'the Flying Mantuan', 'Son of the Devil', and 'The Great Little Man', began his

career in 1923 with motorcycle racing. But he turned his full attention to motor racing in 1929, and as an Alfa-Romeo driver spearheaded Italy's bid for supremacy on the tracks. He invented 'the four-wheel drift' technique on corners. A modest man with a fiery personality, he stood just over 5 ft tall, yet he was the giant of the track in the 1930s. He retired in 1948 at the age of 56.

Belgian driver Jacky Ickx in a Ferrari at Brands Hatch in 1972.

Rindt, Jochen (Austria), once said that he would retire when he won the World Championship. But he was unable to keep his word, because he was awarded the title posthumously, having been killed in practice for the 1970 Italian GP.

After a spectacular victory in a Formula Two race in 1964, Rindt was offered a contract in Formula One by John Cooper. He came third in the 1966 World Championship in a Cooper-Maserati, but it was 1969, at Watkins Glen, before he won his first Championship GP, in a Lotus-Ford. He won 5 GPs in the Lotus before his fatal crash – and fittingly no one was able to overhaul his points total.

Jochen Rindt (right) with Jackie Stewart in 1970, a few months before his death.

Stewart, Jackie (Great Britain), chalked up his record 26th major grand prix victory in the Dutch GP at Zandvoort in July 1973 in a Tyrell-Ford. In August he won the German GP and a month later made sure of his third World Championship, retiring at the end of the season.

A champion at clay-pigeon shooting in his native Scotland, Stewart first took up motor racing in 1960. He was a 'natural' behind the wheel. Driving for Ken Tyrell in Formula Three in 1964, he won 11 of 13 events. He was snapped up by BRM for the 1965 season, won his first GP, at Monza, and finished 3rd in the World Championship. He rejoined Tyrell in 1968 to drive a Matra, and took 6 grands prix in 1969 to gain his first world title; he won another 6 in 1971 in a Tyrell-Ford for his second championship. A thorough professional, whose outside activities netted him as much as his exploits on the track, Stewart has also succeeded in making motor-racing a safer sport.

Mike Hawthorn in a Jaguar leads Stirling Moss (Mercedes) through the Esses at Le Mans during the tragic 1955 race, in which Hawthorn won a hollow victory.

it was, streaking away at the head of the pack, and winning at a record-breaking average speed of 104·04 mph. Quite obviously, Cosworth (an amalgamation of the names Mike Costin and Keith Duckworth) had got it right. They kept on getting it right and the World Champion's car continued to be propelled by a Ford-Cosworth engine well into the 1970s.

The rewards of winning motor races – and making allowances for the fact that you cannot win them all – would not be enough to keep a Formula One team in business. Lotus and Ferrari make big money manufacturing production cars. The other teams exist mostly on sponsorship. Cigarette firms, which are not allowed to spend money on TV advertising, are among the leading patrons. So are the oil companies, and the manufacturers of male cosmetics. The latter presumably imagine that participation in motor racing contributes to the manly image. They may be right.

Sports car racing

One name stands out above all others in sports car racing – that of Enzo Ferrari. Forced to retire from active racing himself in the late 1920s, he started his own racing stable, Scuderia Ferrari, in 1929 with Alfa Romeos, but it was not until after World War II that the first Ferrari made its racing debut. And even Ferrari's grand prix successes have been overshadowed by his continued domination of the sports car scene.

The first World Sports Car Championship was staged in 1953 – and won by Ferrari, with drivers such as Marzotto, Hawthorn, Farina, and Ascari at the wheel of the scarlet red cars. And in 20 years, despite many changes in cham-

pionship format, Ferrari had chalked up some 60 wins and a dozen championships, shared by such motor-racing greats as Fangio, Gonzales, Castelotti, Musso, Taruffi, Gendebien, Gurney, Phil Hill, Graham Hill, Surtees, Bonnier, Rindt, Amon, Ickx, Peterson, and many more.

The World Sports Car Championship takes in about 10 races in Europe and North and South America, with the best 8 counting (only the first car of each particular make can score, however). Points awarded, from 1st to 10th, are 20, 15, 12, 10, 8, 6, 4, 3, 2, 1.

The most prestigious sports car event is the Le Mans 24 Hours, or, to give it its proper name, the Le Mans Grand Prix d'Endurance. First held in 1923, Le Mans has become a French institution, with fun-fairs, shops, restaurants, a cinema, and dance hall in addition to the racing. With the leading cars doing some 300 laps of the 8·45-mile circuit and registering average lap speeds as high as 150 mph, the speed differential between these and lower-class cars can be as much as 80 mph. In the 1920s the 'Bentley Boys' held sway, to be followed by Alfa Romeo (1931–34). Jaguar were successful in the 1950s, but Ferrari dominated the early 1960s with six consecutive Le Mans wins.

Perhaps the toughest sports car race is the Targa Florio, in Sicily, over 11 tortuous 72-km laps and some 9,000 corners. It is not surprising that lap speeds average only 70–80 mph. American events have varied from 6 to 24 hours, and take place at Daytona, Sebring, or Watkins Glen. Most of the other big races are 1,000-km events, held on such circuits as Buenos Aires, Monza, Nurburgring, and Brands Hatch.

Aaltonen, Rauno (Finland),
whose first experiences of high
speeds were on the dirt-track (he
was a speedway international)
and on water (he won the
Finnish powerboat championship
7 times), entered his first rally
with a Mercedes in 1956. He
crashed his Mini Cooper in his
first 'Monte' (1962), and was
saved from death by burning by
his co-driver Geoff Mabbs. He
chalked up numerous successes
in international events, including
the 'Monte' (1967), the RAC,
the Czech, the Polish, and the
Three Cities.

Carlsson, Erik (Sweden),
recorded his first big win in 1957
when, shortly after joining the
Saab works team, he won the
Finnish 1,000 Lakes Rally. In
1960, driving his tiny red Saab
96, powered by an 850 cc two-
stroke engine, he began a
triumphant progress outside
Scandinavia by winning the
RAC — the first of a hat-trick of
victories. The Acropolis followed
in 1961 and the 'Monte' in 1962
and '63. After more remarkable
performances in 1963 and '64 in
his little Saab he virtually retired
from international competition.

Clark, Roger (GB), a consistent
winner and the mainstay of
Ford's numerous successes in
rallying, was first noticed by Ford
talent scouts after a heroic drive
as a private entrant in the 1964
Scottish Rally. He joined the
Ford works team in 1966, and
his major wins have included the
Acropolis (1968) and the RAC
(1972).

Makinen, Timo (Finland),
affectionately known as 'The
Flying Finn', won a reputation as
a wizard on snow and ice. Thrice
winner of the Finnish 1,000 Lakes
Rally (1965–67) and once of the
'Monte' (1965), he lost a second
'Monte' in 1966 on the
controversial 'lights' technicality.
After driving Mini Cooper S's for
a number of years, he joined
Lancia in 1969 and then Ford in
1970. Also highly talented at
power boat racing, he won the
Round Britain Race in 1969.

Rally driving

The basic objective of rallying is to get
from one place to another within a certain time. It is not car racing—the vehicles
are kept apart from one another by staggered starts – but rally drivers claim that
it requires far more endurance than circuit racing. And circuit racers are in-
clined to agree with them; Jackie Stewart
once said that the reason he never took
part in rallies was that they were 'too
dangerous'.

Rallying used to be a social sport; but
nowadays the international scene is
tough, competitive, and highly professional. The classic event is the Monte
Carlo Rally, which takes place annually
in January. The first 'Monte' was
organized in 1911 under the name of 'Le
Rallye International de Monaco', the
idea being to attract visitors to the
Principality in winter. During the years
between the wars, the 'Monte' became
much more complex, with cars converg-
ing on Monaco from all parts of Europe.
Other big international events – such as
the exhausting Liège-Sofia-Liège fixture
and the brutally difficult Alpine Rally –
came on to the calendar, joined post-war
by the Acropolis and the East African
Safari and the acceptance of the RAC as
a major international rally.

*Australia's Snowy Mountains provide a rough
stretch in the 1968 London–Sydney marathon.*

But rallying is far from being confined
to big international events. Most car
clubs have rallies of one kind or another
on their lists of activities. The crew of a
rally car is a driver and a navigator. On
road sections (other than motorways), the
average speed required is not allowed to
exceed 30 mph. On the special stages,
however, there are no limiting factors.
Cases have been recorded of cars reaching 110 mph on rough tracks.

Major car manufacturers usually enter
teams for international events – partly because of the prestige, and partly because
it provides valuable data for development
work. The FIA organizes an International Rally Championship for Makes
and a European Rally Championship for
Drivers.

Motor sport

Moss-Carlsson, Pat (GB), a leading international show jumper, transferred her talents to motor sport in the mid-1950s. Originally taught to drive by her illustrious brother Stirling, she won countless *coupes des dames* as a member of the BMC works team. With Ann Wisdom she won the European Ladies Championship in 1958. They were outright winners of the 1960 Liège-Rome-Liège — the first female crew to win a major international event, and in what was then the toughest of them all. In 1962 she finished 3rd in the East African Safari in a Saab despite hitting an antelope *en route*. She married Erik Carlsson in 1963, and became a mother in 1970, but returned to rallying and recorded her 8th *coupes des dames* in the 'Monte' in 1972.

Pat Moss and Erik Carlsson set off on the 1963 Targa Rusticana.

Hydroplanes race over the waters of Oulton Broad, watched by a large 1956 August Bank Holiday crowd.

Powerboat racing

Although dating back to the early 1900s, powerboat racing did not emerge as an organized sport until the 1960s. The 1959 Florida-Bahamas race inspired activity on the other side of the Atlantic, the *Daily Express* sponsored a Cowes-Torquay race in 1961, and offshore powerboat racing was in business.

The Union Internationale Motonautique governs all forms of powerboat racing, which includes the inland lake variety called circuit or sportsboat racing. A distinct branch of powerboat racing is *hydroplaning*. Hydroplanes are speed craft with a hull designed to give them aerodynamic lift so that they 'plane' across the surface of the water. Particularly popular where large stretches of inland water are available, such as North America and Italy, hydroplane races produce average speeds of some 120 mph. There are world and European championships for a number of classes, with perhaps 10 laps of a 1-mile circuit.

The larger outboard hydroplanes also take part in the marathon offshore powerboat races which now take place in many parts of the world — the European seaboard, the Americas, South Africa, and Australia. One of the more ambitious has been the race first sponsored in 1969 by the *Daily Telegraph*, in which contestants were required to make their way by stages right round the coast of Britain.

Timo Makinen and crew bring Avenger Too home in first place in the 1969 Round Britain Powerboat Race, held over a 10-stage 1,403-mile course for a first prize of £10,000.

Other motor sports

Each branch of motor sport has its own adherents. In America, *drag racing* draws some 6 million spectators a year to watch $\frac{1}{4}$-mile duels from a standing start. Dragsters streak over the track in as little as 7 seconds, a blaze of blinding colour as they fight for traction, reaching terminal speeds of 200 mph and more, before their parachutes bring them to rest. Top stars such as 'Big Daddy' Don Garlits have won huge sums at this sport.

At the other end of the scale are the go-karters, who first appeared in California in 1956. Not a hugely popular spectator sport, *karting* nevertheless spread around the world — even to Russia — one of the beauties being that karts are very cheap to buy and run. With four wheels plus one to steer with, a tiny two-stroke engine, an apology of a seat inches off the ground, and the whole thing held together by an assortment of steel tubes, the kart is by all appearances the most rudimentary automobile ever conceived. Yet speeds of 120 mph are not uncommon with a 250 cc engine, and a circuit such as Silverstone can be lapped at a tidy 80 mph. In 1962 the FIA gave birth to the International Karting Commission and karting now has its own championships and long-distance events, including an incredible 24-hour race at Brignoles.

A more traditional sport is *hillclimbing*, which dates back to 1905 in England. Drivers are timed on difficult uphill runs ranging from $\frac{1}{4}$ to $3\frac{1}{2}$ miles, but more usually 800–1,000 yards. They have to fight all the way, for the sport demands tremendous concentration and driving skill. Cars have varied over the years, from rear-engined models to four-wheel drive specials, and even Formula 5,000 McLaren M10s have proved best. Britain has the very keenly contested Shell-RAC Hillclimb Championship, first staged in 1948. In Europe the sport has an FIA-run Mountain Championship, for sports cars over longer hills, usually dominated by Porsche and Ferrari.

Another motor sport in which cars climb hills is *trials*. In trials, however, time is irrelevant. The hills, or sections, are steep, usually slippery, and have various natural hazards. The idea is to get up each section (usually about a dozen) from a stationary start as far as possible without stopping. A rear-seat passenger, the 'bouncer', helps the driver by shifting his weight and bouncing up and down over the back wheels at the appropriate moments to assist traction. Points are gained for distance covered. Special 'trials' cars may be built for the sport, with a tubular-steel body-chassis unit, 'fiddle brakes' (hand-brakes to operate each rear wheel independently), and perhaps a horizontal steering wheel manipulated with a knob.

Autocross, the first of the off-road speed events, originated soon after World War II. It is a cross between racing and rallying. Cars compete on a closed circuit, usually about ½ mile, in a field – the muddier the better. Cars start in groups, depending on the width of the course, and each is timed separately over the two or three laps of the event. Each competitor has more than one run; usually the best run counts, but in some competitions an aggregate time is taken. Apart from the special techniques required to drive a car round a tight circuit on mud or slippery grass, there is also the problem of visibility, and all sorts of devices are used to keep the windscreen clear of mud.

Autocross gave birth to a number of other sports in England, of which *rallycross* became the most popular. A marriage of rallying and autocross, it was virtually devised for TV in 1966 and continued as a TV sport with the eager assistance of assorted sponsors. Up to four cars start on a track specially prepared to encapsulate the varying surfaces of a rally special stage for the TV camera – tarmac-mud-grass. Time is the deciding factor. Similar motor sports to derive from autocross and rallycross are *sandocross* and *rallypoint*.

Another group of motor sports in which time is the essence includes *autotests* (driving tests), *slaloms*, and *sprints*. They usually take place on a flat piece of ground such as a disused airfield. The autotest course is designed to provide about half a minute of frenzied use of steering wheel, gear lever, and hand-brake to manoeuvre the car through the extremely tight set-pieces. Sprints and slaloms are simplified versions, with marker cones defining the course, which again has to be negotiated in the fastest possible time. Each competitor goes on his own.

A spectacular motor sport that does not always meet with the approval of the authorities is *stock-car racing*. Once a knock-about circus for old bangers whose drivers were primarily concerned with knocking each other off the track, it has branched out in diverse ways in different parts of the world. In America, the land of its birth in the 1930s, it has taken the form of a race over as much as 500 miles of a tight, banked oval track between some 50 production-line saloons pepped up to average as much as 200 mph. In Britain, the sport has retained many of its original features, but whereas a certain amount of 'bumper car' tactics are tolerated, the object is to win the race.

Top: *Karting, or go-karting, at Crystal Palace.* Above: *Harold Bull in his record-breaking 'Mini' dragster, powered by an Austin-Morris 998 cc engine.*

Hillclimbing in 1947 at Shelsley Walsh, Worcestershire, where the sport was born 42 years earlier and was still taking place in the 1970s.

139

Motor sport

Stock-car racing – the knock-about variety – comes to Brands Hatch.

Breedlove, Craig (US), devised a jet-propelled three-wheeler shaped like an arrow, which he built in his father's garage. He called it *Spirit of America*, and came back from Bonneville in 1963 with a record speed of 407.45 mph. But because of the car's unusual design, it was classed as a motor-cycle! It was in a four-wheeled version that he later claimed the LSR.

Campbell, Sir Malcolm and **Donald** (GB), father and son, were two of only three men to hold the world land and water speed records concurrently. All Malcolm's boats were named *Bluebird* after an opera he liked (likewise his son's boats and cars). He broke the LSR 9 times between 1924 and 1935 – 146.16 mph on the first occasion, 301.13 on the last; and the WSR 3 times, from 129.56 mph in 1937 to 141.74 in 1939.
   Donald Campbell inherited his father's ambitions, and in 1955 broke the WSR, which the American Stanley Sayers had usurped in the early 1950s; his new mark – 202.32 mph. In the next 4 years, he made 5 more attempts, and raised it on each occasion. For his attack on the LSR he enlisted the help of industry, building a £1 million car powered by a gas-turbine engine. After misadventures in Australia, he beat John Cobb's 17-year-old mark with 405.45 mph. The same year, 1964, he took the WSR to 276.33 mph, and was killed on Coniston Water in 1967 when attacking this record in the last of the *Bluebirds*, reaching a top speed of 328 mph.

Right: *Donald Campbell at the start of the fatal trials.* Far right: *Two months later, on January 4, 1967, Bluebird 'takes off' on Coniston Water and breaks up at over 300 mph.*

It is about the cheapest form of motor sport, maximums being laid down for the size of engine and amount of money that can be spent on it. Drivers are graded – and paid starting money. Usually some 30 cars begin each heat, which consists of about 25 laps of a ¼-mile tarmac oval. Similar stock-car competitions are held in other European countries, South Africa, and Australasia, where some Australian events are open to women. And in Scandinavia they have developed stock-car racing on ice.

Another rough-and-tumble motor sport to originate in America is *off-road racing*, careering across country point-to-point over total distances of 800 miles or more in California and Mexico. Huge prizes have been won in the Mexico 1,000 (more than 832 miles) over some of the roughest racing terrain in the world, with dune buggies prominent.

At about the same time, the early 1960s, another off-the-road sport was gaining popularity on the northern border of the United States – *snowmobile racing*. More than a million of these petrol-engined caterpillar-tracked vehicles had been sold by the early 1970s. Steered with handlebars operating one or two short skis at the front, snowmobiles attracted sufficient sponsorship to stage 250-entry races in Canada and the United States for prize money as high as £20,000.

At the other end of the motor-sport spectrum, in contrast to the futuristic-looking machines of the snowbound North American wastes, is *vintage car racing*, a sport that developed in Britain in the 1930s and now encompasses both vintage and historic racing and sports cars. There are races, trials, speed hill climbs, and autotests for vehicles that, except for modern safety regulations and the benefit of modern road-holding properties for their tyres, are turned out as close as possible to their original trim.

J. Parry Thomas in his Thomas Special 'Babs' on Pendine Sands, where he twice broke the land speed record in 1926 and died in an attempt to regain it in 1927.

Speed records

The challenge to become the fastest man on land is one that has appealed to a number of people, including Henry Ford, who, in 1904, set up a brief record of 91·37 mph on the frozen waters of Lake St Clare. The driver who began it all was a high-born Frenchman, Count Gaston de Chasseloup-Laubat. In 1898, the Count drove an electric car at the then astonishing speed of 39.24 mph. By the end of the following year – after the record had been broken and re-broken no fewer than four times – Camille Jenatzy had pushed it up to 65.79 mph. The game was on: every year, or so it seemed, one lightning statistic was replaced by another.

In 1904 the Land Speed Record (LSR) went six times, the magic figure of 100 mph being reached for the first time by French enthusiast Louis Rigolly, who travelled at 103.55 mph. The figure of 200 mph had to wait until 1927, when Henry Segrave drove his Sunbeam at 203.79 mph.

The last man to break the record on a public road was an Englishman named Ernest Eldridge, who used a stretch of

French highway in 1924, and returned with a figure of 146.01 mph. After that, the attempts were made on sandy beaches (at Pendine in South Wales and Daytona in Florida) and, latterly, on the saltflats at Bonneville, Utah. Times are taken over a flying kilometre or mile, and the average of two runs in opposite directions taken.

The 1930s belonged to Sir Malcolm Campbell in *Bluebird* whose 301.13 mph in 1935 lasted until George Eyston (*Thunderbolt*) and John Cobb (*Railton-Mobil*) began their duel which took Cobb to 394.20 mph in 1947. This lasted until 1964, when Donald Campbell flashed across the salt beds of Australia's Lake Eyre at 403.01 mph. This was the last LSR to be set by conventional (wheel-driven) cars. The FIA decided to allow jet-propelled cars (Craig Breedlove had already done 407.45 mph in 1963), and in a couple of years Breedlove (*Spirit of America*) and his fellow-American Art Arfons (*Green Monster*) had taken the LSR through the 500 mph barrier, with Breedlove emerging ahead in 1965 with

600.60 mph. In 1950 another American Gary Gabelich touched 650 mph in recording 627.28 in *The Blue Flame*, the rocket engine of which was powered by liquid natural gas and hydrogen peroxide.

Many of the men who have broken the speed record on land have aspired to be fastest on water, and three – Henry Segrave, John Cobb, and Donald Campbell – have been killed in the attempt. The first man to have a water speed record officially recognized was an American named Garfield Wood who, in 1928, piloted his speedboat *Miss America VII* at 92.862 mph. There followed a transatlantic duel between Wood and first Segrave and then Kaye Don, with Wood emerging in 1932 with 124.86 mph in the four-engined *Miss America X*. Sir Malcolm Campbell took the WSR up to 141.74 mph before the war in his *Bluebird*; then, after the war, jet boats came onto the scene. Donald Campbell was killed in one, travelling at over 300 mph when *Bluebird* somersaulted and sank on Coniston Water.

Cobb, John (GB), a specialist in big cars, set about demolishing the LSR after a reasonably successful career racing them. Using a twin-engined Railton-Mobil, he took it up to 350.20 mph in 1938, raised it again in 1937, and yet again (394.20) in 1947. He was killed on Loch Ness in 1952 while attacking the water speed record in his jet-boat *Crusader*.

Cobb (left) *and Segrave.*

Eyston, George (GB), breaker of almost every species of record on land in vehicles ranging from a 750 cc MG Midget to a 73-litre giant named *Thunderbolt*, began on motorcycles and took up car racing in 1923. A year later, he went in for hydroplane racing — with considerable success. With many victories on track and water behind him, he broke the LSR in 1937 in *Thunderbolt* with a speed of 312.00 mph, and in two more steps took it to 357.50 mph.

Segrave, Sir Henry (GB), son of an Irish father and an American mother, won a place in the Sunbeam team in 1921 through sheer tenacity. He justified his claims by winning the French GP of 1923, the first British driver to win a GP in a British car. He twice broke the LSR in a Sunbeam — 152.33 mph in 1926, 203.79 in 1927, and finally raised it to 231.44 in 1929, driving his famous car *Golden Arrow*. In the same year, he won the International Championship for racing boats at Miami, and was knighted on his return to England. He died the following year when his boat *Miss England II* hit a log, but not before he had become the first man to hold the world land and water speed records simultaneously.

MOTOR SPORT 'MOSTS'

The grand prix drivers

World Drivers Championships	5	Juan Manuel Fangio (Arg) 1951–54–55–56–57
Championship GP wins	27	Jackie Stewart (GB)
Grand prix wins in season	7	Jim Clark (GB) 1963
	6	Alberto Ascari (It) 1952 (out of a possible 7)
Consecutive grand prix wins	9	Alberto Ascari (It) 1952–53
Fastest laps	28	Jim Clark (GB)
Pole positions	33	Jim Clark (GB)
Starts	159*	Graham Hill (GB)

The grand prix cars

Constructors' World Championships	6	Lotus (GB) 1963–65–68–70–72–73 (last 2 as JP Special)
Championship GP wins	54*	Lotus (GB)
Consecutive GP wins	14	Ferrari (It) 1952–3

Sports car racing

World championship wins	13	Ferrari (It) 1953–54–56–57–58–60–61–62–63–64–65–67–72
Le Mans wins – car	9	Ferrari
– driver	4	Olivier Gendebien (Bel)
Targa Florio wins – car	11	Porsche
– driver	3	Olivier Gendebien (Bel)

World speed records

Land	630.4 mph†	Gary Gabelich (USA) in *The Blue Flame*, 1970
Water	285.2 mph‡	Lee Taylor Jr (USA) in *Hustler*, 1967
– propeller-driven	202.4 mph§	Larry Hill (USA) in *Mr Ed*, 1971
Drag – rocket-engined	311.4 mph¶	Vic Wilson (Aus) in *Courage of Australia*, 1971
– piston-engined	243.9 mph¶	Don 'Big Daddy' Garlits in *Swamp Rat*, 1972

*To end of 1973.   †Avg of two 1-km runs.   ‡Avg of two 1-mile runs.   §1-km run.   ¶Terminal.

Motorcycle sports

Jim Redman hurtles round Mallory Park on a 250 cc Honda. The London-born Rhodesian won six world titles in the 1960s, two at 250 cc and four at 350.

Agostini, Giacomo (Italy), riding 350 and 500 cc MV machines, won his 13th world title in 1973, more than any other rider since the world title series began in 1949. He joined MV in 1965 after two seasons on 250 machines with Morini. After he gained the 500 title in 1966

from Mike Hailwood (who joined Honda in 1966–67), opposition for the MV rider fell away until 1973, when 350 and 500 Yamaha and Suzuki machines became competitive. MV then enrolled Britain's Phil Read to support Agostini, who retained his 350 title, but lost the 500 crown to Read. Agostini signed for Yamaha in 1974.

Duke, Geoff (GB), was the foremost motorcycle racer of the 1950s. After winning the 350 and 500 cc world championships on Norton machines in 1951 (his third season) and the 350 title again in 1952 (gaining the OBE), he joined Gilera of Italy and won a hat-trick of 500 cc titles.

Right: *Geoff Duke on a Norton.*

Motorcycle racing can be considered as old as the existence of machines, for they were included in the pioneering motor races between capital cities across Europe at the turn of the century. Despite contesting these races successfully – they were usually dominated by Austrian Werner machines – motorcycles were banned after 1903, when accidents during the Paris–Madrid event showed the danger of solo motorcycles competing against cars.

Following this, the Auto-cycle Club de France initiated the International Cup Race as the first event solely for motorcycles in 1904. But the race proved so chaotic, through cheating by organizers and contestants, that the results were declared void! From this chaos, however, came the formation of the FICM (Fédération Internationale des Clubs Motorcyclistes), which organized the next race, near Paris in 1905, with complete success. It was won by an Austrian, Carl Wondrick, on a Laurin-Klement at 54 mph for the 168 miles distance.

Controversial rules stipulating a maximum machine weight of only 50 kg, and no upper limit on engine capacity, encouraged the construction of special racing machines which varied considerably from production design. British manufacturers objected to this and demanded regulations more suited to aiding development of touring machines. When this was refused, Britain withdrew support.

Despite the support of most foreign manufacturers for the British proposal, the FICM persisted with its rules. As a result, in 1906 the 'International' series ended through lack of entries! This effectively ended road racing, particularly for British riders, for there was no alternative – British law did not allow the closing of public roads for racing.

But it did not affect the Isle of Man, where the TT (Tourist Trophy) Races were founded in 1907. Held on a 16-mile course from St John, the first race was won by Charlie Collier (single-cylinder Matchless) at 38.23 mph for 10 laps.

Another great asset to British manufacturers was the opening of the 2.75-mile banked speed-track of Brooklands, at Weybridge, Surrey, in 1909. British machines began a domination of motorcycling that was to hold until the late 1930s.

There was little overseas machine participation at the TT during the 1920s, a decade of intense competition between British manufacturers – Sunbeam, AJS, Norton, Velocette, and Rudge. They also dominated the European GP scene, where classic races by then existed in Belgium, France, Germany, Italy, and the Netherlands.

Racing machine development during this period remained closely allied to production design, but constantly improving performance eventually brought the need for specifically designed racing machines. The cost of such machines is enormous, but BMW and NSU in Germany and Gilera and Moto Guzzi in Italy received considerable government aid. This aid reached its peak in 1939, when a 500 cc supercharged BMW twin won the Senior TT and a supercharged four-cylinder Gilera won the Ulster GP, the first ever race to be won at over 100 mph.

Supercharging was banned by the FIM in 1946, and this gave British manufacturers renewed life for their otherwise obsolete single-cylinder machines. Organization of a world championship (European-based) came in 1949, and the incentive for this urged Gilera and Guzzi to develop 350 and 500 cc racing machines. These, far superior to any British opposition, dominated racing until 1957.

But the cost of this effort, with twin-, four-, six-, and eight-cylindered

Oscar Godfrey in 1911 with the Indian machine on which he won the Isle of Man Senior TT. It was the first year that the still-existent Mountain circuit was used, and the Indian Company sent a team from the United States that finished 1, 2, 3 – all with British riders.

machines, was too great, and after 1957 all but MV Agusta withdrew works support from classic racing. This created something of a repeat situation, for without works machines in contention even classic grands prix scarcely rated world championship status. But the FIM refused to amend its regulations to allow racing to continue more economically with tangible restrictions. With no works opposition, MV overran private entrants in the 125, 250, 350, and 500 cc classes.

This was the position when Japan, led by Honda, came into European racing in 1960. With highly specialized and costly machines, Honda, Suzuki, and Yamaha gained domination of the smaller categories, while MV retained its remarkable hold on the 500 cc class. But the cost of racing on this scale, with the need for special metal such as titanium for engine

Hailwood, Mike (GB), was the leading racing motorcyclist of the 1960s. After gaining 250, 350, and 500 cc national titles in 1959, when he was 19 and contesting only his second season, he won the 250 world championship in 1961, Honda's first racing success. He joined MV in 1962, and took the 500 cc world title from 1962 until 1965. He joined Honda in 1966 to win both the 250 and 350 world championships, a feat he repeated in 1967. Honda then withdrew from racing, and Hailwood turned to motor racing – having briefly flirted with the 4-wheel sport in 1963–64 – but with only minor success compared to his motorcycling activity, which brought him the MBE. Nevertheless, he was good enough to win the European F2 championship in 1972 under the expert guidance of John Surtees. And in 1973 he was awarded the George Medal for gallantry, when he saved fellow driver Clay Regazzoni from certain death in South Africa.

Miller, Sammy (GB), could rank, if there were such a title, as the greatest all-round sporting motorcyclist, for he has shone in all spheres. His greatest success was in trials, where he stood unbeaten as British champion throughout the 1960s and won the first world/European titles (1969–70). Ulster-born, he began his career on grass tracks and scrambles before taking up road racing in 1955. As a works rider with Mondial of Italy, he turned professional and featured in classic events until 1957. He then joined Ariel of Birmingham as a trials rider, and began his unparalleled run of success on the famed 500 cc machine 'GOV 132'. He pioneered the introduction of 250 cc machines as the dominant category in trials when he joined Bultaco of Spain, in 1963. He gave up 'professional' trials riding in 1969, but continued as a development engineer with Bultaco, and then, in 1974, with Honda.

The two giants of motorcycle racing, both riding MV Agustas. Far left: Agostini on his way to victory in the 1972 Junior TT. Left: Hailwood winning the 1965 Senior TT despite an incredible collection of mishaps.

Motorcycle sports

Read, Phil (GB), was the first racing motorcyclist to lap the Isle of Man TT course at over 100 mph on a 250 cc machine (1965). This was a Japanese Yamaha, and on this same marque he gained the 250 world title in 1964–65–68 and the 125 in 1968. Riding his own private Yamaha and not a factory prepared model, he won the 250 title again in 1971. Comparatively old, but vastly skilled and experienced, Read, at 33, joined MV for 1973 – and promptly won his first 500 cc world championship to end the domination of this title by his new team-mate Giacomo Agostini.

Robert, Joel (Belgium), won the world moto cross 250 cc title in 1964 on a CZ before he was 21. It was another 4 years before he won it again, but then he won it 5 years running (1968–72), the last on a Suzuki, bringing his GP wins up to a record 50.

Joel Robert on a Suzuki at Doddington Park in 1971.

Smith, Jeff (GB) famed for his last-lap spurts to victory, contested world title moto cross for BSA from 1954 and won the 500 cc championship in 1964 and 1965. These were the peak years of a long career in which he won 9 national 500 cc titles. He achieved his world success by developing a 500 cc machine from the 250 design that had given him 2nd, 3rd, and 2nd places (1960–62) in the world championship.

components, became too much for the Japanese teams. They were prepared to stand this expense only for so long as it took them to capture world markets. With this achieved, further racing was unnecessary. So MV, which is predominantly an aircraft manufacturer with motorcycle racing regarded as a hobby-interest, were allowed to regain control of the 350 cc class.

However, after 1968, the 250 category became predominant, particularly for development of two-stroke engines. Yamaha continued racing, after disbanding its GP team, with machines based on standard design, and these reached quite remarkable power levels. Development was such that, by 1973, Yamaha, trailed by Suzuki, had developed 250, 350, and 500 cc two-stroke machines derived from standard design that could capably challenge for GP honours.

It was a curious situation of the sport turning a cycle which brought it back to the original object of racing at the turn of the century – racing for the purpose of improving road machines. In the 1970s, these were becoming much larger and more powerful, with 750 cc engines being considered as a GP class.

Moto cross (Scrambling)

Moto cross, or scrambling, is the sport of motorcycle racing over a defined course of rough terrain involving jumps, climbs, descents, adverse cambers, and similar riding obstacles. As moto cross, the sport is sometimes wrongly regarded as having started in Belgium and France in 1946. In fact, the sport originated in Britain, as scrambling, at Camberley, Surrey, in 1924.

Scrambling remained at amateur, club level, and was exclusively British until 1946 when British riders introduced the sport to Europe. Continental promoters soon sensed its business potential and constructed permanent stadiums, with

Sidecar racing, a spectacular branch of motorcycle racing in which a 500 cc world championship has been held since 1949. Dominated at first by British Norton-Watsonian machines – Eric Oliver won four titles – it has since 1954 been won almost inevitably on German BMWs, with Max Deubel (1961–64) and later Klaus Enders (five titles) the most prolific.

receipts which encouraged riders to turn professional.

The success of the sport was enormous, and reflected national interest and prestige with the introduction of the Moto Cross des Nations – an international team contest – in 1947. An individual rider's championship (500 cc) was introduced in 1952. As techniques improved, notably during the 1960s, the previously dominant heavyweight four-stroke OHV 500 cc machines of Britain (BSA and Matchless) and Belgium (FN and Sarolea) were superseded by much lighter two-stroke-engined machines of about 400 cc developed from 250 cc

Moto cross, or scrambling, motorcycle racing over rough cross-country courses.

machines, which, owing to their lightness and easy handling were almost as competitive as 500s. This development was headed by Sweden (Husqvarna) and Czechoslovakia (CZ).

Moto cross reached its peak with the early 1970s, surpassing road racing as the most valuable form of publicity for manufacturers. After supporting classic road racing until 1968, the Japanese industry, led by Suzuki and Yamaha, turned towards moto cross to win further world titles and prestige.

Grass track racing

Grass track racing is a form of motorcycle racing over natural grass surfaces with no additional obstacles. The sport originated in southern England about 1929, and was generally held on circuits of about a mile with left- and right-hand bends. As a club activity, riders used their everyday machines or, as experience increased, machines based on standard road design.

Shortage of land after the war brought inevitable shortening of circuits (Brands Hatch was a 1-mile grass track until 1949), until the present style of $\frac{1}{4}$ to $\frac{1}{2}$ mile ovals became established about 1955. This situation encouraged the development of machines similar to those used in speedway, although grass bikes do have gearboxes and rear suspension.

Grass track racing has remained amateur, but interest has grown in other countries, particularly in West Germany, where long circuits of 1,000 metres are highly popular.

Trials

Motorcycle trials, a form of the sport demanding extreme sense of balance, consists of several riding tests called 'sections'. These involve hazards such as steep gradients, descents, tight turns, adverse cambers, deep mud, streams, and rocks, which riders must negotiate without incurring penalty by stopping or even touching the ground for an instant.

Trials machines are designed specifically for the purpose, but as they are used on open roads (for travelling between sections), they must comply with legal requirements. As a result, trials are the most heavily supported form of motorcycle sport, if not a spectator sport. Sections are invariably difficult to reach, and a trials course may measure several miles per lap.

There are variations, such as 3- or even 6-day events (International Six-Day Trials), where spectators can enjoy following the progress. Since 1966, trials have found considerable interest in Europe, where a championship was introduced in 1969.

Machines are constructed to be as light as possible. The most popular concept is based on 250 cc single-cylinder two-stroke machines, headed by the Spanish Bultaco, developed by Sammy Miller.

Trials consist of special riding tests.

Surtees, John (GB), can claim the unique distinction of winning both motorcycle and motor racing world championships. After dominating British national racing from 1951 on Vincent and Norton machines, he joined MV Agusta in 1956 and promptly won his first world title, the 500 cc, at 22. After a quiet 1957 season when he was not fully recovered from injury, he scored a hat-trick of 350 and 500 cc double victories (1958–59–60) — at which stage of world domination he retired from two wheels. His career was marked with the award of the OBE.

Turning to motor racing, he won the World Drivers Championship in a Ferrari in 1964. A serious crash in 1965 threatened to end his career, but he came back to win the gruelling Monza 1,000 km in 1966 when he surprised the world by even starting. He drove for Honda and BRM before producing his own racing cars in the early 1970s.

Tibblin, Rolf (Sweden), was the first motorcyclist to win both the 250 and 500 cc moto cross world titles. From gaining 2nd place in his first international season (1958), he won the 250 championship in 1959 on a Husqvarna. Turning to 500 cc, he was 3rd in 1960, missed 1961 through a broken leg, but was 1st in 1962 and 1963. Consistent with 2nd, 3rd, and 2nd places until 1966, he retired from moto cross in 1967 after seriously breaking an arm.

MOTORCYCLING 'MOSTS'

World championships

Rider	13	Giacomo Agostini (It)
Manufacturer	38	MV Agusta (It)
Sidecar	5	Klaus Enders (W. Ger)

Grands prix

Rider	108*	Giacomo Agostini (It)
– one season	19	Mike Hailwood (GB) 1966
	19	Giacomo Agostini (It) 1970
Manufacturer	267*	MV Agusta (It)
– one season	29	Honda (Jap) 1966

Isle of Man TT

Rider	12	Mike Hailwood (GB)
– one season	3	Mike Hailwood (GB) 1961 and 1967

Moto cross (Scrambling)

World titles	6	Joel Robert (Bel)
Grand Prix	50	Joel Robert (Bel)
Team titles	17	Great Britain

Speed records

World	224.6 mph†	Bill Johnson (US), Bonneville Salt Flats, Utah, 1962
Road race	134 mph‡	Georg Meier (Ger), Grenzlandring, Germany, 1939

*To end of 1973. †Avg speed of two 1-km runs (unofficial runs of up to 286 mph have been recorded). ‡Race average.

Netball

Korfball, a game very much like netball and basketball but which evolved separately, originated in the Netherlands in 1903. It is a passing game played 12-a-side – 6 men and 6 women – on a 90 by 45 metres pitch. Players are restricted to designated thirds of the pitch, but are rotated after every two goals.

In netball, designated positions are clearly indicated.

A seven-a-side game for women and girls, netball evolved from basketball at the turn of the century in Britain. The first rules were drawn up in 1900–01 by the Ling Association. The game was also popular at this time in Australia and was shortly introduced into New Zealand. In both of these countries it was known as seven-a-side basketball until 1970.

Netball depends even more on team-work than basketball does, because a player may not dribble the ball or take a step with it. But she may pivot on one foot before releasing the ball. Another rule that makes it a fast, quick-thinking game is that a player may not hold the ball for more than 3 seconds.

A totally amateur game even at the highest levels, netball is controlled internationally by the International Federation of Netball Associations, formed in 1960 as the international Federation of Women's Basketball and Netball Associations. The first world championship, scheduled for every four years, took place in 1963 at Eastbourne, in England. Australia won the title, coming top of the 11-country competition run on an all-play-all basis. Most of the countries taking part in those and succeeding championships were members of the Commonwealth.

Netball is played both indoors and outdoors on a court measuring 100 by 50 ft, divided into 'thirds', two goal thirds and a centre third. In each goal third there is a 16-ft-radius semicircle around a 10-ft-high goal post, which is situated midway along the goal line. The goals, 15-in-diameter rings with open-ended nets, are attached to the tops of the goal posts. The ball is 27–28 inches in circumference.

The seven players in each team are restricted to certain areas of the court and have assigned roles as follows: goal shooter, goal attack, wing attack, centre, wing defence, goal defence, goal keeper. Goals may be scored only by the goal shooter and goal attack, who must be in the shooting circle when taking a shot at goal. On the defending side, only the goal keeper and goal defence are allowed inside the shooting circle.

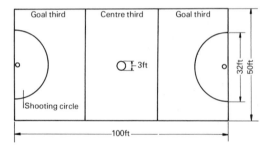

Matches are of 60 minutes duration, divided into four 15-minute quarters, with teams changing ends each quarter. At some levels, two 20-minute halves are played. There are two umpires.

At the beginning of each quarter and after a goal, play starts with a centre pass. It must be received by a player in the centre third, but until the umpire blows for the pass no players other than the centres may move into the centre third.

Players may not throw the ball over a complete third. They may not roll, punch, or play the ball with the foot. Bodily contact is not allowed, and although marking is close, a player may not attempt to defend within 3 ft of the player with the ball. If a player enters a prohibited part of the court, she is offside and her opponents get a free pass. For fouls, a penalty pass is awarded to the other side (the taker is allowed to throw unhindered). A foul in the shooting area is punished by a penalty shot, an unhindered shot at goal.

Olympic Games

The modern Olympic Games, first held in 1896, were the brainchild of Frenchman Baron Pierre de Coubertin. Inspired by the discovery and excavation in the late 1800s of the Olympia complex in Greece, he visualized a modern Olympics that would bring together the youth of the world in friendly competition, all differences in race, politics, and religion to be forgotten.

In Ancient Greece there were many celebrations and festivals in which athletic contests featured. The most notable of these ritual Games was that held at the temple of Zeus in Olympia. The official inauguration of the festival in 776 BC marks the start of the Ancient Olympic Games, the first Olympiad. Held every four years, it gradually grew from a single event – the 'stade' race, a foot race of about 200 yards, the length of the stadium – to a five-day festival that included many kinds of athletic events. To the foot races were added boxing and chariot racing and a pentath-lon which comprised discus and javelin throwing, running, jumping, and wrestling. There were races in armour, horse-races, and special events for boys. In 648 BC an event called the pankration was introduced, a no-holds-barred boxing-cum-wrestling contest in which the participants were often seriously wounded or even killed.

The Ancient Olympics were essentially religious festivals, and the Greeks always proclaimed a sacred truce at the time of the Games. And it was largely due to the waning of religious beliefs that the Games eventually came to an end. As early as the Olympiad of 364 BC the sacred truce and the sanctuary of Olympia were violated by bitter fighting. The Games did not die out with the Roman conquest in 146 BC, but there was much Roman interference, and in AD 65 Emperor Nero competed in the 211th Olympiad and was allowed to receive the victor's crown in the chariot race despite not finishing. Eventually,

A Panathenaic amphora (two-handled jar) from about 525 BC depicts a jumper (with weights), two javelin throwers, and a discus thrower. These events, together with running and wrestling, made up the pentathlon of the ancient Greek Olympics.

*Baron Pierre de Coubertin,
founder of the modern
Olympic movement.*

*In a ceremony in the ruins of
the ancient temple of Altis,
on the plains of Olympia, in
Greece, the flame for the
Olympic torch is kindled from
the rays of the sun. The torch
is then carried by a relay of
runners, often through many
countries and across the seas,
to light the flame at the opening
ceremony of the Olympic Games.*

the Games were abolished, according to most sources as a result of the banning in AD 391 of all pagan cults, by Emperor Theodosius I. The last Olympiad held was reputed to be the 293rd in AD 393, after a period of 1,168 years. The sacred buildings at Olympia were later destroyed, and the ruins submerged by the ravages of earthquakes and floods.

In 1894, Baron de Coubertin established the International Olympic Committee (IOC) to administer the modern Olympics and safeguard their ideals. After the promise of 1896, the celebrations of 1900 and 1904 were reduced virtually to side-shows of trade fairs. The Greeks wished to keep the Olympics in Greece, and held an Interim, or Intercalated, Games in Athens in 1906. But this did not find favour elsewhere, and the Games have always been held in the first year of an Olympiad, or else been postponed.

Women first took part in the Games in 1900, in the tennis and golf, but it was not until later that women's events were included in swimming (1912) and athletics (1928). A separate Winter Olympics was established in 1924 for winter sports (see *Winter Sports*).

The first serious breach of the non-political ideal of the Olympics came in 1936, when the Berlin Games was used as a vehicle of propaganda by the Nazi regime. And strenuous efforts by the IOC since then have not always managed to keep politics out. The expulsion of South Africa from the Olympic movement, the withdrawal of Indonesia and North Korea at Tokyo, the ruthless quelling of the student protests in Mexico City and the Black Power demonstrations in the stadium, the banning of Rhodesia at Munich, and the frightening act of Arab terrorism at the same Games are examples of how politics intrudes, directly or indirectly, in the Olympics or how the Games are used as an innocent tool to further political ends.

Then there is the question of amateurism. No doubt the idealistic views of Avery Brundage, president of the IOC from 1952 to 1972, kept bald commercialism from the Olympic door, but it must be hoped that a 20th-century thinker might be able to rationalize the problems. Overt forms of professionalism such as advertising (the ostentatious display of running shoes or skis in front of the television camera, for example) are obvious contraventions of the code; but what about the professional student and the regular soldier? On this score, as well as for political reasons, many people would consider Russia, for example, ineligible.

And the tremendous growth of the Olympics has brought its own problems. The Games are awarded to a city, rather than a country, and such is the size and expense of the operation that few cities are now capable of organizing an Olympics. There was a movement after the 1972 Olympics to reduce the size of the Games. Some people argue that team games should be dropped. After all, Olympics were not meant to be contests between countries. There will always be a certain amount of chauvinism in sport, but such things as medals tables do not belong in the Games, and the media do a disservice by perpetrating them.

The Olympic movement is a wonderful ideal in a world of few ideals. But it cannot be divorced from the world. It must be above politics and racial and religious discrimination, but it cannot ignore them. Nor can it afford to forget the words quoted by Baron de Coubertin: 'The important thing in the Olympic Games is not so much to win but to take part, just as the most important thing in life is not the triumph but the struggle.'

Athens 1896

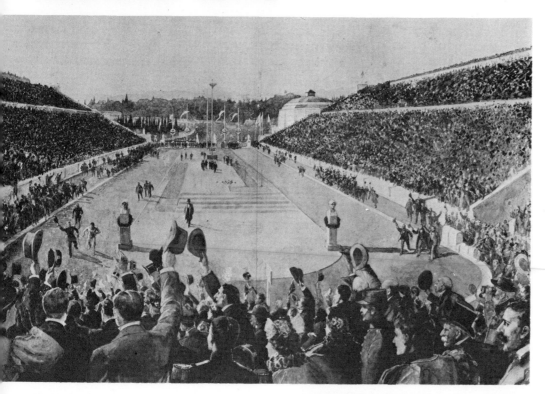

An artist's impression of the finish of the marathon. The Greeks acclaim their only winner of the Games, and the two Crown Princes follow Louis to the finishing line.

There were nine sports in the first Olympic Games. Thirteen nations were represented, most of them with unofficial teams. The 300-odd competitors were all men. For the athletics events, the Greeks restored the 2,000-year-old Pan-Athenaic Stadium of Herodis, rebuilding the ruins in marble. There was room for more than 70,000 spectators round the 400-metre running track, which was long and narrow with very sharp bends.

The 13-man American team won 9 of the 12 athletics events. Three of their number were dual winners – Thomas Burke (100 and 400 metres), Ellery Clark (high and long jumps), and Robert Garrett (shot and discus). Clark's high jump was a creditable 5 ft 11¼ in, and Garrett had never seen a proper discus before. He beat the leading Greek by some 7 inches with his last throw, but the Greeks' disappointment at losing their 'specialist' event was turned to jubilation when Spyridon Louis won the last event, the marathon. The other two events, the 800 and 1,500 metres, had both been won by former Australian mile champion Edwin Flack, resident in England and a member of the London Athletic Club.

In addition to athletics there was cycling, fencing, gymnastics, lawn tennis, shooting, swimming, weightlifting, and wrestling. The cycling produced the first triple gold medallist, Paul Masson

of France, who won the 333⅓, 1,000, and 10,000 metres, and Alfred Guttmann of Hungary won two swimming golds. But the organization and the standard of competition for many of these other sports left much to be desired. Some of the swimming races took place in the ice-cold Bay of Zea, and only three of the entrants turned up for the 500 metres. The tennis singles was won by John Pius Boland, an Irish tourist who just happened to be in Athens. He also won the doubles partnered by a German. These events were held in a shed.

King George of the Hellenes presented all the prizes on the final day of the Games. Winners received a gold medal and an olive branch, runners-up a bronze medal and a laurel branch. The Greeks, who had originated the Olympic idea more than 2,500 years previously, had given the modern Olympics a splendid start.

A photograph of the start of the 100 metres shows the contrasting starting styles of the runners. The one in the centre is balancing on sticks.

Memorable moments in sport

Greek wins first Olympic marathon

Dateline: Athens, 10 April 1896. The hero of the first Olympic Games was, appropriately enough, a Greek. Spyridon, or Spyros, Louis, a shepherd according to some sources, a post-office messenger according to others, was from the village of Marusi, not far from Athens. And although his biographical details might have become obscured over the years, he carved himself a niche in sporting history by climaxing the first of the modern Olympic celebrations with his marathon victory.

The marathon race was the inspiration of French scholar Michel Bréal, who suggested a long-distance endurance test to commemorate the famous feat in 490 BC of the Greek soldier Pheidippides. The latter is said to have carried the news of the historic defeat of the Persians to Athens from the plain of Marathon. After covering the 25 miles, Pheidippides delivered his message and fell dead from exhaustion.

Most of the 17 runners who lined up for the start at the bridge of Marathon were Greek. This was the last of the athletics events, and none had been won by Greeks – to the great disappointment of the huge crowds that had flocked to the newly built stadium at Athens every day. The race was 'sponsored' by various enthusiastic supporters, so that the winner – if he were Greek – would receive a variety of special prizes ranging from jewellery to free haircuts for life.

The early leaders were a Frenchman, Albin Lermusiaux, and the Australian who had won the 800 and 1,500 metres, Edwin Flack. The runners were accompanied by a troop of cavalry, cartloads of

Spyridon Louis, bedecked in national costume and clutching the spoils of victory, looks overwhelmed by all the fuss.

medical personnel, and from time to time groups of peasants. At one stage the Frenchman was so far ahead that he was actually crowned as victor by zealous villagers, but he dropped out after 32 of the 40 kilometres (nearly 25 miles). This left Flack in the lead. But he was soon joined by the moustachioed Louis, and when Flack collapsed 4 km from the stadium Louis surged on alone.

The news of his approach was announced at the stadium, and when he arrived the crowd rose to welcome him. Hundreds of doves were released and Crown Prince Constantine and Prince George of Greece accompanied him on the lap round the track. Five out of the first six finishers were Greeks, and the crowd were jubilant. Louis won by 7 min 13 sec, still the greatest winning margin in an Olympic marathon.

The race not only set the seal on a highly successful first Olympics, but set a pattern for the many dramatic marathons to come.

A photograph of the stadium taken before the start of the Games.

Paris 1900

The second modern Olympics were held in conjunction with the Paris International Exhibition of 1900, and unfortunately many of the Olympic sports played only a secondary role to the exhibition, being spread over a period of nearly six months.

The athletics programme, a five-day affair in the Bois de Boulogne, was haphazardly organized, with an uneven 500-metre track on thick grass and throwing areas restricted by trees.

The United States again sent a small, unofficial team, but mopped up most of the medals in track and field. Their stars were Alvin Kraenzlein, who won four individual gold medals (60 metres, 110 and 200 metres hurdles, and long jump) and Ray Ewry, who took the three standing-jump events. Americans won 17 of the 24 athletics finals despite being

A runner being 'refreshed' in the marathon.

weakened when a number of their team refused, for religious reasons, to take part on Sunday.

One event they did not win was the marathon, held over a 25-mile course that followed the old city fortifications. A controversial race that took place in a temperature of 102°F in the shade, it was won by local baker's roundsman Michel Théato, who beat his compatriot Emile Champion by 4½ minutes, with the rest of the field more than half an hour behind.

British entrants won four of the middle-distance events, and also did well in the swimming, which took place in the Seine. John Jarvis won both the 1,000 and 4,000 metres. A British team won the first Olympic water polo tournament, beating Belgium 7–2 in the final. And Britain also produced the first woman gold medallist of the Olympic Games, in the shape of tennis star Charlotte Cooper, a Wimbledon champion. She won two titles, the singles and the mixed doubles in partnership with R. F. Doherty. The famous Doherty brothers, 'R. F.' and 'H. L.', won the men's doubles and H. L. won the singles.

More than 1,300 competitors took part in the second Olympics, including 11 women. It was regrettable, however, that the French had allowed the Games to be overshadowed by their exhibition. Nevertheless, the new Olympic tradition had been continued, and it would take no less than a world war to halt it.

A rather seedy-looking forerunner of the modern Olympic Village.

Memorable moments in sport

Former cripple wins three Olympic titles

Dateline: Paris, July 1900. American Ray Ewry won three gold medals in Paris, for the three standing-jump events. But to appreciate the magnitude of his achievements, one must go back to his childhood. As a boy he was paralysed, confined to a wheelchair. But choosing to ignore the medical predictions that he would never be able to walk, he devised exercises for himself and stuck to them unswervingly.

As a result, he developed extraordinarily powerful legs, along with the perfect co-ordination and timing that made him the greatest standing jumper in the world.

Jumping from a standing position demanded immense skill and strength, and the long and high standing jumps were on the Olympic schedule up to 1912, the triple up to 1904.

In Paris the 26-year-old former cripple won all his events, the high and triple jumps by substantial margins. Four years later, in St Louis, he successfully defended his three Olympic titles, and in 1908 in London he won the two remaining standing-jump events – taking his collection to eight individual Olympic gold medals. In addition, he won the two standing-jump events at the 1906 Interim Games.

St Louis 1904

For the second successive Games an exhibition was allowed to exploit the Olympic programme. This time it was the Louisiana Purchase Exposition of St Louis, and numerous local events were encouraged to merge with the Olympic competition over a four-month period. Consequently even Missouri schoolboy competitions were designated as 'Olympic' events.

The Games turned out to be the most one-sided in the history of the Olympics. Contributing to the dominance of the American competitors was the fact that few European countries could afford to send full-strength teams across the Atlantic. In the athletics, foreign entrants won only four medals in the 23 events, the only gold-medallist from abroad being the Canadian Etienne Desmarteau in the 56-pound weight. Americans won all the boxing, cycling, and rowing golds. Only in the fencing were they mastered, little Cuba contriving to win five of the six finals. And Hungary and Germany contained them in the swimming.

Star of the track was Archie Hahn, with golds in the 60, 100, and 200 metres sprints. His 21.6 seconds for the 200 metres was perhaps the outstanding performance of the Games, and remained an Olympic record until 1932.

In the athletics events at St Louis only one gold medal left the United States, that for throwing the 56-lb weight, won by Etienne Desmarteau of Canada.

Memorable moments in sport

Marathon runner hitches a lift

The winner, Hicks, receiving attention at 23 miles. He nearly collapsed when Lorz passed him full of running.

Dateline: St Louis, 30 August 1904. The St Louis race produced the now customary drama and controversy that had so rapidly become associated with the marathon. The field, consisting mainly of Americans and Greeks, had to contend with a hilly, 40-km course, a temperature in the nineties, and choking clouds of thick dust and exhaust thrown up by accompanying vehicles.

One of the Americans, Fred Lorz, retired with cramp and accepted a lift. But the car broke down, so he decided to run the last few miles back to the stadium to collect his clothes. When he arrived he was greeted as the winner, and actually stepped up to receive his victor's wreath before he was denounced.

Meanwhile another American, British-born Thomas Hicks, was staggering over the last few miles with the assistance of eggs, brandy, and doses of strychnine administered by his four attendants. He nearly collapsed when Lorz passed him full of running, but revived when persuaded the latter was no longer in the race, and won by 6 minutes.

The surprise of the race was the lone Cuban, postman Felix Carvajal, who had begged his way to St Louis and ran in heavy street shoes, shirt, and serge trousers cut down before the start by an American discus thrower. He finished fourth, and comparatively fresh, after his frequent stops to chat with spectators.

Lorz received a life ban which lasted a year, Hicks survived an objection to his on-course attention, and another runner almost died from a haemorrhage caused by inhaling so much abrasive dust. The Olympic marathon had lived up to its reputation.

Olympic Games

The Olympic flame burns above the flags of the nations.

Athletics has always been the centrepiece of the Olympic Games.

'The most important thing . . . is not so much to win but to take part . . .'
Above left: Japan's Sekini (gold) v Britain's Jacks (bronze), middleweight judo semi-final, Munich 1972. **Above:** Netherlands (7th) v Australia (12th), water polo, 1972. **Left:** Britain's Marion Coakes on Stroller (individual silver), grand prix jumping, Mexico City 1968. **Below:** Hungary's Vilmos Varju (8th), shot put (65 ft 11½ in, or 20.10 metres), 1972.

Swimming (**below**) has been one of the major sports of the Olympics since 1896. Archery (**right**) returned in 1972 for the first time since 1920.

The 1972 US Olympic Trials. Mike Bernard (**above**) was unlucky; Olympic champion Willie Davenport (**below**) qualified, but came fourth in Munich.

Above: Britain's Pat Delafield and Tim Crooks come 5th in the 1972 double sculls. **Below:** Australia (5th) and India (bronze) battle it out in the hockey.

The victors. **Above:** Russia beat Japan in the 1972 women's volleyball final. **Right:** Out on their own in Acapulco Bay, Britain's Pattisson and Macdonald-Smith sail *Superdocious* to victory in the 1968 Flying Dutchman class. **Below:** East Germans Hofmann and Amend win the 1972 Canadian pairs canoeing slalom.

London 1908

The London Games, with 22 sports and 2,000 competitors, was a forerunner of the massive, highly organized celebrations of later Olympiads. But, because of the number of protests from visitors, it was the last Olympics allowed to be run by the host country.

Great Britain, while not dominating to the extent of the Americans in the previous Games, did exceptionally well, winning all the boxing, lawn tennis, rackets, rowing, and yachting gold medals, the soccer, hockey, polo, and water polo events, and most of the swimming, cycling, archery, and motor-boat racing golds.

In the athletics, the Americans again demonstrated their superiority, Melvin Sheppard winning three golds, the 800 and 1,500 metres and the relay. Irish-American 'whale' John Flanagan won his third successive Olympic hammer title. Britain's Wyndham Halswelle won a controversial 400 metres, 'walking over' after the disqualification of an American for hampering him. The only other two finalists were also Americans, and they refused to take part in the re-run.

The marathon, run for the first time over the now standard 26 miles 385 yards, began at Windsor Castle and finished with three-fifths of a lap of the White City Stadium. Won by American John Hayes, it is forever remembered for a gallant loser, Dorando Pietri, who collapsed in sight of the tape and was helped across the line by officials.

Wyndham Halswelle completes the only 'walk over' in Olympic history, in the re-run final of the 400 metres. His time was a highly respectable 50.0 sec.

Memorable moments in sport

The Dorando marathon

Dateline: White City, 24 July 1908. Italian sweet-maker Dorando Pietri – known as Dorando because that was how his name appeared in the programme – became the hero of the 1908 Olympics even though he failed to win a medal. There had been dramatic marathons before 1908 and there have been others since, but the Dorando marathon stands out. The British public have always loved an underdog, and there was a touch of the Charlie Chaplin about Dorando.

The Italian came to the Games with a high reputation as a distance runner, but he also had a record of bad luck and was prone to confusion. His running career, it is said, was started by accident, when as a 17-year-old he ran an errand for an employer, delivering a letter in person instead of posting it, and covering some 30 miles in about four hours in the process.

A diminutive bandy-legged figure, moustachioed and wearing long, bright red shorts, he was the first of the runners to reach the White City Stadium. But, true to form, he started to run the wrong way round the track (the normal direction had been reversed). He was turned round and began to lurch towards the

tape, a pathetic figure now, falling down every few steps but each time picking himself up with tremendous courage and determination.

The crowd were willing him on, but he had to be helped up a number of times, and half carried across the line by officials. This led to his automatic disqualification. Half a minute later the 19-year-old John Hayes finished and was awarded the race. Dorando received a special gold cup from Queen Alexandra when the medals were awarded, and he also won the hearts of the public and earned sporting immortality.

Dorando is helped across the line (above), and receives the special cup from Queen Alexandra (below).

Stockholm 1912

Stockholm was the last Olympics at which the number of competitors per event was almost unlimited. With over 2,500 taking part, it was ably organized by the Swedish hosts and the standard of performance rose accordingly.

Women's swimming events were held for the first time, and a new sport, the modern pentathlon, was introduced. Another brainchild of Baron de Coubertin, it was devised to find the best all-round athlete. The world's best all-round athlete did emerge at Stockholm – although not in the modern pentathlon – in the shape of Jim Thorpe, who won the track and field pentathlon and decathlon, but later tragically lost his medals on a technicality.

The popular hero of the Games was Hannes Kolehmainen, who set the wonderful Finnish tradition in middle- and long-distance running. In winning the 5,000 and 10,000 metres and the 8,000 metres cross-country golds – and a heat in the 3,000 metres team race in world record time – he ran six races in nine days.

Kolehmainen's elder brother Tatu made a strong bid for the marathon, but was finally broken by two South Africans, Kenneth McArthur and Christian Gitsham, who finished first and second. For the first time the race was run on an out-and-back course. But it was still started in the heat of the afternoon, and all the precautions and strict medical supervision arranged by the Swedish authorities could not prevent the worst tragedy to strike an Olympic marathon – Lazaro, a Portuguese runner, collapsed with the heat and died in hospital.

The Americans won their customary lion's share of the athletics medals. They provided five of the six 100 metres finalists, and after eight false starts Ralph Craig won the first leg of his sprint double. The first Olympic 4 × 100 metres relay, however, went to Britain, the Americans being disqualified in the preliminaries. Another unexpected British victory came in the 1,500 metres, won by an individual entrant, Arnold Strode-Jackson of Oxford University.

The 800 metres provided a remarkable blanket finish, with the 19-year-old American Ted Meredith emerging in front in a world record time of 1 min 51.9 sec that stood for 14 years.

Apart from the medallists, three men who were later to excel in other fields also did well at the Games. Philip Noel-Baker, the British statesman who won the Nobel peace prize in 1959, came sixth in the 1,500 metres; Avery Brundage, later president of the IOC, was fifth in the pentathlon; and the American who came fifth in the modern pentathlon, G. S. Patton Jr, later won fame as one of the most colourful generals of World War II. But for his shooting, he would have won a medal!

Memorable moments in sport

Athlete extraordinary

Dateline: Stockholm, 7–15 July 1912. The name of Jim Thorpe is no longer to be found in the official records of the Olympics. Yet in July 1912 he proved himself the world's greatest all-round athlete by winning both the decathlon and the pentathlon at the Stockholm Games. But he lost his medals the following year when it was revealed that he had once accepted payment for playing minor-league baseball.

An American Indian, Thorpe has been called the greatest athlete of all time. His Olympic performances in the newly installed multi-event competitions are without parallel. He won the 10-event decathlon by a huge margin, and in winning the pentathlon finished first in four of the five events. He competed in two other events, coming seventh in the long jump and joint fourth in the high jump. King Gustav of Sweden handed him his medals with the words: 'Sir, you are the greatest athlete in the world.'

Top: *Hannes Kolehmainen, the first of the 'Flying Finns', just passes Jean Bouin (France) at the finish to win the 5,000 metres final. He also won the 10,000 metres and the 8,000 metres cross-country race.*
Above: *Jim Thorpe, whose high-jumping was nearly 3 inches better than the next man in the decathlon and was good enough to earn him joint fourth place in the high jump event.*

Antwerp 1920

The Finns underlined their pre-war athletics prowess in the hurriedly pre-pared Games held at Antwerp, their nine gold medals eclipsing the American tally by one. These Olympics saw the first appearance of the great Paavo Nurmi, the 'Phantom Finn', and Hannes Kolehmainen returned to win the closest ever marathon – by 12.6 seconds.

Nurmi, record-breaker extraordinary, began his prolific Olympic career by

The victory of Jonni Myyra (above) in the javelin, in which Finnish athletes won all three medals, was a sign of things to come in this event.

following Joseph Guillemot home in the 5,000 metres. But he defeated the Frenchman in the 10,000 metres and also won golds in the individual and team cross-country. The Finns also won four field events and the pentathlon.

Britain's Albert Hill brought off a splendid double in the 800 and 1,500 metres, paced in the latter by the runner-up Philip Noel-Baker, who had given similar unselfish assistance to Arnold Strode-Jackson in the previous Olympics. Another track star was America's Charley Paddock, who won the 100 metres with a typically flamboyant finish.

There were many outstanding per-formances in other sports, too, not least that of the 14-year-old American diver Aileen Riggin, who became the youngest Olympic champion when she won the springboard. Hawaiian freestyler Duke Kahanamoku retained the 100 metres title he had won eight years earlier, and another American, Norman Ross, won the 400 and 1,500 metres. Both earned further golds in the 4 × 200 metres relay. Nor was American domination of the

swimming confined to the men, Ethelda Bleibtrey winning a relay and two individual golds, all with world records.

Italian fencer Nedo Nadi set a long-standing record for gold medals in one Olympics with five. American John Kelly (father of film star Grace) beat Britain's Jack Beresford in the single sculls by a second, and joined his cousin Paul Costello to win the doubles with only half an hour's rest between the two finals. And Mlle Suzanne Lenglen added her illustrious name to the Olympic roll of honour with victories in the tennis singles and mixed doubles.

Canada, as expected, won the first Olympic ice hockey tournament, but the United States sprang a major sur-prise by beating France in the rugby.

The Antwerp Games saw the intro-duction of the Olympic flag and the Olympic oath. But two sports that lost sight of the Olympic ideal were soccer and boxing. The Czechs were dis-qualified for walking off the field in the soccer final after a disputed goal had given hosts Belgium a 2–0 lead. And the boxing tournament was riddled with incidents, protests, and disputes.

One of a long line of Irish-American 'whales' who dominated the hammer event in the early 1900s, Patrick Ryan set a world record of 189 ft 6 in in 1913. He had to wait seven years to win an Olympic gold medal, at Antwerp, with 173 ft 5½ in. His world record lasted for 25 years.

Frank Foss (USA) breaking the world record in winning the pole vault with a clearance of 13 ft 5 in.

Paris 1924

The 1924 Games will always be remembered as 'Nurmi's Olympics'. He won three individual gold medals, including a remarkable 1,500 and 5,000 metres double in the same afternoon, and two team golds for his country. Finland again dazzled in the middle- and long-distance events, with eight gold medals. Apart from Nurmi, there was Albin Stenroos, who dominated a relatively incident-free marathon to win by almost six minutes, and Ville Ritola, whose double in the 10,000 metres and the steeplechase did not receive the publicity it deserved owing to the performance of his illustrious team-mate. Ritola, moreover, finished second to Nurmi in the 5,000 metres (by one-fifth of a second), the cross-country, and the 3,000 metres team event. Other Finnish stars were Eero Lehtonen and Jonni Myyra, who retained their respective titles in the pentathlon and the javelin.

The great American tennis star Helen Wills won two gold medals, for the singles and the ladies' doubles (with Hazel Wightman).

Ville Ritola (Finland) leads Edvin Wide (Sweden) in the 10,000 metres, and they finished in that order with Wide half a minute behind. Ritola also won the steeplechase and was second to Nurmi in three other events. If he always had to run in the shadow of his famous team-mate, then Wide was even more unfortunate. In the 5,000 and 10,000 metres, the Swede won three bronze and one silver medal in 1924 and 1928, with no one but the two Finns in front of him.

Memorable moments in sport

Nurmi's Olympics

Dateline: Paris, 8–13 July 1924. Paavo Nurmi's extraordinary exhibition of distance running in the 1924 Olympics has never been surpassed. He remained undefeated in seven races, including heats, over a period of six days, and won five gold medals. The first 'superstar' of the running track, Nurmi, stopwatch in hand, completely disregarded his opponents' tactics – he just ran them into the ground.

On the first and second days he won his 5,000 and 1,500 metres heats. On the third day he won the 1,500 metres by burning off the opposition after 500 metres. Then, less than 90 minutes later, he resisted a similar attempt by his 5,000 metres adversaries to drop him in the first few laps, and gradually left them all behind, except for fellow Finn Ville Ritola who bravely clung to his heels right to the tape.

On the fourth day, Nurmi was first home in a heat of the 3,000 metres team race, on the fifth he won the 10,000 metres cross-country – picking up an extra gold medal for the team event – and on the sixth he led his country to victory in the 3,000 metres team final.

Those privileged to witness Nurmi's triumphs in that week in July 1924 were watching one of the world's greatest ever runners at the peak of his form. They would never forget it.

Nurmi (right) holds off the challenge of Ritola to win the 5,000 metres, some 90 minutes after pulverizing the opposition in the 1,500 metres final.

Amsterdam 1928

400 metres freestyle winner Johnny Weissmuller (centre) flanked by runner-up Arne Borg (right) of Sweden and Australia's Andrew Charlton, who won the 1,500 metres.

Described by General Douglas MacArthur, president of the US Olympic Committee, as a model for future Olympics, the Amsterdam Games saw the introduction of women's athletics events. There were only five, but women's athletics was in its infancy at that time.

Canadian girls won the 4×100 metres relay and the high jump, Ethel Catherwood clearing 5 ft $2\frac{1}{2}$ in. Canada also produced a surprise star of the track, Percy Williams, who brought off the sprint double. The Americans were almost completely eclipsed on the track, failing to win any medals in the 100 and 200 metres, the only time this has ever happened in either of these events.

But it was the Finns again who stole the headlines in the 'glamour' events. There were no team or cross-country races, but the great Paavo Nurmi added to his collection of medals with a gold in the 10,000 metres and silvers in the 5,000 metres and the steeplechase, an event in which he had little experience. Ville Ritola, defending his 10,000 metres title, lost it to Nurmi by six-tenths of a second. But he turned the tables on Nurmi in the 5,000 metres, beating him by 2 seconds. The Swede Edvin Wide came third in both events. Ritola also lost his steeplechase title, failing to finish, but Finns won all three medals.

The tradition of British middle-distance running was maintained in fine style by Douglas Lowe, who successfully defended his 800 metres title and broke the 16-year-old Olympic record.

The future Tarzan, Johnny Weissmuller, again starred in the pool, with golds in the 100 metres and the freestyle relay. This brought his total to five gold medals, a swimming record that stood until 1972.

India began their long domination of Olympic hockey without conceding a goal in the tournament and scoring 29 themselves. Uruguay retained their soccer title, needing a replay to beat Argentina in what was virtually a preview of the 1930 World Cup final. In the rowing, America's Paul Costello completed a hat-trick of double sculls gold medals, this time with a new partner. And Britain's versatile Jack Beresford won a silver in the eights to add to his sculling medals. One of the finest performances of the Games was that of the German fencer Helene Mayer, who won the foil title without losing a bout.

Foil gold-medallist Helene Mayer of Germany.

Lord Burghley (GB) stylishly wins the 400 metres hurdles, breaking the American monopoly in that event.

The United States won 12 athletics titles, 11 of them in the hurdles, relays, and field events. Outstanding was Harold Osborn, who won the high jump and the decathlon. Their only individual track gold on the flat came in the 200 metres, won by Jackson Scholz. It was Britain who shone in the shorter races, through Harold Abrahams (100 metres), Eric Liddell (400 metres), and Douglas Lowe (800 metres). Abrahams scored a shock win in the sprint, becoming the first European to win the event, and still, some 50 years later, the only Briton.

Another great Olympian emerged in the swimming events – the American freestyler Johnny Weissmuller, later to win even more fame in Hollywood as Tarzan. He won the 100 and 400 metres, was in the winning American relay team, and won a bronze as a member of their water polo team. In the men's swimming only the 1,500 metres eluded the Americans. It was won by a 16-year-old Australian, Andrew 'Boy' Charlton, who beat Sweden's Arne Borg by 35 seconds and Borg's newly made world mark by over a minute.

In the absence of Suzanne Lenglen, Helen Wills won the ladies' tennis title, all the golds going to the United States in what was to be the last Olympic tennis tournament. The United States again won the rugby, this time beating France 17–3 in the final. The only other country in the competition, Romania, had conceded a total of 98 points in their two games against the finalists. John Kelly and Paul Costello retained their double sculls title, but Britain's Jack Beresford won the single sculls, Kelly not defending. And British middleweight Harry Mallin became the first boxer to retain an Olympic title.

Los Angeles 1932

Japan's Chuhei Nambu appears to relish winning the triple jump.

Babe Didrikson won the javelin (below) and the hurdles (bottom, seen, far right, in her heat). In the high jump she cleared the same height as the winner, Jean Shiley (USA), but the judges gave the other girl the gold after ruling that Babe's technique was dubious! Apparently to justify this, in the Official Report the winner's jump was recorded as ¼ in or 3 cm more than Babe's, itself a contradiction.

After the near fiasco of the 1904 Olympics in St Louis, the United States were unable to secure another Games until 1932. The Los Angeles Olympics, however, were a success – well organized, highly competitive, with few incidents. And for the first time competitors were housed in a special Olympic 'village'. Nevertheless, there was only half the number of competitors that took part in the previous Games, because few sportsmen from European countries could afford to spend so long away from home.

American athletes reasserted their superiority in the sprints, Eddie Tolan winning the 100 and 200 metres in new Olympic records. Tommy Hampson won Britain's fourth consecutive gold in the 800 metres, and Bob Tisdall, running in Ireland's colours, emulated another Cambridge University man, Lord Burghley, in winning the 400 metres hurdles.

The Italian Luigi Beccali won the 1,500 metres from Britain's Jerry Cornes with the Finns nowhere. But Finland, despite the absence of Paavo Nurmi, still made their presence felt. They were first and third in the 5,000 metres, although the winner, Lauri Lehtinen, apparently impeded runner-up Ralph Hill (US) on the last lap. Another Finn, Volmari Iso-Hollo, won the steeplechase, in which the field ran an extra circuit because an official miscounted the laps. And Finns finished 1, 2, 3, in the javelin, led by Matti Jarvinen, whose brother Akilles won his second decathlon silver medal.

The marathon was a close, exciting race, won by Juan Carlos Zabala of Argentina by 19 seconds from Britain's Sam Ferris. The real drama of the marathon, however, had taken place in the weeks leading up to the Games. The International Amateur Athletic Federation banned Nurmi, alleging that he had infringed his amateur status, despite the protests of the Finnish authorities. The IOC eventually confirmed the ban, and the athletics world was deprived of what Nurmi intended to be a grand Olympic farewell.

A relatively new Olympic power emerged in the jumping events – Japan, who followed up Mikio Oda's gold medal in the 1928 Olympic triple jump with a gold and a bronze this time. Chuhei Nambu, the winner, also came third in the long jump, and Shuhei Nishida narrowly failed to break the American monopoly in the pole vault.

The American women's track and

Juan Carlos Zabala winning the marathon.

field team won five of their six events, and they were morally entitled to claim the sixth, the 100 metres. It was won by Stella Walsh who had lived mostly in the United States since the age of two, but was running under the Polish flag as Stanislawa Walasiewicz. Perhaps the star of the Games was the 18-year-old Mildred 'Babe' Didrikson, who won the 80 metres hurdles and the javelin.

American women also won four of the five swimming events. But it was the Japanese who sprung the shock of the Games by taking five of the six men's.

Other fine performances at Los Angeles included the three gymnastics gold medals of the Italian Romeo Neri and the two golds of British oarsman Hugh 'Jumbo' Edwards in the coxless pairs and fours. Jack Beresford also rowed in the latter, winning his fourth medal in four Olympics. And Australia's Henry Pearce became the first man to retain the single sculls title.

158

Berlin 1936

Apart from the parochial misuse of the early Paris and St Louis Games to further international exhibitions, politics had not yet reared its ugly head in the Olympic arena – that is, not until the Olympics of 1936. Used as an instrument of propaganda to dignify the evil aims of Nazi Germany, the Berlin Games were the biggest and best organized yet. With swastikas lining the massive 100,000-seater stadium, the scene resembled a Hitler youth rally. Thousands of doves were released to signal the opening of the Games by the Fuehrer. The now familiar torch relay from Olympia, Greece, took place for the first time, and the torch was carried into the stadium by a typically blond 'pure Aryan' youth. Perhaps the most ironic gesture of this stage-managed display of Nazi might was the presentation to Hitler of an olive branch by Spyridon Louis, Greek winner of the first modern Olympic marathon 40 years earlier.

Although the Germans, with a team over 400 strong, won more gold medals than even the United States, they won

only five athletics titles, all in the throwing events. The Americans dominated track and field, winning 14 events. And, to the consternation of the Nazi propagandists, it was the black American athletes who shone brightest of all, particularly Jesse Owens, who made his name synonymous with these Games.

The Olympic torch arrives at the Berlin Lustgarten in front of 25,000 German youths. In all, 3,075 runners relayed the flame through seven countries, and elaborate ceremonies were staged in all the big cities.

Jesse Owens, star of the Games, and an embarrassment to the Nazis.

Above: *Korea's Kitei Son, running in Japan's colours, breaks the tape at the end of the marathon.*

Above: *Polo was included for the last time in 1936, the Argentinians winning with ease.* Below: *Double sculls winners Beresford (bow) and Southwood.*

He won the 100 and 200 metres sprints and the long jump, and helped the American sprint relay team to victory in a world record time that stood for 20 years. His duel with the German hero Luz Long in the long jump was a classic, and Long could not have endeared himself to his Fuehrer by his friendly and sportsmanlike attitude to his black adversary.

Negro athletes also won the 400 and 800 metres and the high jump, as well as numerous silver and bronze medals. American athletes also won both hurdles events. But in the 1,500 metres their world mile record holder Glenn Cunningham could not hold New Zealand's Jack Lovelock, who broke the world record in one of the great middle-distance races of all time.

Another classic race was the 4 × 400 metres relay in which the British quartet put on a scintillating display of running to slam the favoured Americans.

One of the finest track performances came in the women's 100 metres, in which the 18-year-old Helen Stephens, the 'Fulton Flash', beat reigning champion Stella Walsh, the 'Polish Flyer', by two yards in 11.5 sec.

The longer track races were once again completely dominated by Finland, whose production line churned out first and second in the 5,000 metres and steeplechase and all three medallists in the 10,000 metres. Volmari Iso-Hollo not only retained his steeplechase title but also won a bronze in the 10,000.

The marathon, however, was a triumph for Japan, with first and third places. The fancied Finns misjudged the early pace and could not catch the first three home – Kitei Son, the British veteran Ernest Harper, and Shoryu Nan. Although running in Japan's colours, Son and Nan were Koreans whose only means of competing was to don the hated vest of the Rising Sun. Another competitor to misjudge the pace was the holder, Argentinian Juan Zabala, who went off too fast and dropped out when caught.

Japan gained a third successive victory in the triple jump and also provided the runner-up. The winner, Naoto Tajima, also won a bronze in the long jump. The Japanese again challenged American supremacy in the pole vault. In a contest that lasted five hours and was completed under floodlights, America's Earle Meadows finally outjumped Shuhei Nishida and Sueo Oe, who shared the silver and bronze medals by cutting them in half.

The men's swimming was another triumph for the Japanese, who won three gold medals and 10 out of a possible 16 altogether. They even won a gold in the women's events, through Hideko Maehata in the breaststroke, who improved on her second place at Los Angeles. The other four women's titles went to the Dutch girls, for whom Hendrika 'Rie' Mastenbroek starred with a 100/400 metres freestyle double, a gold in the relay, and a silver in the backstroke. The United States won 10 of the 12 diving medals, providing the youngest ever Olympic champion, 13-year-old Marjorie Gestring.

Germany – in their best militaristic form – won all the equestrian gold medals, most of the gymnastics, the in-

In the long jump Jesse Owens set an Olympic record that lasted for 24 years.

dividual modern pentathlon, and a share of the shooting medals. One event they did not win was the ladies' foil, in which former Olympic champion Helene Mayer found herself the centre of a *cause célèbre*. A German, then living in America and whose father was Jewish, Miss Mayer had been invited to join the German team only after pressure from the American Olympic Committee. She was placed second, and was said to have thrown a vital bout to spite the Nazis.

The Germans had one of their best triumphs of the Games at Grunau, in the rowing, winning five of the seven gold medals and narrowly missing the other two. In a tremendous finish in the eights, the American boat edged the Italians out by a fifth of a second, with the Germans another two-fifths down. And in the double sculls Britain's pair, the evergreen Jack Beresford and Leslie Southwood, sensationally reversed the result of a heat and beat the Germans by 2½ lengths. For the 37-year-old Beresford it was a fifth Olympics – and a medal in each.

The youngest ever individual Olympic champion, Marjorie Gestring, 13, won the springboard.

There were many heroes of the Berlin Olympics – Owens, Lovelock, Son, Rampling, Beresford, Helen Stephens, Rie Mastenbroek, Marjorie Gestring – but the question must be asked: should the Games have been held? They very nearly were not, for it was only the machinations of Avery Brundage, then president of the American Olympic Committee, that prevented an American boycott. In his innocence, he turned a blind eye to the religious and racial persecution being perpetrated in Germany, and he handed the Nazi regime on a plate a weapon of propaganda they were to use most skilfully. The Fuehrer was projected as the man of the moment; the new German way of life was vindicated in German eyes, and German victories in the Games taken as a triumph for Fascism and totalitarianism; and the Germans were able to demonstrate to the world their new maturity as a nation. Brundage might well say that 'sport transcends all political and racial situations', but this is to give sport a significance that cannot be justified. In the interests of sport, the Berlin Games might overtly have preserved the Olympic tradition in the short term; but in the interests of humanity, it is a tragedy that they were ever allowed to take place.

Lovelock wins classic 1,500

Dateline: Berlin, 6 August 1936. In what was rapidly becoming the Blue Riband of the track, the greatest field to date lined up for the 1,500 metres Olympic final. It included all the Los Angeles medallists – champion Luigi Beccali of Italy, runner-up Jerry Cornes of Britain, and Phil Edwards of Canada – world mile record holder Glenn Cunningham of the United States, the new American ace Archie San Romani, and Jack Lovelock, a New Zealander based in England and former world mile record holder. The only star missing was the British champion, diminutive Sydney Wooderson, prevented by an ankle injury from qualifying.

Lovelock was a runner who believed he could reach his peak only once or twice a year. He had prepared all season for this race, and he planned his tactics to perfection. Cunningham and the Swede Eric Ny cut out the pace, while the crinkly-haired, black-vested New Zealander moved inexorably through the field. Cunningham tried to drop the field on the third lap, but Lovelock went with him, and, with 300 metres to go, he struck – earlier than expected. There was no answer, and he opened up a gap of some 10 yards. And although the brave Cunningham was able to close slightly in the finishing straight, Lovelock hit the tape first in 3 min 47.8 sec, a second inside the world record. Cunningham also beat the old mark, by four-tenths of a second, and he was followed home by Beccali, San Romani, Edwards, and Cornes. The first five smashed the old Olympic record, and only Beccali of the first six failed to produce his best time.

Lovelock finished strongly in world record time, beating world mile record holder Cunningham (746) into second place with 1932 Olympic champion Beccali third.

London 1948

The first Olympics held after World War II were organized in two years on a comparatively low budget. Even so, there were some 4,100 competitors, more than ever before. These austere celebrations were held at already existing venues, the main centre being Wembley Stadium and the Empire Pool, and there was no Olympic village for the competitors. Also missing were the Germans and Japanese, and the Russians were not yet affiliated to the IOC.

The Games were conducted in a friendly atmosphere, and there were no major incidents. Television cameras were present for the first time, although there were few people who could afford sets.

The outstanding competitor at the Games was Dutch housewife Fanny Blankers-Koen, who won gold medals in four events, the two sprints, hurdles, and relay, British girls chasing her home in the first three. Another British runner-up was Dorothy Tyler in the high jump. With the same height, 5 ft 6⅛ in, as the winner, Alice Coachman of the United States, she lost on a failure at that height. Ironically, Mrs Tyler had, as Miss Odam, lost the 1936 gold

The flying Dutchwoman

Dateline: Wembley, 31 July to 7 August 1948. Bursting like a sudden ray of sunshine onto the drab, wet Olympic scene, Fanny Blankers-Koen, the 'Flying Dutchwoman', won an unprecedented four gold medals for a woman at one Games. She set the crowd alight with her explosive start, and rattled off win after win on the Wembley track.

Coming to the Games with seven world records – including the high and long jumps, which she did not enter – she was encouraged by her husband and coach, Jan Blankers, who stung her into action by saying that she was too old. The 30-year-old housewife and mother proceeded to show the world that she was not.

She swept through her heats of the 100 metres, and she beat Britain's Dorothy Manley in the final by three

Top left: Her husband and coach provides shelter from the rain for Fanny Blankers-Koen between races. Left: *A desperately close finish to the hurdles.* Below: *She seems to be flying in the 100 metres final.*

yards in 11.9 sec. She progressed smoothly to the final of the 80 metres hurdles, and, although she lost her hurdling style, just edged out another British girl, Maureen Gardner, in 11.2 sec. She then won a slow heat of the 200 metres, and the mental strain was beginning to tell. But a 'good cry' in the dressing room relieved the tension, she ran an Olympic record 24.3 sec in the semi-finals, and slammed Britain's Audrey Williamson by seven yards in the final. The crowning triumph came in the relay, in which she collected the baton yards down in fourth place and got up to beat Australia's Joyce King at the tape.

Her record stood at 11 races, 11 wins – and 4 gold medals. But it is not for the statistics alone that Francina Blankers-Koen is remembered. She stamped her character and personality on the London Olympics, and the sight of her flying down the track, fair hair streaming behind her, left a memory always to be treasured by those lucky enough to be there.

on a tie, when different rules were operating. Had the rules been changed before the 1936 Games instead of after, she would have won in Berlin.

The men's athletics saw the emergence of the greatest distance runner since Nurmi – Emil Zatopek of Czechoslovakia. He ran away from the 10,000 metres field, completely shattering world record holder Viljo Heino of Finland to win by 47.8 sec. But although he made up some 50 yards on the last lap of the 5,000 metres, he just failed to catch the fading Belgian Gaston Reiff on the line.

The hero of a dramatic marathon was the man who came third, another Belgian, Etienne Gailly. He showed extraordinary courage as, on his last legs, he staggered into the stadium just ahead of Delfo Cabrera of Argentina and Welshman Tommy Richards. But they both passed him on the track, Cabrera winning by 16 seconds from Richards, the third consecutive British silver-medallist in this event.

The Americans were still the most successful athletics nation, with the Swedes taking over 'second place' from the Finns, whose only gold medal came in the javelin. Swedish athletes were first and second in the 1,500 metres, took all three medals in the steeplechase, and won both walks and the triple jump. During the war, Swedish middle-distance runners had rewritten the record book, but their great 1,500 metres stars, Gunder Haegg and Arne Andersson, had been banned for infringing the amateur rules. Yet they still produced Henry Eriksson and Lennart Strand to beat the world at Wembley.

Of the American performers, two stand out – Harrison Dillard and Bob Mathias. Dillard, high hurdles world record holder, failed to make the team in his own event, but qualified for the 100 metres . . . and won it, in a final that contained three sprint world record holders. Mathias, a 17-year-old just out of school, won the punishing decathlon at only his third attempt at the event.

In one of the finest Olympic soccer finals seen, Sweden beat Yugoslavia 3–1. Their brilliant inside-forward trio of Gunnar Gren, Gunnar Nordahl, and Nils Liedholm later made their name in Italian professional football. The Swedes also did well in the canoeing and graeco-roman wrestling, and William Grut won

the modern pentathlon. But although Sweden were placed first in the team dressage, they were later disqualified when it was found that one of their team was not an officer, and thus ineligible to compete.

The Finns, whose athletes had been eclipsed on the track, won four gymnastics events, three of their team sharing the pommel horse gold medal in an un-

Arthur Wint (122) of Jamaica is beaten by America's Mal Whitfield (136) in the 800 metres, but he won the 400, with Whitfield third.

precedented triple tie. In the absence of the Japanese, the Americans regained their former supremacy in the pool, winning all the men's events and most of the women's. In the rowing, at Henley, Britons won the coxless pairs and double sculls, and Mervyn Wood of Australia the single sculls. The fencing was highlighted by a superb performance from the 1936 champion, 41-year-old Ilona Elek of Hungary, who became the first woman to retain the title – and that after a gap of 12 years.

Above left: *A 17-year-old in a man's event, Bob Mathias (USA) took the lead in the decathlon with his discus throw and never relinquished it. He emerged at the end of a gruelling second day the victor by 165 points.* Above: *Two double medallists, Vickie Draves (USA), who won both diving titles, and Reg Harris (GB), who came second in the 1,000 m sprint and the 2,000 m tandem. Harris's was a remarkable performance for he had just recovered from a broken neck and was riding in pain from a broken arm.*

Helsinki 1952

Two of the world's greatest ever distance runners carried the Olympic torch on its final journey to mark the start of the 1952 Olympics, 12 years after the Games had been scheduled to take place in Finland, traditional home of distance running. Paavo Nurmi, a balding, upright figure of 55, brought the 70,000 crowd to its feet as he entered the stadium, torch in hand. After nearly a lap he lit the flame and then handed the torch to the first of the 'Flying Finns', the now 63-year-old Hannes Kolehmainen, who relayed it by lift to the top of the stadium's 250-foot tower to light another flame.

It was fitting, then, that although the Finns themselves could not produce a track star, the hero of the Games should be a distance runner – Emil Zatopek. With an unprecedented triple victory in the 10,000 and 5,000 metres and the marathon, the amiable Czech climaxed four years of world dominance in the distance events. And his wife Dana completed the Zatopek triumph at Helsinki with a win in the javelin.

Other stars of the track included the small Jamaican team. In the 400 metres Herb McKenley again finished second to a team-mate, this time world record holder George Rhoden, and Arthur Wint again followed America's Mal Whitfield home in the 800 metres. In a classic 4 × 400 metres relay, McKenley ran an astonishing third leg in faster than world-record time to snatch a lead that Rhoden maintained for a world relay record 3 min 3.9 sec, finishing a yard in front of the American team.

The American men produced some fine track and field performances, winning 14 gold medals. Outstanding were Bob Mathias, who with a crushing 599-point margin became the first man to win the Olympic decathlon twice, and Horace Ashenfelter, who became the first American to win the steeplechase. Harrison Dillard, reverting to his own event, edged out Jack Davis in an all-American finish to the high hurdles. And surprise silver-medallist in the 1,500 metres Bob McMillen just failed to catch the equally surprising winner, Josy Barthel of little Luxembourg.

Commonwealth athletes won five gold medals in the women's events. Australia's Marjorie Jackson, the 'Blue Streak', completed a world-record sprint double and team-mate Shirley De La Hunty

Josy Barthel (406) was the surprise of the Helsinki Games. Luxembourg's first ever gold medallist, he took the Blue Riband of the track, the 1,500 metres, with another outsider, America's Bob McMillen second, world record holder Werner Lueg (739) of Germany third, and Britain's Roger Bannister (177), unprepared for three races, fourth.

New Zealand's Yvette Williams won the long jump with 20 ft 5¼ in.

Memorable moments in sport

The impossible treble

Dateline: Helsinki, 20–27 July 1952. When Emil Zatopek entered the Olympic Stadium in Helsinki on Sunday 27 July 1952, the crowd rose to him as if they were welcoming one of their own track immortals. The Finns, who had known the great Kolehmainen and the incomparable Nurmi, realized they were witnessing the climax of a feat that had never been accomplished before and would perhaps never be achieved again. As the lone Czech completed the final lap of the last leg of his 'impossible' treble, they gave him what has been described as the greatest sustained ovation ever accorded an athlete. For Zatopek had already won the 10,000 and 5,000 metres gold medals and was now adding the marathon, a distance he had never before run in competition.

Seven days earlier, Zatopek, the undisputed king of long-distance running, had retained his 10,000 metres title with apparent ease, nearly 16 seconds ahead of France's Alain Mimoun. The 5,000 metres, on the 24th of July, had been a rousing affair with Zatopek needing all

Chataway falls on the last bend while leading the 5,000 metres and Zatopek cannot be caught.

Zatopek enters the stadium to an unprecedented reception to complete his 'impossible' treble.

his guile and determination to shake off Chris Chataway, Herbert Schade, and Mimoun on the last bend. Again the Frenchman was runner-up, this time by only four-fifths of a second.

When Zatopek announced his intention to compete in the marathon, there must have been many who thought that he had perhaps overreached himself. Yet the general feeling was one of respect, for although he had never won a marathon before, he was by no means unfamiliar with the distance, having for years maintained long and arduous training schedules. In the event, he ran all the experienced marathon men into the ground, and breasted the tape over $2\frac{1}{2}$ minutes ahead of his nearest rival.

won the hurdles. But for a dropped baton, the Australians would probably also have won the relay, which went to the American girls and was their only athletics gold. South Africa's Esther Brand won the high jump and New Zealand's Yvette Williams the long jump. Russia, competing in their first Olympics since 1912, sent a powerful team of women's 'heavyweights' who dominated the three throwing events and won seven of the nine medals at stake. Only Dana Zatopkova thwarted a Russian clean sweep of the golds.

The swimming was notable for the ascendancy of the Hungarians in the women's events, the only one they failed to win being the backstroke, which went to South Africa's Joan Harrison. Pat McCormick of the United States took both diving events, and American men won both their diving competitions, Sammy Lee retaining his 1948 title. Americans also won four of the six men's swimming events and provided close seconds in the other two.

In the boxing, Hungary's Laszlo Papp moved down a class to take the light-middleweight title, and the middleweight division was won by Floyd Patterson, who eight years later became world heavyweight champion.

Russians won most of the gymnastic medals, with Viktor Chukarin – four golds and two silvers – outstanding. The brilliant and controversial Australian cyclist Russell Mockridge cut into a European preserve with two gold medals. In the fencing, a gallant effort on the part of the 45-year-old women's champion Ilona Elek was checked more by fatigue than by the eventual winner, Irene Camber of Italy. The Mangiarotti family dominated the men's épée, the brothers Edoardo and Dario winning gold and silver in the individual and helping Italy win the team event. Edoardo also won two silvers in the foil events, but here he was overshadowed by a member of another successful family, the young Frenchman Christian d'Oriola. Christian's cousin, Pierre Jonquères d'Oriola, won the individual jumping grand prix on Ali Baba after a five-way jump-off. And it was in the grand prix team event that Britain won her only gold medal. Captain Harry Llewellyn brought what had been a splendid Olympics to a fitting climax with a thrilling clear round on Foxhunter.

Pat McCormick (USA) won both women's diving events at Helsinki, a feat she repeated four years later in Melbourne.

Melbourne 1956

For the first time the Olympics went outside Europe and the United States – to Australia. And it was a marvellously successful Games. Looking down the list of gold-medallists, it is not difficult to discover one of the reasons. For the Melbourne Olympics appears to have had more than its share of sporting heroes. On the track, the remarkable Russian Vladimir Kuts, new king of long-distance running who killed off the rest by means of punishing bursts, won the 10,000 and 5,000 metres by considerable margins; American sprinter Bobby Morrow won golds in both sprints and the relay, demonstrating the faultless style and consistency that led many experts to regard him as the greatest sprinter ever; South America's first field event gold-medallist, triple jumper extraordinary Adhemar da Silva, retained his title; America's Al Oerter, the supreme Olympic competitor, won the first of his four discus titles; and shy Australian 18-year-old Betty Cuthbert became the Golden Girl of the Games with a sprint treble to emulate Bobby Morrow. Other Australian 'all-time greats' to make their

Dawn Fraser (left) and Lorraine Crapp beat each other in the 100 and 400 metres and helped Australia win the relay.

Olympic debut in Melbourne were Dawn Fraser, who won the 100 metres freestyle and relay golds; Lorraine Crapp, not far behind Dawn, who won 400 metres freestyle and relay golds; and Murray Rose, with 400 metres, 1,500 metres, and relay gold medals. The pool also saw America's supreme diver Pat McCormick win both events for the second time. And in other sports there were the Russian gymnasts Boris Shakhlin and Larissa Latynina, both winning the first of their record number of Olympic golds, and Viktor Chukarin, adding three to the four he won in Helsinki; another Russian, Vyacheslav Ivanov, winning the first of his unique trio of single sculls titles; Laszlo Papp, winning his record third boxing gold; Denmark's Paul Elvström, winning the third of his four yachting titles; Sweden's Gert Fredriksson, winning the fourth and fifth of his six canoeing golds; and the nigh unbeatable Christian d'Oriola, retaining his foil title.

In addition to this galaxy of 'superstars', Melbourne was the scene of some outstanding personal achievements from competitors who raised their performance when it mattered most. Third-string steeplechaser Chris Brasher won Britain's first individual track medal for 24 years, but not before surviving a disqualification for alleged obstruction; Irishman Ron Delany came from tenth at the bell with a last lap of 54 seconds to win the 1,500 metres, beating such performers as Australia's John Landy and Hungary's Laszlo Tabori and breaking the Olympic record by nearly 4 seconds; Alain Mimoun won France's third Olympic marathon, with his Helsinki conqueror in two events the great Zatopek, a shadow of his former self after an operation, still managing

Below: The iron man of athletics, Russia's Vladimir Kuts puts in a typical killing burst during the 5,000 metres final and leaves three great British runners labouring in his wake. All some-time world record holders at various distances, they could not stay with the relentless Russian, who won in 13 min 39.6 sec, 2.8 sec outside Gordon Pirie's world record. Pirie (189) finished second, 11 sec behind, with Derek Ibbotson (188) third. Chataway fell right back to 11th. It was a particularly fine effort of Pirie's, who five days earlier had been the only man to stay with Kuts in the 10,000 metres, but had cracked at 8,500 metres and finished eighth.

Bottom: Australia's Betty Cuthbert (466) wins her first title, the 100 metres. She went on to complete a golden treble by winning the 200 metres and the relay. Her more favoured compatriot Marlene Mathews (470) had to be content with bronze medals in the two sprints.

Memorable moments in sport

He also won the hammer title

Dateline: Melbourne, 24 November 1956. Harold Connolly's victory in the Olympic hammer event was somewhat obscured by his romance with the beautiful Czech discus-thrower Olga Fikotova. To many, Connolly's win was just another gold medal for one of the American production line of throwing stars – although it had been 32 years since an American had won this particular event.

It was, however, a triumph over severe handicap, the culmination of years of dedication and determination. For Connolly had suffered a broken arm at birth, which left him with a withered arm. When he was fully grown, his left arm was nearly 4 inches shorter than his right, and he had broken it four times before he was 15. The son of a footballer, he was determined to succeed at sport, although he was 22 before he took up hammer-throwing, having strengthened his arm with weight exercises and tried various other events first.

He came to Melbourne as the new world record holder, having just deprived the Russian champion Mikhail Krivonosov of his world mark. Although the two rivals were well below their best at the Games, they fought a dingdong battle which Connolly won by a

mere 6 inches in a new Olympic record.

Olga Fikotova also won a gold medal at Melbourne, where the two met, and after a romance that regularly made the front pages of the Western press – it did not seem possible that Czechoslovakia's top sportswoman would be allowed to marry an American – they were finally granted permission to wed. The wedding took place in Prague in 1957, with Emil Zatopek as best man.

Although neither of the Connollys won another Olympic medal, Harold set his final world record in 1965 and they both continued to compete in the Games, Harold until 1968 and Olga until 1972, when she carried the flag for the American team at Munich.

Harold Connolly won the hammer with a throw of 207 ft 3¼ in, some 17¼ ft below the world mark he had set in Los Angeles three weeks earlier. But it was good enough to beat Krivonosov, who had set his sixth world record (220 ft 10 in) just 11 days before Connolly's. (Note the difference in size of Connolly's arms.)

sixth place; Bob Richards became the first man to retain the pole vault title, despite failing twice at a low qualifying height; Australia's Shirley De La Hunty retained her hurdles title, won a relay gold, and took her Olympic medal tally to seven, a record for women's athletics; backstroker Judy Grinham became Britain's first swimming gold-medallist for 32 years; Mexico's Joaquin Capilla added a gold to his bronze and silver for the highboard, beating the inevitable American by .03 of a point; Gillian Sheen won Britain's first fencing gold medal with a shock victory over the European favourites; and American hammer-thrower Hal Connolly won a gold medal . . . and a wife.

The Americans, with 15 men's athletics titles, had another successful

Games, but further signs of Russia's emergence as a serious rival in the spurious lists of medal winners were evident in other sports, particularly in gymnastics, wrestling, shooting, rowing, and weightlifting. The Australians had a magnificent Games as hosts, showing the way in swimming and in women's athletics. And a portent for the future was the first entry from both Ethiopia and Kenya.

The Games, which had begun with the entrance of junior mile champion Ron Clarke carrying the Olympic torch, were brought to a close in novel fashion. On a suggestion of a Chinese-Australian schoolboy, competitors from all nations marched together as a single body, and this has since become one of the happiest traditions of the Olympic celebrations.

Rome 1960

Wilma Rudolph wins the 100 metres with gazelle-like grace in a wind-assisted 11.0 sec from Dorothy Hyman (GB). The American won both sprints and a relay gold.

The Rome Games, with more than 5,000 competitors, were marked by some sterling performances in athletics, with Herb Elliott's 1,500 metres outstanding. Unbeaten over the mile or its metric equivalent, and world record holder for both distances, he ran away from the rest of the field after 800 metres, steadily increasing his lead to win by some 20 yards in a new world record.

Rivalling this Australian triumph were two fine New Zealand performances, producing two golds in one afternoon, Murray Halberg winning the 5,000 metres and young Peter Snell the 800. Snell, who was to take over from Elliott as the middle-distance king, beat world record holder Roger Moens in the last few strides.

The marathon, splendidly organized to take the runners back along the torch-lit Appian Way in the evening, was won by barefoot Abebe Bikila of Ethiopia, who finished fresh and undistressed, and beat Zatopek's Olympic mark by nearly 8 minutes. Another popular hero in Rome was Britain's only athletics gold-medallist, the diminutive Don Thompson, christened Il Topolino (the little mouse) when he took the 50 km walk.

European athletes shocked the Americans in the sprints. Armin Hary of Germany, who had recently brought the world 100 metres record down to 10.0 sec – a time accepted with suspicion by many – got his usual perfect start and just edged out America's Dave Sime. In the 200, Livio Berutti set the home crowd alight with a brilliant piece of curve running to equal the world record and become the first European to win this event. And in the sprint relay, the Americans, possibly over-anxious to avenge their previous defeats, made a baton change outside the zone and were disqualified. The race went to Germany, who had finished a metre down in 39.5 sec, equalling the world record. An American, however, won the 400 metres, Otis Davis beating the German Carl

Right: *Herb Elliott (Australia) ran a magnificent 1,500 metres in a world record time (3 min 35.6 sec) that stood for seven years. He won by 20 yards.*
Below: *The great Italian horseman Raimondo d'Inzeo takes Posillipo safely over the water jump. He won the show jumping grand prix from his brother Piero (on The Rock).*

Kaufmann in a photo-finish, both in the world record time of 44.9 sec.

Two Americans fought out a classic long jump, with new world-record holder Ralph Boston beating Irvin Roberson by a quarter of an inch and finally removing Jesse Owens's 24-year-old Olympic record with 26 ft 7½ in. The decathlon produced a magnificent duel between Rafer Johnson and Formosa's Yang Chuan-kwang, with the powerful American's superiority in the throwing events proving the deciding factor.

The Russians won five athletics medals

in the men's events. Their high jumpers eclipsed America's John Thomas, world-record holder, both Robert Shavlakadze and Valeriy Brumel doing 7 ft 1 in. Perhaps Russia's finest performance, though, came from Pyotr Bolotnikov in the 10,000 metres, who kept the title in Russia with a blistering last two laps that left a strong field standing.

The Russian women surpassed their men, winning 6 of their 10 events. The Press sisters took two titles, Irina the hurdles and Tamara the shot, and Nina Ponomaryeva regained the discus title she lost at Melbourne. But the star of the women's athletics was indisputably Wilma Rudolph. Making up for the disappointing showing of America's men sprinters, she raced away with both sprints and anchored the United States team to victory in the relay.

But for the women's breaststroke, won by Britain's Anita Lonsbrough in world record time, Australia and America would have divided the swimming titles between them. Australia won the three men's freestyle titles, although John Devitt's defeat of America's Lance Larson caused a furore over the judging. Murray Rose retained his 400 metres title, but was pipped by fellow-Australian John Konrads in the 1,500. In the women's freestyle, Dawn Fraser retained her 100 metres title, too. Germany's Ingrid Kramer outclassed her rivals in both diving events, and in so doing broke a 40-year-old American monopoly.

The Russians continued their reign of supremacy in the women's gymnastics, with Larissa Latynina outstanding; but Japan maintained their challenge in the men's. They won the team gold and provided nearly as many individual medallists. India lost their 32-year hold on the hockey title, going down 1–0 to Pakistan in the final, and America their 40-year hold on the eights, won by Germany. The boxing roll of honour contained two names for the future. The Italian gold-medallist in the welterweight division, Nino Benvenuti, went on seven years later to win the world middleweight crown, and the light-heavyweight champion was none other than Cassius Clay. And Italy brought the celebrations to a close in fine style by taking first and second places in the individual show jumping through the brothers Raimondo and Piero d'Inzeo.

Two long-distance winners finish at night, Abebe Bikila (left) *in the marathon and Don Thompson* (above) *in the 50 km walk.*

Above: *Romania's Iolanda Balas, with 6 ft 0¾ in, beats the Olympic record by 3¼ in and her nearest opponent by 5½ in to win the high jump.* Below: *Rafer Johnson* (left) *and Yang Chuan-kwang, after a superbly fought decathlon which the American won by 58 points.* Right: *Ingrid Krämer won both diving titles.*

Tokyo 1964

Due to be held in 1940, the Tokyo Olympics were finally celebrated 24 years later. More than 5,000 athletes took part from a record 93 countries. Most of the sports centres were specially built, at a total cost of some £200 million, for these, the first Olympics to take place in Asia. Opened by Emperor Hirohito, the Games were well organized, with much colourful ceremony, but the organizers could do nothing about the weather, and it poured for much of the time.

One man who did not mind the rain was Lynn Davies, who took advantage of the conditions to outjump the defending long jump champion Ralph Boston. This completed a long jump double for Britain, as Mary Rand had already won the woman's event with a world record 22 ft 2¼ in. It was the first time British athletes had won either long jump title, and there was a similar shake-up when American runners won both the 5,000 and 10,000 metres. In the latter, world-record holder Ron Clarke made the pace as usual, and dropped the rest of the field except for the unfancied and unknown Billy Mills and Mohamed Gammoudi of Tunisia. One after the other they led in a frenetic last lap as they threaded their way through lapped runners. It was a magnificent race and had the crowd on its feet, as Mills burst through to win America's first gold medal in a distance event on the track. Both he and Gammoudi, who held Clarke off for the silver, ran a quarter of a minute faster than their best for the distance. Clarke fared no better in the 5,000, setting an erratic pace, but being dropped before the finish. And what a finish! Again it was an American, Bob

Anton Geesink, the giant Dutchman who came to Tokyo and shattered the Japanese by winning the open division of the judo.

The last lap of the pulsating 10,000 metres race. Billy Mills (722), Mohamed Gammoudi (615), and Ron Clarke (12) sweep past Ethiopia's Mamo Wolde. They finished in that order.

Memorable moments in sport

Lynn the leap

Dateline: Tokyo, 18 October 1964. Lynn Davies won the Olympic long jump, beating athletes with far greater claims to the title, because he had the ability to produce his best at the right time; the courage and determination to pull out all the stops at the crucial moment, especially when the odds were against him.

The favourites for the long jump were the American holder of the title and of the world record, Ralph Boston, and the European champion and previous world-record holder, Igor Ter-Ovanesyan of Russia. Both had achieved marks over 27 ft.

The morning of the long jump competition was very wet and very windy – conditions that should have made Davies feel at home. But, after a sleepless night, they served only to make him feel nervous and miserable. The qualifying round of the long jump consisted of three jumps, with the 12 top competitors going through to the six-jump final in the afternoon. Davies had a poor first jump (24 ft 3 in) and fouled his second before he realized that his run-up was wrong – he had measured it 5 ft short! But with the rain pouring down, the run-up badly cut up, and a wind blowing straight into him, Davies jumped 25 ft 6¼ in to qualify with his last attempt. And now he felt fine.

The final took place in the afternoon; it was still raining. After four rounds, Boston led with 25 ft 10 in; Davies was third. As he stood at the end of the runway for his fifth jump, Davies saw the flag at the top of the stadium go limp – that meant the wind had dropped. He hurtled down the runway, hit the board, and soared into the lead with 26 ft 5¾ in, a distance his two rivals could not quite match.

So Davies, from little Nantymoel in Wales, had done it. He'd beaten the world's best, in the world's greatest competition. He was the first British man to win a field event since the 1908 Olympics, the first to win the long jump, and the first Olympic champion from Wales. It wasn't for nothing they called him 'Lynn the Leap'.

In pouring rain and to a backcloth of umbrellas, Lynn Davies makes his winning leap.

Below: *New Zealander Peter Snell, wins the 1,500 metres with ease, completing the first 800/ 1,500 double for 44 years. Josef Odlozil (84) of Czechoslovakia was second, another New Zealander John Davies (467) third, and Britain's Alan Simpson (159) fourth.*
Bottom: *Dawn Fraser wins her third consecutive gold medal in the 100 metres freestyle, a record for a swimmer. Known as 'Granny' because of her advanced age – 27 – for a swimmer, she was suspended for 10 years by the Australian swimming authorities for misbehaviour at the Tokyo Games.*

Schul, who came through with a 54.2 sec last lap to demoralize Michel Jazy of France, who dropped right back to fourth.

America dominated the track as they had never done before, also winning all the sprints, the hurdles, and the relays. Notable performances included 100 metres winner Bob Hayes's explosive anchor leg in the relay and Henry Carr's graceful bend running in the 200 metres. America also provided the two long-legged, gazelle-like winners of the women's sprints, Wyomia Tyus (100 m) and Edith McGuire (200 m). Australia's Betty Cuthbert made a dramatic Olympic come-back to snatch the 400 metres from Britain's Ann Packer, who then proceeded to take the somewhat unfamiliar – to her – 800 metres in confident style.

Yet with all these fine performances and heroics on the track, the man who stood out above all was Peter Snell of New Zealand. He retained his 800 metres title and later stamped his class all over the 1,500 metres field to achieve the first 800/1,500 metres double since 1920.

Abebe Bikila, running in shoes this time, became the first man to retain the marathon title. His world best time of 2 hr 12 min 11.2 sec was even more remarkable in that he had had his appendix removed five weeks earlier. Another great Olympian to triumph over injury as well as his rivals was Al Oerter, who won his third successive discus title despite a dislocated neck and strained rib cartilages!

Other giants of the field were Valeriy Brumel, who improved on his high jump silver in Rome, beating John Thomas, but only on fewer failures; Iolanda Balas, the dominant figure in women's high jumping for the past six years, who retained her title; and the Press sisters, who added another three golds to the two they won in Rome, Tamara with the shot and discus, Irina with the pentathlon, in which she beat Mary Rand into second place.

The most gold-bemedalled competitor of the Games was American swimmer Don Schollander with four, the 100 and 400 metres freestyle and two relays. Americans won 13 of the 18 swimming events. But Australia won three of the men's individual titles, and Dawn Fraser became the first woman in Olympic history to win a title three times running – the 100 metres freestyle. The only European to win a swimming title was the 15-year-old Russian breaststroker Galina Prozumenschikova, who set an Olympic record with her name as well as her swim. The only other European to strike gold in the pool was German diver Ingrid Krämer-Engel, who retained her springboard title but was prevented in the highboard from repeating her Rome double by America's Lesley Bush.

Another competitor to win a third consecutive title was Vyacheslav Ivanov, the Russian single sculler. And in the show jumping, Germany's Hans Günter Winkler, individual champion in 1956, won his third consecutive team gold. The individual winner was Pierre d'Oriola, champion in 1952 and thus the first man to win the title twice. In the water polo, the 37-year-old Hungarian Dezso Gyarmati also won a third gold, in his fifth Games (he also had a silver and bronze).

The Japanese won a total of 16 gold medals to cheer their fans. They dominated the men's gymnastics, with Yukio Endo their star performer. They won five wrestling golds. But their three out of four golds in the new judo events did not include the one that mattered – the open division, won by the giant Dutchman Anton Geesink. The women's gymnastics was a triumph for the Czech girl Vera Caslavska, who won the combined and two other golds. It was a swansong for the great Larissa Latynina, who won a team gold and the floor exercises.

In boxing, the heavyweight division was won by Joe Frazier, who six years later was to become world champion. There were many unpleasant incidents in the boxing. But the usual crop of disputed decisions and complaints about everything from the refereeing to the gloves were overshadowed by the straight left Spanish featherweight Valentin Loren poked at the referee after being disqualified; he was suspended for life.

There had been, however, relatively little controversy in what was a mammoth celebration. But before the Games began, athletes from Indonesia and North Korea had been banned for taking part in the unsanctioned 'political' GANEFO Games in 1963, so both teams withdrew. Perhaps this was a sign of things to come.

Mexico City 1968

The choice of venue for the 1968 Olympics caused lengthy controversy. Standing 7,440 feet above sea level, Mexico City raised an altitude problem for the athletes competing. In the rarefied air, a man normally living at sea level might need a period of anything up to four or five weeks to become acclimatized, and competitors in events that required more than a minute or two of continuous effort might need longer.

The Olympics were dubbed 'The Unfair Games', because competitors from high-altitude countries such as Kenya and Ethiopia would have an advantage. The controversy had originally been sparked off when a Swedish coach forecast 'There will be those who will die'. The IOC refused to budge from their decision, but medical precautions were thorough and there was always oxygen available if a competitor got into difficulties.

In the event no one did die – at least none of the competitors. But the political situation in Mexico at the time was tense, and when protesters and police clashed less than two weeks before the Games were due to start, many people were killed. The IOC were faced with the decision of whether to allow the Games to take place in such an atmosphere, in which the Mexican government were apparently oppressing the people. The Games went on, but the choice of Mexico City was looking more and more unfortunate.

As expected, the competitors from high-altitude countries did well in the endurance events; the lowlanders – at least those who observed the IOC rule of a miximum four weeks' training at high altitude in the three months prior to the Games – were at a distinct disadvantage. In the 'explosive' events, on the other hand, competitors from high and low took advantage of the rarefied air, and new world and Olympic records were commonplace.

But not even the thin air could account for the most remarkable performance of all – Bob Beamon's 29 ft 2½ in long jump, an improvement of 1 ft 9½ in on the world mark. In the sprints, Jim Hines took the 100 metres in 9.9 sec, Tommie Smith the 200 in 19.8, and Lee Evans the 400 in 43.8 – all world records set by American Negroes, who also dominated the relays. But the Games could not shake off the controversy that continued

to dog them – now in the shape of a Black Power demonstration. Smith and the 200 metres bronze medallist John Carlos, after giving an indication of their intentions by running in black socks, each raised a black-gloved hand in the Black Power salute during the playing of their national anthem. They were both sent home, but ugly incident or not, they had made their point: if they win something they are Americans, if they do something bad they are Negroes.

Kenya won three gold medals on the track. Kip Keino won the 1,500 metres and Naftali Temu the 10,000, beating, respectively, the two great athletes and world-record setters of the 1960s, Jim Ryun and Ron Clarke. Ryun, not at his fittest, bravely came second – although he was never in with a chance against the runaway Keino. Clarke, sadly, had no chance in the conditions, coming sixth in a race won in a time nearly two minutes outside his world record, and collapsing at the finish. He needed oxygen, and eventually had to be helped out of the stadium. Behind Temu was

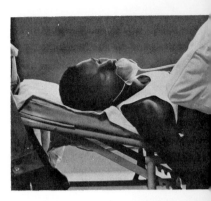

A not uncommon scene at Mexico City, where, although no one died, a number of athletes collapsed either during or after competing, and had to be revived with oxygen.

A more light-hearted Black Power salute from the 4 × 400 metres gold medallists.

Ethiopia's Mamo Wolde, beaten in a sprint finish, and Tunisia's Mohamed Gammoudi, both of whom went on to win fine victories. Wolde kept up Ethiopia's remarkable record in the marathon, taking over from double winner Abebe Bikila, who had to retire after 17 km with an injured leg that would carry him no farther. And Gammoudi outsprinted the two Kenyans Keino and Temu in the 5,000 metres in another all-African finish. Kenya's third gold medal was won in the steeplechase – in remarkable style, or lack of it. Amos

Willie Davenport (USA), winner of the 110 metres hurdles.

Below: *Czechoslovakia's Vera Caslavska set the gymnastics hall alight with her display in the floor exercises to the tune of 'The Mexican Hat Dance', winning four gold medals (one jointly), including the combined exercises.*
Right: *Debbie Meyer (USA) became the first swimmer to win three individual titles at one Games, the 200, 400, and 800 m freestyle.* Bottom: *Britain's David Hemery (402) produced one of the finest performances of the Games with a world record win in the 400 m hurdles.*

Biwott, who had run his first steeple-chase some 10 weeks previously and had won his heat by 70 yards, looked like the novice he was for most of the race. He contrived to jump the water without getting his feet wet, but was 30 yards down and virtually out of the race at the bell, when suddenly the leaders found him flying past them, and hitting the tape just in front of his compatriot Ben Kogo.

One of the finest runs of the Games came from Britain's David Hemery, who outclassed a fine 400 metres hurdles field and knocked a second off the world record, with team-mate John Sherwood third. And Australia's Ralph Doubell equalled Peter Snell's world record in winning the 800 metres.

In the discus, Al Oerter laid claim to being the greatest Olympian of all time, with his fourth successive win, producing a personal best 212 ft 6½ in – as usual, just when it mattered. In the hammer, on the other hand, it was a case of third time lucky for Hungary's Gyula Zsivotsky, twice runner-up, who beat his Tokyo conqueror Romuald Klim of Russia by 3 inches after a see-saw struggle.

The phenomenon of the Games, apart from Beamon's long jump, was the 'Fosbury flop', the backward style of high jumping that won America's Dick Fosbury the high jump. American athletes won 12 of the men's medals, their other victories including Bob Seagren's 17 ft 8½ in pole vault, a height also jumped by the two German runners-up, and Bill Toomey's decathlon. The triple jump produced a most exciting contest, with the first five inside the world record and Russia's Viktor

Kenya's Kip Keino, in his element at the high altitude, toyed with the 1,500 metres field. His winning margin, 2.9 sec, was the biggest in the history of the event.

in the longer freestyle events and Charles Hickcox in the medleys. But both of these Americans were overshadowed by their team-mate Debbie Meyer, who won three freestyle golds. And Claudia Kolb won the two medleys. Dutch girl Ada Kok finally won an Olympic gold when she scraped home in the 200 metres butterfly, a new event. World-record holder for both butterfly events, she had come fourth in the 100, won by Australia's Lyn McClements.

The 'flop' of the pool was America's Mark Spitz, who won 'only' two relay golds, a bronze, and a silver. World-record holder in half a dozen events, he

The supreme competitor, Al Oerter wins his fourth discus title.

Saneyev winning with his last jump.

The women's events produced the first sprinter, of either sex, to retain the 100 metres title – Wyomia Tyus. Australia's girls were among the medals, with bronze and silver in the 200 metres and a gold and silver in the hurdles, 17-year-old Maureen Caird edging out Pam Kilborn. There was a dramatic 800 metres semi-final, in which the favourite Vera Nikolic of Yugoslavia suddenly ran out of the stadium, unable to stand the pressure, and is said to have attempted suicide. Another girl under a lot of pressure was Britain's Lillian Board, popular favourite for the 400 metres. She was beaten on the tape by Colette Besson of France after tying up in the straight.

The women's discus provided a success story to parallel Zsivotsky's in the hammer. Lia Manoliu, a 36-year-old engineer from Romania, finally made it in her fifth Olympics and after two successive bronzes. She beat world-record holder Liesel Westermann by 20 inches.

The swimming was a triumph for American competitors, the men winning 10 of 15 possible titles, the women 11 of 14. Australia's Mike Wenden, however, took the 100 and 200 metres freestyle, and East Germany's Roland Matthes the two backstrokes. And the most popular man in the pool was Felipe Munoz, who gave the home crowd something to shout about with a gold in the 200 metres breaststroke.

Other dual winners were Mike Burton

A desperately close finish to the women's 400 metres, with Colette Besson (France) just getting up to beat the tiring Lillian Board (GB) at the tape.

expected, and was expected, to collect a record haul of golds. He would have to wait another four years, now, to make his dreams come true.

The gymnastics hall was the centre of much attention, with Czech girl Vera Caslavska the popular heroine of the Games. With four gold medals, including the combined, she suitably eclipsed her Russian rivals – 'oppressors' in the eyes of the free world, after Russia's heartless invasion of Czechoslovakia earlier in the year. In the men's events, Japan also outshone the Russians, confirming their supremacy of the last Games.

Britain's yachtsman Rodney Pattisson, crewed by Iain McDonald-Smith, won the Flying Dutchman class by the most convincing margin ever in an Olympic regatta. After having their first-race win ruled out, they proceeded to set Acapulco Bay alight with five firsts and a second. Other British suc-

Memorable
moments
in sport

The man who jumped into the next century

Dateline: Mexico City, 18 October 1968. It's the final of the long jump and the first three have fouled. The tall American Negro comes bounding down the runway, chops his stride slightly before he hits the board, and then soars up, long, lithe arms spreadeagled towards the ground, knees bent but feet stretching forward; he lands crablike in the sand, catapults into an upright position and just stops himself falling backwards.

The sighting device for measuring the jumps won't stretch far enough, so the officials use a steel tape. Someone ventures that it must be all of 28 feet – the next 'magic number' in the long jump list of world records, which had taken 33 years to progress from 26 to 27 feet, and had remained at 27 ft 5 in since 1965.

Suddenly Beamon is seen cavorting about with joy, and the figures light up on the scoreboard – 8.90 metres. As commentators consult their conversion tables, someone says that it's 29 feet $2\frac{1}{2}$ inches. But that's impossible . . . yet it's true.

Beamon has jumped virtually into the next century, for who can believe that his record will be even approached for decades to come. They said that if everything went right for Beamon, he would 'jump out of the pit'. Well, he didn't have style or consistency, but he had bags of natural talent, he was fast, he hit the board at just the right time, with the maximum possible wind of 2.0 metres/sec in his favour, and he soared through the thin air of Mexico City 1 ft $9\frac{1}{2}$ in farther than anyone in history. The 1968 long jump competition was over after only one jump.

A phenomenon that will always be associated with the Mexico City Games is the 'Fosbury flop', perpetrated to perfection by Dick Fosbury (USA), who won a gold medal with a final height of 7 ft $4\frac{1}{4}$ in, and revolutionized high jumping at the same time.

cesses included the three-day event team, with a gold medal, and Marion Coakes, who won a show jumping silver on her tiny pony Stroller, with David Broome third.

A not very convincing, comparative novice won the boxing heavyweight division – George Foreman. Although a certain amount of promise showed through his inexperience, few would have predicted he would be world champion within five years. A more polished winner was Britain's middleweight Chris Finnegan, and he, too, went on to win a certain amount of fame as a professional.

The soccer final was a disgrace to the Olympic movement. A panicky Mexican referee needlessly lost control just before the interval and sent three Bulgarians off. Hungary beat them 4–1, but not without losing one of their men in the same way, and the crowd littered the pitch with cushions in disgust. The match strengthened the argument against team games in the Olympics.

That the Olympic movement survived in 1968 was a testimony to the strength of its ideals. But the signs were there for all to see – the controversy, the politics, the commercialism. The Games had become too big for their own good. How much longer could they continue in their present form?

Munich 1972

Overshadowing everything else that happened in Munich was the violent and premeditated murder of 11 members of the Israeli Olympics team by Arab terrorists. Early in the morning of Tuesday, 5 September, a group of terrorists slipped into the Olympic Village, killing two of the Israeli team and holding others hostage. These were to die at Fürstenfeldbruck air base some time after midnight.

There were strong arguments for cancelling the Games, which were about halfway through. In the event, it was decided to continue. There was a service for the dead sportsmen on Wednesday morning. The world was horrified at the events of the previous night. The Olympic ideal survived, but these Games went on under a dark cloud.

The organizers, while setting out to make this the most impressive Games, had also looked for an image completely divorced from that of the 'Nazi Olympics' 36 years before. So, ironically in view of later events, they called them 'The Smiling Games'. But even before the Games started, the smile was wiped from the face of IOC president Avery Brundage.

Of course, it was politics that reared its ugly head – in the form of a threatened 'black boycott' if the Rhodesian team were allowed to compete. The International Olympic Committee thought that the question had been resolved a year before the Games, when the Rhodesians had agreed to 'participate as a British colony'. But as soon as the Rhodesians – with a 'mixed' team of 30 athletes – arrived in Munich, they were accused of dishonouring the agreement (for one thing, they wore blazers with 'Rhodesia' on, instead of 'Southern Rhodesia'), and their exclusion was demanded. The IOC, obviously reluctantly and by a small majority, voted the Rhodesians out of the Games.

The 84-year-old Brundage, who was handing over the reins of the IOC to Lord Michael Killanin at these Olympics, was perhaps justified in calling this affair 'blackmail'. But when, at the service for the dead Israelis, he attempted to equate the two events, he made a serious error of judgement. For 20 years, he had ruled the Olympics with a rod of iron. He was honest in his aims and rigid in his ideals, but he regularly made the sort of *faux pas* that

exposed his naivety. In an ideal world, his definition of an amateur might have stood up. But, as he was soon to have hammered home to him, the world was far from ideal – and the world of sport could not be completely dissociated from this imperfect 'outside', however hard he tried.

The Germans poured millions of pounds into the Munich Olympics. The majestic acrylic structure that covered the Olympic Stadium itself cost £20 million. The 21 sports were concentrated as far as possible in one centre, most of the venues specially built at immense cost – the £3 million shooting complex, the £2 million artificial canoe slalom, the £8 million rowing course, and so on. More than 7,000 athletes from 122 countries took part.

The striking feature of the contests was the comparative eclipse of the Americans. By normal standards, 33 gold medals cannot be termed failure, but compared with the 50 of the Russians and the 33 shared by the Germans (20 East, 13 West), the American achievement was their poorest for a very long time. Yet it could not so much be attri-

Avery Brundage, IOC president, who retired at the end of the Munich Olympic Games.

The flags fly at half-mast, and the crowd sits in silence during the memorial service for the murdered Israeli sportsmen. The Olympics continued, but 'The Smiling Games' were over.

The clock turned back 50 years, to the days of the great Nurmi and the rest of the 'Flying Finns', as once again Finland dominated the middle-distance events. Lasse Viren won the 10,000 metres, despite falling halfway through the race, and the 5,000 metres (above), beating the holder, Mohamed Gammoudi (904), into second place, with Britain's Ian Stewart (309) snatching the bronze from Steve Prefontaine (USA). In the 1,500 metres (below), the tall, bearded Pekka Vasala strode majestically past the holder, Kip Keino, to give Finland her third gold medal. But the Kenyan did not come away without a title from his last Olympics. For in the steeplechase (right, across page) he stumbled to victory in only his fifth attempt at the event. Ben Jipcho (574), his more fancied team-mate, came second, and the Finns had to be content with the bronze (Tapio Kantanen, 207).

buted to a falling of standards as to slack organization and the most incredible bad luck. Everything went wrong for the Americans. It seemed as if there was an imp – a whole army of imps – sitting on their shoulders just waiting for an opportunity to wreak some mischief.

Two American sprinters, joint world record holders for the 100 metres, arrived too late for their heats and were eliminated. Jim Ryun got himself boxed in during his heat of the 1,500 metres, tripped, and was out. His team-mate Dave Wottle completely misjudged his semi-final run and failed to qualify, so the Americans had no finalist in the 1,500 metres. And Wottle, who had luckily won the 800 metres, again misjudging his run so that he caught Evgeni Arzhanov on the tape only because the Russian fell over, discovered to his own acute embarrassment that he had kept his white peaked cap on during the US national anthem. The antics on the rostrum of the 400 metres gold and silver medallists Vince Matthews and Wayne Collett, however, were not unintentional. And although they were allowed to keep their medals, they were disqualified from this and all future Olympics. With the third runner, John Smith, injured, this meant that the Americans were unable to field a 4 × 400 relay team.

Further disasters hit the Americans in the field events. The holder of the

pole vault, Bob Seagren, found at the last moment – but after a long-drawn-out controversy – that his pole was banned. He was unable to get used to the standard pole in time, managed only 17 ft 8½ in (9¼ in below his world record), and finished 4 inches behind the East German Wolfgang Nordwig. Thus the United States lost the pole vault for the first time in Olympic history. Other titles to elude the Americans for the first time in many years were the shot and discus. Only one American managed to reach the final of the high jump, Dwight Stones, who won the bronze, 2 cm behind the winner, Yuri Tarmak of Russia. But Randy Williams won the long jump with a splendid first jump of 27 ft 0½ in, a do-or-die effort made with an injured leg.

Even America's biggest athletics triumph – Frank Shorter's shock win

in the marathon in the fine time of 2 hr 12 min 19.8 sec – was marred somewhat in the eyes of spectators when a hoaxer (a German student) entered the stadium first, in running kit, and drew the misguided applause of the crowd. Nevertheless, it was the first United States win in this event since 1908, and their other runners were fourth and ninth. Defending champion Mamo Wolde failed to stretch Ethiopia's run of success to a fourth gold medal, but he won the bronze.

Two heroes of the track were Lasse Viren of Finland and John Akii-Bua of Uganda. Viren, despite falling, won a scintillating 10,000 metres, in world-record time, and went on to complete a double in the 5,000, holding off the previous champion Mohamed Gammoudi, Britain's Ian Stewart, and America's Steve Prefontaine on the last lap. Another champion to lose his title on the track was Dave Hemery in the 400 metres hurdles. He was just shaded out of second place by America's Ralph Mann, but neither could approach the fabulous run of Akii-Bua, who chopped three-tenths of a second off Hemery's 'unassailable' record.

Another fine performance was the sprint double achieved by Russia's Valeriy Borzov. He beat the remaining American by a yard in the 100 metres final, and confirmed his worth by smoothly powering to the 200 metres gold in a final that included three Americans.

Kenya's Kip Keino lost his 1,500 metres title by half a second to the strong, bearded Finn, Pekka Vasala – what an Olympics it was for the Finnish middle-distance men after so many years – but still went home with a gold. Unable, because of the programme, to run in the 5,000 metres, he opted for the steeplechase, an event he had run only four times before. And he won it – despite his appalling hurdling – in a time only 2 seconds outside the world record. Team-mate Ben Jipcho was second, with the third Kenyan, defending champion Amos Biwott, in sixth place.

In the women's events, Britain's Mary Peters crowned a long and successful career with a world-record win in the pentathlon, only 10 points ahead of West Germany's long jump winner Heide Rosendahl. Miss Peters was the

Top left: *Russia's sprinting machine Valeriy Borzov allows himself a modest salute after completing the 100/200 metres double.* Top right: *The boxer of the Games, Cuban heavyweight Teofilo Stevenson (right), smashes America's much-vaunted Duane Bobick to third-round defeat in the quarter-finals.*

Above: *16-year-old West German high jumper Ulrike Meyfarth became the youngest ever athletics gold medallist when she 'flopped' over 6 ft 3½ in to equal the world record.* Below: *Mark Spitz (USA) swam to immortality with seven gold medals – and seven world records – an unprecedented feat.*

only woman to prevent a clean sweep of titles by Russia and East and West Germany. In front of their own crowd, the West Germans produced heroines in Rosendahl; the 16-year-old sensation in the high-jump, Ulrike Meyfarth, who 'flopped' over 6 ft 3½ in to equal the world record; and the tall, blonde Hildegard Falck, who won the 800 metres. Two other outstanding performers were East Germany's Renate Stecher, with a fine sprint double, and Russia's Ludmila Bragina, who dominated the new Olympic event, the 1,500 metres, with world records in heat, semi-final, and final.

It was the swimming pool that produced the man of the Games, with perhaps the outstanding performance in any single Olympics. Mark Spitz, multi-world-record holder, but a disappointment in 1968 when he was expected to shine, won four individual gold medals and three more in US teams – an unprecedented haul. He won every event he entered, and each in a new world record. Other fine individual performances almost went unnoticed: Roland Matthes (E. Germany) repeated his Mexico double in the backstroke, so that he also had accumulated four individual Olympic golds; Gunnar Larsson (Sweden) won both individual medleys, the 400 metres by a five-hundredth of a second; and in the women's events Australia's Shane Gould won three golds, a silver, and a bronze, and America's Melissa Belote pulled off a backstroke double and won a third gold in the medley relay.

Although American swimmers did well, with 17 of the 29 golds, they were still not without their troubles. For Rick DeMont, winner of the 400 metres freestyle and one of the favourites for the 1,500, was disqualified after a dope test. An asthmatic, he took a drug banned by the IOC, something that the American team doctors should have spotted.

But perhaps the most sensational setback of all for the United States was their defeat, for the first time ever in the Olympics, in the basketball. After a courageous uphill struggle with Russia in the final, they appeared to have snatched the title by a point with a last-second score ... but that imp was still hanging around. The teams had to return to the court to play three seconds,

which was long enough for Russia to score the winner.

Other sports had their troubles, too. The Pakistani hockey team, outraged by their defeat in the final by West Germany, accused the IHF of fixing the game and behaved so disgracefully at the medal ceremony that the players and officials concerned were banned for life. And in the modern pentathlon, 14 competitors were found to have taken a tranquillizer drug; no action was taken, however.

But if these Olympics had more than their share of tragedy, bad sportsmanship, and controversy, they also had a full quota of outstanding performances. In gymnastics the Russians provided a worthy champion in Ludmila Turistcheva as well as the darling of the Games in 17-year-old Olga Korbut, who won golds on the beam and the floor. At Kiel, in the yachting, Britain's Rodney Pattisson retained his Flying Dutchman title with another crushing performance, winning four out of six races. The British three-day event team also retained their title, and Richard Meade won the individual gold, too. And for the second Games running, a British girl won the show jumping silver medal – Ann Moore on Psalm. New Zealand had their first ever win in the eights, all the other rowing titles going to Eastern Europe. And in an always packed boxing hall, Cubans won three golds, a silver, and a bronze, and their heavyweight Teofilo Stevenson was the outstanding boxer, and the most exciting, of the whole tournament.

The closing ceremony was as spectacular as anything else seen at the Games, with a massive artificial rainbow dominating the night sky. And yet, as seemed to happen all along, something in the presentation went wrong, this time in the form of a message on the giant scoreboard: 'THANK YOU AVERY BRANDAGE'. No doubt Mr Brundage consoled himself with the thought that it was an *amateurish* mistake.

Once again it was a gymnast who was the darling of the Games. Like Vera Caslavska in Mexico City, Olga Korbut delighted the crowds in the gymnastics hall. And the tiny 17-year-old Russian enchanted millions of television viewers all over the world.

THANK YOU AVERY BRANDAGE

OLYMPIC RECORDS

ATHLETICS
Men

100 metres	9.9 s	Jim Hines (USA)	14.10.68
200 metres	19.8 s	Tommie Smith (USA)	16.10.68
400 metres	43.8 s	Lee Evans (USA)	18.10.68
800 metres	1 m 44.3 s	Ralph Doubell (Australia)	15.10.68
1,500 metres	3 m 34.9 s	Kipchoge Keino (Kenya)	20.10.68
5,000 metres	13 m 26.4 s	Lasse Viren (Finland)	10.9.72
10,000 metres	27 m 38.4 s	Lasse Viren (Finland)	3.9.72
Marathon	2 h 12 m 11.2 s	Abebe Bikila (Ethiopia)	21.10.64
4 × 100 m relay	38.2 s	United States	20.10.68
	38.2 s	United States	10.9.72
4 × 400 m relay	2 m 56.1 s	United States	20.10.68
110 metres hurdles	13.2 s	Rod Milburn (USA)	7.9.72
400 metres hurdles	47.8 s	John Akii-Bua (Uganda)	2.9.72
3,000 m steeplechase	8 m 23.6 s	Kipchoge Keino (Kenya)	4.9.72
20 kilometres walk	1 h 26 m 42.4 s	Peter Frenkel (E. Germany)	31.8.72
50 kilometres walk	3 h 56 m 11.6 s	Bernd Kannenberg (W. Germany)	3.9.72
High jump	7 ft 4¼ in (2.24 m)	Dick Fosbury (USA)	20.10.68
Pole vault	18 ft 0½ in (5.50 m)	Wolfgang Nordwig (E. Germany)	2.9.72
Long jump	29 ft 2½ in (8.90 m)	Bob Beamon (USA)	9.10.68
Triple jump	57 ft 0¾ in (17.39 m)	Viktor Saneyev (USSR)	17.10.68
Shot	69 ft 6 in (21.18 m)	Wladyslaw Komar (Poland)	9.9.72
Discus	212 ft 6 in (64.78 m)	Al Oerter (USA)	15.10.68
Hammer	247 ft 8 in (75.50 m)	Anatoliy Bondarchuk	7.9.72
Javelin	296 ft 10 in (90.48 m)	Klaus Wolfermann (W. Germany)	3.9.72
Decathlon	8,454 points	Nikolai Avilov (USSR)	7/8.9.72

Women

100 metres	11.0 s	Wyomia Tyus (USA)	15.10.68
200 metres	22.4 s	Renate Stecher (E. Germany)	7.9.72
400 metres	51.1 s	Monika Zehrt (E. Germany)	7.9.72
800 metres	1 m 58.6 s	Hildegard Falck (W. Germany)	3.9.72
1,500 metres	4 m 1.4 s	Ludmila Bragina (USSR)	9.9.72
4 × 100 m relay	42.8 s	United States	20.10.68
	42.8 s	West Germany	10.9.72
4 × 400 m relay	3 m 23.0 s	East Germany	10.9.72
100 metres hurdles	12.6 s	Annelie Ehrhardt (E. Germany)	10.9.72
High jump	6 ft 3½ in (1.92 m)	Ulrike Meyfarth (W. Germany)	4.9.72
Long jump	22 ft 5 in (6.83 m)	Heide Rosendahl (W. Germany)	3.9.72
Shot	69 ft 0 in (21.03 m)	Nadyezhda Chizhova (USSR)	7.9.72
Discus	218 ft 7 in (66.62 m)	Fainia Melnik (USSR)	10.9.72
Javelin	209 ft 7 in (63.88 m)	Ruth Fuchs (E. Germany)	1.9.72
Pentathlon	4,801 points	Mary Peters (GB)	2/3.9.72

SWIMMING
Men

Freestyle – 100 m	51.2 s	Mark Spitz (USA)	3.9.72
– 200 m	1 m 52.8 s	Mark Spitz (USA)	29.8.72
– 400 m	4 m 0.3 s	Brad Cooper (Australia)	1.9.72
– 1,500 m	15 m 52.6 s	Mike Burton (USA)	4.9.72
– 4 × 100 m relay	3 m 26.4 s	United States	28.8.72
– 4 × 200 m relay	7 m 35.8 s	United States	31.8.72
Breaststroke – 100 m	1 m 4.9 s	Nobutaka Taguchi (Japan)	30.8.72
– 200 m	2 m 21.6 s	John Hencken (USA)	2.9.72
Butterfly – 100 m	54.3 s	Mark Spitz (USA)	31.8.72
– 200 m	2 m 0.7 s	Mark Spitz (USA)	28.8.72
Backstroke – 100 m	56.3 s	Roland Matthes (E. Germany)	4.9.72
– 200 m	2 m 2.8 s	Roland Matthes (E. Germany)	2.9.72
Individual Medley – 200 m	2 m 7.2 s	Gunnar Larsson (Sweden)	3.9.72
– 400 m	4 m 32.0 s	Gunnar Larsson (Sweden)	30.8.72
Medley Relay – 4 × 100 m	3 m 48.2 s	United States	4.9.72

Women

Freestyle – 100 m	58.6 s	Sandra Neilson (USA)	29.8.72
– 200 m	2 m 3.6 s	Shane Gould (Australia)	1.9.72
– 400 m	4 m 19.0 s	Shane Gould (Australia)	30.8.72
– 800 m	8 m 53.7 s	Keena Rothhammer (USA)	3.9.72
– 4 × 100 m relay	3 m 55.2 s	United States	30.8.72
Breaststroke – 100 m	1 m 13.6 s	Cathy Carr (USA)	2.9.72
– 200 m	2 m 41.7 s	Beverley Whitfield (Australia)	29.8.72
Butterfly – 100 m	1 m 3.3 s	Mayumi Aoki (Japan)	1.9.72
– 200 m	2 m 15.6 s	Karen Moe (USA)	4.9.72
Backstroke – 100 m	1 m 5.8 s	Melissa Belote (USA)	2.9.72
– 200 m	2 m 19.2 s	Melissa Belote (USA)	4.9.72
Individual Medley – 200 m	2 m 23.1 s	Shane Gould (Australia)	28.8.72
– 400 m	5 m 3.0 s	Gail Neall (Australia)	31.8.72
Medley Relay – 4 × 100 m	4 m 20.8 s	United States	3.9.72

Facts and figures

Ray Ewry (USA) won 8 individual gold medals in the standing jumps (high, long, and triple) from 1900 to 1908. He also won the two standing jumps at the so-called Intercalated Games of 1906, giving him a total, according to some authorities, of 10 individual gold medals.

Vera Caslavska (Czechoslovakia) won 7 individual gold medals in gymnastics in 1964 (3) and 1968 (4). These include one shared title. She also won 4 silvers, including 3 team medals.

Lydia Skoblikova (USSR) won all 4 women's speed skating titles in the 1964 Winter Olympics. With the two she won in 1960, this gave her a total of 6 individual gold medals.

Larissa Latynina (USSR) won 9 gymnastics gold medals (1956–64). These include three team golds and a shared title. In all she won a record 17 Olympic medals.

Mark Spitz (USA) won 7 gold medals for swimming at Munich in 1972, including 3 relay golds. Having won 2 relay golds in 1968, he retired with a total of 9 gold medals.

Paavo Nurmi (Finland) won 12 athletics medals from 1920 to 1928, including 9 gold medals. Of these, 6 were individual golds, the rest being for team races.

Al Oerter (USA) won 4 successive gold medals in the same event – he won the discus from 1956 to 1968.

Jack Beresford (GB) won medals in five consecutive Olympics (1920–36), 3 golds and 2 silvers, in sculling and rowing.

Dezso Gyarmati (Hungary) won 3 golds, a silver, and a bronze for water polo in five consecutive Games (1948–64)

Hans Günter Winkler (Germany) won the show jumping individual gold in 1956, and 4 team golds from 1956 to 1972.

Ivan Osiier (Denmark) fenced in 7 Olympics (1908 to 1948), refusing to compete at Berlin in 1936 because of the Nazi manipulation of the Games. He won an individual silver medal in the 1912 épée event.

Ellen Müller-Preiss (Austria) fenced in 5 Olympics (1932–56).

Facts and figures (contd.)

She won a gold in 1932 and bronzes in 1936 and 1948.

Oscar Swahn (Sweden) competed at the Antwerp Games in 1920 at the age of 73 — and won a silver medal for shooting, in the running deer event.

Bernard Malivoire (France) won a gold medal as cox in the coxed pairs in 1952 when only 12. It is claimed, however, that an even younger French boy (aged between 7 and 10) coxed the winning Dutch pair in Paris in 1900.

Marjorie Gestring (USA) won the 1936 springboard title at the age of 13 years 9 months.

OLYMPIC RECORDS (contd.)

ARCHERY

Men's Double FITA Round	2,528 points	John Williams (USA)	10.9.72
Women's Double FITA Round	2,424 points	Doreen Wilber (USA)	10.9.72

CYCLING

1,000 metres time trial	1 m 3.91 s	Pierre Trentin (France)	17.10.68
4,000 metres individual pursuit	4 m 37.54 s	Morgens Frey (Denmark)	17.10.68
4,000 metres team pursuit	4 m 15.76 s	West Germany	20.10.68

SHOOTING

Small-bore rifle	points		
— 3 positions	1,166	John Writer (USA)	30.8.72
— prone position	599	Ho Jun Li (N. Korea)	28.8.72
Free rifle	1,157	Gary Anderson (USA)	23.10.68
Free pistol	567	Ragnar Skanåker (Sweden)	27.8.72
Rapid-fire pistol	595	Jozef Zapedzki (Poland)	1.9.72
Clay pigeon	199	Angelo Scalzone (Italy)	29.8.72
Skeet	198	Evgeni Petrov (USSR)	22.10.68
	198	Romano Garagnani (Italy)	22.10.68
	198	Konrad Wirnhier (W. Germany)	22.10.68
Running boar	569	Lakov Zhelezniak (USSR)	1.9.72

Polo

Polo, in its present form, was developed in India under the British raj and was introduced to England in the late 1860s. Its true origins were probably in ancient Persia, although the word itself is derived from the Tibetan word *pulu*, meaning a ball.

The game was not long in finding its way to the United States, being first played there in 1883. Yet if the British and Americans can claim to be early exponents of modern polo, neither nation can claim to be the best in the world. That honour belongs to the Argentinians, for whom the game is a natural extension of their innate horsemanship and skill at ball games.

Polo has been an official Olympic sport on four occasions, Britain winning the first two (1908, 1920), Argentina the next two (1924, 1936). At Berlin, they beat Britain 11-0 in the final.

Polo is played by two mounted teams of four players on a grass pitch measuring 300 × 200 yd (160 yd if 11-inch sideline boards are used). The players carry long mallet-shaped sticks with which they hit a hard white ball ($3\frac{1}{4}$ inches in diameter). Goals are scored by hitting the ball between goalposts set 24 ft apart. Teams change ends after each goal. A game lasts four or six $7\frac{1}{2}$-min periods, called *chukkas*, and ponies can be replaced between chukkas. There is no offside rule, but penalties are strictly enforced for such offences as bumping and riding across another player's right of way.

Since 1909, an international handicapping system has been used to rate players from −2 to 10 goals, although it is no indication of goalscoring ability. It merely establishes a player's ranking and his side's overall handicap in a tournament.

Polo, an equestrian sport that owes its origins, it is thought, to ancient Persia.

Racket sports

Built in 1882, Melbourne's real tennis court is one of only two in Australia. The match is a rubber of the 1969 Bathurst Cup, in which Britain beat Australia 3-0.

The 'father' of racket sports is said to be real tennis, which originated in France. It is first mentioned in French ecclesiastical documents of the 12th century, and was probably first played in a cloister. There are separate entries in this book for the major racket sports (see *Tennis, Squash, Badminton, Table Tennis*).

Real tennis is also known as *royal tennis* ('real' being French for 'royal'). To the uninitiated, it is the most curious and complex of games to understand. The court is marked out with a series of lines with such names as 'Hazard Chase. The Door' and 'Half a Yard Worse than the Last Gallery'. There are sloping roofs called *penthouses*, a buttress called a *tambour*, an opening called the *dedans*, and a *grille*, which is representative of a courtyard hatch. The game is one of skill and delicacy rather than of power, the ball being sliced and cut rather than hit.

In Henry VIII's England there was – and still is – a court at Hampton Court. And there has been a world champion since the mid-1700s. The game is played mainly in Britain and the United States, although there are one or two of the world's 30-odd courts in France and Australia.

Singles or doubles are played, with what looks like a lop-sided tennis racket and a hard ball (about 2½-inch diam., weighing 2½–2¾ oz). Courts vary, the overall floor dimensions being about 96 × 32 ft. Winning points is, not sur- prisingly, involved, being complicated by placements on the floor known as 'laying chases'. Chases are the lines painted on the floor parallel with the net. Scoring is similar to that of lawn tennis, but a set ends with a player (or pair) winning six games unless advantage sets are agreed.

Equally exclusive, but not nearly as complicated, is the game called simply *rackets*. Similar to squash, it is one of the fastest of court games, perhaps only the pelota games being faster. Rackets is played mostly in England, the United States, and Canada, and is recorded as having been played in the London debtors' prisons of the late 18th century. Today it is the sport of a more privileged class.

A rackets court measures 60 × 30 ft, with four walls 30 ft high completely en- closing it. Players enter through a small door in the rear wall. On the front wall there is a service line 9 ft 8 in from the floor, and a 27-inch-high wooden board above which the ball must be hit.

Service must hit the front wall above the service line and rebound, directly or off a side wall, into the opposing service court. The server is allowed one fault, although the receiver may play a fault, making it good. The ball must always be

Atkins, Geoffrey (GB), of Queen's Club, London, became only the third amateur to win the world rackets championship when he challenged and beat James Dear in 1954. He defended it successfully 4 times before retiring in 1970, so passing the record of the great English professional Peter Latham, who was champion from 1887 to 1902. Atkins's success is even more amazing when it is known

that he was only second string in his school (Rugby) pair – and even that for only one year!

Dear, James (GB), held the singular distinction of winning the world championship at both rackets and real tennis. A Queen's Club professional, he beat Canadian Kenneth Chantler for the vacant rackets title in 1947, and held it until Geoffrey Atkins

beat him in 1954. When Pierre Etchebaster gave up his tennis crown in 1955, Dear promptly won the title and held it till 1957.

Etchebaster, Pierre (France), was world champion at real tennis for 27 years, a period surpassed only by J. Edmund Barré (1829–62). Etchebaster, a Basque who excelled at handball and pelota before becoming a Paris tennis professional in 1922, won the title from G. F. Covey in 1928 and held it until he retired undefeated in 1955.

Rackets singles in the Public Schools Championships, first held in 1868. The public schools are the nursery of the game in Britain.

183

In jai alai, reputedly the fastest ball game of all, the ball reaches speeds of 150–160 mph.

hit after one bounce or on the volley. Only the player (or pair) serving can score, and games go to 15 points (aces), with matches being the best of five games in singles and seven games in doubles. The setting of games that go to 13-all or 14-all is similar to that in badminton.

Of the *pelota* games, the fastest is undoubtedly *jai alai*. Though usually known as *pelota vasca*, it is but one of several games played throughout the Spanish-speaking world with a *pelota* (ball) and racket against a wall or walls. These include *frontennis*, *pelota de goma*, and *pelota de cuero*.

Frontennis is played with a hard rubber ball (about the size of a golf ball) and a tennis-like racket. The court consists of two or three walls; if two, the second is on the backhand side of a right-handed player. The ball must not be allowed to

bounce more than once, and rallies continue until one player or side fails to keep the ball up.

Jai alai is not strictly a racket game, being played with a long, curved, basket-like affair known as a *cesta*. With this, the jai alai player catches the small, hard ball on the full or first bounce as it rebounds off the front, side, or back wall; and in the same movement he hurls it at the front wall. The ball may be thrown at tremendous speed (150 mph) or with so much spin that the opposing player is unable to control it. It can be played as singles, doubles, or triples, with matches ranging from 6 to 40 winning points. Jai alai is a spectacular sport, played on a court some 60 metres long, with high (over 40 ft) granite walls. There is heavy betting and spectators can view the game through a screen on the open side.

Roller skating

Above: *Brian and Patricia Colclough (GB), twice world dance champions.* Below: *Roller hockey.*

Most sports on roller skates are basically similar in technique to those on ice skates, with terminology concerning the roller skate's inside and outside wheels corresponding to that describing the ice blade's inner and outer edges. The footwear is much the same for both media. The roller skate has four composite wheels cushioned by ball-bearings, with rubber toe-stops in place of the ice skate's toe-rake. Modern rinks have maple floors surfaced with polyurethane.

Although an early roller skate was invented by a Belgian, Joseph Merlin, in 1760, the first practical four-wheel skate was introduced in 1863 by an American, James L. Plympton, who opened the first public rink in 1866 at Newport, Rhode Island. The sport expanded rapidly after production of the Richardson ball-bearing skate in

1884. European figure championships began in 1921. The International Roller Skating Federation was formed in 1924, and world figure and dance championships began in 1947.

As on ice, speed skating was the earliest competitive sport on rollers. The first British championship was held in 1894. World championships date from 1937. Performed on outdoor oval circuits or open roads, men's titles are contested over 500, 1,000, 5,000, 10,000, and 20,000 metres. The main women's events are 500, 3,000, and 5,000 metres. A skater can cover 500 metres about 4 seconds faster on ice than on rollers.

Five-a-side *roller hockey*, an adaptation of field hockey to roller skates, became properly organized in 1913, with European championships starting in 1926 and world championships in 1936.

ROLLER SKATING 'MOSTS'

World titles – figure

— men	5	K. Losch (W. Germany)
— women	4	A. Bader (W. Germany)
— pairs	4	D. Fingerle (W. Germany)

World titles – speed

— men	6	L. Lazari, G. Venanzi, L. Cavallini, F. Guardigli (all Italy)
— women	16	A. Vianello (Italy)

Roller Hockey

World titles	11	Portugal

Rowing

Rowing as a sport can be traced back to ancient times and is mentioned in Greek literature. In its modern form it dates from the early 18th century, when it began to be practised first in England. The oldest existing sporting event in the world is the annual sculling race for Doggett's Coat and Badge, in which watermen who have recently completed their apprenticeship compete on the Thames in the centre of London. It was established in 1715.

The first rowing regatta on the Thames was held in 1775. The Oxford and Cambridge Boat Race dates from 1829, and Henley Royal Regatta from 1839. Other countries began to take up the sport in the early 19th century. It spread rapidly across Europe and the American continent, and there were races in New York as early as 1811. But the first amateur regatta in the United States was not held until 1872, though the Harvard-Yale race first took place in 1852. In Australia, the Royal Hobart Regatta was inaugurated in 1838, by which time the sport was well established.

Over fifty countries now have their own national federations, and internationally the sport is governed by the Fédération Internationale des Sociétés d'Aviron (FISA), which controls the international rules for racing and organizes world championships for men and women and for boys up to the year when they reach 18. Rowing has been an officially recognized Olympic sport since 1908, and women's events were scheduled to be included in 1976.

For international championship regattas there are eight classes of boat for men's events, both senior and junior, and five for women's. The men's events are for eights; fours and pairs both with and without cox; and single, double, and quadruple sculls. The women's events are for eights and coxed fours and the three sculling events. Quadruple sculls is a new championship event.

Other major regattas are held in many European centres, notably Lucerne, which ranks next in importance to the world and Olympic championships, and Amsterdam, Duisburg, and Ratzeburg. In England, the Nottingham International Regatta, inaugurated in 1973 on the National Water Sports Centre course, is in the same category, while Henley is the most famous regatta in the world. Its trophies are much coveted, especially the Grand Challenge Cup for eights and the Diamond Sculls.

In sculling, an oarsman holds one small oar, or scull, about $9\frac{1}{2}$ feet long, in each hand. In rowing, an oarsman holds a longer oar, usually between $12\frac{1}{4}$ and $12\frac{3}{4}$ feet, with both hands. Sculling boats are light and slender and require more skill to balance than the longer, heavier rowing boats, but even these are light, with smooth skins only $\frac{1}{8}$ inch thick. A modern eight-oared racing shell is about 58 feet long, but is unlikely to weigh more than 250 lb. Oars are also light, being hollowed out inside the shaft, or loom, and weigh about 8 lb. There are no restrictions to the dimensions of boats and oars, except for certain events for inexperienced oarsmen.

Shorter, wider boats are used for coastal rowing and skiff racing. The latter is practised in heavy single or double sculling boats with fixed seats, and is found only in Britain, on the River Thames.

Rowing is one of the most exhausting of sports, because nearly all the muscles are used during each stroke. Height, strength, weight, and exceptional powers of endurance are required to reach the top. The championship distance is 2,000 metres for men, 1,500 metres for boys, and 1,000 metres for women, but the Oxford and Cambridge Boat Race is rowed over a $4\frac{1}{4}$-mile tidal course, and lasts about 20 minutes. The longest race in the world, the Boston Marathon in Lincolnshire, covers 31 miles.

Adam, Karl (W. Germany), rowing coach whose methods revolutionized the sport in the 1950s and 1960s. A former amateur boxer, Adam ignored traditional rowing and coaching methods. He introduced new types of boats and oars, and adopted the training methods of track athletes. For a decade, his Ratzeburg crews dominated international rowing, especially in eights, taking this event in the 1960 and 1968 Olympics. They were four times European champions and twice world champions in this class.

Beresford, Jack (GB), sculler and oarsman, competed in five Olympics between 1920 and 1936, winning a gold or silver medal on each occasion. In 1920 he narrowly failed in the single sculls, but won the title in 1924. He was second in the eights in 1928, won the coxless fours in 1932, and at his last appearance, in 1936, had a remarkable win in the double sculls. Awarded the Olympic Diploma of Merit in 1949, he won the Diamond Sculls at Henley on four occasions and the Amateur Championship of the Thames, the Wingfield Sculls, a record seven successive times, retiring undefeated.

Fairbairn, Steve (Australia), an outstanding rowing coach, made his reputation in England. His influence was world-wide between the two world wars. 'Fairbairnism' was derided by the purists, who disliked the ugly action that arose from allowing the body to work naturally, but the successes of his Thames and London RC crews and of his college, Jesus College, Cambridge, and of his followers on the continent, notably the great Swiss crews of the mid-1930s, eventually commanded respect. A brilliant all-round athlete himself, he rowed four times for Cambridge. In 1926 he inaugurated the Head of the River Race, which today attracts well over 300 eights.

The victorious Oxford crew in the 1966 Boat Race, in which they beat Cambridge by $3\frac{1}{4}$ lengths.

Rowing terms

Best Boat Light racing boat with smooth skin.

Bow Front part of the boat, oarsman rowing nearest front.

Bumping race Race in which boats start at intervals and attempt to 'bump' the crew ahead of them and so gain a position for the next race.

Canvas Thin linen covering at the ends of racing boats; the smallest margin by which a race can be won.

Catch a crab To feather the blade in the water (a serious fault that usually disrupts the boat).

Cox or Coxswain Man at the stern, facing the oarsmen, who steers the boat (coxless boats are steered by one of the oarsmen).

Feathering Turning the blade flat between strokes to reduce wind resistance.

Head of the river race Race decided on times, the crews starting at intervals.

Paddle Row at less than full power.

Rate of striking Number of strokes rowed per minute.

Recovery The return, between strokes, to the position for making the next stroke.

Regatta A meeting over one or more days in which various kinds of rowing and sculling races take place.

Repechage A race in which the losing crews in the first heats race again to qualify for the next round.

Shell Racing boat.

Skiff Heavy boat built with overlapping planks, used in special types of sculling races.

Skin Outer covering of a racing boat.

Slide The sliding seat or the runners on which it travels.

Station A crew's lane or side of the course.

Stern The rear end of the boat.

Stroke The action of pushing the blade through the water, or, more properly, the complete cycle of the rowing action; the oarsman nearest the stern of the boat who sets the rhythm and rate for the rest of the crew.

Washing Unfairly forcing the opposing crew to row in the wake or the 'puddles' left by the blades.

Top: *An idyllic scene at Henley in 1908 – Great Britain, represented by Leander, beat Belgium in the final of the Olympic eights.* Above: *An unusual event, a women's coxed quadruple sculls, in Germany, not racing, but rowing for style.*

Ivanov, Vyacheslav (USSR), won three Olympic single sculls titles, the only man to achieve this feat. He was only 18 on the

first occasion in 1956, and won again in 1960 and 1964. He won the European title four times and was world champion in 1962. His success came from his brilliant judgement of pace and his calmness in a crisis.

The rules of boat racing are clear and comparatively simple. A crew may not receive extraneous assistance and must abide by their own accidents, except within the first 100 metres, when accidental damage can lead to a race being restarted. A crew must remain on their own station. They risk disqualification if they either leave their lane or interfere in any way with another crew.

A crew may be disqualified for a foul when off their proper course if any part of the boat or oars touch the opponents' boats or oars. A crew may appeal for a foul but not for interference, which is at the discretion of the umpire, who has sole jurisdiction over the race after the start.

Oarsmen are divided into status classes according to age or experience, and move up into higher categories as they record more wins.

ROWING RECORDS

Fastest recorded times (2,000 metres)

	Olympic Games		World/European Championships	
	min/sec		min/sec	
Eights	5:54.02	Germany (1964)	5:33.92	New Zealand (1971)
Coxless Fours	6:22.03	USSR (1964)	6:00.72	E. Germany (1971)
Coxed Fours	6:31.85	W. Germany (1972)	6:12.82	W. Germany (1971)
Coxless Pairs	6:53.16	E. Germany (1972)	6:42.55	Netherlands (1964)
Coxed Pairs	7:17.25	E. Germany (1972)	6:56.94	E. Germany (1971)
Single Sculls	6:31.63	USA (1964)	6:15.27	E. Germany (1971)
Double Sculls	7:10.12	USSR (1972)	6:54.18	Czechoslovakia (1961)

Most Olympic titles 3 J. Kelly (US), *P. Costello (US), J. Beresford (GB), †V. Ivanov (USSR)

Most Diamond Sculls 6 ‡S. A. Mackenzie (Australia)

*All double sculls.   †All single sculls.   ‡Consecutive wins.

Memorable moments in sport

Wilson and Laurie

Dateline: Henley-on-Thames, 9 August 1948. Few who witnessed the 1948 Olympic Regatta will forget the performance of two British veterans who won the gold medal in coxless pairs. For behind their masterly exhibition of rowing skill and watermanship lay an equally remarkable story.

In 1938, two Cambridge blues, Jack Wilson and Ran Laurie, on leave after two years in the Sudan, not only surprised everyone by winning the Silver Goblets for pairs at Henley, but also set a new record time.

Both then returned to the Sudan, 600 miles apart, and did not touch an oar again for 10 years. During this time, Wilson was savagely attacked and all but transfixed by a spear. When Laurie heard of his friend's misadventure, he travelled to see Wilson, expecting to find him at death's door, but instead found him up . . . playing tennis.

On leave again in 1948, the two, now in their middle thirties, decided to row again for the sheer joy of it. And despite their long break and only six weeks'

Above: The British pair (left) winning the 1948 Olympic title from Switzerland and Italy. They had recently returned from 10 years in the Sudan – hardly the training for an Olympic rowing event. Inset: Wilson (left) and Laurie at the victory ceremony.

training, they again confounded the sceptics by winning the Goblets, showing all their old skill in doing so.

Their Olympic selection was now assured, though against the world's best their chances were hardly rated. However, as they won first their heat and then their semi-final, excitement at Henley mounted.

In the final, the Swiss shot into the lead from the flag, and, striking a higher rate, maintained this to the halfway mark, with the Italians close behind. Then, to a roar from the partisan crowd, Wilson and Laurie made their effort and nosed ahead. The gallant Swiss fought back, but, showing the perfect cohesion and steering that are the hallmarks of pair-oared rowing, the British pair held off the challenge to win by $\frac{3}{4}$ length and crown an extraordinary career.

Kelly, John B. Sr (USA), Olympic single sculls champion in 1920, also won the double sculls in the same year and in 1924. His 1920 entry for the Diamond Sculls was refused by the Henley stewards because his club, Vesper, were at that time barred from competing, having infringed the amateur rules before the war. But he went on to beat Jack Beresford, the Diamonds winner, at the Olympics. In 1947 and 1949 he had the considerable satisfaction of seeing his son, John B. Kelly Jr, win the Diamond Sculls.

Mackenzie, Stuart (Australia), lost to the Russian Ivanov at his first international appearance, in the 1956 Olympics, but subsequently beat the Russian on two occasions to take the European title, and on two other occasions at Henley, where he recorded a record six successive wins in the Diamond Sculls (1957–1962). He also won the Commonwealth Games title in 1958. A flamboyant character of powerful build, his tactics often led to accusations of gamesmanship and bad sportsmanship, but at his best he ranked with the all-time greats.

Stuart Mackenzie after his record sixth Diamonds win in 1962.

Pearce, H. R. (Bob) (Australia), Australian-born sculler who later became a Canadian citizen, was Australian amateur champion for three years (1927–8–9). In 1928 he became the first Australian to win the Olympic title and repeated this win in 1932. He took the Empire Games title in 1930 and the Diamond Sculls in 1931. Turning professional in 1933, he was world professional champion in the same year and successfully defended the title until retiring at the outbreak of war in 1939. The last of the great professionals, he was the only man to retire undefeated as both amateur and professional champion of the world.

Rugby league

Billy Boston scoring on the 1962 tour of Australia.

If rugby football was born of a rebellious act – William Webb Ellis reputedly picking up the ball and running with it at Rugby School – so rugby league was conceived in rebellion. On 29 August 1895, at the George Hotel, Huddersfield, the representatives of 21 northern rugby union clubs met to bring a little economic commonsense into their game. Far from their mind was the professional game of today. Theirs was still an amateur game played under rules similar to those of rugby union. Indeed, their breakaway movement was to become the Northern Rugby Football Union, a name retained until 1922, when it became the Rugby Football League.

The reason for the Northerners' dispute with rugby union's southern officialdom was what has become known as 'broken time' payment – the recompensing of players for wages lost through playing rugby. This problem was not so applicable to the South of England, where university and former public school men had few problems about taking time off work; if they had to work. But to miners and factory workers, taking time off work meant losing money.

When infringements of the Rugby Union's 'broken time' payments rule led to suspensions of both players and clubs, the men of Yorkshire and Lancashire decided to act. And following the historic meeting in Huddersfield, the new Northern Union became reality on 3 September 1895 at a meeting at the Spread Eagle Hotel, Manchester. Those rebel clubs involved were: Batley, Bradford, Brighouse Rangers, Broughton Rangers, Halifax, Huddersfield, Hull, Hunslet, Leeds, Leigh, Liversedge, Manningham, Oldham, Rochdale Hornets, St Helens, Tyldesley, Wakefield Trinity, Warrington, Widnes, and Wigan. From the first meeting, Dewsbury had withdrawn, but when the first games were played on 7 September 1895, Stockport had joined.

Significant is the fact that professionalism was quickly declared illegal and a ceiling of six shillings put on 'broken time' payments. All players had to have other employment, and this rule still stands.

Northern Union received a big boost in season 1896–97 with the introduction of the Challenge Cup competition, while 1897 also saw the first of the radical law changes. Line-outs were abolished and experiments were made on several new ways of restarting play from touch. In 1898–99 open professionalism was legalized, and three seasons later, in 1901–02, a new league of Lancashire and Yorkshire clubs was formed to become what is now the Northern Rugby League Championship. Season 1905–06 brought in the Lancashire and Yorkshire County

A fierce clash between St George (light strip) and South Sydney in the Sydney Premiership, Australia's major domestic competition. Twelve teams compete in 22 rounds building up to a grand final.

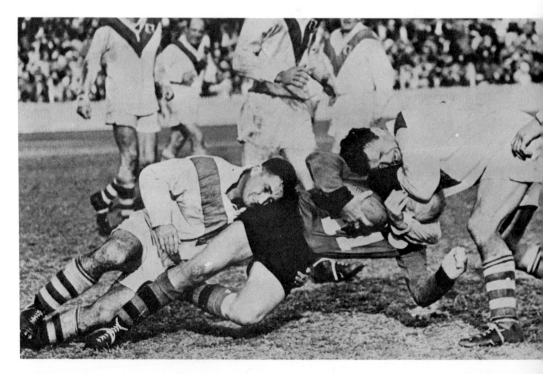

Challenge Cups, and in 1907–08 the now-discontinued County Leagues began. The County Championship had been going since 1895–96.

Perhaps the most important change came in June 1906 with the reduction of teams to 13 players, a move that was to make the game faster, more exciting, and more spectacular. And it was this new rugby that met a team from New Zealand called the 'All Golds' when they toured Britain in 1907–08 under A. H. Baskerville, on the invitation of the Northern Union. With them was the immortal Australian H. H. 'Dally' Messenger, a brilliant threequarter and goalkicker, whom the New Zealanders had played against in Sydney *en route* to England. There were 'broken time' disputes in Australian rugby union at the time, and the 'tests' played with New Zealand led to the rise of rugby league in Australia. Indeed, it was the Sydney sportsmen – now called 'pioneers' – who first used the term 'rugby league'.

Messenger was to return to England the following year with the first Kangaroos, as the Australians are known, and he continued his association with British players when Great Britain made their first tour 'Down Under' in 1910.

Today, matches between Great Brit-

ain and Australia are among the highlights of the sporting world, whether they are in a test series or the World Cup, which was first held in France in 1954. Though lacking the same popularity in other states, rugby league has a great hold in New South Wales and Queensland, with the major clubs, financed by poker machine takings, able to offer lucrative contracts to the best players in both rugby codes.

The contrast between the game in Australia and Britain on the one hand and France and New Zealand on the other could not be more marked. The French Rugby League was founded in 1934 following an exhibition match in Paris between Great Britain and Australia in December 1933, but there, as in New Zealand, rugby league languishes under the shadow of other codes. Even

Nicknamed 'The Wild Bull' and looking the part, Vince Karalius directs operations for Widnes.

Churchill, Clive (Australia), was so highly regarded by Australian fans that he won the accolade 'The Little Master' – after the great Dally Messenger. Though just over 5 ft 7 in tall, the South Sydney fullback was an uncompromising tackler and a strong, powerful runner who made 34 test appearances for Australia, 32 of them consecutive. Churchill toured Britain in 1948–49, as captain in 1952–53 and 1956–57, and as coach in 1959–60.

Churchill, 'The Little Master'.

Fox, Neil (GB), was blessed with the ability and strength to carve or crash his way through the strongest defences. And with a goalkicking accuracy to match his try-scoring feats, the tall, powerful Wakefield Trinity centre not surprisingly was approaching the 5,000 points mark by the end of the 1972–73 season – 4,967 from 2,020 goals and 309 tries. This included a record 20 (7 goals, 2 tries) in the 1960 Cup final against Hull. Fox toured Australasia in 1962 and made 30 international appearances altogether. Surprisingly transferred to Bradford in 1969–70, he returned to Wakefield after a short spell.

A historic Challenge Cup final at Wembley in 1960. Neil Fox (Wakefield Trinity) goes over for a try to score three of the record 20 points he chalked up in Wakefield's record 38-5 victory over Hull.

Gasnier, Reg (Australia), centre supreme, played 36 tests and 3 World Cup matches for Australia, scoring 26 test and 2 World Cup tries. The perfect athlete, with outstanding physique, exceptional speed and courage, Gasnier marked his test debut against Great Britain in 1959 with three tries, an auspicious start to an international career that saw the St George star tour Britain and France three times and New Zealand twice

Jones, Lewis (GB), turned professional after a distinguished rugby union career that saw him capped 10 times for Wales and twice for the Lions. Having joined Leeds for a record £6,000, he continued setting new marks: most points in a season (496 in 1956–57), most points on an Australian tour (278 in 1954), and most goals in an Australian-Great Britain test (10 in Brisbane, 1954). Excellent at fullback, centre, or stand-off, and a prolific goalkicker, Jones played 15 times for Great Britain, including the 1957 World Cup.

Lewis Jones of Leeds in his record-breaking 1956–57 season.

Karalius, Vince (GB), earned the nickname 'Wild Bull of the Pampas' for his crunching tackling on the 1958 Australian tour. A non-stop loose-forward, he captained St Helens to victory in the 1961 Challenge Cup and did the same for Widnes in 1964. He won World Cup honours in 1960.

Messenger, Dally (Australia), toured England with the 1907–08 New Zealand All Golds, returned a year later with the first Kangaroos, and went on to become the greatest player Australian rugby league recognizes. The life-size photo of Herbert Henry Messenger in the foyer of the Australian League headquarters says simply 'The Master' – which is just what this colourful goalkicking centre was. In 1907 he had played union for Australia against New Zealand.

New Zealand (black strip) and France, the 'minnows' of international rugby league, meet in the 1970 World Cup. The Kiwis won this encounter 16–15.

leading international players receive little, if any, payment for club matches. This state of affairs is reflected in the international performances of New Zealand's Kiwis and the French Chanticleers. Success, when experienced, has rarely been consistent, and neither has won the World Cup; Britain and Australia winning this three times each to 1972. Yet strangely, New Zealand and France have won the Courtney Trophy, which is decided on a country's percentage of success over a five-year period.

Since 1948, the International Rugby League Board has been responsible for the international administration of the code, but until then this was done by Britain's Rugby Football League. This body is responsible for all rugby league in Britain, both amateur and professional, although the professional game, consisting of 30 clubs, is controlled by the Northern Rugby Football League, itself responsible to the Rugby Football League's council.

Though the professional game still holds the limelight, it no longer attracts the great crowds it did in the boom years following World War II. Today clubs have had to turn to more social activities to attract fans. Yet the amateur game is gaining popularity in the universities and the South of England, and it may be that, at a time when rugby union in Britain is adopting a more professional approach to coaching and preparation,

rugby league will become even more socially orientated. If so, the wheel could turn, bringing the two codes closer together, perhaps even bridging the bitter gap that has existed in the rugby game for more than three-quarters of a century.

How to play

A rugby league match is played over two periods of 40 minutes between two teams of 13 men each. A team has seven backs and six forwards: fullback, two wing-threequarters, two centre-threequarters, stand-off half (five-eighth), scrum-half; loose-forward (lock), two second-row forwards, two prop forwards, and hooker. Two substitutes can be used for tactical reasons, and in Britain a team can withdraw a substitute and bring back the player he replaced.

As in rugby union, each team attempts to score points by running the ball over their opponent's goal-line and touching down for a *try* (3 pts), or by kicking a *goal* (2 pts, except for a dropped goal in internationals, which is 1 pt). A try gives the scoring side the chance to kick for a goal. This must be taken from a point in line with the touchdown, and the ball must pass over the crossbar and between the posts. *Penalty goals* are attempted from kicks following infringements; *dropped goals* – when the ball is dropped and kicked on the half-volley – can be attempted at any time.

The side in possession make ground by passing the ball to each other, except in a forward direction, or by kicking.

If a player passes forward or *knocks on* – fumbles the ball onto the ground – a scrum is held, unless the opposition gain possession, in which case the referee can apply the *advantage rule*. The defending side stop the attack by *tackling* the ball carrier, but tackling or obstruct-

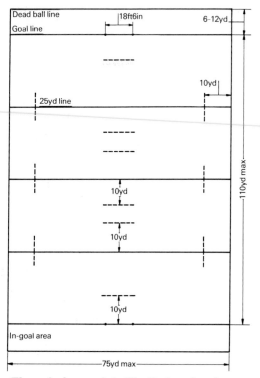

The rugby league pitch. The H-shaped goal-posts have a crossbar at a height of 10 ft above the ground.

ing other players is penalized.

When tackled, the ball carrier *plays the ball* with his foot to a team-mate standing behind him, although he can play it forward for himself provided the ball touches the ground before he gathers it in. Each team is allowed to retain possession in this way for six tackles, after which a *scrum* forms, with the tackling side putting the ball in. Most sides kick to gain ground after the fifth tackle rather than concede the scrum.

If a player tries to kick the ball out of play, the ball must bounce in the field of play before crossing the touch-line, otherwise there is a scrum where the ball was kicked. When the ball bounces out of play, or if the ball-carrier crosses the touchline, play recommences with a scrum 10 yards infield from where the ball went out. If a team elects to kick for touch from a penalty, however, the ball can be kicked out on the full, and then the same side can take a *tap-kick* 10 yards in from the point where the ball went out.

Above: *When a player retains possession after being brought down, he 'plays the ball' back.*
Below: *The unquenchable Alex Murphy walks off the Wembley turf in triumph after captaining his third club to victory in 1974.*

Murphy, Alex (GB), has never ceased to confound his critics, with both the longevity of his playing career and his quest for honours. With a quicksilver burst and a defence-splitting pass, half-back Murphy helped St Helens to their Championship and Cup victories of the 1960s, toured Australia in 1958 and 1960, and was in the World Cup-winning side of 1960. In the twilight of his career he went to Leigh as player-coach and inspired them to their 1971 Challenge Cup win; in 1972–73 he moved to Warrington as manager-player-coach and won both Cup and Championship for them in 1974.

Prescott, Alan (GB), the burly, red-haired skipper of the 1958 tourists in Australia, will be long remembered for his great courage in the Brisbane test of that series, when he played on with a broken arm. But that courageous display also ended his career. The hard-running, hard-tackling St Helens prop turned to coaching, having played in 25 tests and having helped the Saints to their first Challenge Cup win, in 1956.

Raper, Johnny (Australia), brilliant lock (loose-forward), served St George and Australia for a decade with a combination of unerring cover defence and devastating attack. He joined St George from Newtown in 1959, and that same year made the first of three tours to England and France. He remained an automatic selection until 1968, when he led Australia undefeated through the World Cup. He played 33 tests in all.

Risman, Gus (GB), enjoyed an illustrious career that spanned a quarter of a century. A shrewd tactician and accomplished goalkicker equally at home at centre or half-back, Risman was the inspiration of the Salford side that won the Challenge Cup in 1938, were finalists in 1939, and won the Championship in 1932–33. He captained Great Britain on his third Australasian tour, in 1946, and played 15 tests in all.

His son Bev also captained Great Britain, from fullback in the 1968 World Cup. An England and Lions fly-half, **Bev Risman** joined Leigh before winning honours with Leeds.

Rosenfeld, Albert (Australia), arrived in England with the 1908–09 Kangaroos, signed for Huddersfield, and in season 1913–14 raced in for a record 80 tries, still unbeaten 60 years later. A hard-running winger with an enterprising determination allied to a superb eye for the half-chance, Rosenfeld thrived on a profitable understanding with his centre Wagstaff, scoring more than 350 tries as Huddersfield dominated pre-World War I seasons.

Sullivan, Jim (GB), left Wales for Wigan in 1921 at 17 to become perhaps the greatest fullback to grace either rugby code. When he retired in 1946, he had won all possible honours at club, international, and test level, though further acclaim was to greet his coaching of Wigan and St Helens. He toured Australia three times, as captain in 1932, and declined an invitation to tour a fourth time. Sullivan scored 6,192 career points, including a then-record haul of 204 goals in 1934. He kicked more than 100 goals in every season except 1946.

Graeme Langlands scores against Great Britain at Wembley in the first test of the Kangaroos' 1963–64 tour. Australia won 28–2 and went on to sew up the series with a massive 50–12 victory in the second test, at Swinton.

Memorable moments in sport

Prescott's match

Dateline: Brisbane, 5 July 1958. Great Britain, with 11 fit men, beat Australia 25–18 to square the series at a test apiece with one to play. Britain's hero was the captain, red-haired prop Alan Prescott, who broke his arm after 4 minutes but remained on the field to inspire his men to a win as memorable as the 'Rorke's Drift' test victory of 1914.

A record crowd of 32,965 had come to see Australia clinch the series following their 25–8 victory in the first test. They had not reckoned on the courage of Prescott, the skill of scrum-half Alex Murphy, or the superhuman endeavours of Brian McTigue and Vince Karalius.

Yet when Britain lost stand-off David Bolton with a broken collarbone after 18 minutes, their prospects were gloomy, despite a 5–2 lead from a Challinor try and a Fraser goal. Prescott could take no part in the heavy stuff up front, but he never shirked when called on to catch, pass, or tackle. Certainly the Australians found him more than a nuisance.

Nor could they contain the effervescent Murphy. He began both first-half tries – the second by Mick Sullivan – and was in action again straight after half-time, setting up Ike Southward's try, which Fraser converted. It was 15–2. At half-time, Prescott had had a pain-killing injection to keep him going for another 40 minutes, despite warnings of doing lasting damage to his arm, and his presence was now vital, his instructions the rallying cry his tired troops responded to. Southward scored again after a movement Challinor began in his own 25 in answer to an Aussie try and goal, and Murphy and Karalius produced the counter-attack that clinched the game after a further two Australian tries. Fraser converted Murphy's try to make it 25–13, and another Australian try was not enough to rob Prescott and his men of a place in history.

Alan Prescott, 'Captain Courageous', who played almost a whole match with a broken arm and inspired his depleted team to victory.

Above: *David Watkins scored in all 47 games for Salford in 1972–73, kicking a record 221 goals.* Right: *Sidestepping Tom Van Vollenhoven about to score yet again for St Helens.*

RUGBY LEAGUE 'MOSTS'

World Cup – wins	3	Australia, Great Britain

Record score	119	Huddersfield (119-2 v Swinton Pk, NU Cup 1st Rnd) 28.2.14
League	102	Leed (102-0 v Coventry) 12.4.13
Tour	101	England (101-0 v South Australia) 23.5.14
	92	Australia (92–7 v Bramley) 9.11.21
Test	56	Australia (56-6 v France, Brisbane) 2.7.60
World Cup	53	Great Britain (53-19 v New Zealand, Pau, France) 4.11.72

Attendance	102,569	Warrington v Halifax, Odsal Stadium, Bradford, RL Challenge Cup final, replay, 5.5.54
Test	70,174	Australia v Great Britain, Sydney, 1962
World Cup	62,256	Australia v Great Britain, Sydney, 25.5.68

Individual 'mosts'

Test appearances	47	Mick Sullivan (GB)
tries	43	Mick Sullivan (GB)
goals	93	Neil Fox (GB)

Tries			
	season	80	Albert Rosenfeld (Huddersfield) 1913–14
	career	834	Brian Bevan (Warrington, Blackpool Borough) 1946–64
	match	11	'Tich' West (Hull Kingston R. v Brookland R., NU Cup 1st Rnd) 4.3.05
	league	10	Lionel Cooper (Huddersfield v Keighley) 17.11.51
	test	4	Billy Boston (Great Britain v New Zealand, Auckland) 24.7.54
		4	Alex Murphy (Great Britain v France, Leeds) 14.3.59
	tour	39	Cec Blinkhorn (Australia, in England, 29 games) 1921–22
		38	Mick Sullivan (Great Britain, in Australasia, 19 games) 1958
		36	Billy Boston (Great Britain, in Australasia, 18 games) 1954

Goals			
	season	221	David Watkins (Salford) 1972–73
	career	2,955	Jim Sullivan (Wigan and Great Britain) 1921–46
	match	22	Jim Sullivan (Wigan v Flimby and Fothergill, RL Cup) 14.2.25
	test	11	Des White (New Zealand v Australia, Brisbane) 28.6.52

Points			
	season	496	Lewis Jones (Leeds) 1956–57
	career	6,192	Jim Sullivan (Wigan and Great Britain) 1921–46
	match	53	'Tich' West (Hull Kingston R. v Brookland R., NU Cup 1st Rnd) 4.3.05
	tour	285	Dave Brown (Australia, in England and France, 32 games) 1933–34
		278	Lewis Jones (Great Britain, in Australasia, 21 games) 1954

Rugby League Challenge Cup (final)

Wins	8	Leeds
Record score	38	Wakefield Trinity (38-5 v Hull) 1960
individual	20	Neil Fox (Wakefield Trinity v Hull) 1960

Van Vollenhoven, Tom, toured New Zealand in 1956 with the Springboks and changed codes a year later when he signed for St Helens. Leading rugby league try-scorer in several seasons, he was a great favourite in an era when wing play was at its best. His beautifully balanced running and defence-splitting sidestepping brought him 381 tries and Championship and Cup honours.

Wagstaff, Harold (GB), captained England in the historic 'Rorke's Drift' Test of 1914, when England beat Australia 14–6 with only 10 men left at the end. Destined for rugby league immortality from the moment he made his first senior appearance for Huddersfield at 15, Wagstaff was the brilliant individualist centre whose captaincy inspired the magnificent Huddersfield 'Team of All the Talents' prior to World War I. He played in 13 tests.

Watkins, David (GB), established his place in rugby league's hall of fame in 1972–73, when he kicked a world record 221 goals in a season – as well as becoming only the fourth player to score and play in every club game in a season. A convert from rugby union – 21 Welsh and 6 Lions caps – Watkins soon proved he was worth his reputed £14,000 signing-on fee as both 'round the corner' goalkicker and centre. Under his captaincy, Salford emerged as one of the forces of the early 1970s.

Rugby union

'A game for ruffians played by gentlemen' is how some describe rugby union. The description is apt. The hard physical contact of the tackle, the set scrum, and the forward drive seem paradoxical to a game that guards its amateurism with such fervour and jealousy. For in these highly commercial times, rugby union's reward, even at the highest level, is in playing the game and winning. And even the modern dedication to winning would be frowned upon by those men of the public schools and universities who took the embryo that William Webb Ellis supposedly began at Rugby School in 1823 and formulated the rules of the game that is still essentially British.

When Ellis, playing football, took it on himself to pick up the ball and run for the opposition goal, the game was still in its formative stages. Indeed it was not until 1863 that the Football Association was founded. By then, the handling game had spread from Rugby to other public schools, and ultimately to the universities, and it was the old boys of these establishments who dictated the

Football at Rugby School, where the handling code is said to have originated in 1823.

development of rugby. Whether they were also responsible for the evolution of the oval-shaped ball is not clear, as its origins have never been satisfactorily established.

When the FA banned hacking (of an opponent's shins) and running with the ball, Blackheath club, who had formulated rules in 1862 and helped form the

Ireland's Mike Gibson (with ball), the complete rugby footballer, playing for Cambridge Past and Present against the Barbarians in 1972.

FA, withdrew. (In time, however, they, along with Richmond, did away with hacking.) But the handling code continued, and on 26 January 1871, 21 clubs and schools met to form the Rugby Football Union. That same season saw Scotland and England play their first international, at Edinburgh. Each side fielded 20 men, and Scotland won by a goal and a try to a goal. The following season the Scots journeyed south and an international series that grew to be the annual Five Nations (International) Championship between England, Scotland, Wales, Ireland, and France was under way.

As in England, Scottish rugby was established in the schools. And when the Scottish Rugby Union was founded in 1873, it comprised primarily university students and former pupils of public schools. The 'old boy network' was again in charge.

In Ireland, where rugby has provided a unification that politics and religion have failed to achieve, the universities played an important role in Irish rugby's development. Dublin University Football Club, founded in 1854, claim to be the first established rugby club, and have remained a power in the Irish game since the Irish Rugby Union was set up in 1879.

In Wales, New Zealand, and South Africa, however, growth sprung from a different source; one which rugby's social commentators always find indicative of those countries' great successes. True, Llandovery College claims to have introduced rugby to Wales in the late 1860s, but when the Welsh Rugby Union was founded in March 1881, rugby was

the game of working people – miners, mill-workers, and tradesmen. Similarly in New Zealand and South Africa, where the official bodies were founded in 1892 and 1889 respectively, rugby was the game of the entire population. It was classless. Provincial bodies were already strong and the game firmly established long before the NZ Rugby Union and the SA Rugby Board saw the light of day.

In 1888, New Zealand had sent a team of native-born players to Britain, where they played 74 games for a 49 won, 5 drawn, and 20 lost record. Later that year an English team toured Australia and New Zealand, and British sides toured South Africa twice before the turn of the century. In 1905 New Zealand's famous All Blacks made their first tour of Britain; the South African Springboks went there in 1906; and the Australian Wallabies toured in 1908, including among their spoils the rugby gold medal from the London Olympic Games.

For Australia, though, rugby honours were to be few and far between, the reason being the Northern Union code that had split English rugby over 'broken time' payments in 1895 and was to become rugby league. France, too, where rugby union has been played since the 1880s, was to find the professional game a major handicap, but eventually union triumphed over league as the major rugby code.

Despite the time spent in travelling in

The Springbok forwards provide good support for captain Dawie De Villiers against Cardiff in 1969. It was an unhappy tour for the Springboks, who failed to win a test.

Catchpole, Ken (Australia), won his first cap in 1961, that same year captaining Australia in South Africa. His term of captaincy, however, was short-lived. Rated as the best scrum-half Australia has produced, Catchpole allied a swift 'pick up and flick' pass to lightning reflexes and a strong burst around the scrum. He had 27 caps and was still not 30 when injury against the 1968 All Blacks forced his retirement.

Ken Catchpole, with the 1966–67 Wallabies, gets a pass away.

Clarke, Don (New Zealand), first-choice fullback for the All Blacks from 1956 to 1964, tallied a world record 1,851 points in his first-class career. All but 66 of these came from the boot, and 781 were for the All Blacks. More than once Clarke took New Zealand to undeserved victory, notably when his six penalties beat the 1959 Lions 18–17 in the first test and his late try and conversion snatched an 11–8 win in the second. Weighing over 17 stone at times, he could kick goals from his own half, disregarding text-books by placing the ball in an upright position.

Goalkicker extraordinary Don Clarke in familiar action in the 1963 All Black trials.

Dawes, John (Wales and Lions), led the 1971 Lions to unprecedented glory in New Zealand, where they won the series 2–1 (one draw) and were unbeaten by the provinces. A great general rather than a great player, Dawes nonetheless was a talented centre with a fine turn of speed and a beautifully timed pass. His 22-cap career for Wales embraced one of her richest periods, many successes coming under his captaincy.

De Villiers, Dawie (South Africa), captained the 1969–70 Springboks on their unhappy tour of Britain and avenged a disastrous tour of New Zealand in 1965 by defeating the 1970 All Blacks for rugby's unofficial 'world title'. Superb on the blind-side break and at linking with his loose forwards, he somehow lacked the brilliance that could have made him the greatest scrum-half of his day.

Duckham, David (England and Lions), has that enviable gift of being able to sidestep off either foot . . . and the speed to take full advantage of it. Whether at centre or on the wing, he is a thrilling initiator of tries. On tour with the 1971 Lions he scored six tries in one match.

The powerful Frik Du Preez

Du Preez, Frik (South Africa), with 38 caps, is his country's most-capped player. Throughout the 1960s he was the Springboks' first-choice lock forward, a magnificent line-out jumper whose great surging runs in the open led to some memorable tries. He overcame a disappointing tour with the 1969–70 'Boks to power South Africa to victory over the 1970 All Blacks.

those early days of the 20th century, tours became an accepted and anticipated feature of the rugby scene, with the highlights being the internationals or 'tests' between national sides. With jet air transport nullifying the travel problems, short tours became a vogue, with, say, England going to New Zealand for a few weeks only. In addition, air transport has allowed the developing countries of rugby – Japan, Argentina, the highly entertaining Fiji, and Romania – to tour and be toured by the major 'big eight' countries.

Yet for the purist, the big occasion remains the major tour, with the Springboks and All Blacks touring Britain, the British Lions returning those visits, and the mighty, often bitter, clashes between the New Zealanders and the South Africans. The Lions are made up of players from the four British countries, and their brilliant fast-running backs provide a welcome feast for crowds in forward-dominated New Zealand and South Africa.

But if the British were once regarded as easy game by these two countries, times are changing. In 1971, the Lions staggered the rugby world by defeating the All Blacks – only the second time New Zealand had lost a home series – reflecting the improvement brought about by a greater emphasis on coaching and a more competitive approach at domestic level. And then England's unbeaten tour of South Africa in 1972, followed in 1973 by their dramatic victory over the All Blacks on a short, pre-season tour, further emphasized that rugby union was no longer the dominion of the Southern Hemisphere. The game in the land that gave it birth had come of age.

Memorable moments in sport

Morgan fires the Lions

Dateline: Ellis Park, Johannesburg, 6 August 1955. A record crowd of more than 100,000 saw the British Lions win the first test of the four-match series by 23 (five tries) to 22 (four tries). Officially the attendance was given as 95,000, but this figure takes no account of forged tickets and gatecrashers. None of those present will ever forget a match in which the lead changed back and forth and which reached a nerve-racking finale with the South African fullback Van der Schyff having to convert the fourth Springbok try to beat the Lions. The kick, however, went wide.

What is not always remembered about

Cliff Morgan rounds Basie Van Wyk to score the try that sparked a memorable victory for the Lions over the Springboks in 1955.

this titanic battle is that the Lions played almost all of the second half with only 14 men, their forward Higgins having been severely injured. At the time he went off, they were trailing by three points, and such a blow could have proved fatal to their morale. Cliff Morgan, the magical Welsh fly-half, ensured it did not by scoring one of his most brilliant tries.

The depleted Lions pack won a scrum and Jeeps fed Morgan on his left with a long pass that would help him clear of the marauding Springbok back row. Morgan took the ball at speed, and a little outward jink took him through the defence and racing diagonally across the South African 25. Those small piston-like legs that had carried him past the best of British defences now took him arcing gloriously towards the goal-line. The flanker Van Wyk, pounding in pursuit, was unable to prevent him rounding to touch down under the posts.

The tide had turned. The Lions forgot their handicap and swept into a purple spell of attacking brilliance. Cliff Morgan's magic had been the spark that set the Lions alight, and it was fitting that he would captain them to their 9–6 victory in the third test, so ensuring that the Lions could not lose the series.

Wales and British Lions scrum-half Gareth Edwards gets away one of his long, accurate passes against England at Twickenham in 1972, when Wales triumphed 12–3.

Major competitions

Although the Five Nations (International) Championship has existed since the 1880s, internal competition in Britain was for long frowned upon, with the exception of the County Championship (1889) in England. The fiercely competitive French Championship, an immensely popular club competition, has had doubts cast on its amateur status, and trouble in the 1930s led to France's banishment for a decade. Nevertheless, club competition eventually came to Britain, too, in 1972, with the inauguration of the RFU knock-out tournament and the revival after nearly 60

Carwyn James, one of rugby's great coaches, masterminded the British Lions' brilliant series victory in New Zealand in 1971.

years of the Welsh Challenge Cup.

Internal competition flourishes in New Zealand and South Africa. New Zealand's Ranfurly Shield has been played for since 1902. An unusual competition, it is based on challenges – that is, a province holds the trophy until a successful challenge is made. South Africa's Currie Cup for regional sides, on the other hand, is run on a league basis, two divisions each producing a team to contest the final. First staged in 1892, it is now held approximately every two years, depending on international commitments.

A form of competition particularly popular in Britain is 'sevens' – seven-a-side rugby. Knock-out tournaments for this fast, energy-sapping game are held annually in various centres.

How to play

If law changes were indicative of difficulties within a game, rugby union might appear in a rather unhappy state. Few sports have been subjected to as many adjustments in the rules. Yet the game has never lost its essential elements, and the intentions of the lawmakers – the International Rugby Board – are good; wishing to make rugby more flowing and attractive to watch.

For those playing, however, the aims remain the same, despite the subtleties of the Laws. Rugby union is a game to be won by gaining possession and opening the way for points-scoring opportunities.

Points can be scored in six ways: try, goal (try plus conversion), penalty try, penalty goal, dropped goal, and goal from a fair catch. The last three bring three points. A *try* – the grounding of the ball in the opposition in-goal area – is worth four points and gives the chance of an extra two points from the *conversion* kick that follows. The kick is taken from a point in line with the touchdown, and must pass over the crossbar and between the line of the posts. A *penalty try*, given when a player is illegally obstructed from scoring a certain try, is also worth four points, but as the conversion attempt is taken from in front of the posts it is a fairly certain six points.

A team consists of seven backs and eight forwards: fullback, two wing-threequarters, two centre-threequarters, fly-half (stand-off or first five-eighth), scrum-half (half-back); No. 8, two

Edwards, Gareth (Wales and Lions), at 20 the youngest ever captain of Wales, throws the longest pass of any international scrum-half and is one of the hardest to stop on the burst, especially near the try-line. His partnership with Barry John saw Welsh and British rugby at their highest peaks.

Ellis, Jan (South Africa), linked with Tommy Bedford and Piet Greyling to form one of the most dynamic loose-forward partnerships of the late 1960s and early 1970s. A fast, tigerish mover off the side of the scrum, Ellis, with more than 30 caps to his credit, rarely fails to turn in a world-class performance and has few peers in the art of constructive forward play.

Springbok Jan Ellis.

Gainsford, John (South Africa), ended his international career in 1967 with 33 caps, at that time a South African record. And his eight test tries was the most scored by a Springbok. A big strong centre with the ability to swerve and sidestep at top speed, he was rarely absent from the national side following his first appearance in 1960.

Gibson, Mike (Ireland and Lions), deserves nothing less than the accolade 'brilliant'. Few would deny he is the most complete player of his age: impregnable in defence, rapier sharp in attack, cool in crisis, impeccable in his passing. A tall, powerful runner, Gibson made his mark as a fly-half with Cambridge and Ireland, but the Lions, with an embarrassment of quality halves, played him in the centre. If Barry John was king of the 1971 Lions in New Zealand, Mike Gibson was the much respected elder statesman.

James, Carwyn (Wales), made just two appearances for his country, in 1957–58, but the Llanelli fly-half ranks as one of rugby's immortals. New Zealanders certainly shudder at the name, for it was James, as coach of the 1971 Lions, who planned only the second-ever home series defeat for the All Blacks, and in 1972 coached Llanelli to their 9–3 win over the Seventh All Blacks.

Jeeps, Dickie (England and Lions), was uncapped when he played in all four internationals for the 1955 Lions against the Springboks. From then to the early 1960s, though, this chunky, dependable scrum-half was rarely missing behind the England pack, serving his backs with quick dive-passes or nursing his forwards with high, accurate kicks along the touchline. He was first-choice scrum-half for the 1959 and 1962 Lions and later became an England selector.

British Lion Dickie Jeeps gets a kick in under pressure.

John, Barry (Wales and Lions), retired in 1972 while still at the peak of his powers; a supremely confident, elusive fly-half with a genius for ghosting through the tightest defences. A round-the-corner place-kick and a penchant for dropped goals with either foot helped him to a record 180 points from 16 games with the 1971 Lions in New Zealand, where he was nicknamed 'The King'. His 25 appearances for Wales produced a record 90 points as they topped the Championship table every year from 1969 to 1972.

Rugby union terms

Blind side The side of the scrum opposite that on which the backs line out in usual formation.

Dropped goal A goal scored with a *drop kick*, i.e. the ball is dropped and kicked on the bounce; worth 3 points.

Fair catch, or **'Mark!'** A catch from an opponent's kick, knock-on, or forward throw while standing with both feet on the ground and shouting 'mark!'. The catcher must take the kick subsequently awarded, and this must pass through the mark. The opposition may stand on the mark and charge as soon as the ball is placed or the kicker runs to make his kick.

Forward pass An illegal throw that takes the ball nearer the opponents' goal line.

Goal A converted try; worth 6 points.

Hand-off A technique used by the ball-carrier to push away a tackling opponent with open hand.

Knock-on occurs when the ball hits a player's hand or arm and goes forward; in most cases illegal.

Line-out Set-piece for restarting play when the ball goes into touch.

Loose scrum See *Ruck*.

Maul Similar to a ruck, except that the ball is played from hand to hand without touching the ground.

Offside Fundamentally, a player is offside when he is in front of a team-mate who has played the ball.

Penalty goal A goal scored direct from a penalty kick; worth 3 points.

Penalty kick Awarded to the non-offenders after certain infringements. It may be a place kick or drop-kick at goal, a punt, or tap kick. The opposition must retire 10 yards.

Penalty try Awarded when a player is illegally prevented from scoring a try; worth 4 points.

Ruck, also termed a *loose scrum*, involves players from either side, on their feet, pushing each other as in a scrum with the ball on the ground between them. The ball must not be handled.

Set scrum Set-piece for restarting play in certain situations, usually formed by the 16 forwards, the Laws requiring a minimum of 6 players.

Tap penalty One of the penalty-kick options. The ball must be on the penalty mark when tapped forward before being picked up.

Touch Out of play beyond a touch line.

Try Grounding of the ball in the opposition in-goal area; worth 4 points. See *Goal*.

flankers (wing-forwards, side rows, or breakaways), two locks, two props, and a hooker. In New Zealand, the inside of the two centres is termed second five-eighth. One replacement is allowed in internationals and matches against touring teams, but otherwise replacements vary according to domestic laws.

Basically, the forwards are the power-house of the side, winning the ball in the set scrums, line-outs, and loose forays so that the backs, with accurate tactical kicking, crisp passing, and elusive running can set up the scoring opportunities. In practice, however, forwards and backs join together in both attack and defence.

Passes must not go forward, nor must a player catching the ball knock it on, although there are circumstances when a *knock-on* is permitted – for example, if a player charges down an opposition kick without actual loss of control, or if he fumbles direct from a kick and the ball does not hit the ground.

Attacking movements can be stifled by the tackling of the ball carrier, but such dangerous tackles as stiff-arm ones are penalized. The tackled player must release the ball immediately, at which stage the forwards often form a *loose scrum*, or *ruck*, over the tackled player, trying to win possession by driving forward and heeling the ball back.

When play stops for such infringements as a knock-on, a forward pass, or accidental offside, it restarts with a *set scrum*. Though, in theory, only six

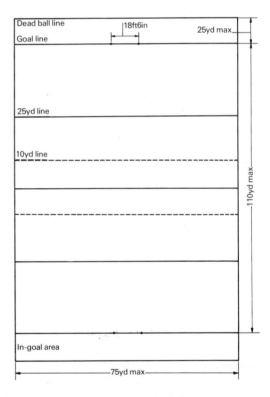

players in all are needed for a scrum, usually both sets of forwards take part, with the front row (props and hooker), locks, flankers, and No. 8 binding together and making a concerted push. The heads of the props and hookers interlock so that adjacent heads belong to the opposing teams. The prop whose head is free is the *loose-head prop*, and it is on his side that the scrum-half puts the ball into the scrum. The locks bind between the hooker and his props while the flankers bind on the side of the locks,

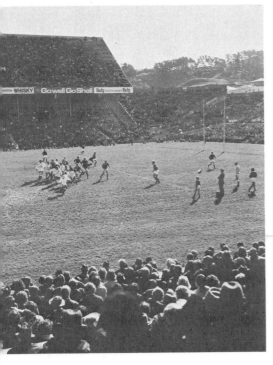

Kiernan, Tom (Ireland and Lions), gained his first cap in 1960, his 54th in 1973, having passed Jackie Kyle's Irish record *en route*. Though by then one of rugby's veterans, Kiernan retained many of the facets that had made him such a distinguished fullback. His positioning was always sound, his handling sure, and his tactical play astute. A reliable goal-kicker, he scored over 100 points in internationals. As well as leading Ireland, he was captain of his second Lions tour of South Africa, in 1968.

Kirkpatrick, Ian (New Zealand), captain of the 1972–73 All Blacks in Britain and France, has few rivals as a world-class flanker. Assured in every aspect of his game, he proved an inspiring captain, dominating the back of the line-out, working solidly in the tight, and moving with awesome power in the loose. First capped in France in 1967, he has rarely failed to impress and has scored some magnificent solo tries.

ready to break away to tackle the opposing backs. The No. 8 binds between the two locks.

When putting the ball into the scrum, the scrum-half stands a yard away from the 'tunnel', down the middle of which he must put the ball so that it touches the ground just past the first prop. None of the front-row forwards must lift his foot before the ball bounces. When the ball is in the scrum, neither scrum-half must advance in front of the ball; if he does, he is offside. Similarly, the backs lined up behind the scrum must not advance ahead of the tail of their scrum.

Japan's Akira Yokoi is just foiled against Wales at Cardiff in 1973, in a match Japan lost 14-62, but which won them many friends.

Above left: *England play Wellington on their first ever rugby tour, in 1963.* Above: *Fast-covering England No. 8 Andy Ripley grabs an Australian at Twickenham in 1973. First capped in 1971, the 6 ft 5 in, high-stepping natural athlete soon became one of the best attacking forwards in the world and was an automatic choice for the 1974 Lions tour.*

It is this Law regarding *offside* that can be one of the most confusing to newcomers to the game. A player is offside when he is in front of a member of his side who has the ball or has kicked it. And he can take no further part in the game until put onside by any team-mate running in front of him from where the ball was last played. Nor must a player in an offside position remain within 10 yards of an opponent waiting to catch

Ian Kirkpatrick

Jackie Kyle

Kyle, Jackie (Ireland and Lions), played a record 46 times for Ireland, a fly-half of undeniable genius, a player of intuition and instinct. Whether sidestepping through a defence, swerving mesmerizingly around a fullback, or popping up in defence, he always seemed to do the right thing. To New Zealanders who saw him with the 1950 Lions, he was 'the greatest'.

Lochore, Brian (New Zealand), made his international debut with the 1963–64 All Blacks and returned to Britain in 1967 as captain of New Zealand and one of the game's finest No. 8 forwards. Under him, the All Blacks had trounced the 1966 Lions; they proceeded to go unbeaten through Britain and France and won 17 successive internationals before losing to South Africa in 1970.

McBride, Willie John (Ireland and Lions), stands without peer in Britain as a second-row forward. The first to make four tours with the Lions when he went to New Zealand in 1971, he set another record in 1974 when he passed Tom Kiernan's number of Irish caps. Inimitably Irish off-field, he brings to his play a Celtic fire that has won him respect ever since he first played for Ireland in 1962, and earned him the captaincy of the Lions to South Africa in 1974 for his fifth tour.

McBride (left) with McLoughlin.

McLauchlan, Ian (Scotland and Lions), was not nicknamed 'Mighty Mouse' for nothing by the 1971 Lions. Only 5 ft 9 in tall, he is a prop in the true Scottish mould — indefatigable and unbending. He was a decisive factor in the Lions' victory over the All Blacks, and a typically non-stop performance in the first test was rewarded with a vital try when he knocked down a clearance.

McLeod, Hughie (Scotland and Lions), shares with flanker Dave Rollo the distinction of being Scotland's most capped player — except that McLeod's 40 caps came in consecutive matches. A stoutly built prop, once described as the 'nearest thing to perpetual motion on the rugby field', McLeod toured with the Lions in 1955 and 1959.

Memorable moments in sport

'For he's a jolly good fellow'

Dateline: Cardiff Arms Park, 15 February 1964. Wilson Whineray's Fifth All Blacks are on the rampage against the Barbarians in their final match. Forgotten is the discipline that took them through Britain and France with only one defeat; forwards and backs are playing with an abandon more associated with the Barbarians than themselves. Unbelievably, the Welsh crowd are urging the New Zealanders on.

With the closing minutes ticking away and the New Zealanders leading 31–6, the Barbarians make a last effort to reduce the margin. But it is not their day. Flynn, their Irish centre, is brought down by the defence, the ball rolls loose and is snatched up by his opposite number, Paul Little. Little darts forward, looks for support, finds Whineray alongside, and passes. Cardiff Arms Park is on its feet at the sight of this mighty front-row forward taking the ball like a threequarter, increasing speed, and racing for the line with team-mates ranged on either side. It is All Blacks power rugby at its most spectacular, and leading the charge is one of the most popular captains to lead a team through the British Isles.

With the Barbarians cover beaten, nothing can stop the All Blacks from scoring, unless Whineray's pass goes astray as he faces the sole defender, Stewart Wilson. But Whineray does not pass. Instead, swinging the ball across his body, he sells Wilson a text-book dummy and races past him to score near the posts.

In the stands pandemonium breaks loose. Welshmen who have come to see the pride of British rugby bring down the All Blacks accord the New Zealand captain a reception few Welsh heroes have received. As Whineray walks back and Don Clarke comes up to make the score 36–6, thousands of voices begin singing 'For He's a Jolly Good Fellow'. And when the final whistle blows, bringing the tour to an end, Whineray is hoisted onto the shoulders of his team-mates and chaired from the field to a momentous ovation. Around the ground more than one New Zealander is seen to brush tears from his eyes. For this to happen at the Arms Park – where Deans was 'robbed' in 1905, where New Zealand were the traditional foe – is indeed the highlight of a memorable tour.

Top: *Willie away! Wilson Whineray streaks for the Barbarians line to climax a magnificent match and a wonderful tour at Cardiff Arms Park.* Below: *The final accolade.*

Above: Rugby league, a code of football played almost exclusively in Britain, Australia, New Zealand, and France. *Right:* Basketball, a universal game, played in some 130 countries and claimed to be the most popular sport to play and to watch. *Below:* Cricket, for long a sport largely for the connoisseur, broadened its appeal with the advent of the one-day game. Gary Sobers (batting) mastered the widely differing skills of batting, bowling, and fielding to an unprecedented degree.

*Jean-Noël Augert of France exhibits the consummate
skill and grace of the alpine ski racer.*

Winter sports, a variety of spectacular activities that take place on snow or ice. *Above:* The biathlon involves a mixture of cross-country (nordic) skiing with stops for rifle shooting. *Right:* Hundreds of competitors start out on the Marcia Longa, an annual Nordic ski race. *Below:* Ice hockey, arguably the world's fastest team sport (USA v Poland, Sapporo Olympics).

Above: Janet Lynn shows why free skating is regarded as the most artistic of all sports with a breath-taking performance at Sapporo.

Below: One of sport's unlucky losers, Australia's Kerry O'Brien, world record holder for the steeplechase, falls at the water jump in the 1970 British Commonwealth Games.

The magnificent, marauding 'Pinetree' Meads, a terrifying sight for those who faced him, ploughs in typical Juggernaut fashion through the North of England defence in 1967.

A dream debut

Memorable moments in sport

Dateline: Cardiff Arms Park, 15 April 1967. England were robbed of a share in the International Championship and the Triple Crown by an 18-year-old fullback playing his first international. Furthermore, Keith Jarrett, four months out of school, was also out of position. His club, Newport, played him at centre. But from the moment his first penalty kick curled in late, hit the far upright, and glanced over, until he converted Gerald Davies's second try, the Welsh gods smiled on Keith Jarrett.

Jarrett scored 19 points that day, equalling Jack Bancroft's Welsh record set in 1910 and becoming only the second Welsh fullback to score an international try. What a try it was too. A vastly improved England had narrowed a 14–6 deficit to 19–15 in an inspired burst after half-time, and looked like overrunning the ragged Welsh. But from the moment McFadyean's kick failed to find touch and Jarrett, near halfway, raced in to take the ball brilliantly on the bounce, head high, England's hopes were dashed. In a trice Jarrett had rounded Savage and fullback Hosen, and was outpacing the English defence over the 50 yards to the left-hand corner, where he touched down. The crowd had still not settled when he had them roaring again with a conversion that was also helped over by the upright.

Nor was that all. Within minutes he was away again, kicking the ball delicately over an opponent's head and catching it with a deftness that belied his size. His rush was stopped, but from a following scrum the Welsh won a tight head and Rebb went over. Jarrett kicked the goal and almost immediately was converting Davies's try. In just six minutes Wales had gone from 19–15 to 34–15. Jarrett had scored 9 of those 15 points and had inspired the Welsh with his amazing try.

England managed to reduce the margin to 34–21, but it was Keith Jarrett's day. Welshmen would always talk of that day at Cardiff Arms Park when a youngster fresh from school kicked two penalty goals and converted five tries, including his own. They might just remember that his only unsuccessful kick at goal hit a post . . . and didn't bounce over.

Jarrett, showing remarkable cool for an 18-year-old débutant, kicks one of his goals.

McLoughlin, Ray (Ireland and Lions), unchallenged as one of the great thinkers of rugby, is also one of the game's foremost prop forwards. First capped in 1962, he was still packing down in the Irish front row more than a decade later. Though injured before the tests and unable to play again for the 1971 Lions, McLoughlin made an enormous contribution to the tour's success with his analysis and understanding of New Zealand forward play.

Meads, Colin (New Zealand), became a rugby legend in his lifetime, a rugby giant in every way. Standing 6 ft 4 in and weighing over 16 stone, 'Pinetree' Meads was ideally built for a lock forward, but allied to his great strength was a turn of speed that made him a formidable opponent in the loose. In the line-out he was rarely bettered.

First capped in 1957, Meads went on to play a world-record 55 matches for his country. Always controversial, he roused both ire and admiration for his uncompromising aggression on the field. Against Scotland in 1967 he became only the second player sent off in an international. His broken arm in South Africa in 1970 severely weakened the All Blacks, but he recovered to captain them against the 1971 Lions.

Meads sent off against Scotland.

Morgan, Cliff (Wales and Lions), played in an era when flat defences and fast-moving loose forwards were allowed to stifle the best half-backs. But Morgan was a wizard, a master of sudden acceleration and of the ability to fade away from the tackle. Ball held tantalizingly before him, he could move sharply off either foot, sell the most acceptable dummies, loose beautifully timed passes, or kick unerringly for the best tactical advantage. His performances at fly-half were a major factor in the 1955 Lions' squaring the series in South Africa 2–2.

Rugby union

All Blacks scrum-half Sid Going is menaced by French No. 8 Walter Spanghero (right). France won this 1973 clash 13–6.

O'Reilly, Tony (Ireland and Lions), went straight into the national side at 18, in his first senior season. Some 15 years later he was recalled to win his 29th Irish cap. In that 15 years, Tony O'Reilly became renowned throughout the rugby world as an entertaining wing-threequarter of flair and speed. In South Africa with the 1955 Lions he scored a record 16 tries; in Australasia with the 1959 side he ran in a record 22.

Prat, Jean (France), played a leading role in France's transformation into a world rugby power, winning 38 caps. A versatile flanker whose try-scoring and goal-kicking were frequent matchwinners, he captained the French to their first ever Championship title (albeit shared), in 1953–54, and that same season crossed the All Blacks line with three opponents clinging to him to defeat the New Zealanders 3–0.

Pullin, John (England and Lions), quiet and unassuming, led English rugby out of the doldrums to two of the most amazing victories in rugby history. On a short tour of South Africa in 1972 his side were undefeated, including an 18–9 win over the Springboks; on a similar tour of New Zealand a year later, they beat New Zealand 16–10. He hooked in three tests for the 1968 Lions and all four for the 1971 side.

Rogers, Budge (England and Lions), played 34 matches for England, passing in 1968 Wavell Wakefield's 42-year-old record. A powerful runner and a devastating tackler, Rogers carried the art of open-side wing-forward play to its ultimate, with the result that the Laws were amended to restrict his ilk. Taking the change in his stride, Rogers forsook the destruction of half-backs for the role of constructive attacker.

Spanghero, Walter (France), ranks alongside Meads, McBride, and du Preez as one of the great lock forwards of the 1960s. Majestic in the line-out, he was equally supreme in the loose, bursting through tackles, doubling in passing rushes, and covering with the speed and enthusiasm of a loose forward — a role he sometimes played in 44 'recognized' matches for France between 1964 and 1973, the latter of these as captain.

the ball. He must retire the statutory 10 yards immediately, until put onside by a team-mate or by an opponent kicking, passing, or dropping the ball. If a player with the ball runs into a team-mate standing in an offside position, it is ruled accidental offside and is punishable by a scrum. All other offside offences are penalized by a kick.

When the ball goes out of play, the game recommences with a line-out, scrum, or drop-kick, depending on the circumstances. If the ball is kicked over the dead-ball line from the in-goal areas or touched down by a defender, the defending side restart play with a drop-kick from their 25-yard line. They do so also if the attacking side kick the ball over the dead-ball line. But if the defending side kick the ball over the dead-ball line from outside the in-goal area or carry the ball over into the in-goal area and touch down, a scrum is held 5 yards out from the goal-line, in line with the place where the infringement occurred.

Under one of the more recent introductions to the Laws, a player cannot kick the ball into touch 'on the full' unless he is kicking from inside his own 25-yard area. If kicking for touch outside that area, he must bounce the ball into touch. In either instance, play recommences with a line-out where the ball goes out, with the opposition throwing the ball in. If the ball is kicked into touch on the full illegally, a line-out is held adjacent to where the ball was kicked.

The *line-out* is a continual source of infringement. The side throwing the

Not an England regular, scrum-half Jan Webster has been the hero of two of his country's greatest triumphs, over South Africa (18–9) in 1972 and New Zealand (16–10), above, in 1973, both single tests on short tours.

ball in determine the length of the line-out, but usually all eight forwards take part, standing a pace from each other. The front man must be at least 5 yards in from the touch-line. The two opposing lines must be straight, and there must be a clear space down the middle. The ball must then be thrown straight down the middle, and the forwards must jump unassisted for it. Until the line-out ends, those players not involved in it must not advance past a 'line' 10 yards behind the line-out. The line-out ends when the ball is passed or knocked back; when the ball touches the ground and a ruck is formed; when a player carrying the ball leaves the line-out; or when the ball is thrown beyond the tail of the line-out.

RUGBY UNION 'MOSTS'

Points*

Internationals	72	France (72-3 v Romania, Olympic Games) 1924
Home Countries	69	England (69-0 v Wales) 1881
touring side	53	South Africa (53-0 v Scotland) 1951
individual	24	Fergie McCormick (New Zealand v Wales) 1969
career	209	Don Clarke (New Zealand)
Touring side	125	New Zealand (125-0 v Northern NSW) 1962
Individual		
match	44	Ron Jarden (All Blacks v Central West, NSW) 1951
season	581	Sam Doble (England and Moseley) 1971–72
tour	251	Billy Wallace (All Blacks in B. Isles and France) 1905–06

Individual tries

Match	8	Rodney Heeps (All Blacks v Northern NSW) 1962
International	4	Ronnie Poulton-Palmer (England v France) 1914
	4	Ian Smith (Scotland v Wales) 1924
	4	Ian Smith (Scotland v France) 1925
	4	Ian Smith (Scotland v Wales) 1925
Career	23	Ian Smith (Scotland)
Tour – All Blacks	42	Jimmy Hunter, in British Isles and France, 1905–06
Springboks	24	Bob Loubser, in British Isles and France, 1906–07
Wallabies	23	C. Russell, in British Isles and France, 1908–09
British Lions	22	Tony O'Reilly (Ireland), in Australasia, 1959

Appearances†

Ireland	57	Willie John McBride (to 1973–74)
New Zealand	55	Colin Meads
France	50‡	Benoit Dauga
Wales	44	Ken Jones
Australia	42	Peter Johnson
Scotland	40	Hugh McLeod; David Rollo
South Africa	38	Frik du Preez
England	34	Budge Rogers
British Isles	13	Willie John McBride (Ireland); Dickie Jeeps (England)

Record attendance

	95,000	South Africa v British Isles, Ellis Park, 1955
British Isles	78,300	Scotland v England, Murrayfield, 1962
Australasia	62,140	New Zealand v South Africa, Eden Park, 1956

Best tour records

All Blacks	P 30 W 30	C. J. Porter's 1924–25 side to British Isles and France
British Lions	P 19 W 19	W. E. Maclagan's 1891 side to South Africa
Springboks	P 31 W 30 L 1	B. J. Kenyon's 1951–52 side to British Isles and France

International Championship

Wins	17	Wales (27, including ties)
Grand Slams	7	England
Triple Crowns	13	England

* Adjusted where necessary to the scoring system now in use.
† Against the eight countries listed and the British Isles (Lions).
‡ Dauga made an additional 13 appearances against other countries.

Thornett, John (Australia), captained Australia through that most successful period of their history (1963–64) when England and New Zealand were beaten by handsome margins and a four-test series in South Africa was squared. First capped in 1955, Thornett made eight Wallaby tours and wore the Australian jersey more than 100 times, winning 37 caps. Originally a lock, he made a highly successful switch to the front row in 1963.

Whineray, Wilson (New Zealand), climaxed a highly successful career as New Zealand's captain with a 3–1 series win over the 1965 Springboks. He had first played for New Zealand in 1957, and the following year was made captain. When he retired in 1965 after 32 internationals, New Zealand had lost only five matches under his command. His greatest success was the 1963–64 All Blacks tour of Britain and France when he proved conclusively that he was a prop forward and leader of the highest calibre. The emotional scenes that followed his classic try against the Barbarians at Cardiff epitomized the regard with which he was held.

All-action Welsh full-back John Williams releasing a pass.

Williams, John (Wales and Lions), is the supreme example of the attacking fullback, looking to run with the ball at every possible occasion, always prepared to commit several tacklers before going down. In addition to his attacking qualities, he is resolute in defence, and both Wales and the 1971 Lions owe much to his bravery and skill in seemingly impossible situations. First capped in 1969, he had 24 caps by 1973 – and was still only 24.

Welsh forward John Taylor scores for Surrey in a County Championship match.

Shooting sports

The shooting of animals with guns, a traditional pastime regarded by some as a true sport, by others as a cruel practice, is as old as the gun itself. But shooting became a regularized and bloodless sport as early as the 15th century, developing along various lines so that a number of sports evolved with a variety of weapons and targets.

Clay pigeon shooting

A sport in which spinning saucer-shaped targets are spring-catapulted through the air to simulate the flight of birds and fired at with 12-gauge open-bore guns, clay pigeon shooting (trench and skeet) derives from competitions near London around 1790, when live pigeons were used. The modern sport dates from 1880, when a Scot, McCaskey, invented a target of clay and pitch basically similar to those used today, and an American, George Ligowsky, introduced the first mechanized target-propelling trap. The British forerunner of the Clay Pigeon Shooting Association was founded in 1893. The sport gained Olympic status in 1900, and the first world championship for men was contested in 1929, and for women in 1962. The governing body since 1947 has been the International Shooting Union (ISU).

Skeet was invented in 1932 by an American, William H. Foster, and introduced to Britain by Charles Bass in 1935. Separate skeet events were added to world championships from 1947 and to the Olympics from 1968.

The black target has a diameter just over 4 inches and weighs $3\frac{1}{2}$ oz. The shotgun used has a 30–32 inch barrel length with an effective range up to 40 yd.

In *trench* events, squads of five shooters stand in line at fixed firing positions. A championship provides 200 targets for each competitor. In *skeet*, each shooter fires from positions round an arc at targets imitating small game flight coming from high and low traps.

Target shooting

A sport with strong Germanic origins, target shooting is today a universal sporting pastime, practised in many forms and with weapons ranging from full-bore service rifles to pistols. Most major competitions are conducted under the rules of the International Shooting Union, which was founded in 1907, the year of the first world championships.

Target shooting has, however, been an Olympic sport since the first modern Games in 1896.

The countries not shooting under ISU rules are Britain and most other Commonwealth countries, Rhodesia, South Africa, and, to some extent, the United States. They conform to the rules of Britain's National Rifle Association (NRA), which was formed in 1860. The NRA enjoyed the patronage of Queen Victoria, whose Queen's Prize is still contested annually at Bisley and is coveted by British Commonwealth marksmen.

Full-bore target shooting under NRA rules is done largely from the prone (lying flat) position, and can be divided, more or less, into three groups – target rifle, service rifle, and match rifle.

Target rifle, for any bolt-action rifle firing 7.62-mm NATO cartridges or .303-in Mk 7 cartridges, is conducted entirely from the prone position at ranges from 200 to 1,000 yd. It usually comprises one or more series of 7, 10, or 15 shots plus two sighters. *Service rifle*, for the 7.62-mm self-loading rifle and the .303-in Lee-Enfield No. 4 rifle without additions or unauthorized alterations, includes standing, kneeling, and 'fires with movement' – rapid and snap-shooting – at ranges of 100 to 500 yd. *Match rifle*, for any rifle fitted with a 7.62-mm barrel and any type of magnifying or telescopic sight, is shot prone from 900 to 1,200 yd.

Under ISU rules, full-bore shooting is done with service-calibre rifles in two classes – *standard rifle* and *free rifle*. The latter class permits such aids to holding as palm rest and hook butt plate, which are not allowed on the standard rifle. Shooting is mainly three-positional at a range of 300 m, with 20 shots in each of the three positions – standing, kneeling, and prone – within a limited time.

Small-bore shooting, for .22-in calibre rifles, is conducted, under ISU rules, in conditions similar to full-bore. Classes are again standard rifle and free rifle. The range is usually 50 m, occasionally 100 m. Under Britain's National Small-bore Rifle Association (NSRA) rules, shooting is usually practised in the prone position at 50 and 100 yd outdoors, and 15 and 25 yd indoors.

Another Olympic target shooting discipline is *pistol shooting*, which includes *free pistol* at 50 m; and, at 25 m, *rapid-*

Grigori Kossych (USSR), who won the free pistol title at the 1968 Olympics and set a world record of 572 (out of 600) a year later. The event comprises six series of 10 shots at 50 metres.

John Writer (USA) shooting at Munich in 1972, when he won the gold medal for small-bore rifle, three positions, an improvement on his second place in 1968. Contestants fire 40 shots in each position – prone, kneeling, and standing – at a range of 50 metres. Writer scored a world record 1,166 (out of 1,200) at Munich and the following year shot 1,167.

Bob Braithwaite (GB), who won the Olympic trench (clay pigeon) gold medal at Mexico City in 1968 with a score of 198 (out of 200). Contestants shoot eight series of 25 'birds' over two days.

fire (automatic) *pistol*, *centre-fire pistol*, and *standard pistol*. Competition shooting under NRA rules is at distances from 7 yd to 50 m.

Sporting rifle shooting at moving targets simulating live game has a limited following, but is included in world championships, with the target being the running boar at 50 m. Any type of sight can be used. Included in the Olympics for the first time in 1972, it produced an entry of 30 from 17 countries. Restricted to .22-in calibre rifles, competitors fired 60 shots at a life-size reproduction of a boar crossing a 10-m gap – 30 times in 2.5 sec and 30 in 5 sec.

Shooting for the Queen's Prize at Bisley, on the 100-target Century Range. Some 1,000 marksmen are narrowed down to 100 finalists in two stages, firing at distances of 200–600 yards. The final consists of 15 shots at each of 900- *and* 1,000-yard targets, the scores being added to the second-stage scores. The winner is carried shoulder-high in the traditional ceremonial chair. The Queen's Prize was first contested in 1860.

SHOOTING 'MOSTS'

	points	(poss.)	
Small-bore rifle			
— three positions	1,167	(1,200)	John Writer (USA), 1973
— prone position	599	(600)	Ho Jun Li (N. Korea), 1972
Free rifle	1,157	(1,200)	Gary Anderson (USA), 1968
Free pistol	572	(600)	Grigori Kossych (USSR), 1969
Rapid-fire pistol	598	(600)	Giovanni Liverzani (Italy), 1970
Clay pigeon — trench	200	(200)	numerous
— skeet	200	(200)	numerous
Running boar	569	(600)	Lakov Zhelezniak (USSR), 1972

Speedway

Briggs, Barry (NZ), won the speedway World Championship four times – in 1957, 1958, 1964, and 1966 – and in a record 18 appearances in the final scored more than 200 points. He first went to England in 1952, and rode for Wimbledon, New Cross, Southampton, and Swindon in a 20-year career in league racing. He retired from league commitments at the end of the 1972 season, but continued to ride in internationals and on the Continent.

Ivan Mauger (New Zealand), leading in the first heat, won his second world title in 1969.

Speedway racing is the gimmick that became an international sport. In November 1923 a young New Zealander, Johnnie Hoskins, introduced short-track motor-cycle racing to the Electric Light Carnival at West Maitland, New South Wales, Australia . . . and speedway was born.

There are earlier claimants to the originators of speedway, notably the South Africans who say that some speedway-type racing was staged as early as 1907 in Pietermaritzburg, but it was from the unlikely beginning at West Maitland that speedway, or dirt-track racing as it was then known, mushroomed. More meetings were held there, carnival or not, and Hoskins was quick and eager to expand. Other tracks were opened in New South Wales, and from there right across Australia.

News of these fearless Australian motor-cyclists quickly spread around the world, and a number of Americans, including the legendary Sprouts Elder, travelled across the Pacific to try their luck. Speedway reached England in the late 1920s, and the first British meeting

was held on 19 February 1928 at High Beech, in Epping Forest. A crowd of 16,000 – situated outside and inside the circuit – saw racing between home riders and were treated to an exhibition of 'broadsiding' by Australian experts Billy Galloway and Keith McKay.

Within weeks speedway had caught on in Britain in a big way, and before the end of the summer the first league competitions had been staged. Expansion and consolidation continued over the next years. Equipment became more sophisticated, with all the major motor-cycle manufacturers producing the

brakeless, gearless 500 cc machines used in the sport.

In 1929 the first test matches were held, between England and Australia. And English riders travelled to Australia for the southern summer to contest series. England and Australia remained the two leading nations, though New Zealand and America also provided some of the most notable pre-war riders.

In 1936 the first individual World Championship was staged, with the final at Wembley. The winner was Australian Lionel Van Praag. A year later Jack Milne became the only American ever to win the title, with Americans filling the other two places. Crowds in the pre-war days were always high, and speedway earned a reputation as a family sport, a feature it has retained up to the present day.

World War II halted organized speed-

Left: *An early meeting at High Beech, the first British track. The rider on the left is the famed Vic Huxley from Australia.*
Below: *Igor Plechanov, the only Russian to have ridden British and Swedish tracks consistently well, finished second in the 1964 and '65 World Finals.*

way, but when the sport began again in earnest in 1946, the crowds were bigger than ever. Englishman Tommy Price won the first post-war World Championship, in 1949.

Although there was a decline in American participation, speedway was now interesting the Continental nations of Europe. The Swedes had banned speedway before the war as being too dangerous; but now there was an upsurge of interest, and from Sweden came the likes of Dan Forsberg and the evergreen Olle Nygren. They were to be the forerunners in a period of great Swedish success. Ove Fundin made his world final debut in 1954, and two years later won the first of his record five world titles.

Sweden also dominated the early years of the World Team Cup, a competition started in 1960, but in later years their grip on the trophy was lost to Poland and then Britain. Poland had emerged during the 1950s as the outstanding nation from Eastern Europe, and later Russia made considerable progress.

Speedway in Britain, however, faced a difficult period during the late 1950s,

Collins, Peter (England), became the new hero of British speedway in 1973. He started riding with Rochdale in 1971, and switched to First Division Belle Vue a year later. Then, in a remarkable 1973 season, he reached the World Final, scored a maximum for Britain when they won the World Team Cup, won the British Junior Championship, and became a regular at international level. This was all achieved as a 19-year-old, and hopes were high that he would be the first Englishman to win the world title since Peter Craven in 1962.

Craven, Peter (England), died from injuries sustained in a crash at Edinburgh in 1963. Aged 29, he was the top English rider at the time and had been World Champion in 1955 and 1962. He had brief spells with Liverpool and Fleetwood before a successful 10-year association with the Manchester Belle Vue team. The diminutive Craven had a remarkable sense of balance and was one of the most spectacular of the post-war riders.

Fundin, Ove (Sweden), considered by many to be the greatest rider of all, won the

World Championship a record five times – in 1956, 1960, 1961, 1963, and 1967. From 1956 to 1965 he was never out of the first three. Fundin rode in league racing in Britain for Norwich for most of his career, but also had spells with Long Eaton and Belle Vue. He won the European Championship five times and had numerous other international successes. He made his last international appearance at Wembley when Sweden won the 1969 World Team Cup, and then retired.

Speedway

Mauger, Ivan (NZ), became the first man to win the World Championship in three successive years. He won in 1968 (Sweden), 1969 (Wembley), and 1970 (Poland), and after finishing runner-up in 1971 he won the title again in 1972 at Wembley. In 1973 he was beaten in a run-off for the title. Mauger's attention to even the minutest detail has contributed to his remarkably consistent success since the late 1960s. He also won the world 1,000 metres championship in 1971 and 1972. He joined Exeter in 1973, having ridden for Wimbledon, Newcastle, and Belle Vue.

Moore, Ronnie (NZ), became one of speedway's most popular riders when he arrived, as a 17-year-old, to ride for Wimbledon in 1950. He reached the World Final that year, and in 1954 became the youngest rider ever to win the title, at the age of 21. He won it again in 1959. Moore rode for Wimbledon until a broken leg forced him to retire in 1963. He returned six years later to ride again for Wimbledon, but retired from league racing in 1972, continuing to ride in internationals and in New Zealand.

Szczakiel, Jerzy (Poland), etched his name into the record books as being the first East European to win the world speedway title. He triumphed at Chorzow in Poland in 1973, and was the biggest outsider ever to win the title. He first rode speedway for his home town track in Opole, 100 miles from Chorzow, in 1968, and reached the World Final in 1971. On that occasion, with the final held in Sweden, he failed to score a point.

Young, Jack (Australia), is arguably the greatest rider to emerge from Australia – a country that produced the likes of Bluey Wilkinson, Lionel Van Praag, and Vic Duggan. While riding for Edinburgh, Young became the first Second Division rider to win the World Championship – in 1951. And a year later – now with First Division West Ham – he was the first man to win the title twice. In all, he rode in seven World Finals.

and declining attendances forced many tracks to close. The Provincial League, formed in 1960, did much to boost morale, for the National League by this time was down to seven tracks. The Nationals and Provincials merged in 1965 to form the British League, and a Second Division of this competition was introduced in 1968. Five years later there were 36 tracks in operation.

After the initial period of experimentation, the basic rules of speedway have been unchanged for some forty years. There are four riders in a race, with the winner gaining three points, second two, and third one. British tracks are between 300 and 420 yards long, and each race lasts for four laps. Some Continental and Australian circuits are slightly longer. Track surfaces have changed considerably since the early days of cinders. Red shale is now the commonest track surface, though granite dust has been tried with success.

The JAP machine has remained in use since the 1930s, but lost its virtual monopoly during the 1960s when Czechoslovakians made the JAWA-ESO. This machine was still being used in the early 1970s by the majority of the world's riders.

Until 1961 the World Championship final was always staged in England, at Wembley. But with interest increasing on the Continent, particularly in Scandinavia and Eastern Europe, the final has since been allocated to Sweden and Poland as well. A series of qualifying rounds and semi-finals determines the 16 riders to compete in the final, where each rider meets all the others just once.

Four teams contest the World Team Cup final. With Sweden inevitably heading the Nordic qualifying group, Britain (including Commonwealth riders) qualifying direct, and Poland invariably qualifying from the European group, it has remained for Czechoslovakia and Russia to battle it out for the other vacant spot. Other major international competitions include a World Pairs Cham-

The 1951 World 1, 2, 3 : Jack Young (centre), Split Waterman (right), and Jack Biggs.

pionship, in which pairs from the competing countries ride as a team.

A popular form of speedway competition is the match race, between two riders. The most famous match race tournament is the Golden Helmet, a trophy raced for regularly in the British league season. The holder has to defend it after a league or cup match against the opposing side's top scorer.

And another form of the sport is speedway on ice. It is held on banked tracks, particularly in Sweden and Russia, with heavily studded tyres on the bikes.

Speedway is governed by the Fédération Internationale Motocycliste, the world controlling body of all motorcycling sport. And speedway is still spreading throughout the world. There is a revival in the United States, notably in California, and speedway machines are again being seen in South Africa and Rhodesia. Australia and New Zealand received a great boost with the formation of the British League, extra opportunities being available to their riders. Most of the Eastern European countries now stage speedway, while in Western Europe, West Germany, the Scandinavian countries, and Italy hold speedway meetings.

And the man who started it, Johnnie Hoskins? In the early 1970s, over 80, he still retained an active interest, promoting at British League Second Division track Canterbury.

SPEEDWAY 'MOSTS'

World Championship		
– wins	5	O. Fundin (Swe)
– points	201	B. Briggs (NZ)
– appearances	18	B. Briggs (NZ)
World Team Cup		
– wins	6	Sweden
European Championships	5	O. Fundin (Swe)

Speedway on ice, a sport which has its own world championships.

Squash rackets

Alauddin, Gogi (Pakistan), third string for Pakistan in 1967 as a 17-year-old, won the English Amateur Championship in 1970–71 and 1971–72, and was a finalist in the 1972–73 British Open. Exceptionally dedicated and the son of a professional, he built up a training schedule that involved running 3 miles, practising two hours, and doing 5,000 skips six days a week.

Barrington, Jonah (GB), the pioneer of 'career squash', has shown that success at the sport can be highly remunerative in winnings, fees for exhibitions and coaching clinics, as a consultant, and in endorsements. A left-hander, he developed a game based on supreme physical fitness, endurance, and tenacity. He won the English Amateur Championship three times in the late 1960s, and the British Open six times between 1966–67 and 1972–73.

Barrington beating Ken Hiscoe in the 1972–73 British Open.

Hiscoe, Ken (Australia), became in 1962–63 the first Australian to win the English Amateur Championship, and remained one of the world's leading players. Six times Australian Amateur Champion, he also showed talent at rugby and surfing.

Hunt, Geoff (Australia), International Squash Rackets Federation (world amateur) champion in the inaugural year 1967, he retained the title in 1969 and 1971, before turning professional. He won the English Amateur Championship in 1969–70 and the British Open in 1968–69. He and Jonah Barrington have vied for the world's No. 1 position since 1967. A devastating hitter and superb stroke-maker, he has come off best overall in their individual duels, winning a 1969–70 exhibition tour with embarrassing ease, 13–2.

Sharing its long ancestry with all racket games, squash rackets evolved in England from rackets, a game played with a hard ball in a large, totally enclosed court. Squash was first played at Harrow School around the middle of the 19th century. Boys waiting their turn to play rackets would knock a ball about in the small, three-sided rectangular space adjacent to the rackets court. Because the rectangle was small and open at the back, the game required a ball slower than the very fast rackets ball. Later, private courts were constructed at country homes, although no standard size was laid down, and this helped spread the game, which became known as 'baby rackets'. Thus squash was born, and by 1886 this smaller-court, soft-ball version of rackets had gained individual recognition.

Primarily because of its close associations with public schools and the armed

Australia's Geoff Hunt (left) and Jonah Barrington of Britain, the world's top two squash players since the late 1960s, in one of their numerous classic encounters. The stylish Australian has usually emerged on top in their duels, but such is the determination of Barrington, he can never be discounted.

forces, squash rackets remained an essentially 'upper class' game until the 1930s. The big breakthrough came, however, in the 1960s. Then a worldwide increase of leisure time, freedom from any control imposed by weather conditions, the amount of exercise that can be obtained in a 40-minute session, and the fact that two minimally talented players of similar skills can sustain long rallies and have an enjoyable game ten minutes or so after playing for the first time led to an explosion in popularity.

Though Britain invented the game, other countries became organized earlier, starting with the formation of the United

Hashim Khan

Khan family (Pakistan). Born in 1916, Hashim Khan was the first of a family who dominated international squash from 1950 to 1962 and was still a major force in the 1970s. He won the British Open Championship a record seven times, his younger brother Azam won it four times, and his cousin and nephew Roshan and Mohibullah captured that prestigious title once each. And Roshan's elder brother, Nazrullah Khan, became the world's shrewdest coach.

McKay, Heather (Australia), is unchallenged as the outstanding woman squash player of all time. Born Heather Blundell, one of a family of 11 children, she grew up in a sporting atmosphere. In 1973, she won her 12th successive English amateur title, having the previous year beaten the record of 10 wins by Janet Shardlow (née Morgan). Her defeats in major competitions have been rare, and few players have even taken a game from her. Yet she started squash just to get fit for hockey.

The 20-year-old Heather Blundell, as she then was, in 1962, prior to the start of her record championship run.

States Squash Rackets Association in 1907 and the Canadian SRA in 1911. The North American game varies considerably from the one met elsewhere in the world, using a very hard ball, different scoring, and a smaller court with different measurements. South Africa's SRA (1910) was the first to adopt the British game officially, the formation of the (English) SRA not coming until 1928.

Competitive squash preceded the SRA; C. R. Read beat A. W. B. Johnson in 1920 for the inaugural professional championship. The amateur championship began in 1922, as did the women's championship.

The first international matches took place at Philadelphia in 1923, Britain beating Canada but losing to America. The first major international event, the British Open Championship, took place in 1930. And the world (amateur) championships – officially, the International Squash Rackets Championships – were inaugurated in 1967 after the formation of the International Squash Rackets Federation. Geoff Hunt of Australia won the individual title and Australia the team.

In 1937–38 F. D. Amr Bey won both the amateur and open championships (for the fourth time), a feat not repeated until Jonah Barrington did it in 1966–67. Barrington turned professional in 1969 and instituted professional exhibition tours with a 15-match series against Hunt – albeit, winning only two. This led to the rapid growth of sponsorship and, in the 1970s, the arrival of commercial, profit-orientated courts.

How to play

A standard squash rackets court is 32 ft long and 21 ft wide. Its front wall is divided into three sections defined by lines running the full width. One is 19 inches above floor level, the section below being made of tin in order to make a distinctive sound when hit by the ball. The second line is 6 ft above floor level, and the service which starts each point must send the ball above this line so that it can fall into the appropriate service rectangle at the back of the court.

Service has to be made from the right service 'box' (5 ft 3 in square) so that the ball will, if allowed to bounce (the receiver may volley it), fall in the left service rectangle, and vice versa. The ball may

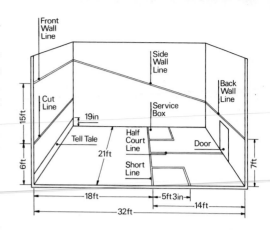

strike side and back walls before landing in the rectangle. As in tennis, the server is allowed one fault; but the receiver may play a fault.

Only the server can add to his score, the receiver taking over service – and the right to score – if he wins the rally. Points are played from alternate service boxes.

A game is won by the player first scoring nine points, unless the score reaches 8-all. In that case play continues either for one more point or until one player wins two of the next three points, 'hand out' (the receiver) choosing which shall apply. Matches are usually best of five games, but may be best of three.

The side and back walls have a line running along them marking the boundaries of the court. Each player endeavours to hit the ball so that it strikes the front wall above the 'tin', falls within the court boundaries, and either evades the opponent or prevents him returning it above the tin before allowing it to bounce twice. A player can also be awarded a (penalty) point if he is obstructed from making a shot by the proximity of his opponent.

The rubber squash balls have a diameter of about $1\frac{5}{8}$ in, with a matt surface. Rackets have a maximum length of 27 in, with the string area not more than $8\frac{1}{2}$ in long and $7\frac{1}{4}$ in wide.

Doubles, on a 45 × 25 ft court, is also played, mainly in the United States, but it can be played on a singles court. Scoring is 15-up, and is similar to that in badminton; in the North American game, singles is also 15-up.

SQUASH 'MOSTS'

World championship	3	G. Hunt (Aust.)
British Open	7	H. Khan (Pakistan)
Women's championship	12	H. McKay (Aust.)

Surfing

Hot-dogging, hanging five, goofy-footer, wipe-out . . . words that swept into the English language in the late 1950s and 1960s, encouraged by pop music and heralding one of the most phenomenal of sporting cults. Surfing had arrived.

What was it that transformed this relatively obscure sport into a world-wide youth craze? As a sporting activity, surfing had been practised and was popular on America's West Coast and Australia's East and around Hawaii, where British seamen first saw it practised in the 1770s. Why, suddenly, were thousands of young people searching for something they called 'the perfect wave'?

The answer is the light, finned, balsawood surfboard, developed by American Bob Simmons in the early 1950s, which led to the plastic foam and fibreglass boards of today. Earlier boards were very heavy, but Simmons's boards could be carried about by women and children. And such was their manoeuvrability that they prompted a new riding style – hot-dogging, making swift changes of direction on a wave.

Surfboard riders go for 'hollow' or 'semi-hollow' waves. A typical semi-hollow wave looks, from the side, like an incomplete tube. The board rider paddles out to catch his wave, avoiding if possible the white water. Once past the break, he turns and lies flat on the board, starting to paddle just before his wave reaches him. As the board begins to move faster than he can paddle, he stands up with knees bent. One foot should be about halfway along the board and some 12 inches in front of the other, both feet facing slightly inwards.

Surfing competitions are judged not only on length and speed of ride and size of wave, but on control of wave and board, manoeuvrability and style. Trick surfing is also a popular and entertaining sport. World championships, for men and women, were first held in 1964.

Boards vary from surf to surf, and generally the bigger the surf the bigger the board. A 6-ft board is fine for small waves about 4 ft high, but surfers tackling waves of 12 ft or more use boards 8 or 9 ft long.

Yet there is more to surfing than board riding. There are many surfing enthusiasts who spurn the board. These people use such disparate equipment as skis, mats (the inflated rubber kind), surfboats, kayaks, handboards . . . and their bodies. Indeed, body surfing seems the most natural activity, requiring little or no equipment but providing all the thrills and exhilaration of the surf. With the correct technique, the body surfer can achieve speeds comparable to those of the board rider.

Above: *Bernard 'Midget' Farrelly in 1965, retaining his Australian surfboard title at Manly Beach, where he had also won the first world championships in 1964.* Below: *A lone surfer at Bude, in Cornwall.*

Swimming

Andersen, Greta (Denmark/ USA), triumphed at both ends of the swimming ladder. In the 1948 Olympics she won the 100 m freestyle and helped Denmark to silver medals in the relay. Later she turned to long-distance swimming and between 1957 and 1964 swam the English Channel six times, set records for crossings in each direction, and won the 1958 sponsored race by over two hours.

Burton, Mike (USA), who set world records at 800 and 1,500 m, was nicknamed 'Mr Machine' by his training companions. A tremendous competitor, he overcame a stomach complaint to win the 400 and 1,500 m freestyle gold medals at the Mexico City Olympics. He retained his 1,500 m title in world record time at Munich in 1972 – the first swimmer to win this event twice.

Crapp, Lorraine (Australia), was responsible for one of the sport's most remarkable swims on 25 August 1956, when she broke the 5-minute barrier for 440 yd and on the way set world records for 200 m, 220 yd, and 400 m. Her 400 m time – 4 min 50·8 sec – bettered the existing record by 9.3 sec. Almost inevitably, she won the Olympic 400 m title later that year, was second to Dawn Fraser in the 100, and collected a second gold in the relay. Altogether she set 16 individual world records.

Fraser, Dawn (Australia), was nicknamed 'Granny' at the 1964 Olympics in Tokyo, where she was 27 years old but still won her third consecutive 100 m freestyle title – the first time a swimmer had completed this kind of hat-trick. An equally significant landmark had come two years earlier when she was the first woman to beat 60 sec for 100 m.
In a stormy career lasting 10 years, Dawn often clashed with officialdom. After Tokyo she was banned from the sport for 10 years because of various escapades at the Games – although she was also awarded the MBE. In all she set 27 world records in individual events, collected 10 gold medals at Olympic and Commonwealth Games, and won 29 Australian championships.

Three great Australian swimmers in 1960: Ilsa Konrads (left), Dawn Fraser (centre), and Lorraine Crapp. Between them, they set a total of 55 individual world records.

Swimming is a sport and pastime that is indulged in as a pleasurable exercise or as a serious athletic pursuit by people of all ages in all countries. It demands little equipment and only the most rudimentary facilities at the lowest level; at its most sophisticated the sport utilizes the latest electronic judging and timing machines. But even the rawest newcomer and the most experienced Olympian share the dual challenge of competitive swimming – the simultaneous competition against a rival and against an alien environment – which gives the sport its unique character.

There was no competitive swimming of any kind in the Greek Olympic Games and the sport was not organized at all in the West until the 19th century. But the Japanese had actually held swimming races as early as 36 BC, and in 1603 an Imperial edict made swimming a compulsory subject in schools. The Japanese flourished in isolation, however, and although swimming has re-

A relay in progress at the Tokyo Olympics, in 1964, in the specially built pool with its impressive scoreboard dominating the scene.

mained one of Japan's leading sports, that country had little influence until the 1930s on the rest of world swimming.

Competition swimming became popular in London in the 19th century, and it was in London that the world's oldest swimming governing body, the direct ancestor of the Amateur Swimming Association, was formed in 1869. But it was not in England but in Australia, according to the French journalist François Oppenheim, that the first modern swimming championship was held: in February 1846 one W. Redmond won a 440 yards championship in Sydney in 8 min 43 sec.

Swimming in Britain soon became amateur, and the importance of the sport was recognized by the inclusion of swimming in the 1896 Olympic Games. Swimming was soon established as an integral part of the Olympics. In 1904 the American championships and Olympic swimming events were held simultaneously, and in 1908 in London a regular programme became established. It was in London in 1908 that the world governing body – the Fédération Internationale de Natation Amateur (FINA) – was formed. And since that date all world swimming has been governed by FINA, who also preside over diving and water polo.

The world's first international com-

Shane Gould getting off to a flying start.

Gould, Shane (Australia), 'retired' from international swimming in July 1973 at the tender age of 16, with 11 world records and 5 Olympic medals (three of them gold) – all in individual events – behind her. Shane set her first world record in April 1971 – equalling Dawn Fraser's 100 m mark of 58.9 sec – and by that December she held every women's freestyle world record. At the Munich Olympics the following year she began her programme with a world record win in the 200 m individual medley and set world records in winning the 200 and 400 m freestyle as well, though she was pushed back to 3rd in the 100 m and 2nd in the 800.

Grinham, Judy (GB), shot into world class in 1956 with her compatriot Margaret Edwards. She took the gold medal in the 100 m backstroke at the 1956 Olympics (with Edwards 3rd) and in 1958 added the European and Commonwealth titles (with Edwards 2nd in each case) – thus becoming the first swimmer to achieve such a treble.

Holland, Stephen (Australia), amazed the sporting world in 1973 when he set world records at 800 and 1,500 m in Australia. His 1,500 m time cut almost a quarter of a minute from Mike Burton's 1972 Olympic winning time. Then, at the world championships – his first international trip – a few weeks later, he reduced his own records in winning the 1,500 m to 8 min 16.27 sec and 15 min 31.85 sec, respectively – and all at the age of only 15.

Konrads, John and Ilsa (Australia), Latvian-born brother and sister, swept through the world freestyle record lists in the late 1950s and were the first young swimmers to grip the public's imagination. John won three golds at the 1958 Commonwealth Games, and Ilsa one, but at the 1960 Olympics Ilsa was past her best and was restricted to a relay silver. John, favourite and world record holder for two events, was pushed back to 3rd in the 400 m but won the 1,500 although hard-pressed by Murray Rose. In all, John set 26 individual world records, Ilsa 12.

petitions were the various national championships, which were normally open to allcomers, as indeed most still are. But the first international events to be organized as such were the Olympics, and apart from dual-meet internationals between individual countries they were the only ones until the first European championships (1926) and British Empire Games (1930). Women's events came into the Olympics in 1912, antedating women's athletics events by 16 years. But swimming's first world championships, incorporating a full Olympic programme of swimming, diving, and water polo, as well as synchronized swimming, were not held until 1973.

Domestically, most countries hold their own national championships once a year, and often these are complemented by early-season short-course competitions (a growing habit in a sport that is tending to divide its season in two). Younger swimmers are encouraged through various age-group events in which children of similar ages are bracketed together and swim only against their contemporaries. And a recent development, which has been prompted by the tendency of swimmers of both sexes to retire from the sport while they are still relatively young, is the 'Masters' competition for older 'age-groupers' – aged 25–30, 31–35, and so on – which began in the United States.

The competitive strokes

The story of competitive swimming is one of constant searches for extra speed. The first swimming style to be used in competition in the early days of the sport in Europe was the *breaststroke*, and it was with this stroke that Captain Webb swam the English Channel in 1875. But breaststroke, with its symmetrical underwater action, was too constricting, and from it came the *sidestroke*, in which one arm recovered (came forward to recommence the propulsive pull) over the water. Developing independently was the *trudgen* stroke (named after John Trudgen who in 1873 in London swam using a breaststroke-like leg-kick and alternately recovering his arms over the water) and the *crawl* stroke popularized by Richard Cavill in Australia around 1900. (In reality, strokes like trudgen and crawl were being widely used by groups such as South Sea Islanders – but not competitively – at much earlier dates.)

For some years, the crawl was confined to sprint events and the trudgen

Larsson, Gunnar (Sweden), was declared the winner of the Munich Olympic 400 m individual medley when the electronic timing apparatus gave him 4 min 31.981 sec against American Tim McKee's 4 min 31.983 sec – a margin of $\frac{1}{500}$th of a second. Larsson followed this with a world record 200 m medley win. The big American-trained Swede had also been prominent in the 1970 European championships, winning the 400 m freestyle and 200 m medley in world record times, and the 400 m medley with a European record. In 1973 he became the first world champion at 200 m medley.

Lonsbrough, Anita (GB), was Britain's most successful swimmer. She started her international career as a breaststroker and had her greatest successes with this stroke, winning the Commonwealth 220 yd (1958 and 1962) and 110 yd (1962), the Olympic 200 m in world record time (1960), and the European 200 m (1962), thus emulating Judy Grinham's treble. After the 1960 Olympics, she broadened her repertoire to include the medley, and in 1962 was 2nd in the European Championships and first in the Commonwealth Games.

Matthes, Roland (East Germany), dominated world backstroke swimming in the late 1960s and early 1970s, winning both the 100 and 200 m titles in the 1968 and 1972 Olympics and in the 1973 world championships. A smooth if angular stylist, he was also in world class in sprint freestyle and butterfly events (European record holder and 4th in Munich at 100 m butterfly), and for a time held the European 200 m medley record.

Meyer, Debbie (USA), achieved a historic treble in the middle-distance events – the 200, 400, and 800 m freestyle – at the high-altitude Mexico City Olympics, which was the first time the 200 and 800 m had been included. She was also a consistent record breaker (16 world records), and in three years reduced the 1,500 m record by almost a minute. Unfortunately, she faded out of swimming while still a teenager and before she could defend her titles in Munich.

Debbie Meyer (below) at Mexico City in the final of the 200 metres freestyle, one of the three events she won.

Memorable moments in sport

Golden boy

Dateline: Munich, 28 August 1972. The 200 metres butterfly is the 'killer' event in swimming. It needs strength of mind and body, stamina, and a perfect technique. But as Mark Spitz lined up for his second Olympic final in this event, it seemed much, much more.

In 1968, as an 18-year-old, he had been favoured to win six golds in Mexico City. Instead, he won only two relay golds and silver and bronze individual medals, and was shamed into eighth place in this event. Even now, four years later, although he stood on the block as world and Olympic record holder, he could not be sure that his 'impossible' dream of seven gold medals in these one Games would not turn into another nightmare. In this race, Spitz was not only racing his seven rivals – he had his own failure in Mexico to haunt him. The others, including his team-mate Gary Hall who had more than once come out best in their encounters, could think of the future; Spitz had the past.

Spitz, lean, 6-ft, 11-stone, black-haired, with a wicked Zapata moustache, slipped into gear as soon as the race was started. At 50 metres he led by a yard; at 100 metres by a yard and a half. And if there were any doubts about his character they were about to be dispelled. He ploughed on to be three yards up at 150 metres and crashed home 2 seconds clear of Hall with a world record time of 2 min 0·70 sec.

The haunting disasters of Mexico City were thus exorcized with one crushing swim on this first day of the Olympic swimming events. Fifty minutes later Spitz was the anchor man in America's 4 × 100 m relay team, which won in a world record time. And from then on there was no stopping the mercurial Spitz. The 200 metres freestyle came next, then the 100 metres butterfly, the 4 × 200 m relay, the 100 metres freestyle, and finally the medley relay – a total, including heats, of 13 swims in the space of 10 days. The result: seven gold medals and seven world records – an unparalleled feat in Olympic history.

dominated the longer distances, but as men became bolder, they increased the distance over which they swam the crawl, and the trudgen was, by the 1920s, virtually extinct as a racing stroke.

Breaststroke, though eclipsed as a 'freestyle' stroke, retained its identity, especially in Europe, and the rules which restricted the swimmer of this style have changed little, the basic idea of the backward thrust of the feet being retained. But it was necessary, in 1952, for the rules to be changed to make swimmers recover their arms under the water. In the 1930s, breaststrokers had begun to recover their arms over the water in a butterfly action; this, being symmetrical,

Memorable moments in sport

Dutch courage

Dateline: Utrecht, 22 August 1966. When Bobby McGregor went to the European championships for the second time, he probably knew that this was his last chance of winning the gold medal that had so far eluded him in the world's major swimming championships. The Scottish sprint freestyler, now 22 years old, could look back on five years of swimming during which he was virtually unbeatable at home, had broken the world 110 yards record four times, but had been a consistent runner-up in international competitions. 1962 – he led the field for 90 metres in the European 100 metres championship, only to fade to fourth and pick up a consolation silver medal in the relay; runner-up to Canada's Dick Pound in the Commonwealth Games in Australia. 1964 – pipped at the post by Don Schollander in the Olympic 100 metres final. 1966, just a few weeks earlier – runner-up again in the Commonwealth Games, this time to the raw Australian newcomer Mike Wenden. Now, with the next major Games two years away, McGregor had his last chance.

The Utrecht final was held in drizzling rain. But the greatest handicap McGregor had to overcome was the starter. The eight men went down, McGregor in lane 5. To his right was Leonid Ilychev of the USSR, the fastest qualifier, to his left Horst Gregor of East Germany. First, Ilychev lost his balance and wavered. Then, perhaps prompted by this movement, Gregor too wobbled. But in any case Gregor took a flier, anticipating the starter. McGregor wrongly assumed the start would be recalled; but seven men are in the water or the air while McGregor's feet have not left the starting block.

McGregor, a yard down already, seems galvanized. There is no panic in his swimming, but steadily and surely he overhauls the others and at 50 metres he is level. There is now no holding him, and he streaks home a yard in front of Ilychev—and wins his gold medal.

Top: *Gregor (lane 6) gets a flier and McGregor is left.*

was then quite legal. Once again breaststroke seemed extinct, until FINA made *butterfly* and breaststroke two distinct strokes, and it is now difficult to see what the two strokes once had in common.

Backstroke swimming has followed a line of evolution similar to the crawl. In the late 19th century a sort of inverted breaststroke – *old English backstroke* – was in use, but it was not long before this was superseded by a supine stroke which became known as the *back crawl*. This, like the front crawl, was characterized by an alternate arm action and flutter leg-kick.

A fifth 'style' of swimming event was developed in America in the 1930s – the

Karen Muir

Muir, Karen (South Africa), was the sports sensation of 1965 when she set a world 110 yd backstroke record of 68.7 sec at Blackpool at the age of just 12 years, 10 months, 25 days – making her the youngest ever world record holder in any sport. Though never tolerated in the Olympic arena, Karen competed all over the world during the rest of the 1960s as one of her country's excellent sporting ambassadors, and set a total of 15 world marks.

Swimming

Rose, Murray (Australia), star of the pool in the 1956 Olympics, won three freestyle gold medals (400, 1,500, 4 × 200 m), and in 1960 in Rome was the first man ever to retain the 400 m title. He became a student in America,

and in 1964, after setting a world 1,500 m record (almost a minute faster than the one he had set in 1956), he was not included in Australia's team for Tokyo – only performances in Australia would count, he was told. So the evergreen Rose, a vegetarian and British-born, retired from the sport to observe the 1964 Olympics from a press seat.

Schollander, Don (1964), claimed not to be a sprinter, but powered his way to the 100 m freestyle title at the 1964 Olympics and followed it with three more first places – the first time this had been done in one Games. He also competed in Mexico City, was beaten by Mike Wenden in the newly instituted 200 m, but claimed a fifth gold in the 4 × 200 relay.

Spitz, Mark (USA), was the Byronic, moustachioed heart-throb of the Munich Olympic Games, in which he won a record seven gold medals – all in world record times – four individual and three team. The only doubt about Spitz had been his competitive ability, considering his 'failure' in Mexico City where, bidding for six golds he won only two relay golds, a silver, and a bronze. But in Munich, after he had won his first event, the 200 m butterfly, he stormed on relentlessly to win the 100 and 200 m freestyle and the 100 m butterfly and help his team to victory in the two freestyle relays and the medley. After Munich he was besieged with film and endorsement offers, and understandably, at the age of 22, turned professional.

medley. An individual medley, as its name implies, is made up of legs of each stroke – butterfly, backstroke, breaststroke, and another stroke (front crawl); a medley relay race is swum in the order backstroke, breaststroke, butterfly, and another stroke (front crawl).

Front crawl is not described in any rule book, and is swum in freestyle races, which have no style restrictions. It is used in freestyle because it is the fastest stroke so far developed.

Long-distance swimming

Long-distance swimming is a description of any open-water (river, sea, lake) race or solo swim of reasonable length – usually in excess of 3 miles. The emphasis is as much on completing the course as on winning. In Britain the sport is amateur, but in America and in some Mediterranean countries large money prizes are paid to the winners of big events.

Certain swims have assumed almost classic status: they include the English Channel, Loch Ness, and Lake Windermere in Britain; the Cook Strait in New Zealand; the Capri-Naples swim in Italy; and the Atlantic City Marathon in the United States.

Other swimming sports

Synchronized swimming is a women-only competitive form of water ballet, in which various graceful movements in the water are performed to music. It has its

SWIMMING 'MOSTS'

Olympic gold medals

Total			
	men	9	M. Spitz (USA)
	women	4	D. Fraser (Australia)
Individual			
	men	4	R. Matthes (E. Germany)
		4	M. Spitz (USA)
	women	3	D. Fraser (Australia)
		3	D. Meyer (USA)
		3	S. Gould (USA)
In one Games		7	*M. Spitz (USA)
individual		4	*M. Spitz (USA)
	women	3	†D. Meyer (USA)
		3	*S. Gould (Australia)
In one event		3	‡D. Fraser (Australia)

Olympic medals

Men	11	M. Spitz (USA)
Women	8	D. Fraser (Australia)

World records

Men	32	A. Borg (Sweden)
	§21	M. Spitz (USA)
Women	39	R. Hveger (Denmark)
	§15	D. Fraser (Australia)

*1972. †1968. ‡Women's 100 m freestyle (1956–64). §At distances currently recognized.

CHANNEL RECORDS

France to England

Men	9 h 35 m	Barry Watson (GB)	1964
Women	9 h 59 m	Linda McGill (Aus)	1967

England to France

Men	9 h 44 m	Davis Hart (USA)	1972
Women	9 h 36 m	Lynne Cox (USA)	1973

Two-way crossing

	30 h 3 m	Ted Erikson (USA)	1965
Most crossings	6	Brojen Das (Pakistan)	
	6	Tom Hetzel (USA)	

The first ever Channel swim: Captain Webb crosses from England to France in 1875.

Synchronized swimming, a form of water ballet that is now highly competitive.

Octopush, a kind of underwater hockey that has its drawbacks as a spectator sport.

Turrall, Jenny (Australia), emerged in 1974 as a natural successor to the prematurely retired Shane Gould. A diminutive 5 ft 2 in, and weighing only 6 st 10 lb, she set world records at 800 and 1,500 metres, and, still only 13, competed in all four

own national championships and international teams in many countries, and a world championship was held in 1973 in Belgrade. 'Synchro', as it is known, is being promoted keenly, as it is thought to provide an athletic outlet for women after their ambitions in the straight competitive field have run out.

The term *underwater swimming* covers a number of different activities, none purely competitive but each physically demanding and mentally satisfying. *Skin diving*, as the name implies, requires the minimum of equipment – mask, snorkel, and fins. It is also used, however, to embrace *Scuba*, or *Aqualung diving*, in which breathing apparatus is used. The increasing sophistication of underwater swimming apparatus, and the consequent opening up of new worlds to explore, has led to the decline of such sports as *spearfishing*, in which world team championships have been held. There have also been competitions for *surface fin swimming*, and in the late 1960s a form of underwater hockey called *octopush*, played in swimming pools, was developed.

freestyle events at the 1974 Commonwealth Games, winning a gold (400 m) and 2 silvers.

Weissmuller, Johnny (USA), was the larger than life sports hero of the 1920s who became a screen idol in the role of Tarzan the Ape Man, his clean limbs contrasting oddly with those of his hirsute companions.

He was a triple gold medallist (100, 400, 4 × 200 m freestyle) and a bronze medallist in the water polo at the 1924 Olympics in Paris, and he retained his sprint title at the 1928 Games, a further relay gold taking his total to five. Weissmuller, whose high-riding style revolutionized the front crawl, also won 18 individual and 5 team US AAU championships, and set 24 world records – a record in itself – at distances from 100 to 880 yd freestyle and even one for backstroke. His greatness is best reflected in the longevity of his records – his 100 yd time of 51.0 sec stood from 1927 until 1943.

Wilkie, David (GB), won the 200 m breaststroke at the 1973 world championships in Belgrade

WORLD SWIMMING RECORDS

Men

Freestyle	100 m	51.22 s	Mark Spitz (USA)	3.9.72
	200 m	1 m 51.66 s	Tim Shaw (USA)	24.8.74
	400 m	3 m 54.69 s	Tim Shaw (USA)	23.8.74
	800 m	8 m 15.88 s	Stephen Holland (Australia)	1.2.74
	1500 m	15 m 31.17 s	Tim Shaw (USA)	25.8.74
	4×100 m relay	3 m 25.17 s	United States	1.9.74
	4×200 m relay	7 m 33.22 s	United States	7.9.73
Breaststroke	100 m	1 m 3.88 s	John Hencken (USA)	31.8.74
	200 m	2 m 18.21 s	John Hencken (USA)	1.9.74
Butterfly	100 m	54.27 s	Mark Spitz (USA)	31.8.72
	200 m	2 m 0.70 s	Mark Spitz (USA)	28.8.72
Backstroke	100 m	56.30 s*	Roland Matthes (E. Germany)	9.4.72
		56.30 s	Roland Matthes (E. Germany)	4.9.72
	200 m	2 m 1.87 s	Roland Matthes (E. Germany)	6.9.73
Individual medley	200 m	2 m 6.32 s	David Wilkie (GB)	24.8.74
	400 m	4 m 28.89 s	Andras Hargitay (Hungary)	20.8.74
Medley relay	4×100	3 m 48.18 s	United States	4.9.72

Women

Freestyle	100 m	56.96 s	Kornelia Ender (E. Germany)	19.8.74
	200 m	2 m 2.94 s	Shirley Babashoff (USA)	24.8.74
	400 m	4 m 15.77 s	Shirley Babashoff (USA)	23.8.74
	800 m	8 m 47.59 s	Jo Harshbarger (USA)	31.8.74
	1500 m	16 m 33.94 s	Jennifer Turrall (Australia)	25.8.74
	4×100 m relay	3 m 51.99 s	United States	31.8.74
Breaststroke	100 m	1 m 12.28 s	Renate Vogel (E. Germany)	1.9.74
	200 m	2 m 34.99 s	Karla Linke (E. Germany)	19.8.74
Butterfly	100 m	1 m 1.88 s	Rosemarie Kother (E. Germany)	1.9.74
	200 m	2 m 13.76 s	Rosemarie Kother (E. Germany)	8.9.73
Backstroke	100 m	1 m 2.98 s	Ulrike Richter (E. Germany)	1.9.74
	200 m	2 m 17.35 s	Ulrike Richter (E. Germany)	24.8.74
Individual medley	200 m	2 m 18.97 s	Ulrike Tauber (E. Germany)	18.8.74
	400 m	4 m 52.42 s	Ulrike Tauber (E. Germany)	21.8.74
Medley relay	4×100 m	4 m 13.78 s	East Germany	24.8.74

* Timed to one-tenth of a second only.

in world record time – 2 min 19.28 sec. Previously bronze medallist in the 1970 Commonwealth Games and runner-up in the 1972 Olympics, he was also third in the 200 m individual medley. His world record was Britain's first in a current Olympic event for 13 years.

Table tennis

Right: *Two great European champions, who enriched English table tennis after the war, Richard Bergmann (left) and Victor Barna.* Far right: *Bergmann teams up with the left-handed Ann Haydon (later Jones) in the 1955 mixed doubles world championships.*

Played on the smallest 'court' of all racket sports, table tennis rose from humble origins as a parlour game to become an all-action world sport played by supremely fit athletes in front of thousands of spectators.

Ping pong or 'Gossima', as the game was first known, evolved as an indoor form of tennis in the late 1800s when a variety of 'rackets' ranging from frying-pans to cigar boxes were used to bat a small cork or rubber ball across the dining-room table. Wooden bats appeared, a certain Mr James Gibb brought back some toy celluloid balls from America, and a craze that lasted from 1889 to 1904 swept across England. It spread to the Continent, and flourished there until World War I. But it was not until after the war that the game developed as a sport. The name Ping Pong had been registered as a trade name, so the game became table tennis, and in 1923 the Table Tennis Association (later the English TTA) was founded. The International Table Tennis Federation was formed in 1926–27, with the Hon. Ivor Montagu as president, a post he ably filled for 40 years.

The season 1926–27 saw the first world championships and the introduction of the Swaythling Cup (presented by Lady Swaythling, mother of Ivor Montagu), the men's team trophy. The corresponding women's trophy, the Corbillon Cup (named after Marcel Corbillon, president of the French federation) did not appear until 1934.

The game was dominated until World War II by Central European countries,

particularly Hungary – with Barna, Szabados, Bellak, and company, and Maria Mednyanszky, who won the first five women's world titles – and to a lesser extent Czechoslovakia (Vana, Kolar, Miss Kettnerova, etc) and Austria (Bergmann, Liebster, etc). Notable exceptions were England's Fred Perry, of tennis fame, who won the world singles title in 1929, and America's Ruth Aarons, who won the women's in 1936 and spearheaded her team's Corbillon Cup victory in 1937.

The same countries continued to feature strongly after the war, with Romania (Rozeanu and Zeller) shining in women's table tennis. Then, in the early 1950s, the Japanese arrived to revolutionize the game, with their sponge bats and all-out attacking penholder style. They won five men's singles titles from 1952 to 1957 (Satoh, Ogimura, Tanaka) and five Swaythling Cups (1954–59). Their women were no less successful, winning seven of the eight single's titles from 1956 to 1969 (Okawa, Eguchi, etc) and six of the nine Corbillon Cups from 1952 to 1963 (Romania won the other three). China entered the world arena in the late 1950s and proceeded to completely overshadow even the Japanese until they disappeared from the scene in 1965 as suddenly as they had arrived. By now the world championships were being held only every two years (since 1957), but the Chinese still managed to collect a prolific number of world titles and team trophies, with three-times world champion Chuang Tse-tung outstanding. In the early 1970s Europe began to come

A spectacular effort from Japan's Sachiko Morisawa during the 1967 world championships, in which she won the singles and doubles.

Chuang Tse-tung (China), an all-round master of the penholder grip and an exceptionally fit athlete, was world champion from 1961 to 1965, although this included only 3 singles titles as the championships had become biennial in the late 1950s. He spearheaded Chinese domination of world table tennis at this time, helping them to Swaythling Cup victories in the same years. He won his 4th Swaythling Cup gold medal in 1971 when the Chinese finally returned to the scene after their self-imposed exile in the mid-1960s.

Leach, Johnny (England), tall and stylish, was the first English-born player since Fred Perry (20 years earlier) to win the world title when he beat Bohumil Vana of Czechoslovakia in the 1949 final. He won it again in 1951 and helped England to Swaythling Cup victory in 1953. He won 152 caps for England.

Rowe, Diane & Rosalind (England), outstanding table tennis twins of the 1950s, won 2 world doubles titles and were beaten in 3 finals. Coached by Victor Barna, the pair won their first in 1951 at 17, and recaptured the title in London on their 21st birthday, in 1954. Their partnership broke up in 1955 when 'Ros' got married (becoming Mrs Cornett), but 'Di', the left-hander of the two, continued into the 1960s, reaching two more world doubles finals. She married West German champion Eberhard Scholer in 1966 and played for the German team.

Rozeanu, Angelica (Romania) completely dominated women's table tennis in the early 1950s, winning 17 gold medals in world events. Mrs Rozeanu (née Adelstein) won 6 consecutive singles titles (1950–55) and took Romania to 5 Corbillon Cup victories. Fast and graceful, with a superb all-round game, the 'queen of table tennis' won all 3 world titles plus Corbillon Cup honours in 1953.

back into world contention, notably Sweden's men and Russia's women.

A table tennis table measures 9×5 ft and stands $2\frac{1}{2}$ ft from the floor. It is divided into two halves by a 6-in-high net 6 ft long, and for doubles is divided lengthwise by a centre line. There are no restrictions on shape or size of bat, but the blade must be of wood and only specified coverings of pimpled rubber or 'sandwich' (pimpled and sponge rubber) are allowed. The white or yellow celluloid ball (diam. 1.46–1.50 in) weighs between 2.40 and 2.53 gm.

The object of the game is to place the ball over the net and in your opponent's court so that he cannot return it into yours. The ball may bounce only once, and volleying is not allowed. Service is made by throwing the ball up from the flat of the hand and hitting it first onto your own court before it bounces over the net into your opponent's; if it touches the net on the way, a 'let' is called. Each player serves for five points at a time; in doubles, the serve alternates every five points among the four players, and service is always from and to the right-hand courts. Games are 21-up, but at 20-all one side must achieve a 2 points lead to win, and services alternate point by point. Matches are usually best of three games, although men's championship table tennis is best of five.

Certain rules have been adopted over the years to counter undesirable trends. The 'expedite' rule limits the duration of a game. If a game is still in progress after 15 min, the umpire calls a let and all succeeding points in the *match* are played with the server allowed 12 strokes after his service to win a point – otherwise, he loses it. Service alternates on every point. An earlier version of the expedite rule was introduced in the 1930s to rid the game of the stonewalling tactics adopted by some players that bored spectators and came to a head in a 1936 Swaythling Cup match when Poland's Ehrlich took 2 hr 5 min to win the first point from Romania's Paneth.

The flat-hand service was introduced in 1937 when an American, Sol Schiff, perfected a finger-spin service that was unpredictable and almost unreturnable. The United States won the Swaythling Cup that year and only the young Richard Bergmann's amazing acrobatics halted Schiff's progress to the world title.

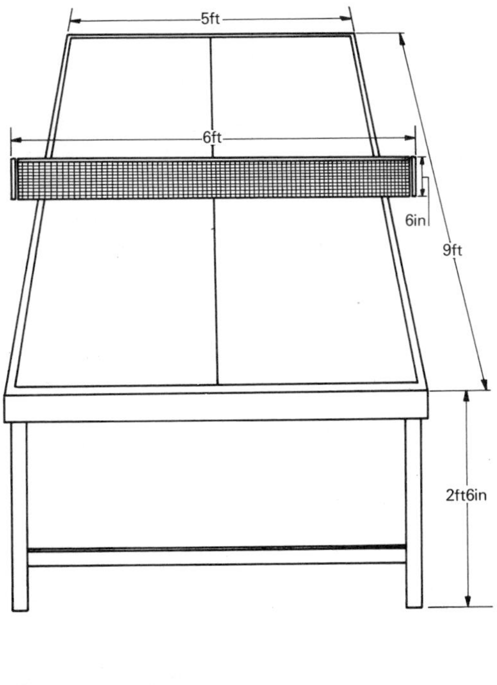

Table tennis table diagram

(diagram labels: 5ft, 6ft, 6in, 9ft, 2ft6in)

TABLE TENNIS – WORLD 'MOSTS'

Singles titles		
Men	5	V. Barna (Hung)
Women	6	A. Rozeanu (Rom)
All titles		
Men	15	V. Barna (Hung)
Women	18	M. Mednyanszky (Hung)
Swaythling Cup	11	Hungary
Corbillon Cup	7	Japan

Tennis

Ilie Nastase of Romania, one of the most exciting players of the 1970s. A fine touch player with superb ground strokes and remarkable speed about the court, he has, however, a volatile temperament, and his remarks have offended officials, opponents, press, and spectators alike. He won his third consecutive Commercial Union (previously Pepsi) Masters Tournament in 1973.

Lawn Tennis, the world's most widely played ball game, evolved slowly. Egyptian illustrations show that bat and ball games existed some 2,500 years ago, and the Persians were playing a game with rackets around AD 400. Tennis, however, mutated from handball, an outdoor game popular in France from the earliest days and which became even more popular indoors in the 14th century.

In the 12th century, powerful hitting had led to the use of gloves, and when these became inadequate protection, thonged binding of the hand replaced gloves. Wooden *battoirs*, similar to the bats used in rounders, came into use in the 14th century. Strung rackets were introduced in the 16th century by an Italian priest. He wrote the first ever book on tennis, *Trattato del Ginoco della Palla*. His diagonal stringing was replaced by today's straight stringing in 1583 by E. Nanteuil.

Confined almost exclusively to the upper classes, tennis was enjoyed by kings and bishops and the like (it is said that Henry VIII had a wicked chop shot) in the cloisters of many churches. And this version of the game is still played on some 30 courts in Britain and elsewhere under the guise of 'royal' or 'real' tennis. Love of sun and fresh air drew some adventurers out into the open, and 'long tennis' was tried on 'courts' as much as 100 yards long. (See *Racket sports*.)

The modern game of 'Lawn Tennis' – the official name, whatever surface is used – evolved in the 1860s when Messrs T. H. Gem and J. B. Perera began playing on a lawn alongside what is now the Manor House Hotel, Leamington Spa, England. There, a metal plaque declares that this is where the first lawn tennis club in the world was formed, in 1872.

Major Clopton Wingfield of Suffolk experimented with the game in the garden of Wingfield Castle, and in 1873 published his first book of rules for 'sphairistike'. He was granted a patent for his 'New and Improved Court for Playing the Ancient Game of Tennis' on 24 July 1874. His court was shaped like an hourglass, 12 yards wide at the baseline and 7 yards wide at the net, which was 14 yards away from each baseline. Gem's court was rectangular, 30 yards long and 12 yards wide.

The game quickly gained support. Members of the All England Croquet Club, Wimbledon, thought that their

Memorable moments in sport

Tennis perfection

Dateline: Dallas, Texas, 12 May 1972. The scene at the Moody Coliseum is the final of the World Championship of Tennis, played indoors, for the richest prize in the world. The protagonists are the two Australian 'veterans': Ken Rosewall, No. 1 pro of the early 1960s, and Rod Laver, the left-handed 'Rockhampton Rocket', who usurped Rosewall's unofficial crown.

Laver, the game's biggest ever money winner, lost to Rosewall in the same final in 1971. He is determined to avenge this. And American TV focuses 500,000 watts of lighting in showing every stroke to the nation.

In tropical heat Rosewall, 37, looks frail. When Laver's blistering attacks take the first set there seems little chance of a repeat. But with near perfect ground strokes, incredible agility, and unquenchable bravery, Rosewall seizes the initiative and destroys Laver's attacks. Laver loses control of his first service.

Leading two sets to one, however, Rosewall slowly droops; those arc lights are draining his energy. Laver takes the fourth set on a 7–3 tie-breaker. Rosewall's last chance appears to have gone. But in the last set, as the unbelievable tops the remarkable in breathtaking stroke play and positioning, tired Rosewall edges away. He is caught. Then he reaches match point at 5–4 but is aced.

They reach six games all and another tie-break. Laver batters his way to 5–4. He serves two thunderbolts, but Rosewall, although tired almost beyond endurance, retains clairvoyancy. Each time he shapes for a backhand even before Laver serves. His first return is superb, the second tennis perfection.

So it is match point to Rosewall again, and even Laver has limits. A netted return and Rosewall is home 4–6, 6–0, 6–3, 6–7, 7–6. Victory earns him $50,000, but honour means so much more that he forgets the cheque and a friend has to return from the hotel to find it.

The honour? Almost in tears, Rosewall can hardly make the winner's speech. Later, much later, he says 'I've been a professional for 16 years . . . It makes you feel the whole thing has been worth while'. So felt all who saw this classic.

Little Ken Rosewall struggles with the massive World Championship of Tennis trophy after defeating Rod Laver in a match that scaled the heights of tennis perfection.

Left: *Henri Cochet (France), 'The Little Man from Lyon'.* Below left: *Jean Borotra (France), 'The Bounding Basque'.* Below: *Maureen Connolly (USA), 'Little Mo'.*

Cochet, Henri (France), 'the Little Man from Lyon' who scorned all orthodoxy, used his native quickness and intelligence to become the world No. 1 from 1928 to 1931. A magical 'touch' player, he was a master of the half-volley. His win over Bill Tilden at Wimbledon in 1927 after trailing by two sets and 2–5 has become a tennis legend.

Connolly, Maureen (USA), perhaps the greatest woman player in history, was unbeaten in any major singles match from September 1951 to July 1954, when she sustained a severe leg injury while horseriding which ended her playing career. The first woman to achieve the 'Grand Slam' of major championships in one year (1953), she was never beaten in singles at the Wimbledon, American, French or Australian championships, a record unparalleled in tennis. A 5 ft 2 in bundle of energy and concentration, she perfected the baseline game. She was nicknamed 'Little Mo' in contrast to the US warship *Missouri*, 'Big Mo'.

Court, Margaret (Australia), amassed more major singles titles than any woman in tennis history. Unquestionably the finest athlete the game has ever known, she became the second woman to achieve the 'Grand Slam', in 1970. This included her third Wimbledon singles title. A supreme example of the success achieved through application and dedication, she chalked up her 22nd major singles title in 1973 with her record 11th Australian win, and took her overall tally of major titles to 57.

Dod, Lottie (GB), Wimbledon singles champion five times and the youngest ever winner (15 years 10 months in 1887), became bored with the lack of tough opponents and quit the game aged 22. She then became the All England all-comers golf champion, a hockey international, an excellent skater, and a crack archer. It is not surprising that she is considered by many to be the greatest woman all-rounder in the history of British sport.

Doherty, H. L. (Laurie) (GB), with his brother R. F. (Reggie), dominated international tennis between 1897 and 1906. H. L. won Wimbledon five times and R. F. four. Laurie quit tennis to please his mother after the game had, she believed, ruined Reggie's health. Possibly the finest stylist in tennis history, he still tops the Davis Cup Challenge Round 'league' with 12 wins in 12 matches for a 100% record.

Jeu de paume (the game with the palm), an ancestor of tennis played in France in the 14th century.

perfect lawns would make an ideal surface, and campaigned for a tournament. So the Wimbledon Championships were inaugurated in July 1877, with a men's singles event won by Spencer W. Gore.

Before then there were at least five major versions of tennis. Wimbledon, then and always in the forefront of tennis progress, decided none was right, and detailed Messrs Julian Marshall, Henry Jones, and C. G. Heathcote to draw up fresh rules. So well did they anticipate the needs of the game, that the rules of today differ only in details from the ones framed.

In particular, they departed radically from other rules then existing in three ways: (1) They fixed the court dimensions at 26 yards long by 9 yards wide; (2) they adopted royal tennis scoring; and (3) they permitted one service fault without penalty.

Until the campaigning of James Van

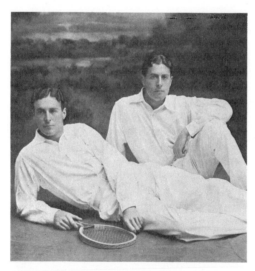

Tennis stars of the distant past. Above left: *Lottie Dod.* Above: *The Doherty brothers, Reggie (left) and Laurie.*

Alen produced in the mid-1960s the 'tie-break' system to end boring marathons, the scoring remained unchanged. The singles-court dimensions and one-fault rule still stand. Only the height of the net and the length of the service court have altered, and then only marginally.

The success of Wimbledon (300,000 in 1973) led to the staging of championships all over the world. By the early 1970s, over a hundred national lawn tennis associations made up the International Lawn Tennis Federation. In America alone there were over 13 million players; more than 130,000 people attended the US Open Championships.

Tennis was originally amateur in spirit as well as fact, but incentives began to creep in around the turn of the century. At first, they took the form of lavish hospitality. In 1921 the Manchester Northern tournament thought the gate would be increased if Suzanne Lenglen were to play. So they approached Papa Lenglen, who agreed she would attend . . . 'but my fee as her manager will be 100 guineas'. So 'shamateurism' was born, though the 'fee' scarcely compares with the £700 or even £1,000 per week commanded by a few world stars when tennis became 'open' to amateurs and professionals in 1968. In six years the then average of £5,000 prize money at tournaments at least doubled, with Wimbledon at £100,000 heading this particular 'league'. Additionally, points acquired by a player at individual tournaments for proscribed achievements were added together in order to fix his bonus from the £100,000 Grand Prix pool backed by the Commercial Union Assurance Company.

Tennis's top two women since the mid-1960s, Billie Jean King (above) and Margaret Court.

Players became millionaires. Rod Laver's winnings exceeded $1 million, and on 20 September 1973 Billie Jean King of America enriched herself by $100,000 when she defeated Bobby Riggs in a man v woman challenge match.

With such money at stake, professional players demanded a say in the government of tennis. ILTF control of the world game was first challenged in 1926 when Suzanne Lenglen signed professional forms and began a tour of exhibition matches. This form of tennis became stronger in the mid-1930s.

After winning Wimbledon and the US Championships in 1947, Jack Kramer turned professional, quickly to prove that his skill as an organizer equalled

his record as the game's all-time No. 4 as a player. His drive and personal integrity led the professional game to immensity and respectability. Inevitably, and with Wimbledon leading the action, the 'apartheid' of amateurs and professionals ended in 1968, the British Hard Court Championships at Bournemouth becoming the first 'open' to all categories of players in tennis history.

Rivalry in organization continued through the activities of Lamar Hunt, an American multimillionaire passionately devoted to sport and the concept of private enterprise. A tennis 'war' between the ILTF and his World Championship Tennis Incorporated ended in 1972, so removing the situation in which money-seeking stars could play off the ILTF against WCT in order to obtain larger fees or prize money.

Gibson, Althea (USA), assured herself of tennis immortality in 1957 by becoming the first black woman to win Wimbledon, a feat she repeated in 1958. Born of extremely poor parents, she proved yet again that a champion's spirit overcomes all obstacles, in her case poverty and racialism. Tall, with a powerful service, she turned professional in 1959 and later became a top-grade competitive golfer.

Gonzales, Richard 'Pancho' (USA), US champion in 1948, was still good enough to win matches against the world's best 25 years later. Six feet 3 inches tall, handsome, and with Mexican lissomness worthy of a cat, he was the world's leading professional during much of the 1950s. His Wembley victory over Frank Sedgman to become the 1956 professional champion ranks as one of the six greatest matches in history.

Hart, Doris (USA), an ailing toddler, might have lived her life as a cripple but for tennis. The knee infection she suffered at 15 months left her slightly lame, and her doctor said she would never be able to run. But her brother Bud wisely bought her a racket. Inspired and enthused, she overcame all handicaps to become a superb stylist, Wimbledon champion in 1951, and before turning professional in 1955 she won 35 singles and doubles titles in the world's four major championships.

Far left: *Rod Laver playing for Australia in the 1960 Davis Cup.*
Left: *Richard 'Pancho' Gonzales.*

Tennis

Hoad, Lew (Australia), won Wimbledon in 1956 and 1957 before turning professional for a then record guarantee of £48,000 in two years. He beat the guarantee in 18 months, and then began the series of arthritic complaints that eventually shortened his playing career. He and Ken Rosewall became the 'Golden Boys of International Tennis' in 1953,

when, both aged 19, they retained the Davis Cup against America's immense challenge, Hoad securing the key rubber with a historic five-set win over Tony Trabert. Blond, with a devastating service, he just missed the 'Grand Slam' in 1956 when Rosewall beat him in the US final.

Jones, Ann (GB), was world No. 2 table tennis player in 1957 as Miss Haydon, but defeats in all three world championship finals earned her the nickname 'Little Miss Runner-up'. Disappointed, she decided to concentrate on tennis, but though she won the French championship in 1961 and 1966, her left-handed baseline game could not get her beyond the Wimbledon final (once) and semi-finals (five times) until 1969. Then she beat Margaret Court and Billie Jean King to win the title, and the MBE, and kill that dreaded nickname.

King, Billie Jean (USA), won the world's biggest prize, £40,000, before the biggest ever tennis crowd, 30,462, by beating Mr Bobby Riggs 6–4, 6–3 at the Houston Astrodome in September 1973. Before that, she had been the first woman in any game to win over $100,000 in one year. An evangelizing 'Woman's Libber', she somehow found time, energy, and skill to win the Wimbledon singles in 1966–67–68–72–73 and reach the final in 1963–69–70. Despite her lack of inches, she developed a powerful serve-and-volley game to which she later added excellent ground strokes. These skills, allied to a ferocious will to win, just gave her the edge over her great rival Margaret Court.

Top left: *Stan Smith (USA) consoles Ilie Nastase after their classic 1972 Wimbledon singles final, which Smith won 6–3 6–3 4–6 7–5.* Left: *A great Australian doubles pair of the early 1950s, Frank Sedgman (left) and Ken McGregor.* Top: *Jack Kramer on the way to his Wimbledon singles triumph in 1947.* Above: *Australia, with Roy Emerson (volleying) and Neale Fraser, play Italy, with Orlando Sirola (left) and Nicola Pietrangeli, in the Challenge Round of the 1960 Davis Cup.*

So about a hundred top men stars founded the Association of Tennis Professionals in 1972. Effectively a trade union, they used the historic weapon, a strike, against Wimbledon in 1973, when some 80 members boycotted the championships in protest against alleged ILTF injustice against Nikola Pilic.

Simultaneously with this conflict, a group of wealthy American entrepreneurs unleashed a plan for inter-city league tennis under franchises granted by their organization, World Team Tennis Incorporated.

Since their format infringed many ILTF laws, suspension faced players who signed forms with WTT. But guarantees of $100,000 a year for five years of play, each covering a mere 16 weeks, drew many stars, headed by Billie Jean King.

As the first woman in any sport to win over $100,000 in a year, she is assured a place in the all-time greats of tennis. How great? Probably behind Suzanne Lenglen, Maureen Connolly, and Helen Wills; possibly after Alice Marble, Pauline Betz, Louise Brough, and Margaret Court, too.

Today television has brought to a peak the cult of the personality, which evolved from the exploits of William Tatem (Big Bill) Tilden in the 1920s, generally rated the world's greatest ever player. Experts usually follow his name with those of Donald Budge, Rod Laver, Jack Kramer, Fred Perry, Pancho Gonzales, Ken Rosewall, Henri Cochet, Rene Lacoste, and Laurie Doherty.

Perhaps the greatest virtue of tennis is that no one can say for sure who was the greatest. Times, heights, lengths, and other measurable criteria do not exist. Only bar-side debates decide such issues . . . and they can go on forever.

How to play

Lawn tennis, the official name of the game whatever the surface, is played outdoors on grass or on hard courts such as clay (ground brick dust) or cement, or indoors on wood, artificial grass, or linoleum. The court is marked out as shown in the diagram, the net posts being 3 ft outside the appropriate sideline (singles or doubles). In clubs, it is customary for these posts to be embedded outside the doubles sidelines, spiked 3 ft 6 in sticks being stuck into the ground 3 ft from the singles sidelines and the net suspended on them when singles are being played.

There are no rules governing the dimensions of tennis rackets, which usually have wood or metal frames, are strung with lamb's gut or a man-made fibre such as nylon, and rarely weigh more than about 14 oz. Tennis balls have a diameter of about $2\frac{5}{8}$ in.

The object of the game is to hit the ball so that it falls within the opponent's court beyond his reach or in a manner that prevents him from returning the ball fairly.

Normally matches are won by the player or players – say, side – winning two out of three sets (best of three sets), but in major men's events this is extended to 'best of five sets' (the first to win three sets takes the match). The set is won by the side first winning six games, unless the score reaches five games all. Then the set continues until one side obtains a clear lead of two games.

Each game is won by the side first winning four points, unless the score reaches three points all. Then play continues until one side is two clear points ahead. But simple 1, 2, 3, scoring is not used in traditional games, although a variation of this was sanctioned in 1973 for experimental use internationally. Traditional scoring uses 15 for 1, 30 for 2, and 40 for 3. When the score in a game reaches 40-all, it is customary for the umpire to call out 'deuce', though the French retain 'quarante a deux' or 'egalité'.

When deuce is reached and one side has to obtain a clear lead of two points, the scoring is called 'advantage server' or 'advantage receiver' according to whoever wins the point after deuce. If the winner then takes the point, it is 'game'.

If the winner loses the point, the score reverts to deuce (40-all), and the two sides again start trying for the two clear points lead.

Players serve games in turn, i.e. A in game 1, B in game 2, A (or C in doubles) in game 3, B (or D in doubles) in game 4, A in game 5, and so on.

Each point begins with the server throwing the ball in the air and hitting it (before it bounces) into the service court diagonally opposite on the other side of the net. Neither of his feet may touch inside his own court before the ball is struck, and the receiver must allow the ball to bounce. The server is allowed a second try if the first is a fault (fails to land in the correct service court). Service is made from the right-hand side for the first point, left-hand side for the second, and so on. If a service hits the top of the net and lands in the correct service court, a *let* is called and the service is played again without fault.

The growth in service-dominated matches and the consequent frequency of marathon sets led to a strong move-

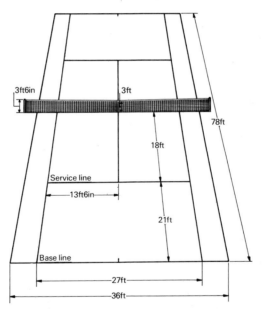

Far left: *Suzanne Lenglen.*
Left: *Helen Wills Moody.*

Tennis

Newcombe, John (Australia), the last winner of the Wimbledon singles (1967) before the game became 'open' in 1968, won it again in 1970 and 1971. And with Tony Roche he formed possibly the best men's doubles pair in history. They won four of the six Wimbledon doubles titles between 1965 and 1970, and Newcombe won in 1966 with Ken Fletcher. At the age of 16 he became the youngest man ever to represent Australia on an overseas tour.

Perry, Fred (GB), probably England's greatest ever player, was the first man since World War I to win the Wimbledon singles three years running (1934–35–36) and was the mainstay of Britain's Davis Cup winning team of 1933–34–35–36. He won the US singles three times and the French and Australian once each in this period. Before that he won the world table tennis championship (1929). He turned professional in 1936 and formed a successful sports clothing company in 1948, becoming radio commentator in the 1960s and 70s.

Fred Perry (England) at Wimbledon in 1936, the year he won his third consecutive singles title. He was the first man to accomplish this hat-trick since before World War I, and no one has done it since. Moreover, he won all his finals in straight sets.

Tennis terms

Ace A service winner that the receiver does not touch.

Advantage Having a point lead after *deuce* has been reached.

Backhand A stroke played with the back of the hand facing the ball.

Chop A stroke played with a downward movement of the racket, imparting backspin.

Deuce When each side has three points in a game the score is called *deuce*; thereafter in that game deuce is called if the scores are equal again.

Drop shot A shot dropped just over the net, usually with backspin to catch the opponent near his baseline.

Fault A service that does not land directly in the proper service court; a player is allowed one fault to each service; two faults – a double fault – and he loses the point.

Foot fault A fault called if the server breaks the rules governing the position of the feet when serving.

Forehand A stroke played with the front of the hand facing the ball.

Ground stroke Any stroke played after allowing the ball to bounce.

Half-volley A stroke played just as the ball touches the ground.

Let Called when a point has to be replayed, most frequently when a service hits the net cord before landing in the proper service court. A let may also be called if a player was not prepared to receive a service or if there is interference from some outside agency.

Lob A high shot played deep into the opponent's court, usually over his head.

Match point The situation when one side requires only one point to win the match; a player needing one game for a match and leading forty–love, for example, is said to have three match points. *Set point* refers to a similar situation regarding a set.

Net cord A shot that strikes the cord at the top of the net and lands on the other side.

Passing shot A shot, usually from the back of the court, played to 'pass' an opponent at the net.

Seeding Separating the best players in the draw so that they do not meet until the later stages of a tournament.

Service The method of starting play for each point. The ball must be served from behind the baseline at one side of the court to the service court diagonally opposite. The receiver may not volley a service.

Smash An overhead stroke played downwards with force, usually on the volley against a lob. The service is, in effect, a smash.

Tie-breaker A means for deciding sets that have reached a certain tied stage, such as 6–6 or 8–8.

Topspin A forward spin imparted by an upward movement of the racket across the ball, making it dip over the net and shoot off the ground; a *topspin lob* is designed to dip over an opponent at the net.

Slice A stroke played with both backspin and sidespin.

Volley Any return played without allowing the ball to bounce.

TENNIS – CHAMPIONSHIP 'MOSTS'

Major* singles
men	12	Roy Emerson (Australia) 2W, 6A, 2F, 2US
women	24	Margaret Court (Australia) 3W, 11A, 5F, 5US

Major* titles
men	28	Roy Emerson (Australia)
women	61	Margaret Court (Australia)

Wimbledon singles
men	7	William Renshaw (GB) 1881–6, 89
women	8	Helen Wills Moody (US) 1927–30, 32, 33, 35, 38

Wimbledon titles
men	14	William Renshaw (GB)
women	19	Elizabeth Ryan (US)

Australian singles
men	6	Roy Emerson (Australia) 1961, 63–7
women	11	Margaret Court (Australia) 1960–6, 69–71, 73

†French singles
men	4	Henri Cochet (France) 1926, 28, 30, 32
women	5	Margaret Court (Australia) 1962, 64, 69, 70, 73

US singles
men	7	Richard Sears (US) 1881–7
	7	William Larned (US) 1901–2, 1907–11
	7	Bill Tilden (US) 1920–5, 29
women	8‡	Molla Bjurstedt Mallory (US) 1915–8, 20–2, 26
	7	Helen Wills Moody (US) 1923–5, 27–9, 31

'Grand slams'*
men	2	Rod Laver (Australia) 1962, 69
women	1	Maureen Connolly (US) 1953
	1	Margaret Court (Australia) 1970

* The major titles: Wimbledon (W), Australian (A), French (F), American (US). All four in one year constitutes the 'grand slam'.

† Since 1925, when they were first opened to all countries.

‡ Including the unofficial 1917 title.

ment pioneered by millionaire American James Van Alen to introduce a shortened system. This led to permissible use of two forms of *tie-break* scoring. Van Alen's method, under the guise of VASSS, normally becomes operative when the game's score reaches 6-all. Then the players contest 9 points. The side whose turn it is to serve (A) serve for two points, then the receiver (B) serves points 3 and 4, A serves on points 5 and 6, and B serves on points 7, 8, and 9. If the score is 4-all and the ninth, deciding point is necessary, the receiving side may elect to receive service in whichever court on their side of the net they prefer.

This system is popular in the United States, but elsewhere there is a preference for the 12-point tie-break conceived in Britain. When used, this normally becomes operative when the game score reaches 8-all. In the 12-point tie-break, player A serves from the right court for point 1, player B from the left and right courts for points 2 and 3, player A in singles (or C in doubles) from the left and right courts for points 4 and 5, player B (or D in doubles) left-right for points 6 and 7, player A left-right for points 8 and 9, and so on. The sides change ends after 6 points have been contested, and again after every 6 points as long as is necessary.

The game and, therefore, the set goes to the first side to win 7 points, unless the points score reaches 6-all. Then play must continue until one or the other side obtains a clear lead of two points.

TENNIS – RECORDS

Longest matches (number of games)

Men's singles	126	Roger Taylor (GB) v Wieslaw Gasiorek (Pol) 27-29 31-29 6-4, Warsaw (1966)
doubles	147	Dick Leach and Dick Dell (US) v Len Schloss and Tom Mozur (US) 3-6 49-47* 22-20, Newport, Rhode Island (1967)
Women's singles	62	Kathy Blake (US) v Elena Subirats (Mex) 12-10 6-8 14-12, Locust Valley, New York (1966)
doubles	81	Nancy Richey and Carol Caldwell Graebner (US) v Justina Bricka and Carol Hanks (US) 31-33* 6-1 6-4, South Orange, New Jersey (1964)
Mixed doubles	71	Bill Talbert and Margaret Du Pont (US) v Bob Falkenburg and Gussie Moran (US) 27-25 5-7 6-1, Forest Hills (1948)
Wimbledon	112	Pancho Gonzales (US) v Charles Pasarell (US) 22-14 1-6 16-14 6-3 11-9 (1969)
Davis Cup	122	Stan Smith and Erik Van Dillen (US) v Jaime Fillol and Patricio Cornejo (Chile) 7-9 37-39 8-6 6-1 6-3, Arkansas (1973)
singles	86	Arthur Ashe (US) v Christian Kuhnke (W. Germany) 6-8 10-12 9-7 13-11 6-4, Cleveland (1970)

Longest singles set

Men	70	John Brown (Australia) v Bill Brown (US), Kansas City (1968)
Women	36	Billie Jean Moffitt (US) v Christine Truman (GB), Cleveland (1963)

Longest time 6 h 23 m

Mark Cox and Bobby Wilson (GB) v Charles Pasarell and Ron Holmburg (US) 26-24 17-19 30-28, Salisbury, Maryland (1968)

Year's winnings

men	$292,717 (£122,000)	Rod Laver (Australia) 1971
women	$180,058 (£75,000)	Margaret Court (Australia) 1973

Biggest attendance†

25,578 Australia v USA, Davis Cup (1st day), White City, Sydney, 27.12.54

Major singles title – age records

Youngest champion	15 yr 8 mth	Lottie Dod, Wimbledon, 1887
Oldest champion	41 years	Arthur Gore, Wimbledon, 1909

Davis Cup

Most wins	24	United States
Individual rubbers	164	Nicola Pietrangeli (Italy), 1954–72 (110 singles, 54 doubles, winning 78 and 42, respectively)
Challenge Round wins	21	Bill Tilden (US), out of 28 rubbers

Federation Cup

Wins	7	Australia

* Longest set in this category.
† 30,462 saw the staged confrontation between Billie Jean King and Bobby Riggs at the Houston Astrodome, 20.9.73

Rosewall, Ken (Australia), was with Lew Hoad one of Australia's 'Golden Boys' in the 1950s. Entrusted with the defence of the Davis Cup in 1953, they beat America 3–2, Rosewall beating Wimbledon champion Vic Seixas in the deciding rubber. He had already won the Australian singles championship (and then the French singles) in 1953 when aged 18. He won it for the fourth time in 1972, this span of 19 years between wins of a major title being the longest in tennis history. A touch player with immense concentration and an unrivalled backhand drive, Rosewall, at under 5 ft 7 in, beat more powerful rivals with his accuracy, fitness, speed about the court, and guile. Twice runner-up at Wimbledon before he turned professional in 1957, he was the leading pro in the early 1960s, and when tennis went 'open' reached another Wimbledon final, losing a five-setter to John Newcombe in 1970. And in both 1971 and 1972 – at 37 – he beat Rod Laver in the final of the £20,000 World Championship of Tennis.

Tilden, William Tatem (USA), 'Mr Tennis' himself, was world No. 1 and unbeaten for six years (1920–25) in major singles competitions. He won the US singles in all of these years and again in 1929, and he won Wimbledon in 1920, 1921, and in 1930, at the age of 37. Ranked by most critics as the greatest player in history, he grew to this stature when loss of the top of his middle finger forced him to remodel his game.

A would-be actor, he possessed immense 'presence' and his matches abounded in incidents. Tall and commanding, 'Big Bill' had every shot. His game encompassed everything from power to consummate finesse. He was a prolific writer, and many of his tennis books remain classics of the game.

Trampolining

An outdoor exhibition of trampolining in a specially built centre with the trampolines set in the ground.

A spectacular test of agility and co-ordination, trampolining can be either an enjoyable leisure activity for people of all ages, or a demanding sport in itself. At international level it has European and world championships for men, women, men's synchronized and women's synchronized, and team.

Trampolines were used by acrobats in the early 1900s, but trampolining as a sport developed in the mid-1930s in America. A sprung-nylon webbed bed 15 × 7 ft supported between a frame 18 × 10 ft, the trampoline enables trampolinists to twist and somersault 20 ft or more in the air. In competitive trampolining, the competitor goes through a routine of 10 bounces, with each bounce beginning a new movement. There are two routines – compulsory and voluntary – and judging is on height, form, and control, with extra points scored for higher-tariff movements.

Paul Luxon (GB), European champion in 1969 and 1971, world champion in 1972.

MOST WORLD CHAMPIONSHIPS

Men	2	D. Jacobs (US); W. Miller (US)
Women	5	Judy Wills (US)

Volleyball

A game developed in the United States for exercise-seeking businessmen, volleyball has a following of some 50 million throughout the world. At Olympic level, it is one of the more recent introductions, coming in for the first time at Tokyo in 1964. However, there have been men's world championships since 1949 – women's since 1952. These are now held every four years between Olympics, so that, in effect, world champions emerge every two years.

Russia's initial domination of both sexes has been seriously challenged by the Japanese, whose women won the Olympic title in 1964 and whose men won it in 1972. Czechoslovakia and East Germany have won men's world titles. In Eastern Europe and Japan, volleyball enjoys a following more associated in Britain with association football, and the game receives enormous support from government bodies.

Volleyball was invented in America in 1895, by William Morgan, a YMCA instructor. Originally played with any number to a team, it is now confined to six players a side, although including substitutes a team can have up to 12 players. A maximum of six substitutions is permitted per set, and no player may be substituted more than once in a set.

The spherical ball has a leather case with a rubber bladder. It is 26–26.8 inches in diameter and weighs between 9 and 10 oz.

Play starts from the service area, behind the baseline. The player serving hits the ball with his hand or arm over the net, while the remaining players adopt frontline and backline positions. Once

The volleyball court, with approximate measurements in feet and inches. The net height is officially 2.43 m (7 ft 11⅝ in) for men, 2.21 m (7 ft 4¼ in) for women, and it is 1 m wide. Overall court measurements are 18 by 9 m and the service area is 3 m wide.

10ft

3ft3in
4ft9in

10ft

Attack line

20ft

30ft

10ft

the ball has crossed the net and is in play, either team is allowed to play it three times with hands or arms before returning it, though no one player may touch it twice in succession. The ball can be returned on the first or second hit, but it is usual tactics to use the first two touches to build up a strong attack and then, with the third hit, attempt to win the rally by smashing the ball down into the opposition court.

The opposing team use two or three players at the net to try to intercept the smash. They do this by jumping up together and reaching over the net to block the ball or force it back into the other court. The other players wait to control the ball if the blockers fail to kill the smash, and they in turn proceed to build up an attack.

Rallies are won by grounding the ball in the opposition court or by forcing the opposition into making errors so that they cannot return the ball fairly or keep it in play.

Only the side serving can score points, so the receiving side must win the right to serve before opening their account. The same player serves until his side loses a rally. A team winning the right to serve must each time rotate their players one place, which means players must have the versatility to play in all positions as the service rotation demands. A set is played to 15, but has to be won by a margin of two points. Club matches go to the best of three sets. Championship and international matches go to the best of five sets, and are conducted by a referee, an umpire, a scorer, and two linesmen.

A typical volleyball situation in which three players leap with arms outstretched at the net to block an opponent's smash.

MOST WORLD AND OLYMPIC CHAMPIONSHIPS

Men	6	USSR
Women	6	USSR

Water polo

One of the most demanding of team games, water polo requires the highest swimming ability, perfect ball handling with either hand, an acute, instant tactical sense, and – although the rules would not seem to make this a necessity – a physical presence and resilience equal to that of a submarine Thai boxer and judoka combined.

The first games organized as water polo took place in Britain in the 19th century, and by 1908 the rules in different countries had been roughly standardized. Water polo has been an Olympic sport since 1900, when Britain won the first of four gold medals. The sport has been dominated by the countries of Eastern Europe since World War II, with Hungary outstanding, having won medals of a kind in every Olympics since 1928. They also won the first world championship, in 1973.

Water polo resembles handball played in the water. Teams comprise 11 players, 7 of whom may be in the water at any one time. Substitutions may be made after goals have been scored or in the three intervals between the four periods of 5 minutes actual play. The object is to score goals by any means except punching the ball. The maximum sized 'pitch' measures 30 × 20 metres, and should ideally be deep enough to prevent standing.

Each team has a goalkeeper who may stand, handle the ball with both hands at once, and punch it, but he may not throw it over the half-way line. The six 'field' players may handle the ball with only one hand at a time. The game is regulated by a referee, who may punish infringements with three grades of punishment: a free throw for ordinary minor fouls (standing, taking the ball under, etc.); banishment from the water until a goal is scored or until a minute has elapsed, for a major foul (e.g. obstruction, repeated minor fouls); a penalty throw at goal from the 4-metre line for major fouls committed within 4 metres of goal. A total of three major fouls excludes a player from the game, though he may be substituted. Total expulsion without substitution is the punishment for brutal fouls such as punching or kicking.

Above: *'Outfield' players may not stand or play the ball with both hands at once.* Below: *The goalkeeper may stand and use both hands – if he can reach the ball.*

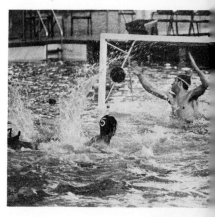

MOST OLYMPIC GOLDS

Team	5	Hungary (1932–36–52–56–64)
Individual	3	G. Wilkinson, P. Radmilovic, and C. Smith – GB; D. Gyarmati and G. Karpati – Hungary

Water skiing

Jumping, the most spectacular of the water skiing events, as demonstrated by Italy's Roby Zucchi.

Allen, Elizabeth (US), became in 1969 the first water skier of either sex to win all 3 individual world titles as well as the overall. This was her second overall title (the first was in 1965) and her seventh title. She also broke the jumping record with 106 ft in 1966.

McGuire, Willa (USA) (née Worthington), the only woman to win 3 world overall titles (1949–50–55), was champion twice in jumping, twice in slalom, and once in figures. She won 8 US national championships and became the most celebrated woman performer, her name to be forever associated with the adaptation of ballet to water skis, epitomized in her difficult but graceful backward swan movement.

Mendoza, Alfredo (USA), gave up a bullfighting career to become the first man to win 2 world overall titles, 1953 and 1955. He was jumping champion both times and also won the slalom on the second occasion. He broke the world jump record 4 times, finally in 1955 with a leap of 116 ft at Cypress Gardens, Florida.

Stewart-Wood, Jeannette (GB), the first Briton to gain a world title, won both overall and jumping in 1967. She also won the European overall, slalom, and jumping gold medals in 1967, and retained the jumping title in 1968. Her jump of 106 ft 3½ in in 1965 was not ratified as a women's official world record because it did not reach the minimum required improvement of 8 in.

Jeannette Stewart-Wood, 1967 world champion, rounds a buoy in the slalom.

Travelling on skis across water, while holding a handle attached to a rope from a towing motor launch, water skiing developed from aquaplaning. It began in veloped from aquaplaning. It began in the in America. It was certainly in America that it developed as a sport. In 1924, Fred Waller patented water skis he had designed, and jumping was first demonstrated in 1928 at Miami Beach, Florida, by Dick Pope Sr, one of the sport's most enterprising pioneers. The World Water Ski Union was founded in 1946. European Championships began in 1947 and world championships in 1949, the latter being dominated by Americans.

Water skiing championships comprise three speciality events – slalom, jumping, and figures (freestyle tricks) – with overall titles awarded to best all-round performers.

The slalom tests skill in timing, turning, and crossing the tow-boat's wake as competitors are pulled through a course containing six diagonally placed buoys, between which a zigzag path is negotiated at speeds progressively increasing to 34 mph. Jumping is achieved at speeds around 50 mph over a 20-foot waxed wooden ramp, 6 ft high for men, 5 ft for women. Figures or tricks are freestyle movements testing the skier's creative ability and skill, featuring different turns on one ski or both, including use of the jump ramp as required.

General purpose skis are made of solid or laminated wood, about 5 ft 9 in long, 6½ in wide, and weighing 15 lb. They have a wooden stabilizing fin on the underside of the blade near the heel. Tight-fitting rubber bindings hold the ski to the foot. For tricks, shorter and

wider skis without fins are used. Jumping skis are slightly longer and heavier. For the slalom, there is a single ski with a large metal fin and bindings for both feet. Clothing consists of a one-piece rubber suit or normal swimwear. The tow-rope, with a maximum length of 75 ft, is usually made of polypropylene.

Crossing the wake of the boat provides one of the sport's greatest pleasures. This is effected by transferring the weight to the same side as the direction of travel, bending the forward knee while slightly raising the dragging foot. The sense of balance and weighting and un-weighting of feet is somewhat similar to that experienced by snow skiers, who thus have an initial advantage when learning the water sport.

Variations of water skiing include *ski racing*, in which the skiers may resume after falling; *long-distance skiing*, over hundreds of miles; and *water-ski flying*, in which jet boats lift skiers thousands of feet.

Skier's visual signals to boat

Cut motor Finger drawn across throat.
Faster Free palm held upwards, or a nod of the head.
Return to base Arm swung down, pointing index finger towards water.
Slower Palm downwards, or thumb-down sign, or shake of head.
Speed ok 'O' made with finger and thumb.
Stop Hand held up with fingers outstretched, policeman style.
Turn Vertical palm turned in direction required.

WATER SKIING 'MOSTS'

World titles

Overall: men	2	A. Mendoza (US)
	2	M. Suyderhood (US)
Overall: women	3	W. McGuire (US)
Titles: men	5	A. Mendoza (US)
Titles: women	8	W. McGuire (US)

Record jump

Men	169 ft	W. Grimditch (US)
Women	111 ft	B. Clack (US)

Record buoys

Men	38	M. Suyderhood (US)
	38	R. Zucchi (Italy)

Speed record

Men	125.69 mph	D. Churchill (US)
Women	105.14 mph	S. Younger (US)

Suyderhood, Mike (USA), twice achieved a world record jump of 162 ft in 1969. One of the only two men to be twice overall world champion (1967, 1969), on neither occasion did he win any of the individual events. Ironically, in 1971, he won both slalom and jumping but finished overall runner-up.

Dutch boy Wille Stahle going through his winning freestyle (tricks) routine at the 1967 European Junior Championships.

Weightlifting

It is natural for man to want to prove himself stronger than his fellow human beings. Throughout history there have been events for strong men who have competed against each other in lifting rocks, barrels, people, or animals. During the 20th century, feats of strength have been regularized in the international sport of weightlifting, which has had a permanent place in the Olympic Games since 1920.

The sport is administered by the International Weightlifting Federation (IWF), which was founded in 1920 and controls numerous competitions – the Olympics, Commonwealth Games, annual world and continental championships, and international matches. Although there was a world championship in London in 1893, it was not truly international. And until the foundation of the IWF, competitions were held on a variety of lifts – many of them one-handed.

For many years there were three lifts for major international events: the *clean and press*, the *snatch*, and the *clean and jerk*. But in 1972 the IWF decided to eliminate the clean and press, which

had caused enormous difficulties in adjudicating.

Before World War II, Germany were the outstanding country in the sport. But since 1946 weightlifting has been dominated in turn by Egypt, the United States – through the exploits of such men as Tommy Kono, Paul Anderson, the 1956 Olympic heavyweight champion,

Jamaican-born mid-heavyweight lifter Louis Martin (GB) was four times world champion (1959–62–63–65). A popular competitor and a fine sportsman, he never won the Olympic gold medal many thought he deserved (3rd in 1960, 2nd in 1964), but he won three consecutive Commonwealth titles (1962–66–70) and set numerous world records.

Super-heavyweight champion Vasili Alexeev of Russia at Munich, where he won the 1972 Olympic gold medal, clinching it with his first jerk. He won his fourth world title in 1973, with a world record total of 417.5 kg (920¼ lb), and he broke the clean and jerk record with 240 kg (529 lb). In the clean and jerk, the lifter first raises the bar in one clean movement onto his shoulders (left) and into a standing position. He then jerks it above his head, sometimes 'splitting' his legs (above) before standing straight.

Alexeev, Vasili (USSR), became the strongest man in history when he won the world super-heavyweight weightlifting title from 1970 to 1973, including the 1972 Olympic gold medal. Weighing over 23 stone, he was the first man ever to raise 500 lb overhead. He was also remarkably consistent in major competitions. In the Munich Games, unlike other equally illustrious Russians who were affected by nerves, he lifted sensibly to set an Olympic total record of 1,410¾ lb (640 kg).

Baszanowski, Waldemar (Poland), was the finest ever weightlifter pound for pound at his zenith during the late 1960s. His flawless technique, suppleness, and strength brought him Olympic gold medals at lightweight in both 1964 and 1968. Not at all heavily muscled, he still possessed prodigious pulling power. He was also splendidly consistent in contests, taking five world titles and two silver medals in the lightweights, the most competitive class, and setting numerous world records.

and Norbert Schemansky, whose Olympic successes spanned the 1948 and 1964 Games – and then Russia. The challenge of the all-round strength of Russia, who have 400,000 competitive lifters, has been led by Poland, with their great lightweight Waldemar Baszanowski, Japan, and during the 1970s Bulgaria, who collected three titles at the Munich Olympics. Britain produced a popular world champion in Louis Martin who won four mid-heavy titles between 1959 and 1965.

The improvement in performances has been phenomenal. Russia's Vasili Alexeev, the 'world's strongest man' in the early 1970s, was lifting 500 lb overhead in the clean and jerk – equivalent to the weight of three ordinary men –

Lightweight champion Waldemar Baszanowski of Poland performing the snatch, an explosive lift that takes less than two seconds from platform to the overhead locked-arms position. The lifter first pulls the bar to about chest height and then to the squat position (left) with the bar at arms' length. The weight must be lowered to the platform.

whereas 20 years previously Canada's Doug Hepburn took the world title with a final lift of $363\frac{3}{4}$ lb. Much of this improvement has been put down to the alleged use of anabolic steroids, and this drug problem has reared its ugly head increasingly in the sport.

Olympic weightlifting requires speed and skill as well as sheer strength. And the complex but fascinating tactics can be used by a shrewd competitor to his considerable benefit. There are nine weight categories, from fly to super-heavy. The more the competitor weighs the greater weight he can usually raise. As a result, most weightlifters are very close to the upper limit of their category.

An event is decided on the aggregate of the best of the three attempts to which a competitor is entitled in each of the two lifts. In the snatch, the evenly weighted bar is pulled overhead in one movement. In the clean and jerk, the bar is raised to the shoulders and then driven aloft with the competitor bending his knees to give the bar initial momentum.

The key to tactics is that, having selected a poundage, a competitor may not take a lighter weight for any subsequent attempt if he proves unsuccessful. If he should fail with all three attempts on either of the two lifts, he is automati-cally eliminated from the competition. The competition is controlled by three referees, and their majority verdict decides the validity of the attempt – they signal with either a white light (successful) or red light (failed).

In addition to the Olympic set, there is the *power set*, which is not held at the Games but features in a number of international events. This consists of *bench press*, in which the competitor lies on his back on a bench and evenly presses out the bar when it is lowered to the chest; the *squat* or *deep knees bend*, with the load resting on the back of the neck; and the *dead lift*, in which the bar is pulled from the ground onto the thighs. Enormous poundages can be run up on these lifts, which require strength rather than skill or speed.

Tommy Kono makes a successful snatch on the way to his 1958 world title at Stockholm.

John Davis near the end of his prolific international career which he began in 1938 at 17.

Davis, John (USA), astonishingly consistent and successful heavyweight weightlifter, won every world or Olympic title for which he competed between 1938 and 1952. Weighing $15\frac{1}{2}$ stone – modest by heavyweight standards – Davis competed initially as a light-heavyweight, taking the world title in 1938. In 1946 he moved into the heavier class, and was not beaten in a major international event until 1953, taking the Olympic gold medals in 1948 and 1952. He was also the first man to lift 400 lb overhead.

Kono, Tommy (USA), a supremely strong weightlifter, varied his bodyweight between lightweight and light-heavyweight, and had a winning run of eight consecutive Olympic or world titles between 1952 and 1959. Of Japanese origin, Kono was pre-eminent as a competitor, often defeating Russian opponents who had totalled more than he had before major events. But Kono was invariably inspired by the big event, and included the Olympic crowns at lightweight in 1952 and light-heavyweight in 1956 among his triumphs. He was the only lifter to set world records in four different bodyweight categories.

Miyake, Yoshinobu (Japan), was the extraordinarily powerful winner of the Olympic featherweight weightlifting titles at the 1964 and 1968 Games. Squat and with lightning-fast movements, he was helped by an intense rivalry with his brother Yoshiyuki, who succeeded him as world champion in 1969. Altogether Yoshinobu collected six world crowns during the 1960s, including the bantamweight in 1962.

WORLD WEIGHTLIFTING RECORDS

		kg	lb		
Flyweight	Snatch	105.5	$232\frac{1}{2}$	Takeshi Horikoshi (Japan)	15.9.73
(52 kg/$114\frac{1}{2}$ lb)	Jerk	140.0	$308\frac{1}{2}$	Mohamed Nassiri (Iran)	15.9.73
	Total	240.0	$528\frac{3}{4}$	Mohamed Nassiri (Iran)	15.9.73
Bantamweight	Snatch	117.5	259	Koji Miki (Japan)	16.9.73
(56 kg/$123\frac{1}{4}$ lb)	Jerk	151.0	$332\frac{3}{4}$	Mohamed Nassiri (Iran)	2.8.73
	Total	257.5	$567\frac{1}{2}$	Atanas Kirov (Bulgaria)	16.9.73
Featherweight	Snatch	125.5	$276\frac{1}{2}$	Yoshinobu Miyake (Japan)	28.10.69
(60 kg/$132\frac{1}{4}$ lb)	Jerk	158.5	$349\frac{1}{4}$	Yuri Golubtsov (USSR)	17.3.73
	Total	277.5	$611\frac{1}{2}$	Yoshinobu Miyake (Japan)	28.10.69
Lightweight	Snatch	137.5	303	Waldemar Baszanowski (Poland)	23.4.71
(67.5 kg/$148\frac{3}{4}$ lb)	Jerk	177.5	$391\frac{1}{4}$	Murkharbi Kirzhinov (USSR)	30.8.72
	Total	312.5	$688\frac{3}{4}$	Murkharbi Kirzhinov (USSR)	30.8.72
Middleweight	Snatch	150.5	$331\frac{3}{4}$	Leif Jensen (Norway)	28.4.73
(75 kg/$165\frac{1}{4}$ lb)	Jerk	190.0	$418\frac{3}{4}$	Nedelcho Kolev (Bulgaria)	19.9.73
	Total	337.5	$743\frac{3}{4}$	Nedelcho Kolev (Bulgaria)	19.9.73
Light-heavyweight	Snatch	161.0	$354\frac{3}{4}$	Vladimir Rizhenkov (USSR)	15.6.73
(82.5 kg/$181\frac{3}{4}$ lb)	Jerk	201.5	444	Vladimir Rizhenkov (USSR)	15.6.73
	Total	355.0	$782\frac{1}{4}$	David Rigert (USSR)	24.12.72
Middle-heavyweight	Snatch	170.0	$374\frac{3}{4}$	David Rigert (USSR)	16.6.73
(90 kg/$198\frac{1}{4}$ lb)	Jerk	213.5	$470\frac{1}{2}$	David Rigert (USSR)	16.6.73
	Total	380.0	$837\frac{3}{4}$	David Rigert (USSR)	5.4.73
Heavyweight	Snatch	177.5	$391\frac{1}{4}$	Pavel Pervushin (USSR)	17.6.73
(110 kg/$242\frac{1}{2}$ lb)	Jerk	224.0	$493\frac{3}{4}$	Valeri Ustyuzhin (USSR)	14.10.72
	Total	400.0	$881\frac{3}{4}$	Pavel Pervushin (USSR)	17.6.73
Super-heavyweight	Snatch	182.5	$402\frac{1}{4}$	Serge Reding (Belgium)	2.6.73
(Over 110 kg/$242\frac{1}{2}$ lb)	Jerk	240.0	529	Vasili Alexeev (USSR)	18.6.73
	Total	417.5	$920\frac{1}{4}$	Vasili Alexeev (USSR)	18.6.73

Winter sports

Ski jumping, the most spectacular of all the winter sports. Yukio Kasaya (Japan) wins a gold medal for the home country at Sapporo in the 1972 Winter Olympics.

Altwegg, Jeannette (GB), an ice skater renowned for good figures, won the Olympic gold medal in 1952, a year after gaining the world title. A calm temperament aided unflappable concentration. Also a junior Wimbledon tennis finalist and private aeroplane pilot, she declined professional offers.

Winter sports – the traditional label for ice and snow sports – are now virtually practised the whole year round in many centres. Refrigerated ice rinks are always available, and with the advent of mechanical ascents to reach very high altitudes, plastic ski slopes, and the development of snow-making machines, skiing of sorts can be enjoyed outside the winter months. Skiing, moreover, has been adapted to grass, with shorter skis on rollers, and annual championships are held.

Winter sports centres in the Alps, in Europe, and in Japan and North America are flourishing holiday resorts. In Scandinavia, skiing is a way of life. In Norway, a major ski-jumping event can draw 100,000 spectators.

Figure skating was the first of the winter sports to be accorded Olympic status, when it was included in the 1908 summer Games. It figured again in 1920, when ice hockey was added (see *Ice Hockey*). Then, in 1924, the first Winter Olympics were staged, at Chamonix in the French Alps.

Now the Olympic programme also includes alpine and nordic ski racing, ski jumping, biathlon, speed skating, bobsledding, and luge tobogganing. The Cresta Run, a form of tobogganing, was included in the 1928 and 1948 Games, which were held at St Moritz. Curling and a similar game called Eisschiessen (which is played mainly in Germany and

Austria) have both featured in Olympics as exhibition sports, as has the 11-a-side bandy, a forerunner of ice hockey which is popular in Scandinavia. A variety of other snow and ice sports exist, with ice dancing and perhaps ski bobbing on the verge of Olympic recognition. Barrel jumping has its adherents in North America, as have the snowmobile (a kind of motorized sled) and dog-sled racing. And to ice yachting belongs the considerable distinction, according to the *Guinness Book of Records*, of having once been man's fastest means of travelling, with speeds of nearly 50 mph in 17th-century Holland.

Figure skating

Figure skating championships are divided into distinct sections. The first, compulsory figures, requires solo competitors to trace with their skates on the ice specific lobed figures, drawn from an internationally recognized schedule.

The second section, free-skating, provides 5 minutes for men and pairs and 4 minutes for women to skate a freestyle programme of their own creation. Soloists and pairs may also have to perform a shorter free-skating programme of specified contents. The free-skating, comprising mainly jumps and spins, is worth 60 per cent of the total marks. The skaters are marked by a panel of judges, whose scoring for each competitor is graded, up to a maximum of six. In free-skating, a contestant is marked separately for technical merit and artistic impression.

The figure skate, made of chromium-plated steel, is distinguished by teeth (the toe-rake) at the front of the blade, to assist spinning. The underneath of the blade is about an eighth of an inch wide, with a hollow ridge making two edges, inner and outer, nearly all movements being made on an edge and not on the flat of the blade.

Each type of jump varies according to the edge, foot, and direction used for take-off and landing. More difficult double and triple jumps derive their names from the number of mid-air rotations made. Most familiar spins are the sit and cross-foot, named after the respective postures assumed while spinning. Pair skating additionally includes various spins while holding and introduces another dimension to skating, the lift, of which there are many kinds.

Probably originating some 3,000 years ago in Scandinavia, skating on ice developed first as a means of transport. Skates were made from animal shank or rib bones, until an all-metal skate was invented in 1850 by E. W. Bushnell of Philadelphia.

The first known club began in Edinburgh in 1742. Mechanically frozen rinks date from 1876, when the first opened near King's Road, Chelsea, in London. The National Skating Association of Great Britain was the sport's first national administration, founded in 1879. The International Skating Union was formed in 1892, and governs both figure and speed skating, with 32 member nations.

The major pioneer of figure skating and proficiency tests was an Englishman, H. E. Vandervell, from whose efforts were evolved the bracket, counter, and rocker figures in the 1880s. World figure skating championships began in 1896, with separate events for women from 1906 and for pair skating from 1908. The three events gained Olympic inclusion in 1908, held separately from the world championships. Originally held outdoors on natural ice, the championships must now take place on indoor, mechanically frozen rinks.

Men's world champions have generally proved durable. A Swede, Ulrich Salchow, was 10 times champion before World War I, and the first Olympic winner, and another Swede, Gillis Grafström, won 3 world and 3

Button, Dick (USA), the first ice figure skater to achieve a triple jump, in 1952, was the only one to hold the world, Olympic, North American, United States, and European titles in the same year, 1948. From 1948 to 1952 he was twice Olympic gold medallist and five times world champion.

Colledge, Cecilia (GB), an ice figure skating perfectionist, won six British titles between 1935 and 1946, in a career interrupted by World War II, in which she served as a driver in the Mechanized Transport Corps. Succeeding Sonja Henie as world champion in 1937, she turned professional eight years later, first to star in London ice shows, then to coach in America.

Memorable moments in sport

The electrifying Canadian

Dateline: Prague, 17 March 1962. Perhaps the most thrilling free-skating performance ever seen climaxed the amateur career of Don Jackson, the dapper, 22-year-old Toronto ice skater whose magnetic personality entranced the world championship spectators in Prague.

Karol Divin, Czech idol of the host nation, led Jackson by 45.8 marks after the compulsory figures, and clearly looked home and dry. The Czech was first of the two to perform the free-skating and was cheered every time his skates left the ice, ending with an aggregate score which, because of the substantial earlier advantage, was obviously safe from anything but a display of unprecedented quality.

The impressive New Sports Hall was hushed as Jackson began his programme, five minutes that were to be a revelation. He leapt magnificently to daring double

and triple jumps, gaining spectacular elevation and punctuating the leaps with shrewdly varied fast spins and dazzling footwork. Every movement of the electrifying display seemed perfect, and the Czech crowd roared with applause. They knew their own hero was eclipsed, but realized they were watching a golden moment of skating history.

The nine judges echoed the appreciation with their marks. There were six maximum sixes for artistic impression and another for technical merit. Jackson scored 67 more than Divin, to finish with 21.2 more overall, but won only by 5–4 judges' majority. Afterwards relinquishing amateur status, Jackson was surely the greatest skater never to win an Olympic title. His scintillating professional performance at Wembley eight years later convinced newer enthusiasts that his 1962 talents have probably never been bettered.

Donald Jackson – unforgettable performance at Prague.

Pair skating – a marriage of art and sport. Above: The Protopopovs, who introduced a ballet-like style to the sport, reigned supreme from 1964 to 1968. Above right: Another Russian pair, Irena Rodnina and Alexei Ulanov, took over from and emulated the Protopopovs, reigning until 1972, after which Rodnina, with a new partner, continued as 'queen'. Right: Popular American pair, Jo Jo Starbuck and Kenneth Shelley.

Goitschel, Marielle (France), an alpine ski racer, headed a dominant French women's team in the mid-1960s. She won Olympic gold medals in 1964 and 1968, and three successive world combined titles (1962-64-66). A professional footballer's daughter, she shared with her sister Christine a unique distinction in the 1964 Innsbruck Olympics, each gaining a silver medal in an event won by the other.

Henie, Sonja (Norway), the beautiful ice figure skater whose film stardom did so much to popularize the sport, won 10 consecutive world titles (1927–36), and gold medals in three Olympics (1928–36). First competing in the Olympics when only 11, she turned her skating skill to lucrative theatrical effect, becoming one of the world's wealthiest women before she died of leukemia, when 57, in 1969.

Free-skating terms

Axel jump 1½ turns in air, from a forward outer edge, landing on the back outer edge of the other skate.
Axel lift Pair movement, with girl turned 1½ times completely over partner's head while man rotates beneath.
Camel spin With torso and free leg parallel with the ice, with back arched.
Cross-foot spin On the flat of both blades, with legs in crossed position.
Death spiral Daring pair movement when man swings partner round at speed, her head all but touching the ice.
Lasso lift Pair movement when man lifts partner overhead, turning 1½ rotations with the man's arms stretched in lasso pose and the girl's legs in split position.
Loop jump Full revolution in air, made from, and landing on, the same back outer edge.
Lutz jump Clockwise mid-air rotation from one back outer edge, landing on the back outer edge of the other skate.
Salchow jump Almost full mid-air turn, from a back inner edge, landing on the back outer edge of the other skate.
Sit-spin From standing position, sinking on skating knee in sitting posture with free leg extended.
Split jump Adopting the split position, from a back edge, landing on a forward edge.
Three jump Elementary half-turn in mid-air, from a forward outer edge, landing on back outer edge of the other skate.

Olympic titles in the 1920s. Austrians then took charge, Willy Böckl winning 4 world titles (1925–28) and Karl Schäfer 7, as well as 2 Olympic golds, in the 1930s. Post-war, the Americans Richard Button (5 world, 2 Olympics), Hayes Jenkins (4 and 1), and David Jenkins (3 and 1) held the stage, before, in the 1960s, the title began to change hands more frequently.

Outstanding among the women has been the Norwegian Sonja Henie, with 3 Olympic and 10 consecutive world victories (1927–36), and half a dozen others have won at least 3 consecutive titles.

In pair skating, a number of countries produced champions, until the Russians won almost complete domination of the sport in the mid-1960s. Particularly successful and popular were Oleg and Ludmila Protopopov, with four world and two Olympic titles.

Ice dancing

An off-shoot of figure skating, ice dancing is more specific in requirements than pair skating, with lifts and certain other tests of physical strength not permissible. Championships comprise three compulsory dances (drawn from nine) plus an original set pattern danced to a specified rhythm, followed by 4 minutes of free-dancing for each couple. Nine ice dances are used in championships, ranging from various waltzes to Latin American rhythms.

Serious ice dancing dates from the waltz-minded Viennese in the 1880s, but gained most impetus in London during the 1930s, when the British developed it as a competitive sport, staging the first national championships in 1937. Although world titles have been contested since 1952 at the same meetings as figure skating championships, applications for adding ice dancing to the Olympic events have been rejected.

British couples have been foremost in the world championships, with Bernard Ford and Diane Towler, four times champions in the 1960s, widely regarded as the most accomplished. The Russians have dominated the 1970s, however.

Speed skating

Speed skating is primarily an outdoor sport staged on mechanically frozen, oval 400-metre circuits. Results are determined solely on times, the skaters racing in pairs and in separate lanes. Speed skates are thinner and longer than those used for figures, and the boots have lower heel supports. World champions are the best overall performers in four races – 500, 1,500, 5,000, and 10,000 metres for men, and 500, 1,000, 1,500, and 3,000 metres for women.

A speed skater can cover 1,500 metres about a minute faster than a track runner, and sprinters can average nearly 30 mph. With long, rhythmic strides, the long-distance racer frequently skates with one hand clasped behind his back to conserve energy.

The frozen canals of Holland helped the Dutch to begin evolving the sport from the mid-1200s. They introduced it to the English Fens, where competitions date from 1814. Officially recognized world championships began in 1893, but the first women's title was not contested until 1936. Men's speed skating figured in the Olympics for the first time in 1924, women's in 1960. Gold medals are awarded for each individual event, with no overall Olympic champion.

The world's reputedly fastest tracks are at Davos, in Switzerland, and Inzell, in West Germany, where most records are set. Many skaters from countries without tracks have to train abroad.

After early successes, Dutch men took a back seat until the 1960s, and then in the 1970s produced the first skater to win all four distances in a world championships, Ard Schenk. Most champions have come from Norway, with Finns and Russians also prominent. From 1948 to the mid-1960s, Russian women dominated the world championships, but since then Dutch and American girls have had considerable success, particularly in the Olympics.

Alpine ski racing

Basically comprising timed descents down steepish snow slopes at one-minute intervals, alpine ski racing is divided into three events – downhill, slalom, and giant slalom. The sport gained its name because terrain in the Alps is generally more suitable than in Scandinavia, where nordic ski racing was born. A senior championship *downhill* course is between $1\frac{1}{2}$ and 3 miles long, with a vertical descent between 2,500 and 3,000 ft. It has no artificial obstacles, and competitors practise on it beforehand. Each participant has one

Above left: *British ice dancers Bernard Ford and Diane Towler completely dominated their sport in the late 1960s, winning the world and the European titles four years running (1966–69). Yet their performances went largely unheralded in their own country, and it was only abroad that they received the star treatment they deserved. In 1969, however, they were each awarded the MBE, and after relinquishing their amateur status they promptly won the professional world championship that same year. Above: The youngest victor at Sapporo in 1972, 16-year-old American girl Anne Henning wins the 500 metres speed skating gold medal. She also won a bronze in the 1,000 m.*

Jernberg, Sixten (Sweden), dominated men's nordic ski racing between 1956 and 1964, collecting 5 individual world titles and 3 relay titles. These included 3 individual Olympic golds – over 50 km in 1956 and 1964 and 30 km in 1960 – and a team gold in 1964. For good measure, he won two silvers and a bronze in the 15 km and another silver in the 30 km. Work as a blacksmith and then a lumberjack helped him build up his immense stamina.

Killy, Jean-Claude (France), the alpine ski racer who dominated the 1968 Grenoble Olympics, won all three events, equalling the record of Austria's Toni Sailer in 1956. Twice world combined champion (1966–68), he also won the first two World Alpine Ski Cup competitions (1967–68), before further successes as a professional.

Monti, Eugenio (Italy), champion bobsleigh driver, won 11 world titles (1959–68), 8 in two-man sleds and 3 with four-man crews. Noted for his sportingly selfless assistance to rivals, he was denied Olympic triumph until his final season, 1968, when he won both gold medals and afterwards became Italian team manager.

Left: *Jean-Claude Killy.*

Memorable moments in sport

Sailer supreme

Sailer winning the special slalom at Cortina for the second of his three gold medals.

Dateline: Cortina, 29 January to 3 February 1956. A 20-year-old plumber from Kitzbühel, in the Austrian Tyrol, Toni Sailer dominated the VIIth Winter Olympics at Cortina with outstanding alpine ski racing that reaped three gold medals. He was the first man to win all three races in the same Olympics, but his manner of performance was more significant than the victories themselves.

First came the giant slalom on the long, fast, and undulating Ilio Colli course, discouragingly named after a skier who had met with a fatal accident. Eighteenth to start in worsening snow conditions, Sailer finished an astonishing 6.2 seconds ahead of his second placed compatriot, Anderl Molterer. Sailer attributes his slalom success to a rare ability to memorize the course so thoroughly that he could still describe the hazards of each gate weeks afterwards.

The next event was the special slalom. His team forgot to bring their race numbers and an official issued spare high numbers. But Sailer was undaunted, and his two runs, the fastest, were together exactly 4 seconds better than Chiharu Igaya of Japan.

Finally came Sailer's favourite event – the downhill. Gusty storms had left such terrible conditions that only 17 of 90 starters got through without falling. Sailer was one of them, 3.5 seconds faster than Raymond Fellay, the Swiss runner-up.

Sailer's three victories, which concurrently earned him the world combined title, were the more notable because of their remarkable time margins, enormous in a sport where world titles are more usually won by fractions of a second. He completely outclassed his contemporaries as could no other racer before or since.

Alpine ski racing requires control, judgement, skill, balance, and courage . . . French skier Patrick Russel grits his teeth as he negotiates a gate at speed.

run only, and best average speeds exceed 50 mph.

Slalom courses, appreciably shorter, contain a series of pairs of poles, known as gates, through which each racer must pass. The gates are set at carefully placed angles and distances to test control, judgement, and skill in turning and pace-checking. A racer who misses a gate is disqualified unless he climbs back to pass through it. Men's courses have 50 to 75 gates and a vertical drop between 650 and 975 ft. Women's are shorter and less difficult. Each competitor has two runs, each over different, roughly matching courses, the fastest aggregate time winning. Entrants must not practise on the course, but have to memorize the gate positions beforehand.

A *giant slalom* course blends characteristics of the downhill and slalom in one event. It is longer than the slalom, with gates set wider and farther apart.

A separate championship title is awarded to the winner of each of the three events, and a fourth title, called *combined*, goes to the best overall performer, calculated on a points basis.

A primitive form of skiing is known to have existed 5,000 years ago. A ski claimed to be nearly as old as this was found preserved in a peat bog at Höting, Sweden. Like skating and sledding, skiing originated as an early form of transport, from which nordic racing emerged before alpine racing. The latter was pioneered by British skiers, primarily Sir Arnold Lunn, who organized the world's first downhill race in 1911 at Montana, Switzerland. The world's first national administration, the Ski Club of Great Britain, had already been formed in 1903. Lunn

invented the modern slalom, first held in 1922 at Mürren, Switzerland.

The first senior open downhill-slalom competition, the Arlberg-Kandahar, was founded in 1928 by Lunn and an Austrian, Hannes Schneider. The first world alpine ski racing championships were staged at Mürren in 1931, when early British prominence was reflected by the success of a British girl, Esmé Mackinnon, the first women's champion in both downhill and slalom. Olympic inclusion began in 1936. A special category of Citadin races, restricted to skiers not resident in mountain resorts, began in 1937.

World Alpine Ski Cup awards date from 1967, based on racers' performances in selected events at different venues through the season. Of the International Ski Federation's 45 member nations, 31 were represented in the 1972 Winter Olympics.

The Swiss, Austrians, and French developed and advanced the best early technique, but most countries have latterly adopted a revised international style based on the best elements proved by individual nations. The modern racer adopts a pronounced forward lean from the waist, with emphasis on hip-swinging when turning. Following the development of suitable courses in South America, Australia, and Japan

Alpine Skiing terms

Christie Swing turn with skis parallel.
Edging Tilting the skis so that the edges dig into the snow to gain a firm hold.
Egg position Crouching stance for downhill, tucking in elbows and hands to reduce wind resistance.
Fall-line Direction of the steepest descent.
Herringboning Method of climbing, with tips of skis turned outwards, leaving fishbone patterns in the snow.
Piste A prepared downhill trail.
Pre-jumping Technique used to ski over bumps.
Safety bindings Mechanical gadgets that release the foot from the ski when falling.
Schuss Fast and straight downhill run.
Seelos Series of three slalom gates specially placed so that the middle gate is at right-angles to the others.
Side-slipping Raising the ski edges to control sliding sideways.
Side-stepping Climbing sideways with the skis parallel.
Stemming Pushing out the rear end of one or both skis to achieve an angle to the direction of movement.
Stem-christie Turn initiated by stemming and ended by a christie.
Traversing Moving directly or diagonally across a slope.
Vorlage Pronounced forward lean.
Wedeln Technique involving a rhythmic series of hip-swinging turns.

Downhill, for the spectator perhaps the most exciting of the alpine racing events, with skiers averaging more than 50 mph as they hurtle down the steep slopes . . . Bernhard Russi (Switzerland) 'takes off' on the way to his gold medal at Sapporo in 1972.

Nepela, Ondrej (Czecho-slovakia), the ice figure skater who first gained fame at 13 as the youngest competitor in the 1964 Innsbruck Olympics, achieved an ambition to become his country's most successful skater. He won the Olympic gold medal at Sapporo in 1972 and ended his amateur career in 1973 with a third successive world title on his home rink at Bratislava.

Nicks, John and Jennifer (GB), brother and sister ice pair skaters, in 1953 won the first world pairs title for Britain since James and Phyllis Johnson in 1912. Also European champions in 1953, they competed in two Olympics, eighth in 1948 and fourth in 1952. Turning professional after their world triumph, John gained distinction as an instructor of prominent Americans.

*Annemarie Proell (now Moser),
downhill racer extraordinary.*

Proell, Annemarie (Austria),
narrowly and surprisingly beaten
by 17-year-old Swiss schoolgirl
Marie-Therese Nadig in both the
downhill and the giant slalom at
Sapporo in the 1972 Olympics,
had to be content with the overall
world championship. Herself only

19 at the time, she put that
disappointment behind her to
establish herself as the best
woman skier of her day, if not of
all time, with her 4th consecutive
World Cup win in 1974. A fine
slalom competitor, she was
virtually unbeatable in the
downhill, recording an
unprecedented 12 consecutive
victories in that event in 1973–74.

**Protopopov, Oleg and
Ludmila** (*née* Belousova)
(USSR), classic husband and
wife ice pair skaters, won four
world championships (1965–68),
and two Olympic titles (1964–
68). Their final victories were
achieved at the ages of 35 and
32, neither having taken up the
sport until 16. They brought a
new ballet-style dimension to
pair skating, and are remembered
particularly for breathtaking
death spiral spins.

Rodnina, Irena (USSR), an ice
pair skater, won an Olympic gold
medal in 1972, and four world
titles (1969–72), all with Alexei
Ulanov. Then she changed
partners and, with a then
relatively unknown skater,
Alexander Zaitsev, won her fifth
world championship in 1973 –
half of it, quite remarkably,
without music. When their
recording stopped, they
continued skating instead of
re-starting.

Sailer, Toni (Austria), alpine
ski racer supreme, won all three
events in the 1956 Cortina
Olympics, each by devastating
margins. Concurrently, he gained
the world combined title and
retained it in 1958 at Bad
Gastein. An artist on skis and
the darling of the crowds, he
turned professional to appear in
films before coaching in America.

and the use of artificially frozen snow to
augment balding patches, leading North
American and European racers are able
to ski for a progressively longer time in
the year by following the snow like international tennis stars follow the sun.

Equipment has advanced rapidly in
recent years. Racers now use different,
specialized skis of metal, wood, and
plastic for each of the downhill, slalom,
and giant slalom events. Skis are a little
longer than the racer's height. Sophisticated precision toe-release and heel-
release gadgets bind the ski to the boot,
which usually has clips where laces used
to be. Ski sticks are used to aid control.
Goggles are essential and protective
helmets compulsory.

Outstanding men have been an
Austrian, Toni Sailer, and a Frenchman,
Jean-Claude Killy, who each won all
three gold medals in one Winter
Olympics. The most prominent women
include Christel Cranz of Germany,
five times world combined champion,
and Marielle Goitschel of France, with
two Olympic titles. The most successful
racers in the 1970s have been an Italian,
Gustavo Thoeni, and an Austrian,
Annemarie Proell, who each won the
World Cup three years in a row, remarkable evidence of sustained consistency.

Nordic ski racing
Also called *langlauf*, nordic ski racing is
long-distance cross-country ski running. It is staged on generally less steep
terrain than that used for alpine ski
racing. The rules stipulate that the
course must comprise constantly varying sections of uphill, downhill, and level
terrain, with no artificial obstacles.
Suitable venues are usually different
from those chosen for the alpine sport,
few areas having ideal ground for both

kinds of skiing. The skis are longer,
narrower, and lighter than the alpine
style. The bindings allow for freer
vertical heel movements and the sticks
are also longer.

Championship events are contested
over 15, 30, and 50 kilometre distances
for men, and 5 and 10 km for women.
There are also relays – for teams of four
men over 10-km legs and three women
over 5-km legs. The roughly circular
course starts and finishes at the same
point. A good racer can average 10 mph.
A strenuous and fatiguing test of
stamina, the longer distances tend to
favour a performer around 30, as in
marathon running. Competitors start at
half-minute intervals, the fastest time
winning. Features of techniques are a
long, rhythmic stride, bending the front
knee and using the sticks to gain added
thrust.

The first records of this oldest form of

*In nordic ski racing, competitors start at
half-minute intervals, so No. 27 is now a full
minute ahead of No. 25.*

competitive skiing date back to 1767 in Norway, where the first club was formed at Trysil in 1861. The sport has thrived mainly in northern Europe, but there has been an increasing following since the mid-1960s in Switzerland and North America. World and Olympic men's championships began concurrently in 1924, with women's events added from 1952. Scandinavians have dominated the men's events, the most successful competitor being a Swede, Sixten Jernberg, who between 1956 and 1964 won five individual world championships, including three Olympic titles, as well as three relay championships. Two Finns, Veikko Hakulinen and Eero Mantyranta, both won four individual championships. Hakulinen, who also helped Finland to win two relay titles, is the only man to have won titles in all three individual events. Russians have dominated the women's events, although in 1968 Toini Gustafsson of Sweden took both titles.

A *nordic combination* event tests the overall ability of skiers in jumping and in 15-km cross-country racing, the winner being determined on a points basis. World and Olympic contests, like other nordic events, began in 1924, and Norwegians have usually proved the most successful performers. Johan Gröttumsbraaten won four world titles between 1926 and 1932, including two Olympic titles.

Ski jumping

In the most spectacular ski sport, the longest jump is not necessarily the best. Five judges award marks for style which, collated with the distances attained, determines the outcome. Ski jumping is a highly specialized sport, in the same way that diving is a speciality in swimming. A jumper can exceed 75 mph as he gathers speed down a long ramp before take-off. Wind resistance prevents use of sticks for balance.

The sport originated in Norway at Iverslokka, near Oslo, in 1866. A hill nearby at Huseby was the focal point from 1879, until Oslo's Holmenkollen jump came into use in 1892. Other important jumps have since been added in Europe and in Japan and the United States. No two are identical in height or construction, making performances at each difficult to compare.

The first world and Olympic titles

were decided concurrently in 1924. In 1964, a second event was added from a lower height. From then on, titles have been contested at jumps from two recognized heights, 90 and 70 metres. Only men compete. The most successful jumper has been a Norwegian, Birger Ruud, who won five world championships in the 1930s, including two Olympic titles.

A separate jumping event, called *ski-flying*, puts full emphasis on distance, and higher jump towers are used, notably at Vikersund (Norway), Oberstdorf (West Germany), and Planica (Yugoslavia). Separate world ski-flying championships began in 1972.

Ski-bobbing

Ski-bobbing is the nearest to cycle racing on snow that one can envisage. A ski-bob looks like a bicycle frame fitted with short skis instead of wheels. The sitting rider wears miniature foot-skis, not much longer than his boots. The foot-skis are fitted with metal claws at the heels to assist braking. More suited to alpine than nordic terrain, ski-bobbing is easier and quicker to learn than skiing. In the interests of safety, separate practice courses have to be used away from ordinary skiers.

The first ski-bob was patented in 1892 by an American called Stevens from Hartford, Connecticut. A development of it was used in Europe as a means of mountain transport for postmen and delivery boys in snow-clad villages in the Alps. Ski-bobbing developed as a competitive sport in the early 1950s, when an Austrian, Englebert Brentner,

Above: *In ski-bobbing, which is easier to learn than skiing, speeds of over 60 mph may readily be attained.* Below left and below: *Ski jumpers can reach speeds of over 75 mph as they accelerate down the long ramp and then soar through the air.*

Russian speed skater Lydia Skoblikova at Innsbruck in 1964, where in four days she won the four gold medals.

Schranz, Karl (Austria), maintained remarkable consistency in an alpine skiing career spanning 19 seasons. Twice winner of the World Alpine Ski Cup (1969–70) and world combined champion in 1962, he gained the Arlberg-Kandahar combined award for a record fifth time in 1969 and won the A-K downhill seven times. Only an Olympic gold medal frustratingly eluded him.

He was controversially banned just before the 1972 Olympics for allegedly contravening the amateur rules.

Skoblikova, Lydia (USSR), became the first person to win four gold medals at one Winter Olympics, coming first over all four speed skating distances at Innsbruck in 1964, all within four days. She also won two gold medals in the 1960 Squaw Valley Olympics, and was twice overall world champion (1963–64). She appeared again in the late 1960s in world and Olympic events, but without her former success.

242

developed a more suitable machine. The International Ski-Bob Federation was formed in 1961. It now has more than 20 member nations. World championships began in 1967, with combined titles awarded for overall best performances in downhill and slalom events. Speeds in excess of 60 mph can be readily achieved, with experts reaching up to 100 mph.

Bobsledding

For seated crews of two or four on winding courses of ice, bobsledding requires the split-second timing, judgement, and courage of a racing driver. Constructed with permanent concrete foundations and sometimes aided by mechanical refrigeration, bobsleigh courses must be not less than 1,500 metres long, with a minimum of 15 banked turns. A championship event comprises four descents for each crew, the lowest time aggregate determining the winner. Speeds sometimes exceed 90 mph. Goggles, crash helmets, and protective padding are essential.

As a sport clearly distinct from tobogganing, bobsledding originated in 1888 in Switzerland, where the first proper bob run was built at St Moritz in 1904. The International Bobsleigh Federation dates from 1923, acquiring its present name in 1957. The first world and Olympic four-man titles were contested concurrently in 1924, separate two-man events being added to the world championships in 1931 and to the Olympics the following year.

The steel and aluminium sleds have streamlined cowlings, with runners on a fixed rear axle and a front axle that turns, steered by ropes or a wheel. The maximum length is 8 ft 10 in for two men and 12 ft 5 in for four men, with crews

The sporting Italian

Dateline: Igls, Austria, 31 January 1964. The Italian bobsleigh driver Eugenio Monti came to the Innsbruck Olympics as the supreme champion – five consecutive two-man world titles from 1957 to 1961 and another in 1963, and four-man titles in 1960 and 1961. Yet he had not won an Olympic gold, as no bobsleigh course had been built at Squaw Valley for the 1960 Games.

Great competitor though he was, first and foremost he was a sportsman. And it was an act of sportsmanship unheard of in modern times that contributed to his defeat at Igls. Among his most dangerous rivals in the two-man event were the British pair Tony Nash and Robin Dixon, whom he had greatly helped and encouraged before the Games. After the first of the four runs, Nash was lying second, but his axle had broken and he had no ready replacement. So Monti, after finishing his second run, whipped off his own axle and gave it to Nash.

The British pair again set the second fastest time, and the following day went on to win the gold, with Monti third behind Italy's second pair. Monti's crew won a bronze in the four-man event, too.

But that is not the end of the story. For four years later, at Alpe d'Huez near Grenoble, Monti, now 40, won both Olympic bobsleigh gold medals to crown his long career. And never was a triumph so deserved, nor so popular with fellow competitors.

Monti (right) congratulates Tony Nash.

seated some 8 inches above the ice. Maximum weights, with crews, are 375 kg (827 lb) for twos and 630 kg (1,389 lb) for fours, which are slightly faster.

The driver or 'pilot' steers; the brakeman, at the back, corrects skidding; and the middle two riders in a four play important parts, particularly in pushing at the start and in weight transference at corners.

Luge tobogganing

Competitive tobogganing is a form of ice sled racing for single riders or crews of two, adopting a backward-leaning sitting posture. Made of wood with twin metal runners, the luge is steered by the feet, a hand rope, and body-weight transference. The single-seater is limited to 1.5 metres in length and 20 kg weight. The double-seater, although longer, has the same weight restriction. The banked courses, usually steeper than for bobsledding, are about 1,000 metres long, with a dozen or more bends. Speeds up to 80 mph have been achieved.

Evolving from primitive ice transport through several thousand years, lugeing as a racing sport dates from the mid-1800s in Switzerland, where British tourists built two runs at Davos in 1879. An International Tobogganing Association was formed in 1913, and European championships began in 1914.

An Austrian, Martin Tietze, gave lugeing a great impetus in the 1930s, inventing a flexible sled with independently moving front runners. World championships started in 1955, with two events for men and single-seater only for women. The present International Luge Federation dates from 1957, and the sport gained Olympic entry in 1964. East Germans have fared particularly well at luge events. In the 1960s Thomas Kohler won five world titles and Ortrun Enderlein won the women's championship three times running.

Cresta Run

A unique variation of tobogganing for single riders, the Cresta Run at St Moritz, Switzerland, is the world's only course. Riders descend prone and head first upon flat skeleton sleds down the 1,213-metre course, with top speeds averaging around 50 mph.

There are no world championships, but the Cresta Run has twice been an Olympic sport, in 1928 and 1948. The major event, the Grand National, dates from 1885 and is staged on the full course. The Curzon Cup, first held in 1910, starts at Junction, a point 888 metres from the finish. The great Italian Nino Bibbia won his first Curzon Cup in 1950 and his eighth in 1969. During the 1960s he also won the Grand National seven times and again in 1973.

Curling

A team game played on ice, curling basically resembles bowls. Disc-shaped granite *stones*, 3 ft in circumference, are propelled towards a 6-ft-radius circle, the centre of which is called the *tee*. The playing area is 138 ft long and 14 ft wide. Each team, also termed a rink, comprises four players, who each deliver two stones, playing them alternately with those of their opponents. Sixteen stones, which have handles, are delivered in each *end*, or *head*, a point being scored for each stone nearer the tee than any of the opponents' stones. A match consists of an agreed number of heads.

The equivalent of bias in bowls is achieved by twisting the handle at the

Bobsledding and tobogganing, sports for men with nerves of steel. Far left: Timing is critical as a two-man bob takes a sharp turn. Left: A two-man luge, a distinctly uncomfortable looking vehicle. Above: Italy's Nino Bibbia winning the gold medal on the Cresta Run in 1948. Bibbia (below) was still winning there 25 years later.

Indoor curling rinks at Winnipeg, in Canada.

moment of delivery, thus 'curling' the stone to the right or left. The direction and speed of the stone is influenced by sweeping the ice in front of it with special brooms. As one player delivers, the *skip* (captain) at the tee end tells his other two players when to *soop* (sweep).

Probably originating in the Netherlands nearly 500 years ago, the sport developed primarily in Scotland from the early 16th century. The first known club was formed in 1510 at Kilsyth, near Glasgow. Curling spread to Canada in 1807. The first American club, at Pontiac, Michigan, dates from 1820.

The international administrative body, the Royal Caledonian Curling Club, was formed in 1838. World championships began in 1959 and have been virtually monopolized by Canada, where more than half a million people play. Curling has appeared as an exhibition sport at a number of Winter Olympics.

Man has devised all kinds of sports to practise on snow or ice, especially in those areas of the world where these elements persist for many months of the year. Left, top to bottom: Eisschiessen, a German form of curling, is demonstrated at the 1964 Olympics . . . Ice yachting, once man's fastest means of travel . . . Skijoring (behind motorcycles and various other vehicles as well as horses) is popular in flat parts of northern countries . . . Dog-sled racing in North America (particularly Canada and Alaska), where some events are staged over 400 mile courses . . . Snowmobile racing in Canada, where events have been sponsored to the tune of $50,000 . . . Ice canoe racing at a carnival in Quebec. And where there is no snow, man has adapted a winter sport and invented grass skiing (below), a sport that now has its own championships.

Winter Olympics

London 1908. Figure skating was included in the summer Olympic schedule 16 years before the first separate Winter Olympics. This was due to skating's very early international organization and the convenience of a suitable indoor rink.

Twenty skaters took part from six nations – Argentina, Germany, Great Britain, Russia, Sweden, and the United States. Ulrich Salchow of Sweden and the British girl Madge Syers became the first solo champions, and the Germans Heinrich Burger and Anna Hübler took the pairs title.

Antwerp 1920. The second figure skating contests were augmented at Antwerp Ice Palace by the Olympic debut of ice hockey. This swelled the total ice event entries to 73 men and 12 women from 10 nations. Seven ice hockey teams competed and, although the Canadian winners and American runners-up outclassed the less experienced Europeans, the sport's interest widened as a result. Sweden's Gillis Grafström won the first of three consecutive gold medals in figure skating.

I Chamonix 1924. Nordic skiers and jumpers, bobsledders, and speed skaters joined figure skaters and ice hockey players in the first separate, self-contained Winter Olympics. Sixteen nations were represented by 283 competitors, comprising 102 skiers, 82 ice hockey players, 39 bobsledders, 31 speed skaters, and 29 figure skaters, the latter including all the 13 women in the Games. Norway dominated the nordic events, winning 11 of the 12 medals at stake.

The outstanding individuals of the Games both won three gold medals. The Norwegian skier Thorleif Haug won both cross-country events and the combined in addition to coming second in the jumping. The Finnish speed skater Clas Thunberg won two events and was placed in the other two, winning his third gold medal because there was an overall award. Last in the women's figure skating was an 11-year-old Norwegian schoolgirl called Sonja Henie.

II St Moritz 1928. There was a sharp increase in entries, 494 from 25 countries. Skeleton tobogganing was introduced on the challenging Cresta Run. The figure skating was memorable for Gillis Grafström's third success and Sonja Henie's first. The Finnish speed skater

Clas Thunberg and the Norwegian skier Johan Gröttumsbraaten each won two gold medals. Norwegians had the lion's share of success, winning 6 of the 13 events. Despite the high altitude, an unseasonably mild spell caused the 10,000 metres speed skating to be cancelled.

III Lake Placid 1932. The first Winter Olympics outside Europe, entailing longer distances and greater expense for the majority, trimmed the entries to 262 from 17 nations. Americans won 6 of the 14 events – all the speed skating and bobsledding.

The status of bobsledding increased with the addition of two-man sleds. William Fiske's crew retained the four-man title and the Norwegian skier Johan Gröttumsbraaten also scored a second successive victory in the nordic combination. The Americans John Shea and Irving Jaffee each gained two gold medals for speed skating, the only time 'pack' starts were permitted instead of timing racers separately, with tactics completely alien to Europeans.

IV Garmisch 1936. Alpine ski racing was included for the first time, with Germans Franz Pfnür and Christel Cranz taking combined titles. A new nordic skiing event, the cross-country team relay, was won by a Finnish quartet.

These 'Hitler Games', organized to impress the world of Nazi efficiency, drew a then record entry of 755 from 28 countries, bolstered by newcomers Australia, Bulgaria, Greece, Liechtenstein, Spain, and Turkey. Ivar Ballangrud, the Norwegian speed skater, took three gold medals and a silver. His compatriot, Sonja Henie, gained her third consecutive figure skating victory. Shock result of the meeting was the ice hockey defeat of Canada, hitherto the acknowledged masters, by an inspired British team captained by Carl Erhardt. It was the first time Canada had lost since ice hockey became an Olympic sport.

V St Moritz 1948. Early post-war problems justified selecting St Moritz for a second time. In the circumstances, an entry only 40 short of the Garmisch figures was heartening, with newcomers Chile, Denmark, Iceland, Korea, and Lebanon among the 28 participating nations. Skeleton tobogganing made its second Olympic appearance on the Cresta Run. The growth of alpine ski racing was underlined by the entry of 25 nations for the downhill, 10 more than in any nordic event.

Two gold medals apiece were gained by the Swedish nordic skier Martin Lundström and the French alpine skier Henri Oreiller. American Dick Button's figure skating success heralded a revolutionary trend in free-skating athleticism.

VI Oslo 1952. More than half a million paying customers attended the first Winter Olympics staged adjacent to a capital city; 623 men and 109 women represented 30 nations, including the debuts of New Zealand and Portugal. In the first Olympic women's nordic ski race, Finns took all three medals, led by Lydia Wideman. A Scandinavian monopoly of the nordic events was overshadowed by the first alpine ski medal to be won by a Norwegian, Stein Eriksen. Andreas Ostler drove German crews to victory in both bob events.

Britain's Jeannette Altwegg, who won the women's figure skating, traced probably the best figures yet seen. Dick Button retained the men's title. But the outstanding individual of these Games was the Norwegian speed skater Hjalmar Andersen, who won three gold medals.

VII Cortina 1956. These Games proved Toni Sailer of Austria to be the most competent and courageous alpine skier yet, outclassing all rivals to win three gold medals in difficult weather conditions. Sixten Jernberg of Sweden was the most successful nordic skier, his medals haul comprising one gold, two silver, and a bronze.

Competing for the first time, the Russians won 7 of the 24 events, including the ice hockey. The Soviet speed skater Yevgeni Grischin won the 500 metres title and shared the 1,500 metres, both with new world record times. Driving the Swiss four-man

The opening ceremony at St Moritz in 1948.

Figure skating gold-medallist Herma Plank-Szabo (Austria) at the first separate Winter Olympics, held at Chamonix, France, in 1924.

245

Surprise double gold-medallist at the 1972 Olympics, 17-year-old Swiss schoolgirl Marie-Therese Nadig competing in the downhill.

bobsled to victory, Franz Kapus, 46, became the oldest gold medallist of all the Winter Olympics. Hayes Jenkins and Tenley Albright won the solo figure skating to stress an ascendancy in American free-skating.

VIII Squaw Valley 1960. This was the first time a complete venue was specially built, appreciably compact, with all events except the nordic skiing within short walking distances. The meeting was a great sporting success, but financially disastrous. The most sensational event was the men's 10,000 metres speed skating, won by Knut Johannesen of Norway, one of five inside the world record. Women's speed skating was included for the first time, and the Russian ice racer Lydia Skoblikova was the only contestant in the Games to win two individual titles outright. Her compatriot Grischin retained his 500 metres title, but again had to share the 1,500 metres gold.

The newly introduced biathlon, combining cross-country skiing and rifle shooting, was won by Klas Lestander of Sweden. The new events partially atoned for not building a bobsleigh run. In the figure skating, Americans David Jenkins and Carol Heiss outmatched all with spectacular jumps.

IX Innsbruck 1964. Nearly a million people saw 27 events contested by 986 men and 200 women from 36 nations. Russians took most medals, 11 gold, 8 silver, and 6 bronze, and the Soviet speed skater Lydia Skoblikova became the first competitor to win four events in one Winter Olympics.

The alpine skiing highlight was a unique women's double by the French sisters Marielle and Christine Goitschel, each coming second to the other in the two slalom events. Sixten Jernberg's 50 km and relay victories brought the Swedish nordic skier's total Winter Olympics medals tally to a record 4 gold, 3 silver, and 2 bronze. Bobsleigh victories by Britain and Canada were noteworthy for countries without a course of their own. Luge tobogganing was included for the first time and the meeting was a triumph of organization at relatively low cost in thawing conditions.

X Grenoble 1968. A record 1,560 competitors from 37 nations took part. The outstanding individual was Jean-Claude Killy, French winner of all three gold medals for men's alpine ski racing, equalling the 1956 feat of Toni Sailer. The most successful woman was the Swedish cross-country skier Toini Gustafsson, taking two golds and adding a silver in the relay.

The bobsledding was a happy career finale for the Italian driver Eugenio Monti, who claimed both golds at the age of 40. Other successful veterans were the Russian pair skaters Oleg and Ludmila Protopopov, who retained their title when 35 and 32 respectively. In the 8 speed skating events, 52 improvements were made on previous best Olympic

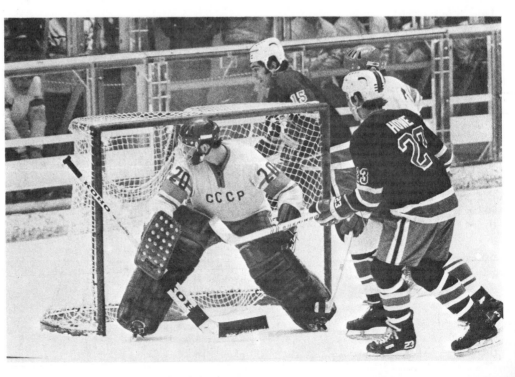

Ice hockey at the 1972 Games, Russia (CCCP) v USA. The Russians won 7-2 and headed their group with 9 out of 10 points to win their third successive Olympic title. The Americans, with 6 points, won the silver medal.

RECORDS ON ICE AND SNOW

Ice skating 'mosts'

World titles	– men	10	U. Salchow (Swe)
	– women	10	S. Henie (Nor)
	– pairs	6	I. Rodnina* (USSR)
	– dance	5	A. Gorshkov & L. Pakhomova (USSR)
Olympic golds	– men	3	G. Grafström (Swe)
	– women	3	S. Henie (Nor)
	– pairs	2	P. & A. Brunet (Fr)
		2	O. & L. Protopopov (USSR)

Speed skating 'mosts'

World overall	– men	5	O. Mathisen (Nor)
		5	C. Thunberg (Fin)
	– women	4	I. Voronina (USSR)
Olympic golds	– men	4	C. Thunberg (Fin)
		4	I. Ballangrud (Nor)
	– women	6	L. Skoblikova (USSR)

Speed skating world records

Men

500 m	L. Linkovesi (Fin)	38.0 s	8.1.72	
	E. Keller (WG)	38.0 s	4.3.72	
	H. Börjes (Swe)	38.0 s	4.3.72	
	L. Efskind (Nor)	38.0 s	13.1.73	
1,000 m	L. Efskind (Nor)	1 m 17.6 s	13.1.73	
1,500 m	A. Schenk (Neth)	1 m 58.7 s	16.1.71	
3,000 m	A. Schenk (Neth)	4 m 8.3 s	2.3.72	
5,000 m	A. Schenk (Neth)	7 m 9.8 s	4.3.72	
10,000 m	A. Schenk (Neth)	14 m 55.9 s	14.3.71	

Women

500 m	S. Young (USA)	41.8 s	19.1.73
1,000 m	A. Henning (USA)	1 m 27.3 s	8.1.72
1,500 m	S. Kaiser (Neth)	2 m 15.8 s	15.1.71
3,000 m	S. Kaiser (Neth)	4 m 46.5 s	16.1.71

Bobsledding 'mosts'
World titles　11　E. Monti (It)

Luge tobogganing 'mosts'

World titles	– men	5	T. Köhler (EG)
	– women	3	O. Enderlein (EG)

Cresta Run

Most Grand Nationals	8		N. Bibbia (It)
Most Curzon Cups	8		N. Bibbia (It)
Record – from Top	54.21 s		P. Marou (It)
– from Junction	43.45 s		B. Bischofberger (Swi)

Alpine ski racing 'mosts'

World combined	– men	2	A. Seelos (Aus)
		2	E. Allais (Fr)
		2	T. Sailer (Aus)
		2	J-C. Killy (Fr)
	– women	5	C. Cranz (Ger)
World titles	– men	7	T. Sailer (Aus)
	– women	12	C. Cranz (Ger)
Olympic golds	– men	3	T. Sailer (Aus)
		3	J-C. Killy (Fr)
	– women	2	A. Lawrence (USA)
		2	M. Goitschel (Fr)
		2	M-T. Nadig (Switz)
World Ski Cup	– men	3	G. Thoeni (It)
	– women	4	A. Proell (Aus)
Arlberg-Kandahar combined		5	K. Schranz (Aus)

Nordic ski racing 'mosts'

World titles	– men	8	S. Jernberg (Swe)
	– women	8	A. Koltjina (USSR)
Olympic golds	– men	4	S. Jernberg (Swe)
	– women	3	C. Boyarskikh (USSR)
			G. Koulakova (USSR)

Nordic combination 'mosts'

World titles	4	J. Gröttumsbraaten (Nor) (also won 2 world, including 1 Olympic, 15 km)
Olympic golds	2	

Ski jumping

Most world titles	5	B. Ruud (Nor)
Longest jump (ski-flying)	169 m	H. Wosipiwo (EG) 1973

Biathlon 'mosts'

World titles	7	V. Melanin (USSR)
Olympic golds	3	A. Tikhonov (USSR)

Curling

World championships	12	Canada

Ice yachting

Record speed	143 mph	J. Buckstaff (USA) 1938

Barrel jumping

Most 'barrels'	17	K. LeBel (USA) 1965

*With two partners

Sonja Henie, the greatest female skater of all time, won 10 world and 3 Olympic titles.

Russian ice dancers Ludmila Pakhomova and Alexandr Gorshkov won their record fifth consecutive world title in 1974 in a sport that had hitherto been the domain of British skaters.

times, Norway's Anton Maier setting a new world record in the 5,000 metres.

XI Sapporo 1972. Sapporo's 13 sports sites were easily accessible from the city. The first Winter Olympics to be held in Asia were sensationally preceded by the late banning of Karl Schranz, the Austrian alpine skier, for alleged contravention of the amateur rules.

King of these Games was the Dutch speed skater Ard Schenk, who bagged three golds in convincing style. The most successful woman was Galina Koulakova, the Russian nordic skier, who also took three golds. Marie-Therese Nadig, a Swiss schoolgirl, was a surprise alpine skiing success, winning both downhill and giant slalom. East Germans took all six medals in the men's and women's luge tobogganing singles, and were joint first and third in the two-man luge. Trixi Schuba of Austria won the women's figure skating with probably the best-ever figures. The Russians won their third consecutive ice hockey title.

Wrestling

'The Wrestlers', in the Uffizi Gallery, Florence, confirms the sport's Graeco-Roman origins.

Perhaps no other sport has had such a long history as that of wrestling. Many of the holds and throws used now in the Olympic and Commonwealth Games and the annual world and European championships are the same as those employed in the competitions of the ancient civilizations of Egypt, Crete, China, and particularly Greece. But wrestling almost certainly precedes even the earliest of these civilizations, since there is evidence that cavemen practised headlocks, throws, and strangleholds to defend themselves.

The sport really developed during the Grecian civilizations; wrestling was introduced to the ancient Olympics in 704 BC – the 18th Olympiad. The winner of the wrestling events was one of the most fêted victors of the Games. There were at least two styles of wrestling – one similar to the present freestyle and *pankration*, in which competitors were allowed to punch, throw, strangle, arm-lock, gouge, and kick; fighters often ended up either mutilated or dead.

The Romans carried on the tradition of the sport and adapted the classical Grecian style to a method called 'graeco-roman', which is one of the three international styles today. There are numerous regional styles of wrestling, which evolved over the last 2,000 years, but there were no truly international events until the end of the 19th century. The sport proved extremely popular in America through the exploits of men such as Bill Muldoon, who claimed the world title in graeco-roman in 1883. The most glamorous figure of this era was the Russian-born George Hackenschmidt, who was the world freestyle champion, and did much to popularize the sport before losing his title to another American Frank Gotch. The top competitors of this 'golden age' were all professional.

But professional wrestling was well aware of the counter-attraction of boxing, and was gradually forced to introduce showmanship to keep the crowds. After World War II it became an entertainment rather than a sport.

Amateur wrestling, which had been part of the first modern Olympics, in 1896, now attracted the serious enthusiasts. The International Amateur Wrestling Federation (Fédération Internationale de Lutte Amateur – FILA) was

The three major internationally recognized styles of wrestling:
Below *freestyle,* below right *graeco-roman,* and bottom *sambo.*

founded in 1921, when the first world graeco-roman championships were held.

Both freestyle and graeco-roman now became accepted as the international styles, and have been held in all Olympics and world championships since World War II. A third style, *sambo*, was recognized by FILA in 1968. World championships are held in this style, and it is scheduled for inclusion in the 1978 Commonwealth Games.

Sambo is a Russian form of jacket wrestling, which is similar to judo, although locks against the knee joint are permitted. Its similarity to judo has meant that many competitors have been successful in both sports.

Although these three are the internationally recognized styles, regional styles still flourish. These include: *sumo*, in Japan, where massive men – inflated by force-feeding and often weighing over 20 stone – attempt to push each other out of the ring in an event which is accompanied by great ceremony and tradition; *glima*, in Iceland, where fighters grasp each other round a harness on the hips and attempt to throw each other; *yagli*, in Turkey, where the wrestlers are covered in oil; and *Cumberland and Westmorland*, in Britain, in which competitors join hands behind each other's backs and attempt to maintain this grip throughout the bout.

Freestyle and graeco-roman
The difference between these two styles is that in graeco-roman a competitor is not allowed to attack an opponent's legs or use his own legs to assist a throw. In freestyle, it is common for a fighter to grab at an opponent's legs and try to sweep them away.

The object of both styles is to achieve a decisive victory through pinning an opponent's shoulders on the mat for a count of one from the referee. But in most major bouts the contest is decided on points. Three officials control a bout. The referee walks round the ring, which for big tournaments is 8 metres square with a free space 2 metres wide round the outside. The judge sits outside the ring. And the mat chairman is in overall charge of the fight.

Bouts are scheduled for 9 minutes – three rounds of 3 minutes each with a minute's rest period between the bouts. The competition system is extremely intricate, but fair. Depending on the

performance of the fighter, he gets a certain number of penalty points ranging from minus 4 for losing by a fall to zero for winning through a fall. A wrestler is eliminated when he has acquired 6 penalty points. As a result, every fighter has at least two bouts.

Wrestlers are not allowed to strangle or armlock an opponent. They use methods of levering and turning an opponent in ground wrestling. In standing work, they either grab at the legs (in freestyle) or hold the opponent round the neck and attempt to throw him to the mat with sudden changes of direction and fast turning moves.

All competitors are divided into 10 weight classes, ranging from light-flyweight (under 48 kg) to heavyweight plus (over 100 kg).

WRESTLING 'MOSTS'

World and Olympic titles
freestyle	8	A. Medved (USSR)
graeco-roman	5	R. Rurua (USSR)
		V. Igumenov (USSR)

Olympic gold medals
	3	C. Westergren (Sweden)
		I. Johansson (Sweden)
		A. Medved (USSR)

Russia's outstanding freestyle wrestler Alexandr Medved won a record eight world titles. These included an unprecedented three consecutive Olympic gold medals, the light-heavyweight in 1964, the heavyweight in 1968, and the super-heavyweight in 1972. The 35-year-old Ukrainian announced his retirement after his third Olympic victory, in which he defeated men much heavier than his own 16½ stone.

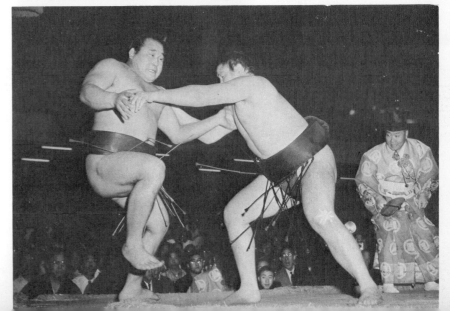

Two of the many kinds of traditional wrestling practised in various parts of the world. Left: Cumberland and Westmorland, a rural pastime for hundreds of years in England's Lake District. Below: Sumo, which is accompanied by much ceremony, is a professional sport in Japan.

Yacht racing

Below: *Eighteen-footer racing, popular in Australia since the early 1900s, has now achieved a more widespread following.*
Bottom: *Eric Tabarly's schooner Pen Duick III, in which he won the 1967 Fastnet Race.*

Whether it be in 80-foot ocean racers or 10-foot dinghies, yacht racing is governed by one set of rules. These, which are annually reviewed, are the result of many years' experience and almost without exception are universally adopted. The International Yacht Racing Union, which controls the sport, meets twice a year, and now only minor changes need to be made to the rules to improve and update them. The Union is also responsible for the administration of the international racing classes, and recommends which of these shall be used for Olympic competition.

Yacht racing has been going on since the reign of King Charles II of England. Then, and for many years, it was the match racing of two or more boats for a purse of several hundred pounds. Only towards the beginning of this century did yacht racing develop as we now know it. And then it took thirty or more years to become popular. Yachts were rich men's toys, run with large crews of paid hands. This state of affairs continued until after World War II.

In the 1920s and 30s, smaller boats were raced entirely by amateurs, and through them the sport began to grow. It was not until 1945, however, that real growth came into small boat racing, and much of this growth can be said to be due to the development of marine plywood and resin glues in the war.

The leisure boom began slowly, and as the roads became stifled, the urge to go sailing was made easier by boats becoming available in kit form. Dinghy racing, which had its origins in the 1920s, came into prominence when amateurs were able to build their own craft. It soon became a hot-bed of talent, so that most of the current batch of top international racing helmsmen started in dinghies. Many more accept the training potential of dinghy racing, and the new Laser class has opened the possibilities of close tactical racing without the necessary boat preparation needed in other classes. Because of this, it has achieved instant popularity with many helmsmen who regard it as a second boat.

The use of glassfibre reinforced plastics (g.r.p.) was a second milestone in yacht racing. This cheap material,

Memorable moments in sport

There is no second

Dateline: Cowes, 22 August 1851. Early in the morning 15 British yachts were at anchor off Cowes in company with the 170-ton schooner *America*. They were due to start in a race round the Isle of Wight for a 100-guinea silver cup presented by the Royal Yacht Squadron. After a cannon had boomed out from the Squadron Castle, activity began on board the seven schooners and eight cutters there to uphold the honour of British yachting. On board the *America*, Commodore John Stevens of the New York Yacht Club was slow to get his crew – under their captain, Dick Brown – under way. The *America* was last of the 16 yachts to head eastwards down the Solent.

At the Nab, only four boats were ahead of her, and in the north-westerly wind the *America* began to pull ahead as she made for the southern point of the island. At one time she was 8 miles clear of her nearest rivals, but the wind fell light on the way up Solent from the Needles (the western point) and the 47-ton cutter *Aurora*, the smallest boat in the race, closed on the big American schooner . . . but too late.

America crossed the finishing line 18 minutes ahead, and a signalman conveyed the result to Queen Victoria aboard the Royal Yacht. She asked him 'Who won the race?' and was answered '*America* first, Your Majesty. There is no second'.

This historic race turned out to be the forerunner of the America's Cup, when the trophy was later put up for challenge. But by the early 1970s, after 22 challenges from Britain, Canada, and Australia, none had been able to relieve the New York Yacht Club of the problem of cleaning the Cup.

requiring only semi-skilled labour for boat building, has again reduced boat costs. Initially, only small boats were built in g.r.p., but now ocean racers are constructed in the material. By the multiple use of the same mould, costs are greatly reduced.

Many of the yachts involved in the 1973 Admiral's Cup series, regarded as the world team championship of ocean racing, were series-produced g.r.p. boats. The Admiral's Cup is a biannual competition based at Cowes, and includes the classic Fastnet Race. There are two other similar competitions – the Onion Patch series in America, which includes the Bermuda Race, and the Southern Cross series in Australia, with its Sydney-Hobart race.

Ocean racing is growing fast, both in numbers of races and in distance travel-led. In 1973 nearly 300 boats took part in the 605-mile Fastnet Race, from Cowes around the Fastnet Rock and back to Plymouth. Shortly afterwards, 20 yachts started in the first Round the World Race, in which there were three stops, at Cape Town, Sydney, and Rio de Janeiro.

Each year most dinghy classes hold national championships, settled over a series of five or more races. Those that have spread internationally hold world championships, although for the chosen six classes these disappear in Olympic years.

Multihulled craft – although not new in concept – failed to make much impression on the yachting scene until the 1950s. Then they first appeared as day-racing craft, and developed into cruising boats. A small offshoot of enthusiasts,

Chichester, Sir Francis (GB), won the first *Observer* single-handed yacht race, in 1960, in *Gypsy Moth III*. Then, at the age of 64, he left Plymouth on 27 August 1966, and stopping only at Sydney sailed around the world in the 53-ft ketch *Gypsy Moth IV*. He returned to Plymouth on 28 May 1967 to a hero's welcome, and later that year was knighted by the Queen. He was not the first yachtsmen to circumnavigate the world alone, but his historic journey with only one stop led to the concept of round-the-world ocean racing.

Elvström, Paul (Denmark), first came to prominence at the Olympic regatta, in Torbay in 1948, when he won a gold medal in the single-handed Firefly class. He was the first yachtsman to realize that physical fitness was important in yachting. He followed his 1948 success with three consecutive wins in the Finn class (1952–56–60). In addition to his Olympic triumphs, he won 10 world championships in 7 major yacht-racing classes between 1957 and 1969: the 5.5 metre, Star, Soling, 505, Flying Dutchman, Snipe, and Finn.

Pattisson, Rodney (GB), gained his first international racing success in 1960, when with his brother John crewing he won the Cadet world championship. But it was when he turned to the Flying Dutchman class that he achieved a reputation of absolute invincibility. He hit the headlines in 1968 by beating the world and European champion John Oakeley for the European title, and went on to take the gold medal in the Olympic regatta at Acapulco, Mexico. Crewed by Iain McDonald-Smith, he sailed *Superdocious* to an unprecedented 5 firsts and a 2nd, despite disqualification in the first race. A dedicated, almost

fanatical yachtsman, he won a second gold (crewed by Chris Davies in *Superdoso*) at Kiel in 1972 (4 firsts in 6 races), having been unbeaten in European and world championships in the intervening years in the Flying Dutchman class.

Stephens, Olin and **Rod,** have been, since the mid-1930s, the major influence on racing yacht design. Brothers and principals of the New York firms of Sparkman and Stephens, they have seen their creations win more prizes than those of any other designer. They have regularly supplied syndicates of the New York Yacht Club with designs to defend the America's Cup, and in ocean racing their one-off and production designs have rarely been equalled.

Tabarly, Eric (France), shy and retiring, surprised many by winning the 1964 Single-handed Transatlantic Race in *Pen Duick II.* It brought him fame in France sufficient for General de Gaulle to award him the Legion d'Honeur. Tabarly tried again in 1968 with a brand

new trimaran *Pen Duick IV*, but failed after a collision one day out with a freighter. In the schooner *Pen Duick III* he won the 1967 Fastnet Race, and two years later in the fifth boat to bear the name he took principal honours in the Transpacific Race.

A race in the 1973 European land yachting championships. Also called sand yachting, the sport has flourished in Europe since the early 1900s and is now also extremely popular in America.

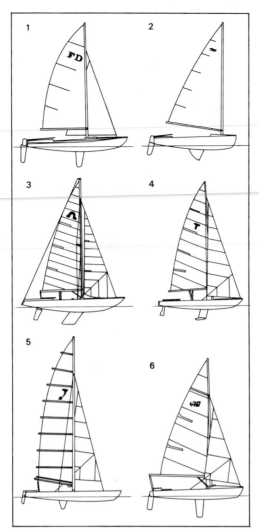

The 1976 Olympic classes : 1 Flying Dutchman, 2 Finn, 3 Soling, 4 Tempest, 5 Tornado, and 6 the 470 class.

Yachting terms

Aft Towards the stern.
Beam Width of boat.
Beat Sail to windward (also, *close-hauled*).
Bermudan Rig with triangular main sail and tall mast.
Boom Spar at foot of sail.
Bow Forward part of the boat.
Catamaran Twin-hulled craft.
Dinghy Small sailing boat, open or partly decked.
Gaff Spar supporting head of four-sided sail, attached to mast.
Gaff-rigged Rig with four-sided main sail supported by gaff.
Genoa Large jib sail overlapping main sail.
Gybe Change course with the wind aft.
Jib Forward sail.
Keel boat Any boat with a *keel* extending below to offer resistance to sideways movement.
Leeward The direction the wind is blowing *to.*
Luff Change course towards the wind.
Port Left-hand side of boat.
Port tack Sailing with wind coming over port bow.
Proper course Fastest course to next mark.
Reach Sail with the wind abeam.
Reef Reduce sail area.
Run Sail with the wind aft.
Sheets Ropes used to control sails.
Spinnaker Light, billowy sail used when running.
Starboard Right-hand side of boat.
Starboard tack Sailing with wind coming over starboard bow.
Stem Extreme point of bow.
Stern Aft part of boat.
Tack Sail zigzag course towards wind, changing from one tack (port or starboard) to the other.
Tiller Handle on rudder used for steering.
Trimaran Three-hulled craft.
Trim the sails Adjusting the sails with the ropes (sheets).
Windward The direction the wind is blowing *from.*

however, founded top competition for catamarans. The Little America's Cup, raced for annually in 25-foot-long craft with 300 square feet of sail, is the principal event for day racers, and there is now much interest in multihulled cruiser racing.

Yacht racing's most famous event remains the America's Cup. While the size of boats may have diminished over the years, the stature of the event has in no way fallen. It is a two-country competition raced on challenge to the New York Yacht Club (the holders) in 12-metre yachts. As these boats cost in the region of half a million pounds, the con-tests are not frequent. Campaigns for the America's Cup cost challenger and defender well over a million pounds each, and they are not taken lightly. For example, Australia, France, and Britain all lodged challenges for 1974, so that a round robin contest had to be arranged to decide which country has the right to race against America.

Yacht racing is now no longer confined to water. Land yachts race within similar parameters regarding classes, and under much the same rules as their water-borne sisters. They race on disused aerodrome runways as well as hard sandy beaches.

YACHTING 'MOSTS'

World and Olympic titles	14	P. Elvström (Den) — 10 world and a record 4 Olympic golds
World titles in same class	12	S. Morris (GB) — International 14 class
World titles in one year	2	P. Elvström (Den) — 1958 (Finn and 505), 1959 (Finn and Snipe), 1966 (Star and 5.5); R. Fisher (GB).— 1966 (Fireball and Hornet)
Fewest penalty points in Olympic series		3, Rodney Pattisson and Iain McDonald-Smith (1968 Flying Dutchman), with 6 firsts (including one disqualified) and 1 second
Fastest speed under sail		29·3 knots, T. Colman (GB) 3.10.73, in *Crossbow*, a 'one-way' proa.

Index

The alphabetical entries in the encyclopedia are shown in the index in heavy type. Also in heavy type are the page numbers of topics that have separate sections and of the pen pictures in the outside columns. Pictures are indicated by a 'p' after the page number. This is not done with major entries and sections, which are invariably accompanied by pictures. Names mentioned in tables and in pen pictures are not as a rule indexed.

For the purpose of the index, unnumbered colour pages have been designated numbers from i to xvi (i-iv between pages 24 and 25; v-viii between pages 88 and 89; ix-xii between pages 152 and 153; xiii-xvi between pages 184 and 185).